SAGE
Criminology &
Criminal Justice:
Our Story

Believing passionately in the **POWER OF EDUCATION** to transform the criminal justice system, **SAGE Criminology & Criminal Justice** offers arresting print and digital content that **UNLOCKS THE POTENTIAL** of students and instructors. With an extensive list written by renowned scholars and practitioners, we are a **RELIABLE PARTNER** in helping you bring an innovative approach to the classroom. Our focus on **CRITICAL THINKING AND APPLICATION** across the curriculum will help you prepare the next generation of criminal justice professionals.

Juvenile Justice

For Simon
—Frank Schmalleger

I dedicate this book to my dad, Rodney Davis. Thank you for letting me be your shining pride.
—Catherine D. Marcum

Sara Miller McCune founded SAGE Publishing in 1965 to support the dissemination of usable knowledge and educate a global community. SAGE publishes more than 1000 journals and over 800 new books each year, spanning a wide range of subject areas. Our growing selection of library products includes archives, data, case studies and video. SAGE remains majority owned by our founder and after her lifetime will become owned by a charitable trust that secures the company's continued independence.

Los Angeles | London | New Delhi | Singapore | Washington DC | Melbourne

Juvenile Justice

An Active-Learning Approach

Frank Schmalleger

University of North Carolina, Pembroke

Catherine D. Marcum

Appalachian State University

Los Angeles | London | New Delhi
Singapore | Washington DC | Melbourne

$SAGE

FOR INFORMATION:

SAGE Publications, Inc.
2455 Teller Road
Thousand Oaks, California 91320
E-mail: order@sagepub.com

SAGE Publications Ltd.
1 Oliver's Yard
55 City Road
London EC1Y 1SP
United Kingdom

SAGE Publications India Pvt. Ltd.
B 1/I 1 Mohan Cooperative Industrial Area
Mathura Road, New Delhi 110 044
India

SAGE Publications Asia-Pacific Pte. Ltd.
3 Church Street
#10-04 Samsung Hub
Singapore 049483

Acquisitions Editor: Jessica Miller
Content Development Editor: Laura Kearns
Editorial Assistant: Sarah Manheim
Copy Editor: Meg Granger
Typesetter: C&M Digitals (P) Ltd.
Proofreader: Jen Grubba
Indexer: Jean Casalegno
Cover Designer: Gail Buschman
Marketing Manager: Jillian Ragusa

Printed in the United States of America

Library of Congress Cataloging-in-Publication Data

Names: Schmalleger, Frank, author. | Marcum, Catherine Davis, 1980- author.

Title: Juvenile justice : an active-learning approach / Frank Schmalleger, University of North Carolina, Pembroke, Catherine D. Marcum, Appalachian State University.

Description: Los Angeles : SAGE, [2020] | Includes bibliographical references and index.

Identifiers: LCCN 2018040425 | ISBN 9781544300412 (pbk. : alk. paper)

Subjects: LCSH: Juvenile justice, Administration of—United States. | Juvenile delinquency—United States.

Classification: LCC HV9104 .S36 2020 | DDC 364.360973—dc23
LC record available at https://lccn.loc.gov/2018040425

This book is printed on acid-free paper.

19 20 21 22 23 10 9 8 7 6 5 4 3 2 1

BRIEF CONTENTS

DETAILED CONTENTS

©iStockphoto.com/ASIFE

RJ Sangosti/Denver Post/Getty Images

REUTERS/Luis Galdamez

©iStockphoto.com/FatCamera

PART III: JUVENILE BEHAVIORS 111

CHAPTER 7. JUVENILES AND GANGS 112

CHAPTER 8. JUVENILES AND VIOLENCE 126

CHAPTER 9. JUVENILES AND CYBERCRIME 140

©iStockphoto.com/KatarzynaBialasiewicz

AB Forces News Collection/Alamy Stock Photo

PREFACE

The purpose of the juvenile justice system is starkly different from that of the adult criminal justice system. Built on the philosophy of rehabilitation and treatment rather than retribution and punishment, the juvenile justice system works to deter delinquency before troubled adolescents make their way into the harsher adult system. The purpose of this book is to provide an in-depth exploration of the history of the juvenile system, as well as to explain how the past influenced the operation of the system today. In addition, this book will address contemporary issues plaguing juvenile offenders.

The book is broken into comprehensive parts. Part I, composed of three chapters, explores the history of the juvenile justice system, the current state of juvenile offender activity, and the theoretical predictors of juvenile delinquency. Part II examines the three main stakeholders who handle juvenile offenders (police, courts, and corrections), including the legal rights afforded to juveniles as they maneuver the system. Part III explores specific juvenile behaviors, such as drug use, gang activity, and online behaviors. Last, Part IV evaluates multiple proactive and reactive juvenile programs that target at-risk or current offenders.

The text is written in a practical tone, discussing the key concepts of each topic in a way that should be easily understood by the student reader. It provides statistics and material from empirical sources to demonstrate the frequency of juvenile behaviors. In addition, a variety of active learning exercises, some individual and some group, are provided to help instructors engage students in the material. All the active learning assignments included in the text were developed by the authors to engage students within their own classrooms (whether ground or electronic) and have proven to be very effective in fostering long-term knowledge about various topics related to juvenile justice. Key words and definitions, discussion questions, and other suggested activities are also provided to enhance student learning.

We are extremely excited about this book. There are multiple juvenile justice and delinquency textbooks in the field, all of which are valuable and informative; however, we believe this book will make its own unique contribution, not only because of the way it presents material but also because of the way it encourages students to engage with the material on a more personal level.

DIGITAL RESOURCES

SAGE edge offers a robust online environment featuring an impressive array of tools and resources for review, study, and further exploration, keeping both instructors and students on the cutting edge of teaching and learning. SAGE edge content is open access and available on demand. Learning and teaching has never been easier!

$SAGE edge™

Log on to http://edge.sagepub.com/schmallegerjj

SAGE edge for Instructors supports teaching by making it easy to integrate quality content and create a rich learning environment for students.

- **ExamView® test banks** save you time and offer a pedagogically robust way to measure your students' understanding of textbook material. Available for both PC and Mac and compatible with most learning management systems, ExamView features a diverse range of textbook-specific test items and options, allowing you to customize exams to your specific needs, as well as create a print or online exam in just minutes!

- **Microsoft® Word® test banks** provide a diverse range of prewritten options as well as the opportunity to edit any question and/or insert personalized questions to effectively assess students' progress and understanding.

- **Editable, chapter-specific PowerPoint® slides** offer complete flexibility for creating a multimedia presentation for the course.

- **Lecture notes** summarize key concepts by chapter to ease preparation for lectures and class discussions.

- **Author-created investigation activities** support chapter content and strengthen the active-learning approach.

- Exclusive access is provided to full-text **SAGE journal articles** that have been carefully selected to support and expand on the concepts presented in each chapter to encourage students to think critically.

- **Chapter-specific discussion question**s help launch classroom interaction by prompting students to engage with the material and by reinforcing important content.

- **Video and multimedia links** include resources that appeal to students with different learning styles.

- **A course cartridge** provides easy learning management system integration.

SAGE edge for Students provides a personalized approach to help students accomplish their coursework goals in an easy-to-use learning environment.

- **Mobile-friendly flashcards** strengthen understanding of key terms and concepts, and make it easy to maximize your study time anywhere, anytime.

- **Mobile-friendly practice quizzes** allow you to assess how much you've learned and where you need to focus your attention.

- **Learning objectives** reinforce the most important material.

- **Video and multimedia links** include resources that appeal to students with different learning styles.

- Exclusive access is provided to full-text **SAGE journal articles** that have been carefully selected to support and expand on the concepts presented in each chapter to encourage students to think critically.

- **Chapter-specific discussion questions** help launch classroom interaction by prompting students to engage with the material and by reinforcing important content.

ACKNOWLEDGMENTS

We would like to extend our sincerest appreciation to the staff of SAGE Publishing for their support and assistance in preparation of this manuscript. We especially appreciate the tireless efforts and encouragement of Jessica Miller and Laura Kearns during the entire publication process.

SAGE gratefully acknowledges the following reviewers for their kind assistance:

Christine S. Barrow, Molloy College

Cindy A. Boyles, University of Tennessee at Martin

Justin DeCecca, University of the Cumberlands

Guy N. Ormes, Golden West College

Doshie Piper, University of the Incarnate Word

Douglas Shuler, Paris Junior College

Clete Snell, University of Houston Downtown

Lacey N. Wallace, Penn State Altoona

Deborah Woodward, University of Central Florida

Lening Zhang, Saint Francis University

ABOUT THE AUTHORS

Frank Schmalleger is Distinguished Professor Emeritus at the University of North Carolina at Pembroke (UNCP). Schmalleger taught criminal justice courses and chaired the Department of Sociology, Social Work, and Criminal Justice for nearly 20 years while at UNCP. He is the author of more than a dozen textbooks in the justice field.

Catherine D. Marcum is the assistant chair of the Department of Government and Justice Studies at Appalachian State University, as well as an associate professor of justice studies. She has over 50 peer-reviewed publications and multiple books in the field of correctional issues, cybercrime, sexual victimization, and juvenile offending and victimization.

PART I

Understanding Juvenile Justice and Delinquency

History of the Juvenile Justice System

After reading this chapter you should be able to

1. Identify how society's perception of children and of their culpability for deviant behavior has evolved over time

2. Discuss the origins of the juvenile court

3. Explain the concept of *parens patriae* and how it has been incorporated into the juvenile court system

Key Terms in Chapter 1

bridewells	*Ex parte Crouse*	*parens patriae*
child savers	houses of refuge	*People v. Turner*
Commonwealth v. Fisher	*Kent v. United States*	Progressive Era
cottage reformatories	nullification	status offenses

INTRODUCTION

In 2017, Judge Raymond A. Jackson of the Federal District Court in Norfolk, Virginia, ruled that the two life sentences that had been imposed on Beltway Sniper Lee Boyd Malvo more than a decade earlier were unconstitutional.[1] Malvo, a Jamaican immigrant, had already spent more than a decade in prison after he and an older man, John Allen Muhammad, went on a shooting spree in the Washington, D.C., area in 2002. The shootings, which took place when Malvo was a teenager, appeared to be totally random and left 10 people dead. Malvo had met Muhammad, a friend of his mother, in Antigua in 1999. The pair immigrated to the United States in 2002 and soon hatched a plan to shoot and kill randomly chosen people in an effort to terrorize the public. Malvo shoplifted a Bushmaster rifle from a gun store and practiced marksmanship in a vacant field. To remain undetected, Muhammad cut a small hole in the trunk of his car, and Malvo used it to shoot people who had no idea they were being targeted. The shooting spree, which lasted 3 weeks, ended when police found a note left at one of the shootings. It led them to Muhammad. Malvo was 17 years old at the time of his arrest and trial but was transferred to adult criminal court instead of being adjudicated delinquent because of the seriousness of his offenses. He and Muhammad were separately tried. Muhammad was found guilty of a capital crime by a Virginia court in 2003 and sentenced to die. Two years later he was extradited to Maryland, where he was convicted of six additional counts of first-degree murder. Because the killing spree had covered a number of different jurisdictions, the District of Columbia also sought Muhammad's extradition from Virginia to try him. Before he could be extradited, however, Muhammad was executed by lethal injection in Virginia in 2009.

The Washington Post/Getty Images

Lee Boyd Malvo, aka "the Beltway Sniper." In 2002, at the age of 17, Malvo joined John Allen Muhammad in a series of sniper shootings that terrified the Washington, D.C., area. In 2017, a judge ruled that the two life sentences Malvo had originally received following his conviction on murder charges were unconstitutional. What caused the judge to rule as he did?

Eight years later, in the wake of a 2012 U.S. Supreme Court decision, *Miller v. Alabama*, Judge Jackson found that Malvo's life sentences were inconsistent with the Eighth Amendment's prohibition on cruel and unusual punishment.[2] The *Miller* decision held that it was unconstitutional to sentence anyone to life in prison without the possibility of parole for crimes committed while they were juveniles. *Miller* represented an expansion of the court's reasoning in the 2010 case of *Graham v. Florida*,[3] in which the justices formally recognized fundamental differences between the neurological development and mental capacity of adults and those of juveniles. In *Graham*, the court held that modern "developments in psychology and brain science continue to show fundamental differences between juvenile and adult minds."

Compare the story of Malvo to that of John Dean, who, at 8 years of age, was publicly executed in England for having set fire to a courtroom in the town of Abingdon in 1629. Justice Whitelock, the judge who sentenced the child to death, is reported to have found evidence of cunning, revenge, and malice in the arson case.[4] The difference in judicial outcome between the case of Malvo and that of Dean is due to almost 400 years of cultural and legal development—a period of time in which Western societies came to recognize crucial differences between adults and juveniles. Today, most countries acknowledge the special status of children, and the legal systems of Western societies treat children separately from adults, acknowledging their relatively undeveloped reasoning capacity, and their inherent ability to change as they mature. The execution of children, however, continues today in some parts of the world. ISIS, with its medieval interpretation of the Koran, is reported to have beheaded or crucified dozens of children in areas under its control over the past few years for "crimes" such as not properly fasting during Ramadan.[5] The practice of executing children also continues today in a number of countries with established legal systems, most notably Iran and Saudi Arabia.[6]

This chapter will explore the historical background of the juvenile justice system in America, beginning with early shifts in perception of the role of the child and the rights of the state. Sanctions developed to meet the special needs of juveniles will be discussed, including institutional reform and the development of a separate juvenile court system.

CHANGING PERCEPTIONS OF CHILDREN OVER TIME

>> **LO 1.1**   Identify how society's perception of children and of their culpability for deviant behavior has evolved over time.

Today's treatment of juvenile offenders in the United States is the result of changes in legislation and practice over the past 150 years. American understanding of children originated in the child-rearing practices and values brought to the New World by English Puritans in the late 1600s. Early practices were harsh by the standards of today, and the belief that youthful offenders should be treated separately from adult offenders took nearly 200 years to develop.

It was not until the 16th and 17th centuries that scholars and medical experts began considering childhood as a period of life that should be treated differently than adulthood. Around that time, some enlightened individuals came to see children as a group that should be shielded from what they saw as the sins of the world, and given education and training that could later benefit them as adults. In addition, as life expectancy grew due to medical advances, the general care of children began to change in regard to nutrition, exercise, and lifestyle.

Unknown child laborer in Mollohan Mills in Newberry, SC. How have views of children changed over the past century?

Soon England began to legislate ages of culpability, and laws were passed recognizing that youths under the age of 7 should not be held responsible for criminal activity; those ages 8 to 14 should be held responsible only if it could be shown that

Changing Views of Adolescents

Cultural views of adolescents have changed considerably over time. Hundreds of years ago, children were seen as young adults and treated as fully grown for the purposes of criminal punishment. In early England, for example, children under the age of 10 were hanged for such simple crimes as stealing a spoon. Although progressive views of children developed slowly, by the end of the 19th century in America, children were seen as a special category of persons deserving of unique protections. Changes in the law continued through the 20th century, when the rights of children were increasingly recognized by the courts. Finally, in the 21st century, the U.S. Supreme Court accepted neuroscientific findings that depicted the adolescent brain as one that is still developing and malleable—meaning that, unlike adults, children (even those who commit serious crimes) could likely still be saved from a life of career criminality through proper handling and treatment. The changing view of adolescents can be seen across generations of Americans living today, and these changes can be documented in a number of ways.

Putting It Into Action

To complete this active learning exercise, document the changing view of children over time in American society by (1) identifying changing portrayals of children in the mass media and (2) interviewing multiple generations of living Americans. To accomplish the former, explore early and mid-20th century feature-length films available on the Internet in which children have central roles or that focus on the lives of children (these can be located through searches for "historical views on adolescence," "early movies starring children," and the like). Create a written record of your perceptions of how views of children can be seen changing over time in American film.

For the second part of this assignment, interview at least three generations of Americans, asking questions about children. The questions might be something like: "What do you think the place of children in society should be?" "How should children be treated?" "How should children who break the law be handled?" Record their answers.

Submit to your instructor the materials you have collected when asked to do so. ●

---

they understood the repercussions of their actions; and children ages 14 and over were considered adults and fully subject to criminal sanctions. However, it was not until the 19th century that the criminal justice system of the Western world began to change its handling of delinquent children.

Children and the Criminal Justice System

Prior to the 19th century, Western criminal justice systems treated children like adults—and in some cases even more harshly. In Colonial times, the Puritans saw the family as the cornerstone of the community, and they believed that parents should be allowed to punish their children as they saw fit. If corporal punishment or other sanctions by the parents did not have the desired effect, disobedient children could be sent to community officials for more punishment, based on the same rules used for adult offenders. This could even mean sentencing children to death, though this was rarely done. Since the criminal justice system did not have uniform standards to deal with juveniles, some children were punished quite severely and others not at all. Courts had the option of invoking **nullification**, which meant refusing to enforce sanctions against children due to the dearth of common-law standards and statutes applicable to them.

In the early 19th century, American industries attracted immigrants who often joined the ranks of the poor when they arrived. As cities grew and crime became a bigger problem, authorities developed vocational training programs to help the poor learn marketable skills. Many of these programs were directed at poor children in particular, because the young were viewed as more malleable.

Ingraham v. Wright, 430 U.S. 651 (1977)

In October 1970, Assistant Principal Solomon Barnes administered corporal punishment to Roosevelt Andrews and 15 other boys in a restroom at Charles R. Drew Junior High School, located in Dade County, Florida. Andrews had been accused of tardiness, and when he resisted paddling, he was struck on the arm, back, and across the neck. Five days later, Principal Willie J. Wright removed James Ingraham and other disruptive students from the classroom and paddled many of them in his office. When Ingraham refused to allow paddling, Wright called Barnes and another assistant principal to hold Ingraham while he paddled him 20 times. Ingraham's mother later took him to the emergency room for a hematoma.

Ingraham and Andrews filed suit against the school administration, as well as the Dade County School System, for deprivation of constitutional rights and damages from corporal punishment. The suit was dismissed, stating there was not enough evidence to go to jury. The U.S. Court of Appeals for the Fifth Circuit reversed the decision, holding that the students' treatment violated the Eighth and Fourteenth Amendments, and noting that the students were denied due process. An en banc court later rejected the Fifth Circuit ruling and confirmed the original decision.

In a decision written by Justice Lewis Powell, the U.S. Supreme Court ruled that the Eighth Amendment does not prevent corporal punishment in schools and due process was not violated in the Dade County case. However, Justice Powell warned against severe corporal punishment in schools and recommended that school staff use restraint when administering punishment to students.

1. **Do you agree with the final ruling?**

2. **What legal rights should juveniles have?**

3. **In your opinion, would this ruling be the same today?**

Online Case Opinion

https://caselaw.findlaw.com/us-supreme-court/430/651.html ●

Houses of Refuge

Programs for impoverished children actually originated in England. **Bridewells**, founded in London in the mid-16th century, housed poor and delinquent youths and worked to train them in specific skills. Reformatories opened in the United States in the early to mid-1800s and followed this general model. The purpose of the reformatory was to instill a strong work ethic in its charges. During this era, criminological theory began attributing crime to poor living conditions, and some reformers called for changing offenders' environment as a way to change their behaviors.

In America, new **houses of refuge** offered skills training, education, discipline, and religious teaching to juveniles in an attempt to change the direction of their lives. The thinking was that these facilities could make up for what poor families had failed to provide. By learning the value of hard work and useful skills, these youths could become productive members of society. The courts would give errant youths indeterminate sentences in houses of refuge, and the houses would then develop

Nineteenth-century bridewells, such as the one featured, became the home to many offenders. What purpose did bridewells serve?

Liszt Collection/Newscom

individualized improvement plans for each child. After only a few months, some children would be deemed reformed and released, while others might be held for years. However, confinement generally ranged from 6 weeks to 2 years.

Life in these facilities was entirely institutionalized. On arrival, each child was given the same haircut and the same clothing as the others. They followed a strict schedule, and lessons involved reciting material in unison. Those thought to be troublemakers were given a diet of bread and water, and even more severe punishment involved solitary confinement without food.

Houses of refuge were opened in the largest cities of the early United States: New York (1825), Boston (1826), and Philadelphia (1828). In the 1830s, more than 20 more facilities were built, and 40 more in the 1840s. Most of these institutions housed male juveniles, with capacity ranging from 90 in Lancaster, Massachusetts, to 1,000 in New York. Often these houses were built next to workhouses and jails for adults, giving the youths a chance to interact with career criminals and to learn from them.

Many of these houses eventually lost sight of their original purpose and lapsed into mere institutions of control. Residents were overwhelmingly boys, who had little contact with girls and were held under a strict military model, with uniforms, drilling, and corporal punishment. These boys might be sent into communities on apprenticeships to learn skills, but they were often put on isolated farms or ships, where many were ignored, beaten, and forced to work long hours.

Houses of refuge became, in effect, a type of prison. Though they were meant for youths, many facilities began accepting adults who were impoverished or criminal. Many soon became overcrowded, and the initial goals of moral education and training were forgotten. To deal with overcrowding, reformers built **cottage reformatories**, which were small facilities that mimicked a large family. On farms removed from the criminal enticements of the cities, surrogate parents were supposed to provide a nurturing environment focused on education, discipline, and training.

By mid-century, reformers began to rethink this harsh system in hopes of improving the juveniles' chances of reintegrating into adult society. In Massachusetts in 1841, the concept of probation was introduced. Probation involves release of an offender from detention following a period of good behavior, but under supervision in the community. Instituted first for adults, probation was seen as both a way to rehabilitate offenders and a way to cope with overcrowded jails.

John Augustus, whom some refer to as *the father of probation*, developed a community supervision system for hundreds of adults convicted of nonviolent offenses. This process, which initially depended on volunteer probation officers, became so successful in Massachusetts that it came to be supported by the state government. In 1869, the Massachusetts Board of Charities implemented probation for youthful offenders as well. It was a different system than we have today, with probation officers used as aids to juvenile court judges rather than as community overseers. Such early probation officers would assist judges with adjudication decisions and help determine placement of youths and arrange for apprenticeships.

Youth activists in the United States in the early 1900s protest child slavery. How do contemporary views of children differ from those of the past?

Despite innovations like probation, 19th century systems continued to be overcrowded, and juvenile offenders were often mixed in with dangerous offenders. Soon state legislatures reduced funding, forcing many institutions to cut services. This created custody and control issues. Facilities came to be plagued with insurrections, arson, sexual misconduct, and truancy.

Female juveniles constituted a very small proportion of the delinquent population. They were often housed in the same institutions as male offenders, and meager resources were dedicated to their care. In the mid-19th century, however, a few institutions dedicated to reform emerged, such as the Lancaster State Industrial School for Girls in Massachusetts. Girls held there were generally from poor immigrant families and were put in a cottage atmosphere, where they were instructed on parenting, housework, and other important feminine qualities of the time. Some graduates went on to marry and have children. However, much like male juvenile facilities, Lancaster became overcrowded, and its focus shifted from reform to control and discipline.

CREATION OF THE JUVENILE COURT

>> LO 1.2   Discuss the origins of the juvenile court.

In America in the late 19th century, immigrants flooded into cities, often settling in impoverished areas, and delinquency rates mushroomed. Lacking community organization and collective efficacy, youths in low-income areas joined criminal enterprises. In the **Progressive Era** (1880–1929), middle- and upper-class reformers were concerned about these developments and pushed for changes in how juveniles were managed. A widespread **child savers** movement began, and individuals such as Louise Bowen and Julia Lathrop set out to restore the values of the American family by rescuing delinquents from the streets, emphasizing respect for parental authority, and domesticating young women to make them ready to become wives and mothers (see Figure 1.1).

Enforcing mandatory schooling, regulating working conditions, and implementing a juvenile justice court system were some of the most prominent Progressive reforms. Many jurisdictions began experimenting with separating juveniles and adults in the court system. In 1870, Massachusetts established separate court dockets, hearings, and records for children under age 16. Colorado operated a quasi-juvenile court in the late 1800s, and New York provided separate trials for juveniles beginning in 1892. In 1899, the first fully separate juvenile court was created in Cook County, Illinois, which includes Chicago.

The Cook County Juvenile Court was established through legislation reflecting a new attitude that children should be treated differently due to their undeveloped cognitive and emotional status. This court operated in a less formal manner than adult courts, discouraging what could be interpreted as intimidating features such as opposing attorneys, adversarial testimony, and merely objective legal terminology (see Table 1.1). Judges shifted from indifferent disciplinarians to a paternal and caring role, providing delinquent youths with resources rather than formal punishment.

FIGURE 1.1

Timeline of Juvenile Court Development

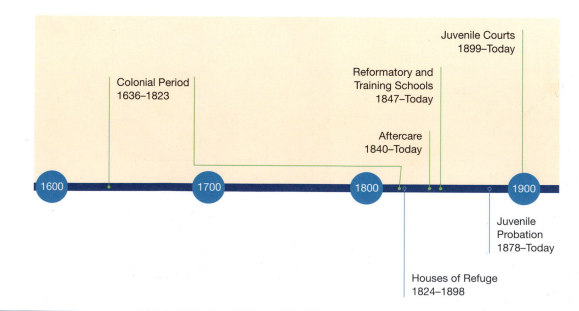

TABLE 1.1

Juvenile Justice Versus Adult Court System Terminology

JUVENILE JUSTICE SYSTEM	ADULT COURT SYSTEM
Custody	Arrest
Petition	Indictment
Hearing	Trial
Adjudication	Conviction
Commitment	Sentence
Delinquent	Offender

The new juvenile courts, charged with handling people under the age of 16, were expected not only to reform youths who had committed criminal acts but also to give assistance to those in poor living conditions.

These courts could deem the child-rearing practices of poor immigrant families deficient and remove their children from the home, sending them to public institutions.

Cook County and other new juvenile courts used a probationary model, which meant keeping most of their charges in the community rather than having them serve time in a correctional facility. Probation officers could act in a positive, mentoring role for youths who might otherwise be subject to criminal influences. The government began paying probation officers, and in 1912, the U.S. Children's Bureau was established to oversee the juvenile justice system, including probation officers.

The juvenile courts also expanded their authority. In 1903, Illinois legislation allowed the juvenile justice system to intervene with **status offenses** such as curfew violations and incorrigibility, in addition to their existing mandate to deal with youths engaged in criminal acts or subject to dependency and neglect findings. These early courts accumulated a long list of delinquent behaviors (see Table 1.2). In 1909, the first court-affiliated guidance clinic was created in Chicago by William Healy, a leading supporter of the juvenile court. Healy called on the courts to individually assess each youth and to identify the interventions needed. By 1931, more than 200 guidance clinics were created to assist the juvenile justice system.

A typical juvenile court. How does juvenile court differ from adult court?

©iStockphoto.com/imagnima

TABLE 1.2

Examples of Delinquent Behavior Found in Early Juvenile Codes

Habitual truancy	Consumption of liquor
Begging	Running away from home
Use of vile/obscene language in public	Engaging in immoral conduct in public
Associating with immoral persons	Curfew violations
Running away from a state institution	Visiting a house of ill repute

The transition to juvenile courts, however, was far from seamless. Many initial court employees—including judges, probation officers, and clinicians—were untrained volunteers, some court proceedings were not even recorded, and some courts meted out especially harsh sentences.

PARENS PATRIAE AND THE JUVENILE COURT

>> **LO 1.3**   Explain the concept of *parens patriae* and how it has been incorporated into the juvenile court system.

FIGURE 1.2

Historical U.S. Supreme Court Cases in Juvenile Justice

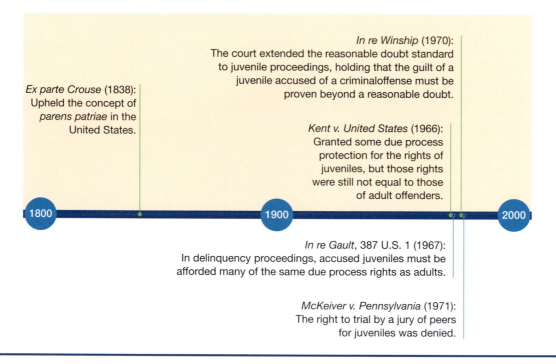

Ex parte Crouse (1838): Upheld the concept of *parens patriae* in the United States.

In re Winship (1970): The court extended the reasonable doubt standard to juvenile proceedings, holding that the guilt of a juvenile accused of a criminaloffense must be proven beyond a reasonable doubt.

Kent v. United States (1966): Granted some due process protection for the rights of juveniles, but those rights were still not equal to those of adult offenders.

In re Gault, 387 U.S. 1 (1967): In delinquency proceedings, accused juveniles must be afforded many of the same due process rights as adults.

McKeiver v. Pennsylvania (1971): The right to trial by a jury of peers for juveniles was denied.

Early juvenile courts often forcibly removed children from their homes in the belief that doing so was in the best interest of the child. Opponents argued that this approach violated a juvenile's basic rights as well as the rights of parents to manage their home as they saw fit, but proponents said the benefits to the child outweighed the loss of parental rights.

Proponents cited an English legal standard set in the Middle Ages called **parens patriae**—a Latin term for "parent of the nation." *Parens patriae*, which became the guiding principle of the juvenile court, made the court the children's guardian. As far back as 1838, American courts upheld the doctrine of *parens patriae* in the case of **Ex parte Crouse**, which involved the incarceration of Mary Ann Crouse at the request of her mother but without the approval of her father (see Figure 1.2). The father argued his daughter deserved a jury trial, but the Pennsylvania Supreme Court ruled that the state had the power to intervene, no matter the reason, if it could provide help that the family could not provide. The court stated:

> [The state] has a paramount interest in the virtue and knowledge of its members, and that of strict right the business of education belongs to it. That parents are ordinarily entrusted with it, is because it can seldom be

put in better hands; but where they are incompetent or corrupt, what is there to prevent the public from withdrawing their faculties, held as they obviously are, at its sufferance? The right of parental control is a natural, but not an inalienable one. (*Ex parte Crouse*, 1838)

Critics of the *Crouse* decision contended that the state offered the child nothing more than incarceration, while the father could have provided education, training, and nurturing care. Indeed, this argument prevailed in the 1870 ruling of the Illinois Supreme Court in **People v. Turner** (1870), which upheld parents' rights to care for their children without government intervention. The court stated:

In our solicitude to form youths for the duties of civil life, we should not forget the rights which inhere both in parents and children. The principle of the absorption of the child in, and its complete subjection to the despotism of, the State, is wholly inadmissible in the modern civilized world. The parent has the right to the care, custody, and assistance of his child. The duty to maintain and protect it, is a principle of a natural law.

In subsequent decisions, however, most jurisdictions ignored *Turner* and followed the standards set in *Crouse*. In the 1905 case of **Commonwealth v. Fisher**, the Pennsylvania Supreme Court settled the issue of child and parental rights by citing the intent of intervention—that is, by explaining why the courts needed to intervene. It said:

There is no probability in the proper administration of law, of the children's liberty being unduly invaded. Every statute which is designed to give protection, care, and training to children, as a needed substitute for parental authority, and performance of parental duty, is but a recognition of the duty of the state, as the legitimate guardian and protector of children where other guardianship fails. No constitutional right is violated.

The Pennsylvania court ruled, in effect, that a child not only might *need* court intervention but in fact had a *right* to intervention. As a result, juvenile courts were given the freedom to deal with juveniles as they saw fit, and parents had virtually no legal recourse to defy them.

The legal standard established by *Fisher* went undisputed for decades. In the 1960s, however, the U.S. Supreme Court altered the treatment of juvenile delinquents in a series of rulings. Its 1966 **Kent v. United States** decision granted some protection for the rights of juveniles, but their rights were still not found to be equal to those of adult offenders. To this day, juveniles are treated as a special class of persons and courts still have the ability to intervene on their behalf in many circumstances. ●

NAVIGATING THE FIELD 1.1

Parens Patriae and the Juvenile Court

In 1899 the Cook County (Illinois) Juvenile Court opened its doors. The court, which was the first of its kind in the country, was based on the classic principle of *parens patriae*. *Parens patriae* is a Latin term that this chapter says means "parent of the nation." However, phrases from antiquity, such as *parens patriae*, are not always easy to define, and their definitions often vary from one source to another.

Putting It Into Action

Use the Internet to search for other definitions of *parens patriae* (and possibly other spellings). Gather those definitions into a single file. Add to the file your comments on what you think the significance of the varying definitions might be for juvenile court philosophy.

Submit that file to your instructor when asked to do so. ●

SUMMARY

>> **LO 1**   **Identify how society's perception of children and of their culpability for deviant behavior has evolved over time.**

It was not until the 16th and 17th centuries that scholars and medical experts began to think that children should be treated differently than adults. Prior to that time, children as young as 5 years old could be forced to perform hard physical labor, often at the behest of their caregivers. In addition, they could be punished for criminal offenses in the same manner as adults. With the advent of Enlightenment thought, however, increasing recognition was given to the emotional and physical needs of children. England began legislating ages of culpability and enacted laws that protected young children. These new laws did not hold young children to the same standards of responsibility as older teenagers or adults. With this change in mindset, the methods of handling juvenile offenders changed and began to move toward rehabilitation rather than punishment.

Key Terms

bridewells   6   houses of refuge   6
cottage reformatories   7   nullification   5

>> **LO 1.2**   **Discuss the origins of the juvenile court.**

The child saver movement, which began in the late 1800s, advocated rescuing juvenile delinquents from the streets and providing them with social services—instead of punishing them harshly for problem behaviors such as running away from home. The first juvenile court in Cook County, Illinois, was built around a less formal and less adversarial model than adult courts. In addition, the state of Illinois extended the jurisdiction of the court to manage dependent and neglect cases as well.

Key Terms

child savers   8   Progressive Era   8   status offenses   9

>> **LO 1.3**   **Explain the concept of *parens patriae* and how it has been incorporated into the juvenile court system.**

In America in the late 1800s, *parens patriae* became the guiding principle of the juvenile court, meaning that the juvenile court could assume the role of parent or guardian for youths who did not come from stable homes or who had parents who were unable to make appropriate decisions for them. Juvenile court principles required the court to make decisions in the best interest of youths in regard to residency, education, and other matters.

Key Terms

Commonwealth v.   *Ex parte Crouse*   10   *parens patriae*   10
  Fisher   11   *Kent v. United States*   11   *People v. Turner*   11

DISCUSSION QUESTIONS

1. Compare the treatment of youths in the American colonies with that of children of other cultures and countries around the same time. Has the viewpoint of the role of the child changed throughout the world or just in Western societies?

2. Explain the idealistic concept of cottage reformatories. If implemented as intended, would these reformatories be successful in the 21st century? Why or why not?

3. Did the U.S. Supreme Court do an adequate job of defining constitutional rights of juveniles and their parents? Do you agree with the ruling of *Kent v. United States* in regard to the ability of the state to intervene in the lives of children?

EXPLORING JUVENILE JUSTICE FURTHER

1. Explore the creation and development of the juvenile justice system in your particular state. Make a timeline of the important events that occurred during its development, such as the creation of the first juvenile court or implementation of a juvenile residential facility.

2. Interview an employee of a child social services agency in your area, focusing specifically on his or her involvement with the juvenile justice system and his or her satisfaction with the treatment of juveniles in your jurisdiction.

$SAGE edge™

Give your students the SAGE edge!

SAGE edge offers a robust online environment featuring an impressive array of free tools and resources for review, study, and further exploration, keeping both instructors and students on the cutting edge of teaching and learning. Learn more at **edge.sagepub.com/schmallegerjj**.

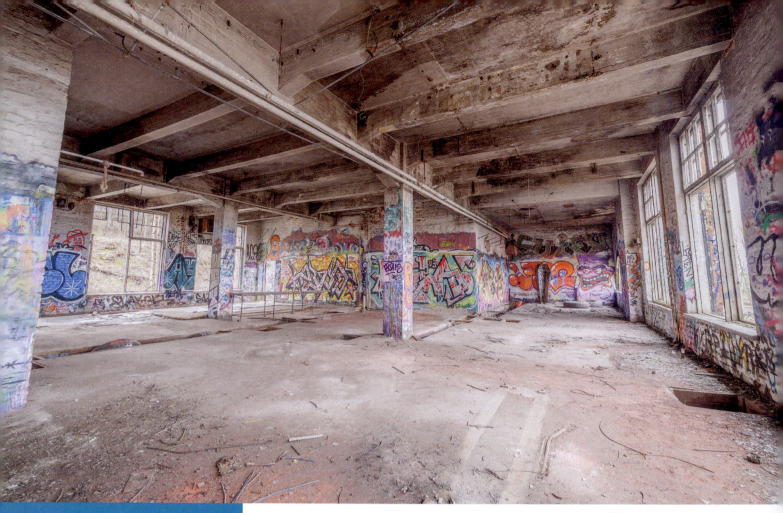

2

Measurement of Juvenile Crime

After reading this chapter you should be able to

1. Explain the concept of the age–crime curve and the stages of juvenile offending
2. Identify the primary methods used to gather juvenile arrest statistics, as well as the limitations of the data collected
3. Identify the primary methods used to gather juvenile court statistics
4. Identify the primary methods used to gather juvenile correctional statistics
5. Discuss the differences between self-report and victimization data

Key Terms in Chapter 2

age of onset
age–crime curve
Children in Custody Survey (CIC)
clearances by arrest
dark figure of crime
desistance
Juvenile Court Statistics (JCS)

Monitoring the Future Survey
National Council on Crime and Delinquency (NCCD)
National Crime Victimization Survey (NCVS)
National Juvenile Court Data Archives

National Survey of Youth in Custody
National Youth Survey
persistence
reliability
self-report studies
Uniform Crime Report (UCR)
validity
victimization studies

INTRODUCTION

In 2018, a Wal-Mart store in Neptune Township, New Jersey, received a call during which the caller claimed that a bomb had been planted in the store and would soon explode.[1] Emergency services responded quickly, and police, firefighters, and medical assistance were at the store within minutes. The building was quickly evacuated, and bomb-sniffing dogs worked their way through every part of it. Thankfully, the call was a prank, and no bomb was found. Prank calls can be tough to trace though, as anyone who has ever received robocalls will agree. Anyone with a bit of knowledge and the right software can spoof caller ID systems into showing misleading information on the phone receiving the call. In the case of the Wal-Mart caller, police had some trouble identifying where the call originated, and the caller might have gotten away without anyone knowing who he was. With the help of the phone company, however, the police were eventually able to identify the caller—and it turned out that he was an 11-year-old boy who had gotten the idea for the call from something he had seen on the Internet. After juvenile authorities took the boy into custody, Monmouth County prosecutor Christopher J. Gramiccioni issued a statement to the press. "Prank calls about bomb threats or guns are not a laughing matter. Resources are deployed at a cost to taxpayers. Parents have a responsibility to monitor what their children do on the Internet where these ideas can be cultivated," he said.

In this case, the prankster was eventually caught, but not all offenders are identified or apprehended. This is especially true in cases of cybercrime (discussed later in this text), where victims sometimes don't even realize they have been victimized. Undiscovered victimization, unreported crimes, and offenders who remain anonymous and unidentified all contribute to inaccuracies in official crime statistics.

In the United States, a variety of strategies are used to try to piece together an accurate representation of the true crime rate—including crimes committed by juveniles. While we may never know the actual amount of crime that occurs, we can gather information from multiple sources to get a clearer picture of what is going on and where crime is occurring.

This chapter explores the various kinds of data used to understand juvenile crime rates. Law enforcement, the courts, and other government agencies collect data on direct interactions with juvenile offenders. However, higher levels of criminal activity are shown in data based on self-reports from offending juveniles and crime victims. No one type of data provides a complete picture of crime, but this chapter should help the reader gain a better understanding of juvenile crime rates.

AGE–CRIME CURVE AND STAGES OF DELINQUENCY

>> LO 2.1   Explain the concept of the age–crime curve and the stages of juvenile offending.

Before exploring the various types of data that attempt to piece together the juvenile delinquency puzzle, it is important to understand patterns of juvenile offending. There is a universal trend in Western nations that shows an increase in the commission of delinquent acts during late childhood, generally peaking between the ages of 15 and 19 years old (Figure 2.1). For the majority of individuals, this offending behavior decreases in their early 20s. Otherwise known as the **age–crime curve**, this phenomenon indicates that as a child grows into the teenage years, he or she is more likely to take risks, be impulsive, and behave in ways that may seem irrational to a grown adult. However, as a person ages, he or she matures out of such behaviors and moves toward a more settled life without the presence of criminality.[2] While this is not the case for every person (as many people commit crimes throughout their entire adult life), it is a well-identified trend characteristic of most people.

There are different versions of the age–crime curve, depending on the individuals involved and the type of criminal behavior. For instance, the property crime curve will peak earlier than a curve depicting violent crimes.[3] Females are more likely to peak earlier than males.[4] Last, the age–crime curve is more likely to be higher and wider for young males (often minorities) growing up in high-crime, disadvantaged neighborhoods.[5]

It is important to understand the terms associated with the initiation, continuation, and ceasing of delinquent behavior, otherwise known as the stages of delinquent behavior. **Age of onset** is the age a juvenile first begins committing delinquent acts. For example, if a female commits her first act of shoplifting at age 13 by stealing a candy bar from a grocery store, 13 years old is her age of onset. Research has indicated that juveniles who begin offending at an earlier age are more likely to continue offending into their adult years.[6] A juvenile who begins offending at age 14 is more likely to continue criminality as an adult, compared with an individual who begins at age 17. Age of onset can differ depending on the type of crime. The average age of onset for gang membership is 15.9 years old, followed by marijuana use at 16.5 years old and gun carrying at 17.3 years old.[7]

Persistence is the continuation of delinquent behaviors as a youth ages, often with an escalation of seriousness in the criminal offending.[8] The previous example of the shoplifter would demonstrate persistence

A juvenile offender. Why do juvenile offenders often feel hopeless and alone?

FIGURE 2.1

The Age–Crime Curve

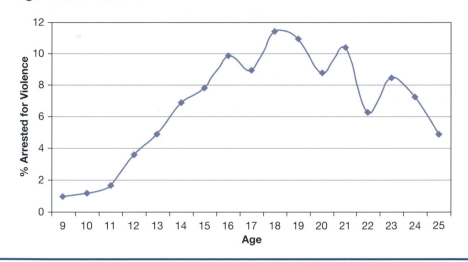

Source: National Institute of Justice.

if she continued shoplifting, potentially moving on to bigger and more expensive items. She may begin stealing electronics, purses, or other expensive material items. Or she may begin stealing motor vehicles. Not all offense categories have the same rate of persistence. For instance, studies have shown drug dealing and weapons possession have one of the highest likelihoods of persistence into adulthood compared with other minor offenses.[9]

Last, **desistance** is quitting the delinquent behavior. As indicated in the age–crime curve, the majority of juveniles will cease offending by their early 20s. Those juveniles who do persist and continue offending into adulthood will increase the severity of their offending and often have a higher likelihood for committing lethal violence.[10] This violence is often directed at individuals of the same age.

JUVENILE ARREST STATISTICS

>> LO 2.2 **Identify the primary methods used to gather juvenile arrest statistics, as well as the limitations of the data collected.**

Reports of criminal offending rates were erratic and unreliable for decades until jurisdictions began to formalize reporting procedures. Authorities in Maine, Massachusetts, and New York were the first to collect official crime statistics. Other states and localities attempted to publish crime rates, but the information was not valid enough to determine the actual crime level. In other words, the method of measuring and collecting the data did not allow for an accurate representation of the crime rate. Federal record keeping began in 1870, when Congress created the Department of Justice; however, many law enforcement agencies ignored the department's requests for data.

A juvenile offender under arrest. How do most juveniles enter the system?

In the early 20th century, the International Association of Chiefs of Police formed the Committee on Uniform Crime Reports to improve data collection. Seeing the need for a regulated method of collecting data, the committee worked toward a uniform method of gathering and reporting data on criminal activity. In 1930, the U.S. Attorney General made the Federal Bureau of Investigation (FBI) responsible for collecting and publishing data for the **Uniform Crime Report (UCR)**, an annual compilation of crime data from all law enforcement agencies in the United States. It listed all **clearances by arrest**, which are arrests made because an offender confessed to a crime or was implicated by other evidence or witnesses. While nonparticipation is not a punishable offense, the majority of law enforcement agencies regularly report to the UCR, making it one of the most used datasets to describe and explain crime rates. Since 2006, the UCR has been published electronically each year on the FBI website under the title *Crime in the United States* (CIUS).[11]

CASE STUDY

Montgomery v. Louisiana, 577 U.S. 503 (2016)

Henry Montgomery was 17 years old in 1963 when he killed Charles Hunt, a police officer in East Baton Rouge, Louisiana. A jury found him guilty and sentenced him to death, but that decision was overturned in 1966 by the Louisiana Supreme Court due to claims of public prejudice. Montgomery received a new trial and was again convicted and sentenced to life imprisonment without parole. This decision was affirmed by the Louisiana Supreme Court. For decades, Montgomery was a model prisoner and was very active in mentoring other inmates. After the U.S. Supreme Court decision of *Miller v. Alabama* (2012), which found it unconstitutional to sentence children to life without parole, Montgomery made a motion to have his sentence reduced. The Louisiana Supreme Court again weighed in, stating *Miller* could not be applied retroactively.

Montgomery's attorneys appealed to the U.S. Supreme Court, and in January 2016, the court ruled in favor of Montgomery. Written by Justice Anthony Kennedy, this decision said that the decision in *Miller* could be applied retroactively. Justice Kennedy wrote that "prisoners like Montgomery must be given the opportunity to show their crime did not reflect irreparable corruption; and if it did not, their hope for some years of life outside prison walls must be restored." As of February 2018, Montgomery's request for parole had been denied and he was still incarcerated in Angola Prison.

1. Do you agree with the ruling in *Montgomery v. Louisiana*?

2. Should a murder committed by a juvenile be deserving of a life sentence without any possibility of release from confinement?

3. In your opinion, would this ruling be the same today?

Online Case Opinion

https://caselaw.findlaw.com/us-supreme-court/14-280 .html ●

The UCR is divided into Part I and Part II offenses (see Table 2.1). Part I offenses include the following serious criminal behaviors: aggravated assault, arson, automobile theft, burglary, larceny, murder, rape, and robbery. Part II offenses include nonviolent offenses, such as buying and receiving stolen property, carrying and possessing weapons, counterfeiting, forgery, fraud, prostitution, and simple assault. It lists the age, sex, and race of offenders and each person's arrest charge or number of crimes committed. While the UCR is a very useful tool for examining crime rates, it has some problems with validity and reliability. **Validity** is the degree to which a measure reflects what is really going on, but the UCR can report only crimes known to the police. It cannot show the **dark figure of crime**, the crime that is unknown to police. Also, because juveniles are usually arrested only for serious crimes, the other crimes juveniles have committed are usually not part of the UCR. Similarly, **reliability** indicates consistency of a measure. Since crimes are not reported in the same way in all jurisdictions, there will be underreported crimes and overreported crimes.

TABLE 2.1

UCR Crime Classification

PART I CRIMES	PART II CRIMES
Aggravated assault	Buying and receiving stolen property
Arson	Carrying and possessing weapons
Auto theft	Counterfeiting
Burglary	Forgery
Larceny	Fraud
Murder	Prostitution
Rape	Simple assault
Robbery	

The following findings were reported by the CIUS in the year 2017:

- There were 620,264 juvenile arrests in 2017.

- The highest number of arrests for juveniles was for larceny-theft 15.7% of all juvenile arrests), followed by simple assaults (14.7%) and drug abuse violations (11.6%).

- Juvenile arrests for property crimes constituted 13.4% of all property crime arrests.

- Almost 33% of individuals arrested for arson in 2017 were juveniles, with over half of those youths under the age of 15.

Table 2.2 highlights types of juvenile arrests in 2017. As can be seen from the data, property crimes and drug offenses are higher than any other category.

TABLE 2.2

UCR Data Showing Juvenile Arrests in 2017

	AGES UNDER 15	AGES UNDER 18
Murder	58	685
Rape	1,148	2,989
Robbery	2,824	14,703
Aggravated assault	6,991	21,485
Burglary	7,425	23,569
Larceny-theft	25,846	91,715
Motor vehicle theft	2,983	12,466
Arson	998	1,738
Vandalism	11,353	28,130
Weapons offenses	4,173	14,088
Drug abuse violations	10,813	72,334
DUI	88	4,593
Curfew and loitering	6,900	23,461

Source: 2017 Crime in the United States, Uniform Crime Report, FBI.

JUVENILE COURT STATISTICS

>> **LO 2.3**   **Identify the primary methods used to gather juvenile court statistics.**

The Office of Juvenile Justice and Delinquency Prevention, a branch of the Department of Justice, annually publishes the ***Juvenile Court Statistics* (JCS)**, which provides information on children who appear before juvenile courts. It was launched in 1929 by the Department of Labor, describing cases handled by 42 courts in 1927. For the next 10 years, the Children's Bureau would gather cards completed by the juvenile courts that showed each delinquency, dependency, and status offense, as well as the age, gender, and race of the juvenile, reason for the referral, and adjudication and disposition of each case. Due to the cost, the tabulation system ceased, and until the mid-1970s JCS reports were based on simple counts reported by the courts. The method of data collection changed over the next few decades, to the point that now JCS has become a sound method of data collection and reporting.[12]

The unit counted by the JCS is a case, which represents a juvenile processed by a juvenile court on a new referral, no matter the number of violations contained in a referral. For instance, a juvenile charged with four arsons in a single referral would represent one case. When a case is disposed, it means action has been taken on the referral, but it does not necessarily mean the case is closed.

JCS is prepared annually by the National Center for Juvenile Justice, which is the research division of the National Council of Juvenile and Family Court Judges. The gathering and preparation of the data are supported by an annual grant from the Office of Juvenile Justice and Delinquency Prevention. JCS caseload statistics for 2005–2016 are shown in Figure 2.2.

Another source for juvenile court statistics is the **National Juvenile Court Data Archives**. In 1979, the National Center for Juvenile Justice began collecting data from 15 states or large jurisdictions with automated data systems, representing more than 80% of the juvenile population.[13] According to the National Juvenile Court Data

FIGURE 2.2

Delinquency Caseloads for All Offense Groups in 2016

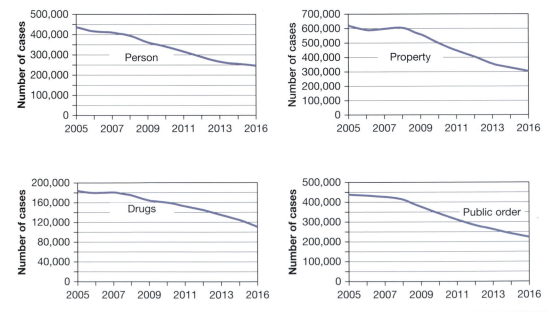

Source: Hockenberry, Sarah, and Puzzanchera, Charles. 2019. *Juvenile Court Statistics* 2016. Pittsburgh, PA: National Center for Juvenile Justice.

Archives, truancy cases accounted for over half (55%) of the status offense petitioned cases in juvenile court in 2016, followed by liquor law violations (12%). In addition, about 71% of delinquency cases in 2016 were either handled informally or not adjudicated.[14]

REPORTS OF JUVENILES IN CUSTODY

>> **LO 2.4** **Identify the primary methods used to gather juvenile correctional statistics.**

The entrance to a social services agency. What kinds of services are available to juveniles and their families?

©iStockphoto.com/sshepard

Historically, data collected on juveniles under correctional control have been less accurate than court data. In the early 1970s, the U.S. Census Bureau launched the **Children in Custody Survey (CIC)**, a twice-yearly survey of public and private correctional facilities. While the Census Bureau survey has a response rate of almost 100% from the public juvenile facilities, the rate from private facilities is lower. In the past, it was difficult to make valid inferences from these numbers, due to growth of private corrections facilities, lack of standardized legal codes across jurisdictions, and aggregation of the data rather than reporting individual cases.[15]

To supplement the CIC survey, the Bureau of Justice Statistics in 2000 launched a survey using a random sample of juveniles in secure facilities. This survey, the **National Survey of Youth in Custody**, is now conducted by Westat, a private professional services company. It collects more detailed data on the types of juveniles in facilities, personal factors that have influenced their behaviors, and conditions of confinement.[16] Findings from the National Survey of Youth in Custody are reported in the Bureau of Justice Statistics' Prison Rape Elimination Act report. At the time of the publication of this text, the most recent data collection was from 2012. In 2012, about 9.5% of youths in state-run facilities reported one or more incidents of sexual victimization within 12 months of taking the survey. Those assaults were most likely to have been carried out by staff members at the facility. Of the 1,390 youths who reported victimization by staff, 89.1% were males who reported sexual activity with female staff. In addition, of those youths who were victimized by juvenile facility staff, over 20% had been given drugs or alcohol to coerce them into sexual activity.[17]

The **National Council on Crime and Delinquency (NCCD)** field-tested a data collection method on juveniles annually admitted to state-operated commitment facilities. It covered individual information, allowing for better policy analysis.[18] However, not all states provided data, short-term detention facilities did not report, and it mainly captured information on very serious offenders and others incarcerated for long periods. The Office of Juvenile Justice and Delinquency Prevention has since stopped data collection through the CIC and NCCD. The Census Bureau was then recruited to complete an analysis of all juveniles in facilities originally covered by the CIC. In addition, the National Jail Survey provides periodic information on juveniles admitted to jails.[19]

SELF-REPORT STUDIES

>> **LO 2.5** **Discuss the differences between self-report and victimization data.**

As noted previously, official data reported by law enforcement and court systems do not accurately portray the amount of juvenile crime in the United States. One way to improve accuracy is using self-report studies, in which juveniles report their own delinquent acts. For about 50 years, the results of **self-report studies** have been challenging the assertions made by official report data. These studies indicated that juvenile crime was not carried out mainly by minorities in lower-class neighborhoods, as was supposed, but was more widely distributed.[20] Recent studies also show that delinquency rates are much higher than previously assumed. Research on male juveniles shows that as much as 82% of total crime was self-reported delinquency, while only 35% of total crime came from official juvenile justice system reports (some self-report data overlaps and includes official data).[21] Similarly, research on female juveniles between the ages of 12 and 17 found that there were on average three times as many self-reported offenders as those in official reports.[22]

Many small-scale studies have gathered data on juvenile delinquency, but the most influential data have come from two nationwide studies. The **National Youth Survey**, conducted seven times from 1976 to 1987 by the National Institute of Mental Health, collected data about deviant behaviors from a representative sample of young people. The **Monitoring the Future Survey** is an ongoing project collecting data on the behaviors, attitudes, and values of about 50,000 eighth-, tenth-, and twelfth-grade students, followed up by questionnaires mailed to a sample of each graduating class.[23] The Monitoring the Future Survey revealed in 2017 that there was a significant increase in marijuana use for eighth, tenth, and twelfth graders. The year 2017 was also the first year vaping was measured, including nicotine and marijuana vaping. One in 10 twelfth graders reported vaping, and 19% of the same grade level reported nicotine vaping.[24]

The validity of self-report studies has been questioned. The veracity of juveniles who commit many delinquent acts can be called into question, and different methodologies are used to gather the data.

While the results of self-report studies vary somewhat, the following conclusions can be made:

1. Delinquent rates are considerably lower in police reports and court data than in self-report studies.

2. Data from self-report studies show smaller differences in crime commission based on race, ethnic origin, and gender than do data from official reports.

NAVIGATING THE FIELD 2.1

Self-Report Studies

This chapter describes self-report studies as an alternative source of information about juvenile misbehavior. Self-report studies are especially important in documenting juvenile crime that has either not been detected by the authorities or not been reported by the public.

Putting It Into Action

For this active learning exercise, make a list of activities in which you were involved as a teenager that might be considered delinquent. Describe those activities in some detail, but do not include your name or other personally identifiable information. Were those activities ever discovered by the authorities? By your parents? Were they known to your friends? If so, what role did your friends play? Did they encourage you or discourage you from involvement? Would you repeat those same activities today, given the chance?

When asked to do so, submit to your instructor a description of what you have learned from this exercise, but in that description do not include the details of your misbehavior. ●

3. Juveniles in the lower and middle classes have a high level of delinquency.

4. Juveniles commit a higher number of serious crimes than what is reported by law enforcement.[25]

VICTIMIZATION STUDIES

Victimization studies, another way to better understand juvenile delinquency, collect data from individuals on their experiences with crime victimization, rather than offending behaviors. One of the most notable measures is the **National Crime Victimization Survey (NCVS)**, an annual survey conducted by the Bureau of Justice Statistics. The U.S. Census Bureau began the NCVS in 1972 as a way to supplement official arrest data such as the UCR.

A parent hugs his child following a school shooting. Why is school violence so common today?

RHONA WISE/AFP/Getty Images

The NCVS surveys almost 135,000 households and 224,520 individuals ages 12 and older on their experiences with crime victimization, including rape, robbery, assault, and domestic violence (see Figure 2.3).[26] Each household was interviewed twice in 2016. The study projected that this population experienced 5.7 million violent victimizations, representing 1.3% of the total population, and 15.9 million property crimes, or 8.8% of the total. These rates were similar to those in 2015.

One notable finding of the NCVS was that individuals ages 12 to 24 years had the highest rate of violent victimization of any other group (see Table 2.3). Males, blacks, and people in lower income levels were more likely to be victimized than females, other races, or people in higher income levels.

Based on official arrest data and victimization data, the following conclusions can be made:

1. The crime rate reported in victimization surveys is higher than that reported by law enforcement.

2. Though the NCVS and the UCR report very different numbers for categories of offenses, these categories maintain basically the same rank order.

3. Juveniles and young adults are more likely to commit property crimes than are other age groups, but they have a higher rate of victimization in both property and personal crimes than do other age groups.

4. Racial minorities are overrepresented both as offenders and victims compared with their share of the general population.

The NCVS has issues with validity and reliability, much like the other measures of crime. Respondents may define victimization differently, such as what constitutes the act of rape. For instance, although incorrect, some respondents may consider only rape that occurs between a male offender and female victim. In addition, respondents who are questioned more than once sometimes provide different answers based on the ability to recall events accurately. ●

FIGURE 2.3

National Crime Victimization Survey: NCVS-1 Basic Screen Questionnaire

NCVS-1   Implementation Date: (07-01-2016)

OMB No. 1121-0111: Approval Expires 08/31/2018

NATIONAL CRIME VICTIMIZATION SURVEY

NCVS-1 BASIC SCREEN QUESTIONNAIRE

NOTE: Questions are listed in the order asked. Skips in question numbering are due to questionnaire changes over time.

MOBILITY QUESTIONS

33a. TIMEATADDRESS   `506`   _____ Years (Round to nearest whole year)

Before we get to the crime questions, I have some questions that are helpful in studying where and why crimes occur.

Ask or verify -
How long have you lived at this address?

(Enter 0 if less than 1 year.)

If = 0 ASK 33b
If = DK or RF SKIP to 33c
Else SKIP to 33d

33b. MONTHSATADDRESS   `505`   _____ Months (1-11) - SKIP to 33e

How many months?

33c. TIMEATADDRESSPROBE

Have you lived here...

Read categories 1-4:

1 ☐ **More than 5 years** - If HHLD Respondent ASK 34, else SKIP to 36a.
2 ☐ **Less than 5 years, but more than 1 year**
3 ☐ **Less than 1 year, but more than 6 months**   SKIP
4 ☐ **6 months or less**   to 33e
5 ☐ Don't Know

33d.   **CHECK ITEM A**   How many years are entered in 33a?

☐ 5 years or more - If HHLD Respondent SKIP to 34, else SKIP to 36a
☐ Less than 5 years - ASK 33e

33e. TIMEMOVEDIN5YEARS   `508`   _____ Number of times -   If HHLD Respondent ASK 34, Else SKIP to 36a

Altogether, how many times have you moved in the last 5 years, that is, since _____, 20 ___?

Enter number of times.

BUSINESS OPERATED FROM SAMPLE

34. BUSINESS (Asked of Household Respondent Only)   `530`   1 ☐ Yes - ASK 35

Does anyone in this household operate a business from this address?   2 ☐ No - SKIP to 36a

35. BUSINESSSIGN (Asked of Household Respondent Only)   `531`   1 ☐ Yes (Recognizable business)

If this is a PERSONAL visit - Fill by observation.   2 ☐ No (Unrecognizable business)
If this is a TELEPHONE contact - Ask.

Is there a sign on the premises or some other indication to the general public that a business is operated from this address?

RESPONDENT'S SCREEN QUESTIONS

36a. SQTHEFT

I'm going to read some examples that will give you an idea of the kinds of crimes this study covers.

As I go through them, tell me if any of these happened to you in the last 6 months, that is since _____ _____, 20 _____.

Was something belonging to YOU stolen, such as -

Read each category.

(a) **Things that you carry, like luggage, a wallet, purse, briefcase book -**

(b) **Clothing, jewelry, or cellphone -**

(c) **Bicycle or sports equipment -**

(d) **Things in your home - like a TV, stereo, or tools -**

(e) **Things outside your home such as a garden hose or lawn furniture -** (Asked of Household Respondent Only)

(f) **Things belonging to children in the household -** (Asked of Household Respondent Only)

(g) **Things from a vehicle, such as a package, groceries, camera, or CDs -**

OR

(h) **Did anyone ATTEMPT to steal anything belonging to you?**

Ask only if necessary | 532 |

Did any incidents of this type happen to you?

1 ☐ Yes - ASK 36b

2 ☐ No - If Household Respondent ASK to 37a; Else SKIP to 40a

36b. SQTHEFTTIMES | 533 |

How many times?

_____

Number of times (36b)

36c. SQTHEFTSPEC

What happened?

Briefly describe incident(s)

_____

_____

_____

_____

If Household Respondent ASK 37a; else SKIP to 40a

37a. SQBREAKIN (Asked of Household Respondent Only)

(Other than any incidents already mentioned,) has anyone -

Read each category.

(a) **Broken in or ATTEMPTED to break into your home by forcing a door or window, pushing past someone, jimmying a lock, cutting a screen, or entering through an open door or window?**

(b) **Has anyone illegally gotten in or tried to get into a garage, shed, or storage room?**

OR

(c) **Illegally gotten in or tried to get into a hotel or motel room or vacation home where you were staying?**

Ask only if necessary | 534 |

Did any incidents of this type happen to you?

1 ☐ Yes - ASK 37b

2 ☐ No - SKIP to 38

37b. SQBREAKINTIMES (Asked of Household Respondent Only) | 535 |

How many times?

_____

Number of times (37b)

37c. SQBREAKINSPEC (Asked of Household Respondent Only)

What happened?

Briefly describe incident(s)

_____

_____

National Crime Victimization Survey.

TABLE 2.3

Rate of Violent Victimization and Percentage Reported to Police Based on Demographic Characteristics

VICTIM DEMOGRAPHIC	RATE OF VIOLENT CRIME PER 1,000 PERSONS AGE 12 OR OLDER	PERCENTAGE OF VIOLENT CRIME REPORTED TO POLICE
Total	21.1	42.1
SEX		
Male	21.4	44.3
Female	20.8	40.0
RACE		
White	20.5	40.1
Black	24.1	39.8
Hispanic	20.2	51.6
AGE		
12–17	30.9	27.7
18–24	30.9	35.7
25–34	31.8	38.9
35–49	22.9	49.8
50–64	16.1	49.1
65+	4.4	60.4
MARITAL STATUS		
Never married	29.8	33.5
Married	12.4	50.8
Widowed	10.7	48.1
Divorced	30.1	53.8
Separated	67.5	43.2
HOUSEHOLD INCOME		
Less than $10,000	35.8	47.3
$10,000–$14,999	35.6	50.2
$15,000–$24,999	32.9	45.3
$25,000–$34,999	21.0	44.2
$35,000–$49,999	20.4	34.0
$50,000–$74,999	17.6	42.4
$75,000 or more	15.7	39.4

National Crime Victimization Survey.

Families and Schools Together (FAST)

Media reports often describe crimes committed by juveniles, but sometimes they also highlight delinquency prevention programs, especially when those programs have been shown to be successful. Families and Schools Together (FAST) is one such program. FAST targets at-risk youths in urban areas who have been exposed to violence. It is a multifamily group intervention program that provides parents the tools needed to help protect their children and to build supportive parent peer groups. After 8 weeks of training, follow-up meetings are initiated and run by the families for 2 years with juvenile involvement. Youths involved in FAST have scored lower on the teacher aggressive behavior scale compared with other students who have not been exposed to the program. In 2017, news outlets reported that the state of Wisconsin had received funding from multiple sources to implement FAST in the Madison area. The intention was to increase student success for adolescents in high-crime areas.

Putting It Into Action

Using your Internet search engine, research the FAST program to better understand its implementation. Explain why you feel this program would or would not be successful in reducing future violent behavior among youths in Madison, as well as other high-crime areas. ●

SUMMARY

>> **LO 2.1** **Explain the concept of the age–crime curve and the stages of juvenile offending.**

The age–crime curve is a universal trend showing that the prevalence of committing delinquent acts will increase during late childhood, generally peaking between the ages of 15 and 19 years, then decrease into the early 20s. There are three stages of juvenile offending: (1) age of onset, or the age at which juveniles first commit offenses; (2) persistence, or juvenile offending that continues as a youth ages, most likely with increasing severity; and (3) desistance, or the cessation of criminal offending.

Key Terms

age of onset 16	desistance 17
age–crime curve 16	persistence 16

>> **LO 2.2** **Identify the primary methods used to gather juvenile arrest statistics, as well as the limitations of the data collected.**

The Uniform Crime Report (UCR), created by the International Association of Chiefs of Police, is the most prevalent source of offender arrest data. All U.S. law enforcement agencies are expected to report arrest data annually. Offenses are divided into two categories based on seriousness. However, since not all crime is reported to law enforcement, the validity of the data is under question. And since not all agencies report data, or report it inconsistently, the reliability of the measurement is of concern.

Key Terms

clearances by arrest 18	Uniform Crime Report
dark figure of crime 18	(UCR) 18
reliability 18	validity 18

>> **LO 2.3**   **Identify the primary methods used to gather juvenile court statistics.**

The Department of Labor has been collecting juvenile court data since 1929. Data measurement has changed over the years, and the current method involves examining each case in the system. The department's National Juvenile Court Data Archives provide a robust source of past and current juvenile delinquency trends.

Key Terms

Juvenile Court Statistics
(JCS)   20

National Juvenile Court
Data Archives   20

>> **LO 2.4**   **Identify the primary methods used to gather juvenile correctional statistics.**

Juvenile correctional data have been somewhat unreliable for decades due to their limited origins. For instance, the Children in Custody Survey has had robust response rates from public juvenile facilities but not from private juvenile facilities. More recent collection efforts have used random sampling of institutions along with more detailed data on juveniles under correctional control.

Key Terms

Children in Custody Survey
(CIC)   21

National Council on Crime
and Delinquency
(NCCD)   21

National Survey of Youth in
Custody   21

>> **LO 2.5**   **Discuss the differences between self-report and victimization data.**

In addition to official data, other methods of gathering information on juveniles' offending behaviors provide a clearer picture of actual crime rates. Self-report studies are based on individuals' own reports on their offending behaviors. Victimization studies are based on the experiences of crime victims. These reports have consistently shown a much higher juvenile offending rate than data from law enforcement.

Key Terms

Monitoring the Future
Survey   22

National Crime
Victimization Survey
(NCVS)   23

National Youth Survey   22
self-report studies   22
victimization studies   23

DISCUSSION QUESTIONS

1. Why might law enforcement agencies overreport or underreport arrest rates?

2. Are there better ways of more accurately reporting crimes not collected by law enforcement, known as the dark figure of crime?

1. Investigate the juvenile crime rates in your state, and compare them with a different state in another region of the country. For example, if you live in the Southeast, choose a state in the Northwest. What differences and similarities do you see in regard to personal versus property crime? Male versus female crime?

2. Create a self-report survey to gather data on offending behaviors of students at your university, specifically focusing on their offending behaviors as high school students and then college undergraduates. Administer the survey to your classmates. What do you expect to find?

3. Read through the report in Appendix A "Girls in the Juvenile Justice System." What important trends do you notice? Why do you think girls account for less than one-third of all juvenile arrests? What is the one crime where they have a higher proportion of arrests than boys? What conclusions can you draw from this about the dynamics of female juvenile delinquency?

$SAGE edge™

Give your students the SAGE edge!

SAGE edge offers a robust online environment featuring an impressive array of free tools and resources for review, study, and further exploration, keeping both instructors and students on the cutting edge of teaching and learning. Learn more at **edge.sagepub.com/schmallegerjj**.

Theories of Delinquency

After reading this chapter you should be able to

1. Explain the importance of theory and research
2. Explain the differences between classical and biological theories of delinquency
3. Describe how psychological factors affect criminality
4. Discuss developmental and sociological theories of criminality

Key Terms in Chapter 3

anomie
antisocial personality
   disorder
atavistic
biological school
biosocial theory
causation
Chicago school
classical school
collective efficacy
concentric zones
concordance
containment theory
correlation
developmental theories
differential association
differential reinforcement
dopamine
ecological fallacy
empirical research

the Enlightenment
focal concerns
free will
general strain theory
general theory of crime
hedonistic calculus
inner containments
labeling
Minnesota Multiphasic
   Personality Inventory
   (MMPI)
modeling
neoclassicism
neurotransmitters
nonspurious
operant conditioning
outer containments
phrenology
positivism
primary deviance

psychoanalysis
psychological school
rational choice theory
reintegrative shaming
routine activities theory
secondary deviance
serotonin
social bond
social disorganization
social ecology
social learning
soft determinism
somatotypes
strain
subculture
symbolic interaction
techniques of
   neutralization
theory
time sequence

INTRODUCTION

The causes of crime and delinquency have not been understood until relatively recently. In the town of Salem, Massachusetts, for example, witchcraft trials held in the late 1600s resulted in the execution of 20 people—14 of whom were women. Five other people, including two infants, died in prison. The witchcraft hysteria began in 1692 when two children, 9-year-old Betty Parris and 11-year-old Abigail Williams, experienced what might today be described as seizures. The two girls soon claimed that they were the victims of witchcraft—and they named women who they said had initiated spiritual attacks against them. Soon arrest warrants were issued for more than 40 people, charging them with "afflicting others with witchcraft" and "making an unlawful covenant with the Devil." Proof of witchcraft was pretty simple and consisted largely of the testimony of the young girls who had brought the accusations. The girls described seeing demons and hearing sounds from the underworld, and their testimony came to be referred to as "spectral evidence." At trial, "touch tests" were also entered into evidence. Such tests relied on the testimony of people who were present when the girls experienced seizures. If the seizures went away when they were touched, then the person who had touched them was assumed to be in league with the Devil. This is one of dozens of explanations that have, in the past, been advanced as a cause of juvenile criminality.

An engraving showing the Salem Witchcraft trials. What role did children play in that trial?

THE IMPORTANCE OF THEORY AND RESEARCH

>> **LO 3.1**   Explain the importance of theory and research.

Spiritual explanations of criminality have existed for thousands of years, but it was not until the 18th century that they fell into disfavor and not until the 19th century that scientific research was used to study the causal relationships involved in deviance and delinquency. It was only within the past 150 years that the testing of **theory** became an integral part of explaining criminal behavior. Theories posit relationships between observable phenomena and attempt to explain why those relationships exist. Theories are either validated or invalidated by **empirical research**, which is used to test whether a theory is credible. The research either supports or debunks the theory.

An effective criminological theory can demonstrate **causation**. Causation shows that a certain factor results in an effect. So, for example, tests of a theory that says poverty leads to crime can be conducted to see whether the theory is true. While it may be true that poverty is sometimes associated with criminal behavior, such a relationship does not necessarily prove that poverty *causes* crime. To demonstrate causation, four factors must be present. First, there must be a sound theoretical rationale as to why a causal relationship would exist. Second, there must be **correlation**—or demonstration of the fact that changes in the purported cause and effect occur in relation to each other. For example, research may indicate that drug abuse significantly increases the likelihood of a person committing a crime. If the crime rate and drug use rate are rising at the same time, that is a correlation. However, it is important to note that correlation does not necessarily imply causation. In other words, two variables can be correlated, or occur together, but that does not equate to a cause-and-effect relationship. If the number of puppies in the United States is rising and the crime rate is declining, these variables are correlated but that does not necessarily mean the existence of more puppies is causing a lower crime rate.

Third, there must be a demonstrated **time sequence** between the purported cause and effect. A theory must indicate which variables are the cause and identify their effects. Last, a **nonspurious** relationship must be present; that is, it must be possible to show that the relationship between the purported cause and effect exists without requiring other factors. The association of drug abuse with crime, for example, may be a spurious relationship, because other factors could be in play.[1]

This chapter will explore various criminological theories introduced since the 18th century, and each theory will be explained and critiqued. Keep in mind that some theories are more accepted than others as a way of explaining juvenile delinquency. Take time to consider the usefulness of each theory as you read about it.

THE CLASSICAL SCHOOL AND BIOLOGICAL THEORIES

>> **LO 3.2**   Explain the differences between classical and biological theories of delinquency.

It was in the mid-1700s, during a time of historical upheaval and change, when the first modern criminological school of thought emerged.[2] This was when the age of the **Enlightenment**, ending the Dark Ages, sparked changes in philosophical thought and scientific innovation. With the introduction of the **classical school** of criminology, Cesare Beccaria (1738–1794) and Jeremy Bentham (1748–1832) revolutionized the way society viewed the cause of criminal behavior. Rather than looking to spiritual explanations, these thinkers asserted that human beings are rational and make choices based on their own **free will**. Decisions to commit criminal acts are based on the expectation of a favorable rather than a painful outcome, they argued.[3]

The juvenile justice system consistently tries to balance justice with rehabilitative programming to treat the offender. What kinds of programs might work best?

Beccaria opposed the erratic and severe methods of punishment that then existed, such as stoning people to death for stealing a loaf of bread or a silver spoon. Beccaria asserted that if individuals could appreciate a clear set of statutes that indicated definite punishment, they would be more likely to refrain from committing a crime. For legal sanctions to be an effective deterrent for future criminality, he believed they must be swift (occurring almost immediately after commission of the crime), certain (all offenders who committed a crime should be punished), and not overly harsh.

Bentham held that since humans are hedonistic (pleasure-seeking), they use free will to make decisions that bring them the most benefit. In every decision, he said, humans intuitively use a **hedonistic calculus**—a mental (and perhaps less than fully conscious) calculation of the pleasure and pain associated with a particular behavior. A person who is considering robbing a bank, for instance, will weigh the benefits (money and material possessions) against the detriments (arrest and prison time). A rational person will then make a choice that he believes will produce the best results[4] for himself.

Contemporary Applications of the Classical School

The classical school led to new approaches, such as **rational choice theory**. Rational choice theory, introduced in the late 20th century, assumes that offenders make a choice to commit crime based on the opportunities that are available to them in their surroundings. Much like Bentham's hedonistic calculus, this theory posits that offenders weigh the pros and cons of participating in the behavior to make a decision. However, rational choice recognizes that some behavior is spontaneous, resulting from past experience and the routine of daily life.[5]

Similarly, **routine activities theory** (or lifestyle theory) focuses more on explaining what increases a person's likelihood of victimization, rather than on offending behavior. Routine activities theorists Lawrence Cohen and Marcus Felson describe three components in the commission of a crime: (1) a motivated offender, (2) a suitable target, and (3) lack of capable guardianship. Suitable targets—people who are desirable and available victims—may, for example, post on a social networking website that they are going on vacation, unwittingly signaling to motivated offenders that their home will be unguarded. The potential victim may also have failed to arrange for *capable guardianship*, such as bringing in a caretaker, putting a lock on a door, setting an alarm, or creating a strong password for an online account. Motivated offenders can also take advantage of lifestyle routines, such as leaving the house at the same time for work or leaving a car unlocked in the driveway at night.[6]

Positivism

Almost a century after the introduction of the classical school, **positivism** put a new spin on explaining criminality. Positivists believed that criminality did not result from individual choice but from factors beyond an individual's control. Positivists acknowledged that many factors cause people to commit crime, so each person must be assessed individually. Much like a doctor assesses a person's symptoms before creating a treatment plan, positivism holds that each offender must be properly assessed to identify the root causes of deviancy. Only then can a customized rehabilitation and treatment plan be developed. There cannot be a "one-size-fits-all" treatment plan.[7]

Positivism was the dominant school of thought in the late 1800s, shaping attitudes about criminology as well as sociology, medicine, and psychology. The juvenile justice system was particularly affected, as positivism called for identifying the specific causes of delinquency in each youth, rather than treating every problem adolescent the same way. However, our current juvenile justice system has largely built on the Classical viewpoint and created what is called **neoclassicism**. Advocates of neoclassicism assert that individuals have some degree of free will in choosing their actions but these choices are limited because some factors are outside their control. This is called **soft determinism**. Soft determinism says that individuals have a limited number of choices available to them, and these choices determine how much free will is in play.

The Biological School

The **biological school** of criminology, which emerged in the mid- to late 1800s, proposed another theory of crime causation. Instead of relying on philosophical pondering, this school used scientific testing to support or debunk theoretical assertions, looking for possible biological and genetic components of criminality. This school believed that criminality can result from an inherited predisposition to be deviant or genetically determined physical attributes that affect behaviors. Franz Gall, for example, applied **phrenology**, the study of the shape of the skull, to predict criminality.

Physical Appearance

Cesare Lombroso, a representative of the biological school, is considered by many to be the father of criminology, but he had very different views from most modern criminologists. He believed that criminal offenders were evolutionary throwbacks to previous stages of human evolution who hadn't physically and mentally developed to the level necessary to fit in with modern society. Most criminals exhibit, he said, poorly developed physical traits, or **atavistic** characteristics, such as a protruding

Yulia Ryabokon/Alamy Stock Vector

Biological theorists often believed that offenders were evolutionary throwbacks, not completely developed human specimens. How did such theorists explain criminal behavior?

jaw, close-set eyes, excess hair, or a high forehead. Lombroso viewed individuals who had apelike characteristics as "born criminals," while other offenders were "criminaloids" or simply "insane." Criminaloids committed crime due to a convergence of factors such as physical, social, and mental conditions, while insane offenders had severe mental and psychological deficiencies.[8],[9]

Like the positivists who used scientific research to test theories, Lombroso examined incarcerated offenders and concluded that more than 40% of them exhibited at least five atavistic traits. However, Lombroso's findings were later called into question because he did not use control groups. That is, he did not validate his conclusion by comparing his research group of offenders to a control group of other people in the general public. Subsequent studies using control groups found little physical difference between offenders and non-offenders. This prompted Lombroso to look for other characteristics that might cause deviant behavior.[10]

Body Types

Despite problems with the approach of early biological school theorists, further research in the mid-1900s found a relationship between physical composition and criminal behavior. William Sheldon, observing residents in a juvenile facility, identified three **somatotypes** (body types) that he felt were related to deviant behavior. *Endomorphs* had heavy, soft bodies or short stature, which Sheldon associated with viscerotonic personalities that were easygoing and fun-loving. *Ectomorphs* were skinny and delicate, and likely to be anxious introverts who complained frequently. And *mesomorphs* had an athletic build, exhibiting a muscular composition and somatotonic (dynamic and aggressive) personalities.

Based on his findings, Sheldon asserted that mesomorphs were the most likely to commit delinquent acts.[11] This approach was taken up by the Gluecks[12] and Cortes over the next 25 years, but it had methodological problems. Determinations of body type were subjective, often based only on viewing photographs of delinquents. Researchers did not consider that many delinquent youths were mesomorphic because their athletic build made them preferable recruits for criminal acts. Also, as youths grow, their body type often changes, a factor that these studies didn't consider.

CASE STUDY

In re Winship, 397 U.S. 358 (1970)

Samuel Winship was 12 years old when he was arrested for breaking into a woman's locker and stealing $112 from her purse. The charge also noted that if Winship had been an adult, he would have been charged with larceny. Section 744(b) of the New York Family Court Act affirmed that juvenile guilt should be based on preponderance of the evidence. Winship was found guilty. His appeal to the Appellate Division of the New York Supreme Court and in the New York Court of Appeals was denied.

The U.S. Supreme Court ruled that the standard of guilt "beyond a reasonable doubt" must apply to juveniles and adults. With the majority opinion written by Justice William Brennan, Jr., the court stated that using the preponderance of the evidence standard to determine guilt was denying defendants a fundamental constitutional protection. As long as an individual is facing potential loss of liberty, age variations should not matter with the standard of evidence for determination of guilt.

1. **Do you agree with the ruling?**

2. **What standard of evidence do you think should be used with juveniles: the preponderance of evidence or reasonable doubt standard? Why?**

3. **In your opinion, would this ruling be the same today?**

Online Case Opinion

https://caselaw.findlaw.com/us-supreme-court/397/358.html ●

Genetic Inheritance

One of the core components of biological theory is the idea of a genetic predisposition to commit crime. Biological theorists of the late 20th century looked for variables that were related to criminality, such as poor self-control, and attempted to relate them to physical features. To identify genetic propensities toward deviance, researchers studied twins. Comparing monozygotic (MZ) twins, those who shared the same egg, with dizygotic (DZ) twins, those who were fertilized in two separate eggs, researchers found a higher degree of deviant behavior in the MZ group.[13]

However, while the twin studies indicated support for genetic inheritance of criminality, they did not consider environmental influences. To deal with this issue, adoption studies in the late 1900s examined the relationship between the criminality of biological parents and their children who were adopted, and found a higher **concordance**, or similarity, in criminality for the adopted children of offending parents. In addition, a recent meta-analysis of twin and adoption studies revealed a significant relationship between heritability and criminality. The studies did not show, however, that the criminal behavior itself was inherited but only that a propensity to commit crime was. In other words, burglars might not produce offspring who committed burglary, but they were more likely to produce descendants who were deviant in some way.[14]

Biosocial Criminology

Early biological school assertions have been challenged recently by a new **biosocial theory**. In recent decades, biosocial criminologists have merged the original idea of genetic predisposition as a predictor of crime with environmental factors to create a modern explanation of criminality. One's genetic makeup impacts the composition of the brain, but environmental factors also influence how the brain responds. When specific biological conditions converge with surrounding environmental factors, they may lead to deviant behavior. For example, some individuals with attention deficit disorder may be easily frustrated and can be disruptive in social situations. If these people encounter a particularly frustrating situation, such as waiting hours to see a doctor or to get assistance at a government agency, they may become aggressive.[15] In other environments, however, they are likely to remain sociable and react positively to those around them.

Multiple factors have been linked to delinquency in biosocial studies. Not surprisingly, alcohol and drug use are often linked to criminal behavior. Biosocial criminologists have suggested that alcohol, which can diminish a person's inhibitions, can also prompt aggression or irritability. Drug use has also been correlated with violence based on its biological effect on users,[16] but it can also bring about criminality in people who are under pressure to steal to get the money to buy drugs.

Hormones and aggressive behaviors have been often linked in criminological theory. Androgen, the male sex hormone in testosterone, has been linked to aggressive and violent behaviors. Epinephrine and norepinephrine, both responsible for flight or fight reactions in the body, due to increases in adrenaline and increased energy rates, have also been linked to aggressive behaviors. However, while all these hormones can be triggered by environment, they are not necessarily required for criminality. Other body chemicals have also been associated in empirical research with criminal behavior. **Neurotransmitters**, or chemicals responsible for transmission of impulses in the nervous system, can alter the behavior of an individual by impacting the processing of information in the brain. Two specific neurotransmitters, **serotonin** and **dopamine**, have been correlated with aggression. Serotonin controls impulse and hyperactivity, and low levels of serotonin have been associated with aggression and behaviors related to low self-control. Dopamine is a pleasure-inducing chemical, and behaviors that increase levels of this neurotransmitter can also be associated with law violation.[17]

Free Will and the Classical School

The classical school gives choice and the exercise of free will a central role in human behavior—claiming that people choose what they do, and saying that when people make bad choices they should suffer the consequences of those choices. Recently, a number of social media challenges have been making the rounds on the Internet, starting with the Ice Bucket Challenge some years ago. One of the contemporary challenges asks you to wait until you are hungry and then go shopping for the things you most like to eat. If, for example, you crave tacos when you get hungry, then you will shop for the ingredients that allow you to go home and prepare a taco (or two).

Putting It Into Action

This active learning exercise asks you to do just that: wait until you are hungry, go to the grocery store and buy something that you'd like to eat, and take it home and prepare it (unless no preparation is necessary and it can be eaten just as it comes). Then, once it has been prepared, instead of eating it, give it away—perhaps to a family member or roommate. Don't eat something in its place, but wait for at least an hour before considering what else to eat.

After you've performed the exercise, write down whether you were successful or not. Did you give the food away as instructed? Did your appetite get the best of you, and did you eat it anyway? What did you feel while performing this exercise? Try to describe the pushes and pulls you may have felt. On the basis of what you experienced, assess how much free will you actually have.

Answer each of these questions in what you write, and submit your paper to your instructor when asked to do so. ●

Contemporary views on biosocial criminology are an improvement over the old assertions of the biological school, but they still meet with criticism. For example, some of the relationships asserted in biosocial studies have problems with time order and often do not consider other important contributing factors of criminality, such as social factors, environment, and other forces.

PSYCHOLOGICAL APPROACHES

>> **LO 3.3** Describe how psychological factors affect criminality.

Developed from the fields of biology, psychiatry, and physiology, the **psychological school** examined the effect of early life experiences on deviant behavior. Some early psychologists (especially psychotherapists) asserted that criminal behavior is a result of psychological problems not identified or treated during childhood and adolescent years. However, diagnosis is very individualistic. That is, different individuals may exhibit the same behaviors, such as multiple personalities or antisocial behaviors, but the root cause of these symptoms varies for each person. Psychological school advocates assert the importance of treatment and rehabilitation, rather than taking a punitive stance, when handling these offenders. This next section will investigate the varied pathways of psychological schools and how they predict and explain offending behavior.

Psychoanalysis

Psychoanalysis attempts to uncover the instinctual, subconscious factors that underlie a person's deviant behavior and to determine conscious therapeutic methods for dealing with such issues. The psychoanalyst Sigmund Freud, for example, described three distinct aspects of human personality and explained how they affect behavior. The *id*, he said, is the pleasure-seeking portion of the psyche, consumed only with what benefits "me." The *superego* is the result of early moral teachings and distinguishes between right and wrong. Last, the *ego* is the balancing act between the first two parts, and determines the person's actual behavior. The strength of the id or the superego will essentially determine what behavior will be permitted by the ego.[18]

While psychoanalysis may be useful in uncovering unconscious cognition, it comes into play only after the behavior has already taken place. The purpose of psychoanalysis is to determine why the individual behaved a certain way and what can be done to correct it in the future. However, psychoanalysis assumes that once a person reaches adolescence, it is difficult to shift his or her behavior, because the superego has already cemented the person's morals and values, and it does not consider other environmental and social factors in a person's life. Such criticisms raise doubts about the actual value of psychoanalysis in criminology.

Learning and Imitation

Some psychological theories focus on learning and examine how an individual learns. They also seek to identify what promotes appropriate learning. **Modeling**, or imitation, is the simplest form of learning. It involves mimicking the behavior of another person and is seen primarily in children, who copy the behaviors of persons closest to them. These people can be real, such as parents or siblings, or fictional, such as superheroes.[19]

Operant conditioning describes the process of reinforcement of behavior with rewards and punishments. Early examples such as B. F. Skinner's experiment with rats demonstrated how easy it is to use rewards to condition behavior.[20] Children who receive a piece of candy or money for performing a chore will hypothetically continue to perform the positive behavior. If a response to an act is pleasurable (positive reinforcement) or removes a painful experience (negative reinforcement), the act will be repeated in the future. In addition, if children perceive that a person exhibiting a certain behavior is not punished for it, they may decide that it is appropriate behavior. For instance, if Batman physically assaults the bad guys and receives adoration from the citizens of Gotham, then a child may believe it is acceptable to hit someone on the playground.

Mental Illness and Mental Disability

Psychologists have linked mental illness with deviant behaviors in children and adults. Many adult offenders and juvenile delinquents exhibit traits of mental illnesses listed in the *Diagnostic and Statistical Manual of Mental Disorders*, 5th edition, or the DSM-V, published by the American Psychiatric Association. For example, serial and violent offenders often exhibit **antisocial personality disorder**, or behavior that violates social norms. A person with antisocial personality disorder may be charismatic but manipulative and not demonstrate remorse for harming or violating the rights of others (see Table 3.1).[21] Environmental and genetic conditions apparently contribute to this disorder,[22] but it is extremely difficult to treat, generally requiring medication, and it is usually not identified until adulthood. While this diagnosis can be helpful in classifying adults in the corrections system, it may not help in identifying problem juveniles.

TABLE 3.1

Characteristics of Antisocial Personality Disorder[23]

Disregard for right and wrong	Reoccurring criminal behavior	Poor relationships
Pathological lying	Lack of empathy and remorse	Failed or abusive relationships
Arrogance	Hostility and aggression	Consistent irresponsibility

Kohlberg, L. (1981). *The philosophy of moral development.* San Francisco: Harper and Row.

A diagnostic tool often used to connect mental illness with deviancy is the **Minnesota Multiphasic Personality Inventory (MMPI)**, which has more than 500 true/false questions that measure personality dimensions. While the test may be useful for treating offenders, critics argue that the results cannot explain past acts or even predict future behavior. In addition, critics point to the fact that refinements of the tool have been based on the life experiences of incarcerated individuals rather than the general population.[24]

Mental disability, also known as *deficiency*, has also been linked with deviancy. Mental ability, also known as the intelligence quotient, or IQ, is based on performance on a standardized test. Questions are geared toward a variety of different age groups, and older individuals are more likely to answer more difficult questions. Multiple studies have indicated that incarcerated individuals are often less educated and have lower scores on academic achievement tests, but it is not clear whether this indicates a low IQ. Even so, many criminologists say there is an indirect link between low IQ and delinquency. Juveniles with low IQ have been tied to poor school performance, truancy, and rebellious behavior, including criminal acts.[25]

DEVELOPMENTAL AND SOCIOLOGICAL EXPLANATIONS

>> LO 3.4 Discuss developmental and sociological theories of criminality.

Similar to Lombroso's theory of stunted physical development, many psychological theorists claim that criminality results from arrested emotional development. That is, the person never reaches an appropriate level of maturity. **Developmental theories** focus on an individual's conception of right and wrong that emerge over a period of time (particularly in childhood). Psychologist Lawrence Kohlberg identified six stages of moral development, beginning with basic childhood recognition of obedience and rules for self-preservation, and ending in a final stage of development that is often not reached, in which adults make decisions to benefit all parties involved and recognize these decisions to be morally right (see Table 3.2). Kohlberg asserted that deviants were individuals whose moral development was incomplete. They did not reach the same levels of development as those who refrained from criminal activity. Adults who do not consider the effect of their behavior on others would be considered to have stunted development.[26]

A child learning spatial skills. How do children learn?

©iStockphoto.com/MarsYu

One concept used to assess development is Interpersonal Maturity Levels (I-Levels). These are a continuum from the child's consciousness of "me" and "everyone else" to the often unattained final stage of development, where adults make decisions to benefit all parties involved. There are seven I-Levels, and deviant behaviors generally occur in Levels 2 through 4 (see Table 3.3). Individuals may even commit deviant behaviors to cope with stress or to act out against authority.[27]

Social Disorganization

The theories discussed earlier in this chapter posit that crime results from individual choice or from genetic and mental abnormalities. However, the **Chicago school** of criminology says that criminal behavior does not result from individualistic characteristics but, rather, from environmental challenges. **Social ecology** is a related concept that involves the interaction of social groups competing for resources in the same area. Sociologists Robert Park and Ernest Burgess examined waves of new immigrants from around the world who settled in Chicago in the

TABLE 3.2

Kohlberg's Stages of Moral Development

LEVEL 1. PRECONVENTIONAL LEVEL	
Stage 1	Obedience to authority figures and avoidance of punishment.
Stage 2	Focusing on own needs, allowing others to do the same.
LEVEL 2. CONVENTIONAL LEVEL	
Stage 3	Behavior is regulated by the approval of others.
Stage 4	Behavior is regulated by authority and recognition of social norms.
LEVEL 3. POSTCONVENTIONAL LEVEL	
Stage 5	Social contract between self and society is recognized, and behavior is based accordingly.
Stage 6	Individual acts are based on universal ethics and morality.

Sullivan, C., Grant, M., & Grant, J. (1957). The development of interpersonal maturity: Applications to delinquency. *Psychiatry, 20*, 373–385. Reprinted with permission from Taylor & Francis.

1920s. The people studied were found to exhibit a variety of cultural norms, impeding the development of an organized community with shared norms, focusing on things such as religious beliefs, food preferences, languages, and expectations of right and wrong.[28]

Park and Burgess mapped the city of Chicago into five **concentric zones** (Figure 3.1) to highlight a variety of environments. Since most immigrants were poor upon arrival in Chicago, they generally settled in the same area of low-income housing that was close to factory jobs. Once financially stable, they would move to more desirable neighborhoods and new immigrants would move into the low-income area, which Park and Burgess referred to as the zone of transition (also known as Zone 2).

Almost twenty years later, Clifford Shaw and Henry McKay applied the concept of concentric zones to understand juvenile delinquency. What they called the "zone of transition" was the area with the least **collective efficacy** (the ability of the neighborhood to control the behaviors of its residents). That area had the highest rates of juvenile delinquency, no matter the nationality of its inhabitants. Their work proposed that an environment exhibiting **social disorganization** and lack of cohesive social norms fostered criminality. While this theory has been continuously used to

TABLE 3.3

Interpersonal Maturity Levels (I-Levels)

Level 1	Individuals learn to discriminate between themselves and others.
Level 2	Individuals start to differentiate between persons and objects, partly on the basis of their own needs and what they can control.
Level 3	Individuals begin to learn rules and can manipulate their environment for their own benefit.
Level 4	Individuals perceive events from the viewpoint of others.
Level 5	Individuals become aware of behavior patterns and relationships.
Level 6	Individuals can distinguish between themselves and the roles they play.
Level 7	Individuals can perceive different methods for handling the world and make appropriate choices based on experience and benefits for others.

National Center for Biotechnology Information. (2010). *Antisocial personality disorder.*

FIGURE 3.1

Map of Concentric Zones

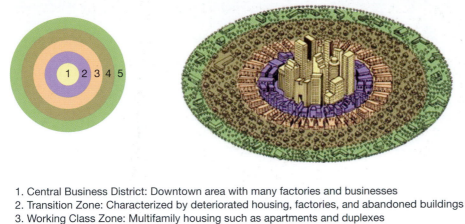

1. Central Business District: Downtown area with many factories and businesses
2. Transition Zone: Characterized by deteriorated housing, factories, and abandoned buildings
3. Working Class Zone: Multifamily housing such as apartments and duplexes
4. Residential Zone: Single family homes with yards/garages
5. Commuter Zone: Suburbs

Rubenstein, James M., *Contemporary Human Geography*, 3rd edition. Copyright © 2016. Printed and electronically reproduced by permission of Pearson Education, Inc., New York, New York.

explain delinquency, it has been criticized for its tendency toward **ecological fallacy**. While the crime rate may be higher in low-income areas, that does not mean that every person who lives in government housing and is on the poverty line will be delinquent.[29]

Strain

Strain theories, which developed about the same time as social disorganization theories, predicted criminal behavior based on the amount of pressure that individuals feel to obtain societal goals and successes. According to the strain theorists, success is measured in terms of achievement—such as college education, career and financial success, and positive relationships—and individuals often experience stress (or **strain**) when trying to obtain those goals. Strain occurs when individuals feel unable to reach such goals through legitimate (legal) means. They may then experience **anomie**, an inability to handle the resulting strain, and then react with delinquent behavior.

Robert Merton believed that there were five ways a person could adapt to anomie. They are (1) *conformity,* which is the acceptance of socially approved goals and legitimate means to obtain them; (2) *innovation,* or the pursuit of illegitimate means to obtain acceptable goals, such as stealing or selling drugs to afford the cars or homes desired; (3) *ritualism,* where individuals do not invest in socially approved goals but adhere to legitimate means—for example, a person who has no religious faith but continues to go to church because it is expected of him or her; (4) *retreatism,* or a lifestyle that focuses on a temporary high or relief, rather than long-term success—for example, alcoholics and drug addicts; and (5) *rebellion,* or an attempt to replace accepted goals and means with new standards that provide more opportunity for all members of society.[30]

A contemporary application of Merton's assertions was introduced by Robert Agnew in 1992. He proposed **general strain theory**, which asserts that individuals who commit crime use it as a coping mechanism to deal with strain. Agnew believed that strain would be induced by (1) removal of or the threat to remove positively valued stimuli or (2) introduction of or the threat to introduce noxious stimuli.[31]

©iStockphoto.com/Mixmike

Two girls sharing leisure time. Why are adolescents susceptible to learning deviant behaviors from friends?

Social Learning

One of the most influential criminological theories was developed by Edwin Sutherland. It involves the concept of **social learning** and holds that delinquency involves learned behaviors. That is, said Sutherland, individuals learn how to commit crimes in the same manner they learn to tie their shoes or drive a car. They learn in interaction within intimate peer groups promoting this behavior. Sutherland noted that individuals learn the most from people with whom they spend the most time and in whom they have the most interest. When individuals are in a peer group that supports deviant behavior, they are likely to follow along. Sutherland termed this process **differential association** and described it in nine propositions (see Table 3.4). His initial ideas were criticized for lack of clarity—for instance, what does "excess of definitions" mean, and how is "frequency" defined? Nevertheless, Sutherland's ideas continue to be influential today.[32]

The concept of **differential reinforcement** was later added to Sutherland's theory of differential association to explain the importance of learning. That is, if a person steals a sweater from a store and does not get caught, the shoplifting behavior is reinforced. But if the shoplifter is arrested or suffers public humiliation, then that person will be less likely to want to shoplift again.[33]

Labeling

Another criminological school of thought involves the idea of **symbolic interaction**, in which individuals are thought to create a self-image based on their reaction to the surrounding world. To explain juvenile delinquency, theorists of **labeling** hold that juveniles' self-perceptions are based on how they are thought of by others and how they are treated by people around them. Calvin Cooley called this the *looking-glass self*. Juveniles who commit an initial act of delinquency, called **primary deviance**,

TABLE 3.4

Sutherland's Nine Propositions of Differential Association

1. Criminal behavior is learned.
2. The learning occurs in interaction with other persons in a process of communication.
3. This takes place within intimate groups of people.
4. Learning includes (a) crime techniques, which can be quite simple or very complicated, and (b) specific motives, drives, rationalizations, and attitudes.
5. The direction of motives and drives is learned from definitions of the legal codes as favorable or unfavorable.
6. Individuals become delinquent because they accept more definitions favorable to violating the law than definitions favorable to following the law.
7. Differential associations may vary in frequency, duration, priority, and intensity.
8. Learning criminal behavior by associating with criminal and anticriminal patterns involves the same mechanisms involved in any other learning.
9. Criminal behavior is a result of needs and values, but it is not explained by those needs or values.

Sutherland, E. (1939). *Principles of criminology* (3rd ed.). Philadelphia: Lippincott.

are labeled delinquent by the juvenile justice system. They then perceive that society sees them as "bad" and continue to commit more delinquent acts, or **secondary deviance**. Their attitude is, "Why should I try to do better when everyone thinks I am bad?"[34] Moreover, society often denies them the opportunity for self-improvement once they have been negatively labeled.

The rehabilitative strategy of **reintegrative shaming** is related to labeling. Using this strategy the juvenile justice system shows disapproval of bad behavior but provides forgiveness and reintegrates offenders back into society. For instance, juveniles who vandalize a school are required to clean up what they did but then, in an act of forgiveness, are reintegrated into society.

John Gress/Corbis News/Getty Images

A group of Chicago men gather on the street. What role do violent subcultures play in the development of adolescent behavior?

Subculture Theory

A **subculture** is a smaller group within a larger culture that provides an identity for its members. In the United States, subcultures contribute to a melting pot of language, customs, and values. Subcultures can also foster criminality that often includes aggressive and violent behavior. While the dominant culture views such acts as deviant behavior, members of a particular subculture, such as a gang, may embrace them as their values.

Looking at lower-class boys involved in gang subcultures, Albert Cohen observed that the boys encouraged each other to commit delinquent acts because they believed they could not meet middle-class standards. When they became involved in the juvenile justice system, they acquired negative self-esteem and felt that they were failures in the eyes of the larger society. Cohen believed that delinquents did not necessarily commit crime for personal benefit but as a vengeful act for being left with feelings of inadequacy.[35]

Walter Miller developed a theory of behavior that he applied to all males in lower-class subcultures. He said that lower-class males had a set of values and beliefs that was different from those of other groups. He called such values and beliefs **focal concerns**. The goal of the delinquent, he said, was not to act out against the middle class but to embrace a distinctive yet different lifestyle, which included the following aspects:[36]

1. Autonomy—independence and lack of control by other people

2. Excitement—activities that provide immediate gratification or thrill

3. Fate—allowing what happens, rather than planning, to determine life choices

4. Smartness—relying on wit and street savvy rather than intelligence

5. Toughness—showing masculinity and physical skill

6. Trouble—getting out of trouble, which becomes very time-consuming

According to Miller, these values are integral to the daily lives of the lower class, much like eating and breathing, and are essentially acts of defiance.

The three subcultural theories discussed here were introduced at the same time, but only Miller's approach implies that members of the lower class try to meet the expectations of their subculture and of the middle class at the same time. Sykes and Matza believed that while juveniles commit delinquent acts based on lower-class expectations, they still wish to fit into the middle class at least superficially. They do not believe they are less respectable than the middle class. Sykes and Matza said that lower-class juveniles use **techniques of neutralization** to justify deviance and crime when faced with the expectations of a law-abiding culture (see Table 3.5).[37]

TABLE 3.5

Techniques of Neutralization

TECHNIQUE	EXAMPLE
Denial of responsibility	"It's not my fault."
Denial of injury	"She will never notice." "He can afford it."
Denial of victim	"He deserved it—he is a jerk."
Condemnation of the condemners	"Who is he to judge me? That police officer speeds all the time."
Appeal to higher loyalties	"My gang leader expects it from me."

Sykes, G. & Matza, D. (1957). Techniques of neutralization: A theory of delinquency. *American Sociological Review, 22*, 664–670.

Social Control

Rather than investigating predictors of delinquent behavior, social control theorists try to identify factors that keep individuals from committing deviant acts despite having opportunities to do so. Walter Reckless, an early control theorist, developed **containment theory**, which identifies two types of forces that can control behavior. Factors of **outer containments** provide direct controls over an individual's behavior and consist of things such as family, peers, and other individuals who provide mentorship. Factors of **inner containments** are the values, beliefs, and level of self-control that an individual refers to when deciding on behavior. Both forms of containment can help a person avoid deviant behavior, but that person has to cope with external factors that might lead to deviance. These include *external pushes* (anxiety, discontentment), *external pressures* (unemployment, poverty), and *external pulls* (deviant peers, subcultural expectations). The continuous battle between containment and the external pulls and pushes determines whether a person will engage in criminal activity.[38]

One of the more popular social control theories is Travis Hirschi's **bond** theory. Hirschi believed that an individual's bonds to his or her community develop in early childhood and encompass four elements: attachment, belief, commitment, and involvement (see Table 3.6). Juveniles, he said, were more likely to become delinquent if social bonds were weak—a conclusion based on research on some 4,000 high school boys. He found that delinquent behavior among those boys was significantly related to the following personal characteristics: weak attachment to parents and education (attachment), low respect for the police (belief), lack of aspiration toward measures of legitimate success (commitment), and activities driven by boredom (involvement). However, Hirschi's theory did not adequately explain how the social bond between the juvenile and society was broken, and it did not clarify whether all or just some of the components of the bond must be broken for delinquency to occur.[39]

TABLE 3.6

Elements of Hirschi's Social Bond

ELEMENT	EXAMPLE
Attachment	Concern for the opinion of others
Belief	Values common with those of the community
Commitment	Investment in conventional activities
Involvement	Participation in conventional activities

Hirschi, T. (1969). *Causes of delinquency*. Berkeley: University of California Press.

A more recent school of thought, the **general theory of crime**, also links low self-control to criminal behavior. It holds that self-control develops at an early age through parental management and is the determining factor for participation in deviant behaviors. The general theory emphasizes that parents are responsible for the formation of self-control through proper socialization. Individuals with low self-control are impulsive, risk-taking, and lack the ability to see long-term consequences, which makes them more likely to participate in delinquency. The general theory has been used to explain personal, property, and cybercrimes, but it does not explain behavior changes later in life.[40] ●

NAVIGATING THE FIELD 3.1

Techniques of Neutralization

Review the examples of the five techniques of neutralization in Table 3.5. These techniques are denial of responsibility, denial of injury, denial of victim, condemnation of the condemners, and appeal to higher loyalties.

Putting It Into Action

Collect deviant narratives from fellow students, asking them to talk about times when they broke social norms. Also ask them to explain either (1) why they did something they knew to be wrong or (2) why they believe they didn't do anything wrong (even though others did).

Use the assembled narratives to identify techniques of neutralization in the accounts of your fellow students. Are they similar to the neutralization techniques described in this chapter? If yes, how so? Do they provide any excuses or justifications not described in this chapter?

Submit your conclusions to your instructor when asked to do so. ●

SUMMARY

》》 LO 3.1 Explain the importance of theory and research.

A theory proposes relationships between variables and attempts to explain how and why those relationships exist. Criminological theories specifically try to provide predictive factors of criminality, which hopefully allows policymakers and lawmakers to develop programs and laws to proactively and reactively address crime. For a theory to be valid and demonstrate a cause-and-effect relationship, it must possess the following factors: theoretical rationale, correlation, time sequence, and nonspurious relationship.

Key Terms

causation 32	empirical research 32	theory 32
correlation 32	nonspurious 32	time sequence 32

》》 LO 3.2 Explain the differences between classical and biological theories of delinquency.

These first criminological schools of thoughts challenged earlier assumptions that crime was a result of demonic possession or spiritual influences. Classical school criminologists believed that criminal behavior resulted from the exercise of free will and the use of rational choice. In addition, as historical punishments were overly severe and generally not effective deterrents, these theories stressed the importance of the punishment fitting the crime. Biological school theorists believed that criminality was inherited and rooted in instinct, often a result of genetic maldevelopment. Multiple factors relating to crime were suggested, including body type, physical attributes, and hormonal imbalances. During this time period, empirical research that examined theoretical assertions was introduced.

Key Terms

atavistic   34
biological school   34
biosocial theory   36
classical school   32
concordance   36
dopamine   36
the Enlightenment   32

free will   33
hedonistic calculus   33
neoclassicism   34
neurotransmitters   36
phrenology   34
positivism   33
rational choice theory   33

routine activities
    theory   33
serotonin   36
soft determinism   34
somatotypes   35

» LO 3.3   Describe how psychological factors affect criminality.

Psychological theories use multiple explanations for criminal behavior. Criminality can be a result of the inability to achieve certain stages of moral development or can flow from mental disability or instability. In addition, reward and punishment can be used to influence a person's choices to commit crime or to conform to acceptable social standards.

Key Terms

antisocial personality
    disorder   38

Minnesota Multiphasic
    Personality Inventory
    (MMPI)   39
modeling   38

operant conditioning   38
psychoanalysis   37
psychological school   37

» LO 3.4   Discuss developmental and sociological theories of criminality.

Criminological theories introduced in the 20th century focused on a variety of factors. One of them, social disorganization, identified lack of community organization and efficacy as a causal factor in crime. Strain theory blamed a lack of the ability to cope with the expectations of conforming others. Social learning theories identified association with deviant peers as the determining factor in criminality. More recent criminological theories, including labeling and the impact of negative labels, have provided a variety of explanations for delinquent behavior. Self-control, seen in terms of social pressures and pulls, can also affect a person's criminality.

Key Terms

anomie   41
Chicago school   39
collective efficacy   40
concentric zones   40
containment theory   44
developmental
    theories   39
differential association   42
differential
    reinforcement   42

ecological fallacy   41
focal concerns   43
general strain theory   41
general theory of
    crime   45
inner containments   44
labeling   42
outer containments   44
primary deviance   43
reintegrative shaming   43

secondary deviance   43
social bond   44
social disorganization   40
social ecology   39
social learning   42
strain   41
subculture   43
symbolic interaction   42
techniques of
    neutralization   43

DISCUSSION QUESTIONS

1. In your opinion, which of the theories discussed in this chapter provides the best explanation of juvenile offending? Explain your answer.

2. Why do people choose to rationalize bad behavior? Have you ever used techniques of neutralization in your own life?

3. Do you believe that labeling theory provides a better explanation for juvenile offenses or for adult crime? Why?

1. Create a program for at-risk youths in a violent, urban area based on the concepts of one of the criminological theories. The program should be an after-school program for both male and female juveniles.

2. Create a program for at-risk youths in a rural area based on the concepts of one of the criminological theories. The program should be a residential program for either male or female juveniles.

$SAGE edge™

Give your students the SAGE edge!

SAGE edge offers a robust online environment featuring an impressive array of free tools and resources for review, study, and further exploration, keeping both instructors and students on the cutting edge of teaching and learning. Learn more at **edge.sagepub.com/schmallegerjj**.

PART II

Navigating the Juvenile Justice System

4

Juveniles and the Police

After reading this chapter you should be able to

1. Discuss the historical changes involving police interactions with juveniles

2. Describe important aspects of police-juvenile interaction

3. Describe the processing of juveniles who are taken into police custody

4. Identify some of the constitutional rights of juveniles

5. Describe the proactive measures used by police to prevent juvenile crime

6. Identify trends in juvenile arrests

7. Explain police discretion and identify the choices available to police who work with juveniles

8. Describe some proactive methods that police use to prevent juvenile crime

Key Terms in Chapter 4

community policing
community-based
    interventions
confession
discretion
due process
exclusionary rule
fingerprints

gang detail
gang unit
gang-based interventions
hands-off doctrine
interrogation
juvenile bureau
lineup
police process

problem-oriented policing
reasonable suspicion
school resource officers
    (SROs)
search and seizure
youth service program

INTRODUCTION

In 2014, a witness called 911 and said that a juvenile was brandishing a weapon in a Cleveland park. Officers Timothy Loehmann and Frank Garmback arrived at the park, with Garmback driving the police cruiser onto the grass beside the table where 12-year-old Tamir Rice sat with what appeared to be a handgun. It was later revealed that the 911 caller had said that the weapon was probably fake (it was a plastic pistol), but that was not relayed to the officers. Less than two seconds after the cruiser pulled in, Officer Loehmann (a trainee at the time) shot and killed Rice. Loehmann was later fired by the city for making a false statement on his police employment application, but a grand jury decided not to bring charges against the officers. Eventually, however, the city settled a civil lawsuit with the family for $6 million.[1]

Not every interaction between juveniles and police officers is this tragic. However, a youth's first interaction with the juvenile justice system typically begins with law enforcement and can often take him in a direction that has a dramatic effect on his future. The purpose of this chapter is to explore the history of police interaction with juveniles, as well as to examine the current methods of handling minors. Legal rights afforded to juveniles will be discussed, as well as measures that are currently being taken in hopes of reducing juvenile crime.

Pacific Press/Sipa USA/Newscom

The mother of an incarcerated youth protests mass incarceration. Why are racial tensions between police and youth so prevalent in many communities today?

HISTORY OF POLICE INTERACTION WITH JUVENILES

》 LO 4.1   Discuss the historical changes involving police interactions with juveniles.

For centuries, the control and socialization of juveniles were based on the idea that it takes a village to raise a child. In the United States, early Puritan communities allowed not only the family but also the church and community members to take an active role in correcting and punishing a deviant child. However, as cities grew and employment opportunities increased with the growth of factories, the need for formal social controls became necessary. Immigration created larger and more diverse populations that led to social disorganization, with increases in street crime and prejudicial violence. Governments created full-time police forces[2] in reaction to these trends.

The first police forces were implemented in the more populated urban areas—New York, Philadelphia, and Boston—in the 1830s and 1840s. By the end of the 19th century, all major cities and some small cities had full-time police officers patrolling the streets. The introduction of police officers created tensions within the community that continue to this day. These officers had full discretion to handle juveniles as they saw fit. Some of them developed personal relationships with juveniles and mentored them into a crime-free lifestyle. Other officers sent problem juveniles to their parents or church elders for punishment, while still others simply arrested and beat them.

Some police agencies began focusing on the need to combat juvenile crime, seeing it as a special category of police work. In the early 20th century, police chiefs in New York City; Portland, Maine; and Washington, D.C., came up with creative ways to deal with juvenile delinquency. Female officers were hired specifically to communicate with runaways and truants, and to patrol locations—often crime-ridden—where these juveniles were likely to hide. Welfare officers were assigned to more crime-infested districts, employment agencies were designated for young men, and relief programs provided resources to poor children. In the 1960s and 1970s, police agencies developed programs to provide youths with a positive perception of police rather than one of suspicion or fear. Police officers spoke at schools. Newly formed youth programs tried to develop leadership skills and worked to combat drug and alcohol use among young people.[3]

©iStockphoto.com/asiseeit

A school resource officer talks to elementary students. Can such talks build positive relationships between children and the police?

These efforts, however, were initially not well organized. In 1914, Chief August Vollmer of the Berkeley, California, Police Department implemented the first **juvenile bureau**. This office—which in other departments may be called the juvenile division, youth aid bureau, or juvenile control bureau—was assigned the task of monitoring juvenile crime and maintaining organized efforts to work with youths. Specially trained police officers, known as juvenile officers, staffed such divisions. The Central States Juvenile Officers Association and the International Juvenile Officers Association, founded in the 1950s, created standards and procedures for those working with juveniles and started empirical research on training and programming.[4]

Unfortunately, budgetary restrictions from the 1970s to the 1990s forced police departments to reduce efforts to combat juvenile crime. Funds were used instead to focus on neglected and abused children. **Community policing** and **problem-oriented policing** became popular in the 1990s and early 2000s, but these efforts focused on improving police relations in communities as a whole, rather than focusing on juveniles.

THE CURRENT ROLE OF POLICE IN THE JUVENILE JUSTICE SYSTEM

>> **LO 4.2**   Describe important aspects of police-juvenile interaction.

Today's police officers attempt to form a different relationship with juveniles than with adult offenders. Rather than being a harsh agent of crime control, law enforcement agencies work to provide a wide range of services within the juvenile justice system—effectively serving as a multifaceted tool to address the needs of juveniles and lower the risks of the juvenile offender.[5]

Law enforcement agencies also serve as a conduit between juveniles and the juvenile court system. Police discretion (discussed later in the chapter) allows an officer to use discretion in handling an event informally or referring a case to the juvenile court. Police officers also deal with a variety of noncriminal juvenile offenses. Running away from home, skipping school, and violating curfew are not against the law; however, they are considered status offenses for juveniles. Status offenses are violations of a code of behavior that applies only to minors. When a juvenile commits a status offense, law enforcement officers will often return the juvenile to a parent or guardian rather than formally processing the youth.

In a sense, law enforcement officers act as social workers when dealing with many juveniles. They may be called to help youths who are in an abusive or neglectful situation, find relevant social services, and provide temporary foster care or even medical treatment. They sometimes rescue young people who have been abandoned in a home or locked in a hot car. In addition, police work to identify at-risk youths in crime-ridden communities. They can direct youths to prosocial programs that provide a respite from violence, such as a YMCA or Big Brothers Big Sisters community center.

Last, law enforcement agencies sometimes provide education and training for both juveniles and adults. It is not uncommon, for example, to see law enforcement officers lead antigang or antidrug programming at public schools, or participate in community events. They also provide training and education to faculty on Internet safety and drug and alcohol abuse, and teach child caregivers to recognize signs of sexual and physical abuse.

Snapshot of Police–Youth Interactions

The Bureau of Justice Statistics found that youths between the ages of 16 and 24 years old are more likely to interact with the police than any other age group. However, these interactions are not always due to a young person breaking the law. The Office of Juvenile Justice and Delinquency Prevention (OJJDP) organizes police–juvenile interactions into four categories.[6]

Youth-initiated contact with the police usually involves a young person reporting a crime or requesting police help with a noncriminal issue. These contacts are voluntary on the part of the youth. Conversely, *police-initiated contact* may not be a voluntary interaction for youths. These are often interactions resulting from a traffic violation or stopping a youth on the street. *Contact resulting in arrest* accounts for only a small portion of the interactions between youths and police officers.

The last category of police–youth interaction is *contact due to victimization*. This may or may not be voluntary on the part of the youth. Police are notified of youth victimization due to child abuse or neglect, school or community violence, or property crime. About 25% of victims of serious violent crimes known to police are individuals under the age of 18, indicating that this type of contact is of particular importance to law enforcement.

No matter the category, all police–youth interactions are influenced by a variety of factors. Environmental factors, such as community organization and crime rate, affect the types of interactions that occur between law enforcement and juveniles.[7] Areas with high rates of crime, especially violence, have higher rates of police and youth interaction. Individual officer characteristics, such as race, age, and gender, have also been shown to affect interactions. For instance, younger officers are more likely to arrest juveniles, compared with more experienced officers.[8] The extent of an officer's educational and ethical training influences the type and quality of police–youth interaction as well.[9] Occupational attitudes toward the use of punitive, authoritative actions versus rehabilitative actions similarly affect interactions between these two groups.

POLICE DISCRETION AND THE HANDLING OF JUVENILES

>> **LO 4.3**   **Describe the processing of juveniles who are taken into police custody.**

If officers proceed beyond a verbal warning when interacting with a problem juvenile, they have several options for what is termed the **police process**. During *informal processing* at the police station or youth bureau, the juvenile is brought in to have a discussion with an officer or counselor. That conversation is likely to involve parents or guardians and to focus on appropriate behavior. It is at this time that juveniles receive warnings about actions that could be taken against them if their problem behavior continues. The officer or counselor could also refer juveniles and their families to mental health counseling, anger management, drug or alcohol treatment, or special education programs in conjunction with the public school system. Neglected or abused children could be referred to child protective services for guardianship or other assistance. The youths could also be taken into custody or arrested, but might still be handled in some of the informal ways that have been discussed.[10]

A formalized interaction between a juvenile offender and law enforcement, on the other hand, begins with an arrest. A juvenile is then taken into police custody and brought to the police station for booking. During booking, a juvenile's personal information (e.g., full name, date of birth) is recorded and a criminal history is run. The juvenile is also fingerprinted.

After booking and fingerprinting, the juvenile can be released to parents or guardians for supervision. That might be the end of the case, or it could be referred to juvenile court. In some cases, the youth could also be placed in a secure juvenile detention facility or jail to await a preliminary hearing or trial. Or, if the offense is serious enough, the youth can be transferred to adult court, something that is discussed further in Chapter 5.

CONSTITUTIONAL RIGHTS OF JUVENILES

>> **LO 4.4**   **Identify some of the constitutional rights of juveniles.**

Until the mid-20th century, juveniles were considered to have few legal and constitutional rights due to the informal and rehabilitative nature of the juvenile justice system. Under the **hands-off doctrine**, the courts left juvenile facilities alone to handle administrative issues. In the 1960s, however, the U.S. Supreme Court clarified the constitutional rights of both adult and juvenile offenders.

Applying the Fourth Amendment

The Fourth Amendment of the Constitution of the United States, which protects one's privacy against unreasonable **search and seizure**, is one of the most well-used bases for appeals by accused and convicted offenders. The amendment reads as follows:

> The right of the people to be secure in their persons, houses, papers and effects, against unreasonable searches and seizures, shall not be violated, and no Warrants shall issue, but upon probable cause, supported by Oath or affirmation, and particularly describing the place to be searched, and the persons or things to be seized.

That is, **due process** must be followed before searches and seizures, to ensure the safety and security of individuals.

Two Supreme Court rulings determined the appropriate application of search and seizure rules. In 1961, *Mapp v. Ohio*[11] introduced the **exclusionary rule**, which stated that evidence seized without a proper search warrant (and *probable cause*, indicating that a crime has been committed) could not be used in court against adults accused of criminal offenses. In 1967, judges in the New Jersey court case of *State v. Lowery*[12] applied the ban against unreasonable search and seizure to juveniles. The court ruled that New Jersey juveniles must be presented with a search warrant before their person or their home could be searched, unless the juvenile waived this right or was caught in a criminal offense.

Limits to privacy are affected by the location of the interaction between the officer and juvenile. On the street, an individual has the least amount of privacy and officers can use discretion based on the situation. For instance, an officer is entitled to stop and question juveniles, but they do not have to answer and can leave the area if not detained. If an officer has **reasonable suspicion** that a youth is carrying a weapon or has been involved in criminal activity, the officer is justified in performing a Terry[13] stop, which involves patting down a suspect. Weapons recovered from the pat-down can be seized, and at that point the officer would have probable cause to search the person for more contraband. Last, juveniles who are under arrest and charged with a crime are not free to leave custody.

A juvenile who is operating a motor vehicle has certain protections against unreasonable search and seizure. Police officers must have a justifiable reason to pull a vehicle over, such as for speeding, a broken taillight, or erratic driving. At a traffic stop, the officer can search without a warrant for anything in *plain view*.

However, if the officer smells alcohol or marijuana, or has reasonable suspicion to believe there is something dangerous in the glove compartment (or elsewhere), the officer may proceed to search the vehicle. Also, to protect the officer and other occupants of the car, anything that is unlocked and within reach of the person being stopped can be searched.[14]

The Fourth Amendment makes it more difficult for an officer to search a juvenile's home, but officers may do so without a warrant if an authorized person, such as a parent or guardian, gives them permission. Once the officer is in the home, contraband can be seized without a warrant if it is in plain view. And with the permission of a parent or guardian, an officer may search a juvenile's room. Police officers also may enter a home without a warrant if they have probable cause to believe a crime is currently being committed there, someone is in danger, or evidence may be destroyed before a warrant can be obtained.[15]

Kansas City Star/Tribune News Service/Getty Images

Police officers prepare to search an apartment. What are the most common offenses committed by juveniles?

Juveniles also have Fourth Amendment rights at school, where they might spend more time than in their own homes. Police or school resource officers are more likely now than ever to operate in public schools. School administration may use drug dogs, video cameras, metal detectors, and routine searches of backpacks, purses, and other personal property to find illegal contraband, including dangerous items. In fact, juveniles have very limited privacy rights within a school setting. In 1985, the Supreme Court ruled in *New Jersey v. T.L.O.*[16] that school searches do not require a warrant or probable cause. Instead, the legality of the search is dependent on the (1) scope of the search, (2) gender and age of the student, (3) behavior of the student at the time of the search, and (4) reasonableness of the search. The legality of these searches continues to be upheld in appeals courts, especially when pertaining to drugs and guns.

IN THE MEDIA 4.1

A Witch Hunt for Drugs

A year or two ago, local news media in rural Georgia featured a story from Worth County, Georgia, where Sheriff Jeff Hobby put the Worth County High School on lockdown while his officers searched the school for drugs. Unfortunately for the sheriff, none were found, and he is now facing a federal lawsuit for invasive groping and other illegal search procedures.

Putting It Into Action

In this active learning exercise, you should respond to the question of whether students should have at least a minimal and legitimate expectation of privacy in their person and their personal belongings—including

assigned desks and lockers. Also provide your opinion about how much leeway law enforcement officers should have to search students and their property, even when the students have not been accused of any illegal activities.

Be sure, however, that the opinions you put into writing are supported by a review of court decisions relative to school searches, and name at least some of those cases. You can find such decisions by performing an Internet search.

Submit your opinions to your instructor when asked to do so. ●

Only recently did the Supreme Court make a ruling on limiting searches in schools. In the 2009 case of *Safford Unified School District v. Redding,*[17] a 13-year-old girl was forced to expose her breasts and pelvis for a search that uncovered two tablets of Advil. The court determined that the search was unreasonable because the quantity and potency of the drug were not dangerous enough to warrant such an intrusive and humiliating search.

Applying the Fifth Amendment

The U.S. Constitution, in the Fifth and Fourteenth Amendments, also addresses due process and equal protection rights afforded to a juvenile in regard to **interrogation** and **confession**. The Fifth Amendment asserts that "no person shall be compelled in any criminal case to be a witness against himself, nor be deprived of life, liberty, or property without due process of law." For this protection to be in effect, the questioning must take place when juveniles are in police custody and they do not feel free to leave. When juveniles are not in police custody and make incriminating statements, those statements can be used against them in a court of law.

The 1966 Supreme Court case of *Miranda* v. *Arizona*[18] provides protections for juveniles and adults if two conditions are met: a juvenile is in custody and a juvenile is about to be interrogated. Once arrested and before being questioned, all individuals must be read the following Miranda warning:

You have the right to remain silent. If you give up that right, anything you say can and will be used against you in a court of law. You have the right to an attorney. If you cannot afford an attorney, one will be provided to you at no cost. During any questioning, you may decide at any time to exercise these rights, not answer any questions, or make any statements.

Any confession given by juveniles in custody before Miranda rights are read to them cannot be used as evidence, unless the confession is made willingly and without interrogation.

Adults have the ability to waive their Miranda rights and proceed with police questioning without the presence of an attorney. However, many appeals courts have weighed the matter of a juvenile's intellectual capability to understand the impact of waiving these rights. Factors such as age, language barriers, and mental capacity have also been considered. Decisions have varied in regard to standards of capability, but the 1979 Supreme Court case of *Fare* v. *Michael C.*[19] used the "totality of the circumstances" approach to the interrogation of juveniles. In other words, each individual case is different, and the entirety of the factors involved must be considered when making a decision about a juvenile's understanding of the impact of waiving Miranda rights.

This basic legal approach was used in the 1948 Supreme Court case of *Haley v. Ohio*,[20] which found there was excessive police coercion in interrogations of a 15-year-old. After 5 hours of interrogation by several police officers, without his parents or an attorney present, Haley confessed to robbing and shooting a store owner. The Supreme Court ruled that "greater protections must be accorded children when they are interrogated, and courts must rigorously consider youth in assessing whether a child's statement was voluntary under the totality of the circumstances." Some jurisdictions have ruled that someone acting in the best interest of the child (loco parentis), such as a parent or attorney, must be present during police interrogations. *Commonwealth v. Guyton* (1989)[21] determined that the interested party must be an adult, excluding relatives who are minors.

Other Supreme Court cases have addressed the conditions of interrogations and how they relate to constitutional rights. *In re Gault* (1967)[22] applied to juveniles the right to counsel and protection against self-incrimination, which had previously been interpreted as a constitutional right that applied only to adults. The case of *Brown v. Mississippi* (1963)[23] held that physical force cannot be used in police interrogations to obtain confessions.

A juvenile probation officer interviews a client. What proactive police strategies might be used to prevent delinquency?

TOOLS USED BY LAW ENFORCEMENT DURING INVESTIGATION

>> LO 4.5   Describe the proactive measures used by police to prevent juvenile crime.

Each person has a unique set of **fingerprints**, often making them a useful form of evidence in criminal cases. When individuals are arrested and booked, their fingerprints are recorded and placed in a nationwide database for use by law enforcement. In addition, applicants for government positions are often fingerprinted and their prints are recorded. Some stakeholders in the juvenile justice system, however, say that fingerprinting denies juveniles a clean slate before they reach adulthood. The use of fingerprints provides a permanent record of delinquent activity.

In dealing with this controversial issue, some states allow police departments to record fingerprints routinely when juveniles are taken into custody, while other states prohibit fingerprinting of juveniles unless a judge gives permission. Some states also require judges to control access to fingerprint records and call for their elimination once the juvenile enters adulthood.[24]

The legal system also governs how juveniles are treated in a police **lineup**, where witnesses or victims are asked to pick out the suspect from a small group of individuals,

Young men in a police lineup. Are juveniles accorded special treatment by police?

including the suspect. Identification of a suspect in a lineup can be used as evidence in court. Police are not allowed to coach the witness or victim to identify a particular person.[25]

In addition, suspects in a lineup are entitled to *the right to counsel*, which means having an attorney present during questioning. The presence of an attorney ensures that identification is not biased. In *United States v. Wade* (1967) and *Kirby v. Illinois* (1972), the Supreme Court upheld the right to counsel during lineups and directed that this right must be accorded as soon as an indictment is issued. *In re Holley* (1970),[26] a case involving a youth convicted of rape was reversed because the juvenile did not have counsel during lineup identification.

Photographs can be substituted for lineups. A victim or witness is shown photographs of many individuals and is asked to pick out the suspect. To protect the rights of the suspect, police are not allowed to bias the process by showing only one photograph and pressing for identification. In addition, some states give police the opportunity to take photographs of juvenile suspects but do not allow them to provide them to the media, because the youths could be stigmatized if they are found not guilty. As with fingerprints, some states require that photographs of juveniles be destroyed when the subjects reach adulthood.[27]

TRENDS IN JUVENILE ARRESTS

>> LO 4.6   Identify trends in juvenile arrests.

Let's start with a recent snapshot of juvenile crime in the United States and then go back in time. In 2017, there was a 61% decrease in arrests of juveniles in the United States compared with 2007. Juvenile arrest rates for robbery, aggravated assault, and drug violations have dropped, but arrest rates for murder have increased. Overall, arrest rates for male and female juveniles, as well as all racial groups, have decreased. Table 4.1 highlights the offenses for which juveniles are most frequently arrested. Most arrests involved males; blacks were arrested more often for personal crimes, while whites were arrested more frequently for property and nonindex crimes.[28]

Police officers in a crime-ridden area. What might explain high crime rates in such areas?

This trend in dropping arrest rates has been occurring since the early 21st century. There was an almost 35% drop in juvenile arrests between 2003 and 2013. As a result of fewer arrests, as well as more use of community diversionary programs, the number of juvenile commitments to residential facilities (discussed in Chapter 6) has dropped almost 50%. However, even though the arrest rate is dropping, the rate of black youth arrests has grown compared with white youth arrests. When comparing these two racial grounds, they have the same likelihood of participating in physical altercations, carrying weapons, and having involvement in selling and using drugs. Furthermore, although black youths are more likely to commit violent crimes, this accounts for only 5% of arrests.[29] So why the sizable difference between the groups? Has the variable of race and ethnicity always been a correlate in police interactions?

TABLE 4.1

Juvenile Arrests in the United States, 2017

OFFENSE	NUMBER OF ARRESTS	FEMALE	UNDER AGE 15	WHITE
Murder	850	9%	9%	36%
Aggravated assault	28,060	26%	32%	54%
Robbery	19,200	11%	19%	29%
Burglary	31,990	12%	30%	55%
Larceny	134,180	41%	27%	60%
Motor vehicle theft	15,720	19%	23%	47%
Simple assaults	128,930	37%	39%	58%
Vandalism	39,120	17%	40%	69%
Drug abuse violations	98,490	23%	15%	75%
Curfew and loitering	34,180	30%	29%	56%

Source: C. Puzzanchera, "Juvenile Arrests, 2017," *Juvenile Justice Statistics, National Report Series Bulletin* (Washington, DC: U.S. Department of Justice, December 2018).

Note: Most recent data available at the time of publication

POLICE AND JUVENILE RELATIONSHIPS AND ATTITUDES

>> **LO 4.7** Explain police discretion and identify the choices available to police who work with juveniles.

Shaping Police Decisions

Many of today's police officers share an overall concern for youthful offenders, with the aim of averting them from paths to crime. Police agencies nationwide support proactive mentoring and diversionary programs meant to gain the trust of at-risk youths and give them opportunities to succeed. However, police officers sometimes experience occupational hazards that make it challenging to maintain a positive attitude toward juveniles. Some officers feel that violent juveniles are a real source of danger, with few young people stopping to consider the consequences of their actions.

Police are allowed some **discretion** when dealing with juveniles. Since an arrest by an officer will likely label a youth as a delinquent, much of the time officers simply warn juveniles who are loitering or involved in a brief physical altercation, and ask them to leave the area. However, certain juvenile behaviors require police intervention.

Police officers have to consider the *seriousness of any offense* before making a decision on how to proceed with an official intervention.[30] Nonviolent and less serious offenses can often be handled informally. However, *citizen complaints* can also affect how police proceed with an intervention, even in a minimal offense. If a citizen asks police officers investigating a case of trespassing, for example, to make an arrest, formal juvenile processing is more likely. And if there is *community-wide pressure* to crack down on juvenile crime, more formal processing is likely to take place.

Demographic factors and *individual characteristics* of the juvenile can affect a decision about formal processing. Research has indicated that male juveniles are more likely than females to be arrested. Whether race is a factor is disputed in the research, but more recorded serious offenses are committed by ethnic minorities than by whites, and juveniles of lower socioeconomic status are more likely to be arrested and processed than are middle- and upper-class juveniles. Furthermore, disrespectful or aggressive youths are more likely to be taken into custody than are youths who are compliant and respectful.[31]

CASE STUDY

J.D.B. v. North Carolina, 564 U.S. 261 (2011)

J.D.B. was a 13-year-old male student enrolled in special education classes in the state of North Carolina in the year 2005. The police suspected he had committed neighborhood burglaries, thus visiting him at his school for interrogation. They had received information that he was in possession of a digital camera that was reported stolen from one of the burglaries. He was not read his Miranda warnings, nor was his legal guardian contacted before interrogation. J.D.B. was interrogated by an investigator, uniformed police officer, and other school officials. The student eventually confessed to the crimes. During his trial, any motions by the defense to suppress statements made by J.D.B. were denied because he was not considered in police custody. He was convicted of the burglaries.

In December 2009, the North Carolina Supreme Court ruled that neither his age nor his special education status should be considered a factor when determining if he was in police custody; therefore, he was not entitled to Miranda warnings. The case was then heard by the U.S. Supreme Court. While not a unanimous decision, the Supreme Court reversed the lower court order and sent the case back to the state court system to determine the custody status of the youth during interrogation. Justice Sonia Sotomayor wrote the majority opinion, stating, "It is beyond dispute that children will often feel bound to submit to police questioning when an adult in the same circumstances would feel free to leave. Seeing no reason for police officers or courts to blind themselves to that commonsense reality, we hold that a child's age properly informs the Miranda custody analysis."

1. **Do you agree with the ruling?**

2. **Do you feel that minors have a different perception of police authority than do adults?**

3. **In your opinion, would this ruling be the same today?**

Online Case Opinion

https://caselaw.findlaw.com/us-supreme-court/9-11121 .html ●

Police must be as guarded in interactions with juveniles as they are with adults because, as alluded to earlier, some juveniles can be violent. In addition, some juveniles are well versed in their legal rights and know how far they can push an officer. In accordance with the law and court precedent, police must limit themselves to appropriate verbal and physical reactions to juveniles and refrain from overreacting.

Some police officers feel that ongoing juvenile crime and gang activity in urban areas are due to the leniency of the juvenile justice system. Because of the rehabilitative nature of the juvenile legal codes, officers believe that many juveniles will not be sanctioned unless they commit very serious offenses.

Weighing Juvenile Opinions

There have been decades of studies on the attitudes and perceptions of juveniles toward the police. Though the studies indicate that youths today often have more positive perceptions of police officers than in the past, the most negative perceptions of police come from juveniles who have had encounters with the police.[32] Generally, younger children and girls have a better attitude toward law enforcement than do older children and boys. African American youths and those of lower socioeconomic status are much more likely than others to have negative attitudes about law enforcement.[33]

PROACTIVE POLICE METHODS OF PREVENTING JUVENILE CRIME

>> **LO 4.8**   **Describe some proactive methods that police use to prevent juvenile crime. Describe some proactive methods that police use to prevent juvenile crime.**

A primary goal of the juvenile justice and criminal justice systems is to curtail offending behavior. This goal would reduce resources needed to supervise offenders and could free up resources to provide a better quality of life for at-risk populations. At-risk juveniles are considered an especially important population because they are often viewed as more likely to be rehabilitated than adults. Law enforcement attempts to deter juvenile crime through interventions in three areas: the community, schools, and gangs.

Community-based interventions can be an effective way to control juvenile crime. They involve forming positive relationships with organizations that serve juveniles, such as the YMCA, Boys and Girls Clubs, local youth centers, and local schools, as well as local businesses. In addition, police try to help parents and youths feel comfortable working with law enforcement.

Youths should not see the police as an enemy who is out to get them. This can partly be accomplished by providing helpful services such as locating missing children, recovering stolen bikes, locating stolen phones, and so on. The Amber Alert system, a program that has been used to recover hundreds of missing children,[34] was initiated by Dallas–Fort Worth broadcasters in 1996 after the abduction and murder of 9-year-old Amber Hagerman.

Police officers also enforce curfew ordinances and drug and alcohol use laws. Juveniles often view these measures as an annoyance, but they can prevent future delinquent behavior. Officers are also involved in the protection of certain groups—such as minority races, LGBTQ youths, and religious groups—from hate crimes, which can demonstrate an interest in the welfare of these groups.[35]

Specialized Interventions

Community-Based Policing Operations

While some policing programs are designed to improve police–youth relationships, others are designed to decrease crime committed by juveniles. These efforts, often beginning with the word *operation*, are intense initiatives that target a specific type of criminality. For instance, Operation Ceasefire is a policing program in Boston, Massachusetts, implemented with the goal of reducing gang and gun violence, as well as illegal gun possession. The program uses comprehensive strategies to apprehend and prosecute gun offenders, acting as a deterrent for juveniles considering similar behaviors. Evaluations of Operation Ceasefire found a reduction in calls for service and youth homicide, and an increase in recovery of illegal firearms.[36] This program led to the development of Operation Peacekeeper, a similar program implemented in Stockton, California.[37]

A speaker at the Boys & Girls Club of America. How can such organizations provide a positive outlet for at-risk youth?

AP Photo/Paul Morigi

Another example of a community-based policing operation is Little Village Gang Violence Reduction Project (GVRP). This Chicago program had two purposes: (1) the reduction of individual gang member violence and (2) the reduction of aggregate gang violence. GVRP used the Comprehensive Gang Model, which contained five core elements: (1) community mobilization, (2) social intervention, (3) provision of social opportunities, (4) suppression, and (5) organizational change and development of local agencies and groups. While property crime arrests did not significantly decrease, GVRP was successful in reducing arrests for violent and gun crimes in the city.[38]

Gangs

Gang-based interventions are implemented in certain urban areas that have increased gang activity. A **youth service program** is a temporary intervention to address a specific gang issue and is not the primary responsibility of the police, but officers are involved in a **gang detail** and **gang unit**. In a gang detail, officers are pulled from juvenile, detective, or other units to work on gang issues. Gang units are permanent divisions in a police force that use confidential information and intelligence, and work with gang members.[39]

Gangs are a major cause of violence and drug distribution in an urban area. Juveniles who have no steady family or support in their lives can be strongly attracted to gangs. The Gang Resistance Education and Training (G.R.E.A.T.) program, implemented in schools across America in 1991, was meant to counteract the attraction of gang membership. The program provides a curriculum for elementary and middle school students, as well as family and summer programs. More than 6 million students have graduated from the program, and 12,000 police officers have been certified as G.R.E.A.T. instructors. Empirical research has not shown that G.R.E.A.T. reduces gang involvement, but the program has led to more positive attitudes toward law enforcement.[40]

Schools

McGruff the Crime Dog's advertising campaign to "take a bite out of crime" launched in 1979, focusing to a large extent on school-age children. Similarly, "Officer Friendly" programs, popular in the 1960s and 1970s, brought police officers into schools to help develop positive attitudes toward law enforcement. Since then, police departments have sponsored school-based programs on issues such as bicycle safety, bullying, drug and alcohol abuse, and gangs. Though not all programs have been successful, some have demonstrated evidence of crime prevention and community acceptance of the police.

Police have a relatively high profile in public schools, and not just in areas with high crime rates. The Office of Community-Oriented Policing in the U.S. Department of Justice has awarded more than $700 million to about 2,900 law enforcement agencies to hire **school resource officers (SROs)**. SROs not only provide law enforcement services but also act as problem solvers and community liaisons. They may teach classes on substance abuse and gang prevention, mentor at-risk students, facilitate community service projects, or simply serve as a positive presence in the school.

Some school-based programs have been shown to be successful in improving attitudes toward police and reducing delinquency in youths. The Law Enforcement Education Program, run by a private nonprofit group in Michigan, offers educational programs and scholarships in law enforcement for children. These programs, which focus on child safety, have had a positive impact on juveniles' attitudes toward citizenship. The School Program to Educate and Control Drug Abuse, developed in New York City in the 1980s, uses counselors and police officers as role models to assist fifth and sixth graders in developing skills to resist drug involvement and has been strongly linked to positive changes in children's knowledge of and attitudes toward drugs.[41] ●

NAVIGATING THE FIELD 4.1

Safe Streets Baltimore

The Safe Streets Baltimore program targeted four violent neighborhoods in the city, using outreach workers and law enforcement officers to connect with high-risk youths and young adults during evenings and weekends to provide them with positive services that were intended to lower their involvement in delinquency. One aspect of the program focused on developing an organized community with strong social bonds through a focus on public education, faith, and community mobilization—along with positive involvement by criminal justice personnel. Since implementation of the program began, there has been a significant reduction in shootings and homicides in all four Baltimore neighborhoods. After participating in the program, community members are found to be much less likely to use firearms as a method of dispute resolution.

Putting It Into Action

Using your Internet search engine, research this program and its implementation.

Explain how such a program might be used in other urban areas to reduce violence.

Submit what you've learned to your instructor when requested to do so. ●

SUMMARY

>> LO 4.1   Discuss the historical changes involving police interactions with juveniles.

The early citizens of the United States allowed the family and community to manage juvenile behavior and punishment. However, once immigration began to increase, a more formalized method of law and order was developed, and uniformed, organized police officers started policing the country's towns and cities in the mid-19th century. In the early 20th century, the first juvenile bureau was created. It specialized in managing troubled juveniles.

Key Terms

community policing   52

discretion   59

juvenile bureau   52

problem-oriented policing   52

>> LO 4.2   Describe important aspects of police-juvenile interaction.

Law enforcement agencies nationwide are advocates of proactive mentoring for juveniles, with the intention of steering at-risk youths away from a life of crime. However, not all youths are willing participants in police-sponsored efforts. Police are allowed some discretion when taking juveniles into custody, especially if no violence is involved in their behavior. Various factors can affect officer decisions, including demographics, behaviors, and community pressures.

Key Terms

confession   56

due process   55

exclusionary rule   55

fingerprints   57

hands-off doctrine   54

interrogation   56

lineup   57

reasonable suspicion   55

search and seizure   55

>> LO 4.3   Describe the processing of juveniles who are taken into police custody.

Police officers can use discretion to determine how to handle juvenile offenders, especially those involved in nonserious offenses. They may choose to send them home with their parents, or recommend that they participate in a mentoring program. Neglected children may also be referred to social service agencies. Youths who are formally processed, on the other hand, will be arrested and taken into custody. Some may be released to parents, while others may be placed in a juvenile facility to await adjudication.

Key Terms

confession 56	hands off doctrine 54	reasonable suspicion 55
due process 55	interrogation 56	search and seizure 55
exclusionary rule 55	police process 54	

≫ LO 4.4   Identify some of the constitutional rights of juveniles.

Many of the constitutional rights afforded to adults are shared by juveniles, such as protection against the use of illegally seized evidence in court. Like adults, youths are protected against interrogations without Miranda warnings, and they have the right to an attorney. Court rulings have also addressed other areas, such as the use of photographs and lineups

Key Terms

fingerprints 57	lineup 57

≫ LO 4.5   Describe the proactive measures used by police to prevent juvenile crime.

There are many intervention programs available to at-risk youths to prevent future criminality. Community-based interventions often involve programs with mentoring opportunities. Larger urban areas employ gang-based interventions to decrease the appeal of gang life for youths. Public and private schools also have programming and have recently begun introducing school resource officers to build trust between law enforcement officers and juveniles.

≫ LO 4.6   Identify trends in juvenile arrests.

Since the beginning of the 21st century, arrest rates of juveniles have been decreasing. However, Black youth are still more likely than White youth to be arrested, despite the similarities in their criminal behavior.

≫ LO 4.7   Explain police discretion and identify the choices available to police who work with juveniles.

A variety of factors are considered when law enforcement make decisions on the management of interactions with juvenile offenders. Officers weigh the seriousness of the offense, the attitude of the offender, and perception of the community of that particular behavior. Law enforcement utilizes a wide range of discretion when determining how to move forward, considering formal processing or informal management of cases.

≫ LO 4.8   Describe some proactive methods that police use to prevent juvenile crime. Describe some proactive methods that police use to prevent juvenile crime.

Law enforcement uses a variety of methods as proactive measures of combating juvenile crime. Implementation of community programming that provide prosocial options as well as gang-specific interventions are helpful. In addition, school resource officers are placed in many public schools to encourage a positive relationship between youth and law enforcement.

Key Terms

community-based interventions 61	gang unit 62	school resource officers (SROs) 62
gang detail 62	gang-based interventions 62	youth service program 62

1. How can positive perceptions of law enforcement officers by juveniles be enhanced?

2. Current limitations on search and seizure involving juveniles impede effective law enforcement, but are they necessary to protect the constitutional rights of juveniles? Which is more important? Explain.

3. Antidrug programs such as the "Just Say No" campaign have not shown much success. What tactics can law enforcement and public schools use to reduce juvenile drug use?

EXPLORING JUVENILE JUSTICE FURTHER

1. Investigate what community policing programs are available in your jurisdiction, especially those targeting juveniles. Choose a program you believe would be the most successful no matter the jurisdiction (urban, suburban, or rural). In your opinion, what components of the program make it successful?

2. Find an example from the recent media that depicts negative police and juvenile interaction. Based on the details of the negative interaction, develop a police training program that could improve it. For instance, the program could focus on firearms training or ethics.

3. Read through the report in Appendix B "5 Ways Law Enforcement Agencies Can Use Data on Juveniles." Out of these five strategies, choose the one that you think would be the most effective. Explain why you have chosen this strategy. Find an example of a police department that has utilized this strategy. What was the result?.

⑤SAGE edge™

Give your students the SAGE edge!

SAGE edge offers a robust online environment featuring an impressive array of free tools and resources for review, study, and further exploration, keeping both instructors and students on the cutting edge of teaching and learning. Learn more at **edge.sagepub.com/schmallegerjj**.

The Juvenile Court System

After reading this chapter you should be able to

1. Describe the juvenile court system, including some of the personnel who work in the system

2. Show how pretrial procedures impact the handling of delinquency cases

3. Describe adjudicatory and dispositional hearings in the juvenile justice system

4. Identify the constitutional protections applicable to juvenile proceedings

5. Explain judicial transfer procedures as they apply to juvenile court

6. Define status offenders and offer recommendations on their management

Key Terms in Chapter 5

1974 Juvenile Justice and Delinquency Prevention (JJDP) Act
adjudicatory hearing
bail
bifurcated system
blended sentence
concurrent jurisdiction
consent decrees
crossover youths

deinstitutionalization of status offenders (DSO)
deinstitutionalize
detention hearing
determinate sentencing
dispositional hearing
indeterminate sentencing
informal probation
intake process
judicial waiver
nonjudicial adjustment

petition
plea bargain
predisposition report
presumptive diminished responsibility
preventive detention
prosecutorial discretion
release on recognizance
reverse waiver
statutory exclusion
youthful offender programs

INTRODUCTION

On September 2, 1961, 16-year-old Morris A. Kent, Jr., broke into a house in the District of Columbia and raped and robbed a woman. At the time of the offense he was on juvenile probation for an offense committed in 1959, when he was 14 years old. Kent had been fingerprinted following his 1959 arrest, and his prints matched those found in the woman's home. He was taken into custody 3 days later and was charged with three counts of housebreaking and robbery, and two counts of rape. Interrogated by the police without counsel, he admitted not only to the current offenses but also to several previous offenses.[1]

After his first interrogation, he spent the night at the Receiving Home for Juveniles and returned the next morning for more questioning. There is no record of when Kent's mother was informed of his detention, but she did not retain counsel for him until the second day. At that time, the social services director for the juvenile court met with Kent's counsel to discuss the possibility of waiving the case to adult court. The attorney opposed the waiver and requested a psychiatric evaluation, which revealed that Kent suffered from severe psychopathology. An affidavit asserted that Kent could be rehabilitated if adequate treatment was provided. Nonetheless, his case was transferred to adult court, where he was convicted and sentenced to 30 to 90 years of detention. Following conviction he was sent to Saint Elizabeth's Hospital—a secure facility in Washington, D.C.—for psychiatric treatment.[2]

The juvenile court's decision to transfer him to the jurisdiction of adult criminal court was challenged by Kent's defense counsel in the 1966 case of *Kent v. United States*. In arguments before the U.S. Supreme Court, Kent's counsel argued that his client's

St. Elizabeth's Hospital in Washington, D.C. This photo shows the oldest part of the hospital and is the place where Morris A. Kent, Jr., was sent following his conviction in adult court in the early 1960s. What did the case of *Kent v. U.S.* establish?

transfer to adult court violated his due process rights, which guaranteed fair treatment for everyone processed through the justice system. The lawyer argued that, in Kent's case, the juvenile court judge failed to rule on some of the motions made by the defense, did not make reference to those motions when making the transfer, did not discuss the case with Kent or his parents, and did not act on reports of Kent's deteriorating mental state. The Supreme Court agreed that the transfer decision violated due process, and held that Kent's interrogation and detention without access to an attorney were illegal. The court held that Kent's rights had been violated when he was not read his Miranda rights, and also ruled that he had the right to attend his transfer and waiver hearing.

NAVIGATING THE JUVENILE COURT SYSTEM AND ITS STAKEHOLDERS

©iStockphoto.com/feixianhu

A juvenile courtroom. What are the stages involved in the processing of juveniles by the justice system?

>> LO 5.1   **Describe the juvenile court system, including some of the personnel who work in the system.**

The juvenile court system varies widely in its structure depending on the jurisdiction. Juvenile courts in large urban areas have employees solely dedicated to managing cases involving minors. Smaller cities and rural jurisdictions often use judges who try adult cases as well, or they use family court judges, who have a variety of responsibilities. Quite often the juvenile court is part of a district, superior, or circuit court that also handles general trials or lesser criminal matters. Ideally, juvenile courts should stand apart from other court systems, but limited resources often won't allow that. Despite the differentiation, juveniles often encounter similar types of personnel as they navigate the system, as indicated in Table 5.1.

TABLE 5.1

Juvenile Court Personnel

PERSONNEL NAME	RESPONSIBILITIES
Juvenile judge	Determines legal issues presented to the court
Referee	Acts as primary hearing officer in many states
Prosecutor	Pursues cases against juveniles but is still expected to ensure their constitutional rights
Defense attorney	Advocates for the juvenile and assists court staff on issues pertaining to the juvenile
Probation officer	Assesses the needs of juveniles and writes reports on their conduct
Support staff	Carries out administrative work on a voluntary or paid basis in social service and other agencies

PRETRIAL STEPS IN THE JUVENILE COURT PROCESS

>> **LO 5.2** **Show how pretrial procedures impact the handling of delinquency cases.**

As already mentioned, the juvenile court can handle a variety of cases, including delinquency, dependency, and neglect. Children's courts can be responsible for adoption, termination of parental rights, and issues involving guardianship and financial support. This particular section will address delinquency cases and the pretrial procedures followed by juvenile courts.

Juvenile courts in the United States handled about 850,500 cases in 2016.[3] Between 1960 and 2016, juvenile court delinquency caseloads more than doubled. Table 5.2 displays statistics on juvenile court cases for 2016. In addition, juvenile courts supervised more than 31 million juveniles in 2014, and 79% of these youths were ages 10 to 15. Table 5.3 provides a profile of offense categories by age group.

TABLE 5.2

Highlights of 2016 Juvenile Delinquency Court Cases

OFFENSE	NUMBER OF CASES	YOUNGER THAN 16	FEMALE	WHITE
Homicide	1,000	32%	13%	29%
Forcible rape	7,900	62%	4%	53%
Robbery	20,300	47%	11%	12%
Aggravated assault	26,200	54%	25%	31%
Simple assault	158,700	61%	37%	41%
Burglary	55,300	54%	11%	37%
Larceny-theft	126,800	51%	39%	46%
Vandalism	41,900	62%	18%	52%
Drug violations	107,400	37%	23%	56%
Public order offenses	214,700	49%	28%	41%

Source: Sarah Hockenberry and Charles Puzzanchera, *Juvenile Court Statistics 2016* (Pittsburgh, PA: National Center for Juvenile Justice, 2018).

TABLE 5.3

Offense Categories by Age Group

OFFENSE CATEGORY	AGE 15 OR YOUNGER	AGE 16 OR OLDER
Drugs	10%	17%
Person	31%	22%
Property	35%	34%
Public order	24%	27%

Source: OJJDP *Statistical Briefing Book.*

IN THE MEDIA 5.1

Pennsylvania's "Kids-for-Cash" Judges

In 2019, Luzerne County, Pennsylvania, became the site of significant media attention when the nonprofit Juvenile Law Center (JLC) in Philadelphia identified two juvenile court judges as corrupt. The judges, Mark Ciavarella, 58, and Michael Conahan, 56, were accused of taking kickbacks from juvenile facilities to which they committed adjudicated delinquents. JLC claimed that at least 5,000 children, over a 5-year period, appeared before Judge Ciavarella and that he took money from private detention centers and wilderness camps to send them some of these juveniles. Each judge was proven to have accepted kickbacks in excess of $1 million. The scandal began in 2002, when Judge Conahan closed a state juvenile detention center and funneled millions of dollars from the Luzerne County budget into the building of expensive private facilities. In 2009 Ciavarella pleaded guilty in federal court to charges of fraud and tax evasion; Conahan pleaded guilty to the same charges. In 2011 Ciavarella was sentenced to 28 years in federal prison—a sentence that was upheld by an appeals court in 2013.

Putting It Into Action

In this active learning assignment, you should schedule an interview with a juvenile court judge, prosecutor, or attorney who specializes in the handling of juvenile cases.

Ask the professional you interview how judges such as Ciavarella and Conahan could have gotten away with the crimes they committed—and see if they can identify systems that are in place today to prevent such things from happening again. Create a file containing what you learned, and submit it to your instructor when asked to do so. ●

Detention Hearings

A **detention hearing** determines whether a juvenile will be detained. The hearing must be held shortly after arrest, generally within 48 to 72 hours, not including weekends and national holidays. In large urban areas, 24-hour intake units may make detainment decisions within a few hours of arrest. These hearings can occur at three points: (1) at the time youths are brought in by law enforcement; (2) during or after a review to determine if referral to juvenile court is appropriate; or (3) after the adjudicatory hearing.[4],[5]

Police officers must often place juveniles in a lockup or local jail while parents are being notified. While most youths are released to their parents or guardians, some may be further detained based on their classification. Serious offenders or status offenders with abusive or neglectful home situations may be detained for the protection of society or for their own protection—a practice known as **preventive detention.**

Police also have the option to bring youths to intake personnel at the juvenile court, who will determine whether juvenile court referral is appropriate. In addition to the need to protect society or for their own protection, preventive detention may be ordered for juveniles who are waiting for adjudicatory or disposition hearings. Some of these juveniles may be sent to a shelter, a public or private detention center, or in-home detention.

A detention home is physically restrictive, meaning that the juvenile cannot leave the premises. Shelter care is not restrictive and is available for youths who cannot be placed in a home. In-home detention is preferable because youths can stay at home while being supervised by a court staff member. The youths can also be put in police lockup or jail, but this is the least desirable.

Critics of juvenile detention have argued that putting delinquent youths together increases recidivism by allowing them to learn new methods of offending, and impairs successful reintegration into society. Detention can also stunt maturation and educational attainment, damage the psychological and physical health of mentally ill juveniles, and incur much higher expenses than in-home supervision.

Pretrial Release and Preventive Detention

Bail is not a sanction. For adults, **bail** is a method of pretrial release that seeks to ensure that defendants will return for trial proceedings. In the juvenile system, bail is used to help ensure the appearance of the accused youth at the adjudicatory hearing. The court will determine the appropriate amount of bail at an early intake hearing, basing it on current and past behavior, as well as relationships with peers and family. Once the appropriate amount is set, a family will typically pay about 10% of that amount to a bondsman and the juvenile will be released into parental custody.[6]

Bail is not a guaranteed constitutional right for juveniles, per the U.S. Supreme Court ruling in *ex parte Crouse*. However, many states assume that as the juvenile justice system is based on reuniting families and rehabilitation for the juvenile, it is also safe to assume that juvenile court procedures and due process are sufficient enough to guarantee early release for appropriate juvenile offenders. States such as Hawaii, Kentucky, and Oregon prohibit bail completely for juveniles, while West Virginia, Oklahoma, Colorado, and Georgia allow it. In 2018, California abolished monetary bail, leaving it up to judges and other experts to assess the dangerousness

NAVIGATING THE FIELD 5.1

The Equal Justice Initiative

In April of 2017, the Equal Justice Initiative (EJI) released a report concluding that black students have disproportionately higher rates of arrest by police and also suspension and expulsion from schools. In reaching its conclusion, the EJI used data from the U.S. Department of Education.

Putting It Into Action

Using your Internet search engine, examine the EJI data and the conclusions that it reached. Remember that a mere demonstration of disproportionality is not necessarily an indictment of justice system processing. That's because there may actually *be* higher rates of inappropriate or delinquent behavior among some

groups—and it would be inherently unfair to target members of the other groups simply to make the numbers "match."

While exploring the EJI site, decide whether disproportionate rates reflect actual biases and if the site provides the data necessary to reach that conclusion in an objective fashion.

Also examine how the EJI is attempting to reduce the potential for bias in the juvenile justice system, and describe your perception of the effectiveness of these efforts.

Put your conclusions into a document that you can submit to your professor when asked to do so. ●

of a defendant before deciding whether or not to release the defendant prior to his or her next scheduled court appearance.

The Eighth Amendment protects adults from excessive bail, but it can be legally difficult to determine what is considered excessive. Some states that allow bail for juveniles require higher courts to review bail set by lower courts to ensure that excessive amounts are not posted. Some juvenile justice experts have suggested using **release on recognizance**, which is based on a verbal promise to return for proceedings, rather than setting monetary amounts for bail. Other experts have suggested simply issuing a summons for the youth to return to court at a specific day and time.

The use of preventive detention for juveniles has been an extremely controversial topic because it involves individuals who have not yet been adjudicated for a crime. It reverses the maxim of our criminal justice system, "innocent until proven guilty." While it refers to the behavior the juvenile is accused of and is supposed to protect society, it has a punitive connotation. Research has indicated that youths who were placed in preventive detention were more likely to receive the sanction of out-of-home placement, which counters the goal of rehabilitation and reunification.

The U.S. Supreme Court weighed the use of preventive detention for juveniles in *Schall v. Martin* in 1984.[7] An appeals court in New York had ruled that the New York Family Court Act was unconstitutional because it allowed the preventive detention of juveniles for unadjudicated acts. The U.S. Supreme Court reversed the decision, with Justice William Rehnquist stating that preventive detention legitimately protected juveniles and society from the potential of pretrial criminal activity.

Intake

The **intake process** serves to classify and manage youths before adjudicatory proceedings. At intake, it is determined if cases should be sent to the juvenile court or other social service agencies. The process controls the use of detention and diverts what would otherwise be an unmanageable number of cases in the juvenile court. The deployment of the process itself is, however, dependent on the resources available to a particular juvenile court. Larger probation departments will have intake units for juveniles, while smaller departments use juvenile probation officers to make intake decisions.[8]

When intake officers begin to work on a case, they may meet with police officers, the prosecutor, parents, and legal counsel for the youth. Cases may be dismissed and the youth sent home if the case is weak, the cited behaviors are not covered by state law, the juvenile is a first-time offender and the offense is relatively minor, or parents successfully intervene.

If a youth is a status offender, the intake officer may choose to apply a **nonjudicial adjustment**, or intervention without the use of the juvenile court. This can include a simple warning to the juvenile and release to the parents or guardians. The offender may be asked to pay restitution to the victim, or be referred to a diversion program where social services are available to help the juvenile with his or her issues.

Intake officers have several alternatives to sending a youth to a juvenile court. Youths can be placed on **informal probation**, which is release back into the community with certain supervisory conditions, such as curfew, employment, and community service. Once the youth serves the specified amount of time, his or her case

Law enforcement will fingerprint children as a community safety initiative. Why is such fingerprinting a valuable service?

report is forwarded to the court and, if no additional behavioral problems have been identified, is dismissed. However, if the youth has problems following the required conditions, a **petition** can be filed sending the youth back to court. Authorities can also issue **consent decrees**, which are an intermediate measure between probation and nonjudicial adjustment. For a case to be dismissed in this way, the youth must fulfill conditions such as restitution, supervision, or community service.

ADJUDICATORY AND DISPOSITIONAL HEARINGS

>> **LO 5.3** Describe adjudicatory and dispositional hearings in the juvenile justice system.

After the pretrial proceedings are complete and when the juvenile has not yet signed a plea bargain, an **adjudicatory hearing** will be held. An adjudicatory hearing is equivalent to a trial for adults. The hearing is the fact-finding stage of the process that includes the juvenile's plea, presentation of evidence by prosecution and defense, and a ruling by the judge. The hearing is not as formal as an adult trial and may last from 5 minutes to an hour or more, and may be extended by continuances that are required to receive evidence from social service agencies or forensics specialists.[9]

In today's juvenile courts, due process and procedural requirements are followed much more carefully than in the past. Written petitions are required, hearsay cannot be used as evidence, and proof must be "beyond a reasonable doubt." Youths are protected against self-incrimination, and cross-examination of all witnesses is permitted. Attorneys are generally present on both sides to protect the interest of the state and of the juvenile. If a juvenile has not retained an attorney by the time of the adjudicatory hearing, then a public defender will be appointed to represent him or her without cost. Last, jury trials are an option for juveniles in some jurisdictions. Some states require a jury trial for juveniles who request one at the adjudicatory hearing or if institutional confinement is a potential sanction.

A **dispositional hearing** is the equivalent of a sentencing hearing in the adult criminal justice system. In some instances, it occurs during the adjudicatory hearing. The judge discusses the case with the juvenile, the family, and the attorneys, then reviews the case report provided by social service agencies. Once these two stages are complete, the judge will decide what is the most effective sanction and treatment for the juvenile.

A second type of hearing is a **bifurcated system**, or separation of the adjudicatory hearing and disposition hearing. Generally, the disposition hearing will occur 1 to 2 weeks after the adjudicatory hearing. The judge requests all relevant information about the juvenile, even if it would be inadmissible in the adjudicatory hearing stage, to make the best possible decision for the youth. This arrangement prevents the judge from making a prejudicial decision of guilt or innocence based on certain types of information, but also allows the judge to use the information to make a decision for effective punishment and treatment.[10]

The use of the bifurcated system also gives the juvenile probation department ample time to compile the predisposition report. The **predisposition report** is a comprehensive document that provides a full background report on the juvenile, for the judge to use during the disposition hearing. It includes the juvenile's past and current involvement with the juvenile justice system, including offense history, violent and aggressive behaviors, and successes and failures with past sanctions and treatments. This information is gathered from law enforcement agencies, juvenile court, and related agencies. The probation officer also collects information on the juvenile's psychiatric and medical history from physicians, schools, and social service agencies. A juvenile may also be referred for a psychological evaluation for current assessment of his or her mental state. Last, the report provides information on the youth's personal history including abuse, relationships with family and friends, and school and work history (see Figure 5.1).

FIGURE 5.1

Standard Contents of a Predisposition Report

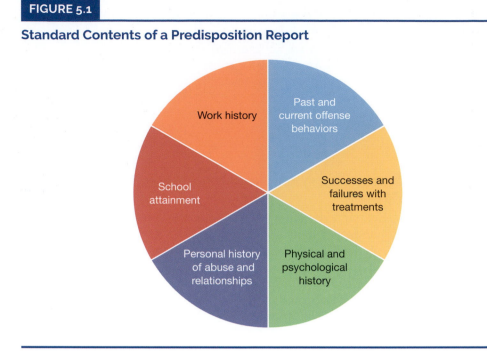

Source: Institute of Judicial Administration and American Bar Association, *The Juvenile Probation Function: Intake and Predisposition* (1980), https://www.ncjrs.gov/pdffiles1/ojjdp/83585.pdf.

Once the report is complete, it is reviewed by a judge. The probation officer recommends a course of action, possibly including punitive sanctions and treatment resources. Once the judge has fully reviewed the report, the hearing commences with the juvenile present, and the judge orders disposition. Generally, the judge follows the recommendation of the probation officer in the disposition report. However, the judge also independently considers the seriousness of the offense and past violent history of the juvenile. In addition, past research has indicated that other factors can affect the decision, such as the judge's values, social and racial background of the juvenile, demeanor of the juvenile, and pressure from the community.

The Option of the Plea Bargain

In the adult criminal justice system, plea bargaining is a vital part of the court system. About 90% of adult criminal cases end with a plea bargain rather than going through the complete trial process. A **plea bargain** is an agreement made between the prosecutor and defense attorney that allows a defendant to plea to a lesser charge and serve a less severe sentence. This agreement may be in exchange for testimony against other involved defendants or simply to get the case closed and off the docket.[11]

Plea bargaining has also become more common in the juvenile justice system, typically with the aim of using the more rehabilitative sanction of community-based corrections or reducing the caseload. However, critics assert that this option may encourage innocent youths to plead guilty to a lesser charge to avoid a harsher sentence. On the other hand, youths who are serious or violent offenders and are guilty may not get the appropriate care needed in a plea bargain.

Juvenile Sentencing Options

Much like in the adult criminal justice system, the judge has several sentencing options. **Indeterminate sentencing**, a traditional form of sentencing, is focused on rehabilitation and sets an indefinite term of incarceration that can be shortened based on good behavior. For instance, a judge may sentence a juvenile to 5 to 8 months in a detention center, allowing the juvenile to earn early release with good behavior. **Determinate sentencing** sets a specific amount of time to be served for a specific crime, and the time is often mandated by statute. Another option is a blended sentence, allowing a judge to mix and match sentencing options.

Table 5.4 lists all the judicial alternatives generally available to a juvenile court. Which one is used often depends on how the judge can administer and on the availability of resources in the area. Judges in larger urban areas generally have every option available to them, but judges in smaller areas may have only a few.

Children at work cleaning up a neighborhood. How do sentences of community service repair damage and rebuild bonds with the community?

Life Without Parole

Until recently, the United States stood alone as a nation that sentenced juveniles to life without parole for violent crimes.[12] Of the states that allowed the sentence, Pennsylvania, Michigan, and Louisiana accounted for about two-thirds of the life without parole sentences for juveniles. In 2017, more than 2,000 juveniles had received a life without parole sentence. However, the Supreme Court ruling of *Miller v. Alabama* (2012), overturned mandatory life without parole sentences. Since 2012, almost 30 states and the District of Columbia have altered their laws for

TABLE 5.4

Judicial Alternatives for Juvenile Courts[13]

JUDICIAL ALTERNATIVE	DEFINITION
Adult facility or youthful offender facility	Facilities for youths who commit serious offenses and are viewed as too violent for juvenile facilities
Community-based residential programs	Residential facilities in a juvenile's community, such as group homes or halfway houses
County/city institutions	Facilities for juveniles who need more security than available with probation but are not suited for long-term placement
Day treatment programs	A popular but not frequently available alternative that allows a youth to stay overnight at home
Dismissal	Judicial determination to dismiss the case, even if facts indicate guilt
Foster home placement	Placement of youth in a different home, often used for status offenders or dependent youths
Institutionalization in a mental hospital	Commitment to a mental hospital, occurring after a doctor's referral based on the results of a psychiatric evaluation
Outpatient psychiatric therapy	Treatment-oriented decision that includes a mental health clinic or private therapist
Probation	Sanction that involves serving time in the community under specific requirements and supervisory conditions (most popular judicial alternative)
State or private training school	Residential facilities reserved for serious offenders; and can be minimum, medium, or maximum security
Restitution	Paying the cost of the delinquent behavior, either through direct payment or working off the debt

Bartollas, C. & Miller, S. (2017). *Juvenile Justice in America* (8th ed). Boston, MA: Pearson Education.

juveniles convicted of homicide. States such as Nevada and West Virginia provide mandatory minimums for a chance of parole after 15 years.

The recent *Montgomery v. Louisiana* (2016) ensured that the Miller decision could be applied retroactively. In fact, Montgomery asserted that life without parole as a sentencing decision for juveniles should be applied only when offenses reflected "irreparable corruption." It is recognized that brains are not fully developed until a person is in his or her 20s, indicating that a juvenile cannot completely comprehend the seriousness of a crime. In addition, the environment of juveniles who are given life without parole is often violent and disorganized, and these juveniles often experience abuse.[14]

The Right to Appeal

Juveniles have no constitutional right to appeal. However, the U.S. Supreme Court established just such a right for juveniles in *In re Gault* (discussed further in the next section), and states have followed suit with statutes enshrining the same right.

Juveniles and their parents are generally the only parties allowed to appeal. In some circumstances, states have been permitted to appeal, but this rarely occurs. States usually permit the appeal of final orders, such as confinement in a secure facility as a sanction. Most states send cases directly to an appeals court, and few states order a whole new trial. During the appeal, juveniles have the right to an attorney and transcripts of court proceedings.

CONSTITUTIONAL PROTECTIONS OF JUVENILES

>> **LO 5.4**   **Identify the constitutional protections applicable to juvenile proceedings.**

Early supporters of the juvenile court movement stressed the importance of processing youths in an informal, relaxed fashion, rather than using formalized, stringent processes—as is the case in adult criminal courts. Instead of being stigmatized and shamed, youths, they said, should receive all the help necessary to make choices that would steer them away from future criminal behavior.

Critics, however, have argued that this idealistic picture is often unattainable. Some juvenile crimes are so violent, they say, that any sort of therapeutic management of cases would fail to deter future criminality, and it is also unfair to allow anyone, even minors, to get away with heinous crimes. Critics also argued that many jurisdictions do not have enough resources to undertake serious juvenile rehabilitation and that the juvenile court's use of rehabilitative options may even be distorted due to discrimination based on race or sex.

The *Kent* decision, which provides this chapter's opening story, was the first of several important court decisions that secured the constitutional rights of juveniles processed in juvenile and adult courts (Figure 5.2). *In re Gault* (1967), another landmark case, further addressed due process rights for juveniles during the court processing. Gerald Gault, a 15-year-old in Arizona, was taken into custody after a neighbor complained that he made lewd comments to her on the phone. Gault's parents were not notified that he was in custody, much less what charges had been brought against him. Gault was not advised of his right to counsel or his right to

©iStockphoto.com/jaflippo

The United States Constitution. What rights do juveniles who are involved with the justice system have?

FIGURE 5.2

Requirements for Attendance for Juvenile Hearings by State

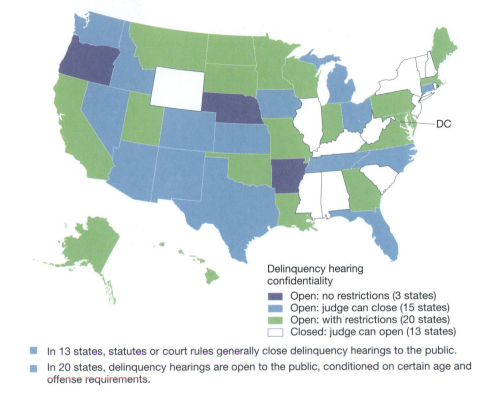

Delinquency proceedings are open in some states, closed in others, and in some states, it depends on the type of case

DC

Delinquency hearing confidentiality

- Open: no restrictions (3 states)
- Open: judge can close (15 states)
- Open: with restrictions (20 states)
- Closed: judge can open (13 states)

■ In 13 states, statutes or court rules generally close delinquency hearings to the public.

■ In 20 states, delinquency hearings are open to the public, conditioned on certain age and offense requirements.

Source: From "Juvenile Justice Trends in the U.S. Could Provide Lessons for China's Courts (Part 2 of 2)," *Human Rights Journal: Current Issues in China's Criminal Justice System,*" January 26, 2017, Dui Hua Foundation. Map created using data from "The Come Back States: Reducing Youth Incarceration in the United States," National Juvenile Justice Network & Texas Public Policy Foundation, June 2013.

remain silent, nor was he afforded the right to attend any of his hearings. The judge sentenced him to the State Industrial School until age 21, despite what some said was lack of clarity about his actions.[15]

In re Gault, considered one of the most influential cases in the area of juvenile justice, addressed the basic constitutional rights that juveniles must have when institutionalization is being considered. The Arizona Supreme Court had dismissed a request by Gault's lawyer for a writ of habeas corpus pleading unlawful detention. In response, the U.S. Supreme Court found that the following rights, many of which were not afforded to Gault, should apply to juveniles based on the Fourteenth Amendment:

1. To receive notice of the charges filed against them

2. To have representation by legal counsel

3. To confront and cross-examine witnesses

4. To avoid self-incrimination

Essentially, *In re Gault* identified what due process rights must be provided to juveniles. The court stopped short of ruling that juveniles were entitled to transcripts of proceedings or to appellate review, but this was because the high court did not want to transform the juvenile courts into the adversarial system of adult courts.

While Kent and *In re Gault* secured the constitutional rights of juveniles, other landmark cases affected processing of juveniles by the system. In the case of *In re Winship* in 1970, the Supreme Court ruled that juveniles are entitled to adjudication of a crime based on the "beyond a reasonable doubt" standard of proof. Winship was a New York juvenile adjudicated for petty larceny and sent to a state training school. The lower court decision was based on the "preponderance of the evidence"—a standard of proof that the Supreme Court ruled was unreasonable when charging youths with acts that would be considered criminal if committed by adults.[16]

In 1971, the Supreme Court decided three cases that had to do with a juvenile's Fourteenth Amendment right to a jury trial. The first, *McKeiver v. Pennsylvania*, involved 16-year-old Joseph McKeiver, who was found delinquent by a lower court for robbery, larceny, and receipt of stolen goods. McKeiver was denied a jury trial and placed on probation.[17] Meanwhile, *In re Terry* involved the assault and battery of a police officer by 15-year-old Edward Terry in Pennsylvania. He was also denied a jury trial and adjudicated on the charges.[18] Then in the case of *In re Barbara Burruss*, Burruss and 45 other African American youths received a juvenile court summons in North Carolina for publically protesting school assignments without a permit in 1968. All of them were denied a jury trial and placed on probation.[19]

Hearing these three cases together, the Supreme Court determined that juveniles do not have a right to a jury trial and do not have access to all constitutional rights. The court reasoned that jury trials could turn the juvenile system into the adult adversarial system, with its formal style, frequent delays, and backlogs of caseload. The court allowed that a state could permit use of jury trials if it so chose, but this was not a guaranteed right. Currently, 11 states and the District of Columbia have statutes specifying that juveniles have no right to a jury trial. The states are Colorado, Florida, Louisiana, Maine, Montana, Nebraska, New Mexico, North Carolina, Texas, Wisconsin, and Wyoming.

The Supreme Court then ruled in *Breed v. Jones* (1975) that juveniles, much like adult offenders, still have constitutional protection against double jeopardy, which states that an individual cannot be tried again on the same charges and the same facts. Jones was taken into custody for robbery and detained for a hearing. The juvenile court found the allegations to be true, but at the disposition hearing, the judge did not believe Jones could be helped by juvenile services and waived him to adult court, where he was found guilty of robbery. The Supreme Court ruled that this sequence of events amounted to double jeopardy and that to avoid this, juveniles must be transferred to adult court without an adjudicatory hearing in juvenile court.[20]

JUVENILE TRANSFER PROCEEDINGS

>> **LO5.5**   Explain judicial transfer procedures as they apply to juvenile court.

Chapter 1 described the evolution of the system's views on the accountability of children who commit criminal and deviant behavior. Initially, when minors had adult roles, such as working a full-time job or being married, they were treated as fully developed adults who could understand right and wrong. Moreover, minors as young as age 5 who committed crimes could be punished with the same severity as adults.

Over time, the criminal justice system recognized that young people were unable to fully conceptualize right and wrong or to understand the repercussions of their behaviors as adults could. Research showed that juveniles and young adults had underdeveloped moral and cognitive abilities. *In re Gault* affirmed a standard for juveniles of **presumptive diminished responsibility**, which states that juveniles should not be held fully responsible for their actions due to a lack of cognitive formation. The role of the juvenile justice system is to address the needs of delinquent and neglected youths, punish appropriately when necessary, and use rehabilitative programming to try to deter future deviant behavior in adulthood.

In recent times, however, our juvenile justice system has been dealing with youths who commit very adult, brutal crimes. Juveniles who have barely begun adolescence have been arrested for murder, rape, violent assault, and other serious offenses. This continued increase in serious offenses by young people exposes possible errors in our current methods of managing juvenile delinquents and suggests that a tougher stance may be needed. Returning to some of the earlier stances on punishment, our juvenile justice system now directs that selected youthful offenders may be transferred to the adult criminal justice system. Still, some stakeholders argue against punishing any youths as adults. Table 5.5 provides a comparison of the arguments for and against diminished responsibility.[21]

TABLE 5.5

Arguments for and Against Presumptive Diminished Responsibility for Juveniles

ADVOCATE FOR JUVENILE RESPONSIBILITY IN MID-ADOLESCENCE	ADVOCATE FOR PRESUMPTIVE DIMINISHED RESPONSIBILITY
Recognition of right and wrong	Different cognitive decision-making skills than adults
Recognition of remorse and guilt	Lower moral and cognitive development
Emotionally mature	Difficulty understanding legal language, such as the Miranda warning
Socially conscious and mentally aware	Psychological immaturity that affects compliance with authority

Scott, E. & Grisso, T. (1998). The evolution of adolescence: A developmental perspective on juvenile justice reform. *Journal of Criminology and Criminal Justice, 88*, 137–74.

Laws in every state allow youths to be *transferred* or *waived* (the words mean essentially the same thing) to adult court for prosecution. All told, more than 200,000 juveniles are prosecuted in adult court each year.[22] States have a variety of policies on transfers, involving both age and the offense being considered. For example, Iowa and Vermont set the minimum age for transfer or waiver at 10 years old, while Kentucky and New Jersey set it at 14 years. The criteria for all 50 states, including minimum age and certain types of offenses, are displayed in Table 5.6.

There are multiple ways a juvenile can be waived to adult court, as shown in Figure 5.3. The most common method of transfer is **judicial waiver**, which is made by judicial staff during the intake process. Depending on the state, the decision is made by the juvenile court judge, prosecutor, or intake officer, but some states allow the judge or prosecutor in adult court to make the decision. The decision is made based on several criteria: offense severity, age of offender, maturity of child, relationships with peers and family, and other relevant variables.[23]

Prosecutorial discretion, the decision made by prosecutors to send juveniles directly to adult court, exists in states with concurrent jurisdiction. Such transfers are known as waivers. **Concurrent jurisdiction** allows more than one court to exercise judicial review of a case at the same time. Some states use **statutory exclusion**, an automatic transfer to adult court for certain offenses. Other states have amended existing legislation to allow for waivers based on age. In Indiana, for instance, children age 10 or older are automatically waived to adult court for trial.

Conversely, some states have implemented measures to bring juvenile offenders back into juvenile court. **Reverse waiver** is the process of sending youths, who are over the maximum age of jurisdiction, back to juvenile court in certain cases. The judge's decision on this may be based on evidence provided by the prosecutor or defense.

A **blended sentence** imposes adult and juvenile court sanctions for serious juvenile offenders. Some states impose a set amount of time to serve. The juvenile sanction is applied until the youths reach adulthood, and then they are transferred to an adult correctional facility to serve out their sentences. In other states, the juvenile court judge can order juvenile and adult sanctions for youths who have received a direct file, or mandatory or prosecutorial waiver. The juvenile sanction is served first, and if it is successfully completed, the adult sentence is dismissed. Unsuccessful completion means the youths must complete adult sentencing conditions.

TABLE 5.6

Offense and Minimum Age Criteria for Juvenile Waiver

STATE	MINIMUM AGE FOR JUDICIAL WAIVER	JUDICIAL WAIVER OFFENSE AND MINIMUM AGE CRITERIA							
		ANY CRIMINAL OFFENSE	CERTAIN FELONIES	CAPITAL CRIMES	MURDER	CERTAIN PERSON OFFENSES	CERTAIN PROPERTY OFFENSES	CERTAIN DRUG OFFENSES	CERTAIN WEAPON OFFENSES
Alabama	14	14							
Alaska	NS	NS	NS			NS			
Arizona	NS		NS						
Arkansas	14		14	14	14	14			14
California	14	16	14		14	14	14	14	14
Colorado	12		12		12	12	12		
Connecticut	15		15	15	15	15	15		
Delaware	NS	NS	15		NS	NS	16	16	
District of Columbia	NS	15	15		15	15	15		NS
Florida	14	14							
Georgia	13		15	13		15			
Hawaii	NS	14	14		NS				
Idaho	NS	14			NS	NS	NS	NS	
Illinois	13	13	15					15	
Indiana	NS	NS	NS		12			16	
Iowa	10	14	10						
Kansas	12	12	12			14		14	
Kentucky	14		14	14	14				
Louisiana	14				14	14			
Maine	NS		NS		NS	NS	NS		
Maryland	NS	15		NS					
Michigan	14		14						
Minnesota	14		14						
Mississippi	13	13							

JUDICIAL WAIVER OFFENSE AND MINIMUM AGE CRITERIA

STATE	MINIMUM AGE FOR JUDICIAL WAIVER	ANY CRIMINAL OFFENSE	CERTAIN FELONIES	CAPITAL CRIMES	MURDER	CERTAIN PERSON OFFENSES	CERTAIN PROPERTY OFFENSES	CERTAIN DRUG OFFENSES	CERTAIN WEAPON OFFENSES
Missouri	12		12						
Nebraska	14	16	14						
Nevada	13	16	14		13	16			
New Hampshire	13		15		13	13		15	
New Jersey	14	14	14		14	14	14	14	14
North Carolina	13		13	13					
North Dakota	14	14	14		14	14	14		
Ohio	14		14		14	16	16		
Oklahoma	NS		NS						
Oregon	NS	15	15		NS	NS	15		
Pennsylvania	14		14		14	14			
Rhode Island	NS		16	NS	17	17			
South Carolina	NS	16	14		NS	NS		14	14
South Dakota	NS		NS						
Tennessee	NS	NS							
Texas	14		14	14				14	
Utah	14		14		16	16	16		16
Vermont	10	16	10		10	10	10		
Virginia	14		14		14	14		14	
Washington	NS	NS							
West Virginia	NS		NS		NS	NS	NS	NS	
Wisconsin	14	15	14		14	14	14	14	

Source: Office of Juvenile Justice and Delinquency Prevention OJJDP *Statistical Briefing Book*, https://www.ojjdp.gov/ojstatBB/structure_process/qa04110.asp?qaDate=2015&text= (accessed October 15, 2017).

Note: Ages in the minimum age column may not apply to all offense restrictions but represent the youngest possible age at which a juvenile may be judicially waived to criminal court. "NS" indicates that no minimum age is specified.

OJJDP Statistical Briefing Book.

FIGURE 5.3

Types of Juvenile Waivers

STATE	JUDICIAL WAIVER			PROSECUTORIAL DISCRETION	STATUTORY EXCLUSION	REVERSE WAIVER	ONCE AN ADULT ALWAYS AN ADULT	BLENDED SENTENCING	
	DISCRETIONARY	PRESUMPTIVE	MANDATORY					JUVENILE	CRIMINAL
Number of states	45	15	15	15	29	24	34	14	18
Alabama	■				■		■		
Alaska	■	■			■		■	■	
Arizona	■			■	■	■	■		
Arkansas	■			■		■	■	■	■
California	■	■		■	■	■	■		■
Colorado	■	■		■		■	■	■	■
Connecticut			■			■	■	■	
Delaware	■	■	■	■	■	■	■		
District of Columbia	■								
Florida	■			■	■		■		■
Georgia	■		■	■	■	■			
Hawaii	■						■		
Idaho	■		■		■		■		■
Illinois	■	■	■		■	■	■	■	■
Indiana	■		■		■		■		
Iowa	■				■	■	■		■
Kansas	■	■					■	■	
Kentucky	■		■			■	■		■
Louisiana	■		■	■	■		■		
Maine	■	■					■		
Maryland	■					■	■		
Massachusetts					■			■	■
Michigan	■			■	■		■	■	■
Minnesota	■	■			■		■	■	■

STATE	JUDICIAL WAIVER			PROSECUTORIAL DISCRETION	STATUTORY EXCLUSION	REVERSE WAIVER	ONCE AN ADULT ALWAYS AN ADULT	BLENDED SENTENCING	
	DISCRETIONARY	PRESUMPTIVE	MANDATORY					JUVENILE	CRIMINAL
Mississippi	■				■	■	■		
Missouri	■						■		■
Montana				■	■	■		■	■
Nebraska	■			■		■			■
Nevada	■	■			■	■	■		
New Hampshire	■	■					■		
New Jersey	■	■	■						
New Mexico					■	■		■	■
New York					■				
North Carolina	■		■				■		
North Dakota	■	■	■				■		
Ohio	■		■		■	■	■		
Oklahoma	■		■	■			■	■	■
Oregon	■				■	■	■		
Pennsylvania	■	■			■	■	■		
Rhode Island	■	■	■				■	■	
South Carolina	■		■		■	■	■		
South Dakota	■				■	■	■		
Tennessee	■						■		
Texas	■						■	■	
Utah		■							
Vermont	■		■	■	■	■	■		■
Virginia	■			■	■	■			■
Washington	■				■		■		
West Virginia	■		■						■
Wisconsin	■				■	■	■		■
Wyoming	■			■		■			

Source: Patrick Griffin, Sean Addie, Benjamin Adams, and Kathy Firestine, *Trying Juveniles as Adults: An Analysis of State Transfer Laws and Reporting* (Washington, DC: Office of Juvenile Justice and Delinquency Prevention, 2011), p. 3. https://www.ncjrs.gov/pdffiles1/ojjdp/232434.pdf (accessed January, 5, 2018).

Roper v. Simmons, 543 U.S. 551 (2005)

In 1993, 17-year-old Christopher Simmons concocted a plan with two younger friends, Charles Benjamin and John Tessmer, to break into the home of Shirley Crook and murder her. Although Tessmer decided at the last minute not to participate, Simmons and Benjamin broke into her home, tied her up, and then drove her to a state park and threw her off a bridge. Simmons confessed to the crime, and later a court found him guilty of murder. The jury recommended a death sentence. Simmons filed a motion claiming ineffective assistance of counsel and asking for the jury to delay sentencing and consider his age and troubled background. The motion was denied, as well as his appeals, until the Supreme Court ruling of *Atkins v. Virginia* (2002), which overturned the death penalty for an intellectually disabled man. Simmons filed a new petition for post-conviction relief, and the Supreme Court of Missouri changed his sentence to life imprisonment without parole, saying that the national consensus was that execution of juveniles violated the Eighth Amendment.

The state of Missouri then appealed the decision to the U.S. Supreme Court. The court ruled that under the "evolving standards of decency" test, it was cruel and unusual punishment to sentence a person to death who committed a murder at the age of 17 or younger. Writing for the majority, Justice Anthony Kennedy stated that juveniles are immature and have a diminished sense of responsibility compared with adults.

1.   **Do you agree with the ruling?**

2.   **Do you feel there is that much of a difference between the behavior and maturity level of a 17-year-old compared with an 18-year-old?**

3.   **In your opinion, would this ruling be the same today?**

Online Case Opinion

https://www.supremecourt.gov/opinions/04pdf/03-633 .pdf ●

Waiver Hearings

Prior to the U.S. Supreme Court rulings of *Kent v. United States* and *Breed v. Jones*, juveniles could be waived (i.e., transferred) to adult court without hearings, evidence, or the benefit of an attorney. These cases guaranteed the same due process rights given to adults before waiver to adult court could be allowed. Most states now require waiver hearings before transfer to adult court, but some states allow the prosecutor to make the waiver decision or allow youths to be automatically sent to adult court, where mandatory legislation is in place. In states where a hearing is required, *Kent v. United States*[24] directs use of the following criteria:

1.   Consideration of whether the alleged offense was aggressive, violent, premeditated, or willful

2.   Determination if the alleged offense was against persons or property, with greater importance placed on personal crimes, especially if personal injury resulted

3.   Consideration of whether the alleged offense is serious enough to threaten the safety of the community

4.   Determination if there is a criminal record for the juvenile

5.   Consideration of the emotional maturity and life circumstances of the juvenile

6.   Determination if there is prosecutorial merit of the charges and evidence

7.   Determination if a trial is desirable

The waiver process begins when a prosecutor files a motion with the juvenile court judge to send the juvenile to adult court. Then there is a hearing for probable cause in front of the judge in which everything is stated under oath. The judge first explains the nature of the hearing to the youth and the parents or guardians. Then the prosecutor presents the state's case against the juvenile, including submission of evidence of the crime and citation of statutory requirements for waiver on age and offense. The defense attorney then can challenge the prosecutor's assertions, and both sides can examine witnesses.

If probable cause is determined, the judge determines whether the juvenile must be transferred to adult court and presents options and sanctions so the youth can receive all possible resources. If probable cause is not found, the case is dismissed or the juvenile is referred to juvenile probation.

When the case is waived to adult court, the prosecutor reviews the case to ensure it meets the standards of legal sufficiency. If the prosecutor determines the case does not meet those standards, it is sent back to juvenile court. But if the case remains in adult court, it may be presented to a grand jury or an arraignment date may be set, depending on each state's requirements. The youth is accorded the same due process rights as an adult offender.

TYPES OF JUVENILE OFFENDERS

>> **LO 5.6** Define status offenders and offer recommendations on their management.

Status Offenders

Juveniles can be charged with offenses that are considered criminal for people of any age under federal, state, or local law. However, one factor that makes the juvenile system unique is that juveniles can be taken into custody and adjudicated for behaviors that are illegal only for non-adults, called status offenses. There is a wide range of status offenses that can include behaviors that apply to specific statutes, such as underage drinking and consumption of tobacco products, truancy, or running away. They can also involve violations of omnibus statutes, such as acting immorally, incorrigibility, and behavior that parents have been unable to control. Depending on the state, status offenders can be classified as one or more of the following:

- Children in need of supervision (CINS)
- Families in need of supervision (FINS)
- Juveniles in need of supervision (JINS)
- Minors in need of supervision (MINS)
- Persons in need of supervision (PINS)[25]

There has been a movement in the juvenile justice community to **deinstitutionalize** status offenders, or reform the management of them by handling these youths with sanctions and treatment that don't entail juvenile detention and other forms of institutionalization. This nationwide movement was sparked by passage of the **1974 Juvenile Justice and Delinquency Prevention (JJDP) Act**. For states to continue receiving federal funding for juvenile justice programs, the act requires status offenders to be housed in separate areas from juvenile delinquents in detention facilities and institutions. In addition, placement of juveniles in adult facilities must be strictly limited.[26] Juveniles who are confined for any length of time are prohibited from having any sight and sound contact with adult inmates.

The **deinstitutionalization of status offenders (DSO)** section in the JJDP Act effectively changed laws and policies that had previously placed many status offenders in secure confinement. Rather than stigmatize and institutionalize status offenders, the DSO calls for the use of social services, mental health treatment, and community agencies to address problematic behavior by juveniles. While punitive measures have been shown to actually increase such behaviors, rehabilitative measures have been successful in reducing them.[27]

Bryan Chan/Los Angeles Times/Getty Images

Police officers and adolescents interact. What are status offenses?

There has also been serious debate over the appropriateness of juvenile courts having jurisdiction over status offenders. Juvenile court judges have argued that if jurisdiction is removed, status offenders will have no one to protect them, and agencies have few ways to provide a nurturing environment to juveniles that would substitute for a home. On the other hand, some have called for the removal of status offenders from the court's jurisdiction, arguing that

1. lack of clarity in the statutes that are supposed to define status offenders creates an unconstitutional vagueness and often results in discriminatory outcomes in the treatment of juveniles, especially with regard to gender;

2. the procedures of processing and confining status offenders are not in the best interest of the child and do not follow the *parens patriae* role of the court to intervene on behalf of a juvenile's best interests; and

3. status offenders are often housed with serious and career offenders, even though they have not committed a criminal offense. This special group of youths should be handled differently from those who have committed a mainstream crime.[28]

A few states have provided support for the DSO movement by decriminalizing status offenses. Maine, New York, and Washington have removed status offenders from the jurisdiction of the juvenile court. However, Maine and Washington have repealed parts of their legislation, giving juvenile court jurisdiction over abandoned, runaway, and endangered children. Many juvenile experts believe it is unlikely that decriminalization will become a popular option for states, noting that the majority of stakeholders support juvenile court jurisdiction over status offenders. The consensus is that these youths are likely to participate in more serious and destructive behavior, so it is important to have options for treatment that best serve their needs. Placing youths in mental health service facilities, private facilities, or on juvenile probation can be an impetus for improving the life course of a child.

Juveniles Supervised by Multiple Agencies

A special group of juveniles are overseen by multiple agencies based on their behavior and needs. These juveniles—also referred to as dual-jurisdiction cases, dually adjudicated youths, **crossover youths**, or cross-system cases—are seen as victims when managed by the child welfare system and offenders when under the care of the juvenile justice system. Unfortunately, little coordination occurs between the two systems, and it is not unusual for one agency to close a youth's case if the other system becomes involved.[29]

Crossover youths usually experience a combination of mental health problems and drug and alcohol abuse, which are often left untreated in both systems. They are more likely to have low grades, drop out of school, and commit status offenses and criminal acts. The juvenile justice system often puts them in out-of-home settings, such as group homes. Not surprisingly, crossover youths who are minorities are often in the welfare system. The Annie E. Casey Foundation found that while there is no disparity among races in the abuse of these youths, minority children tend to be placed in foster care more often and receive fewer services than white children.[30]

Some successful practices in the juvenile court system involving interactions for crossover children provide lessons. First, it is extremely important to screen and assess youths, not only at intake but also when courts and welfare systems manage them. The strengths, risks, and needs of juveniles change frequently. Second, effective case management is key for collaboration. All dependency and delinquency hearings should involve agency coordination and attendance. In addition, case managers should work with multidisciplinary panels of professionals so youths' needs in both areas are met. Last, judges should ensure that financial responsibility for the care and treatment of crossover youths is shared by both the juvenile justice and child welfare systems. Putting the burden on one system will result in subpar resources.[31]

Youths in Prison and Youthful Offender Programs

According to the Office of Juvenile Justice and Delinquency Prevention, more than 4,000 juveniles were in state jails in 2014[32] and slightly fewer than 1,000 were in state prisons in 2015.[33] While these numbers are small compared with the number of adults in custody, adult correctional facilities are not intended to meet the needs of young people. These facilities may be extremely overcrowded, and they contain violent and manipulative inmates. Juvenile inmates are at higher risk for physical and sexual abuse and are more likely to consider and attempt suicide. These juveniles are also less likely to receive the educational, medical, and mental health services required by law.

Youthful offender programs, first introduced in Colorado, are an alternative to adult correctional facilities. These programs, often called intermediate or third systems programs, impose strict adult-level sanctions on violent youth offenders and yet still focus on rehabilitation. This approach has been called "shock sentencing." Youths get a sentence severe enough to show the seriousness of the offense and are told that next time they are sentenced they will go to an adult correctional facility.[34]

The rehabilitative component of these programs is supposed to provide an employable skill through vocational training and use role models to teach reaching out to the community, better decision making, rule enforcement, and self-esteem. Youths should be given the opportunity to understand the consequences of their behavior, make better choices, and join a positive environment upon release.

Juveniles, Capital Punishment, and the Law

Only in the 21st century were authorities barred from imposing the death penalty, the most severe sanction of all, on juveniles. While there has been a long history of disputes over the constitutionality and application of the death penalty, many changes occurred just in the past 30 years.

In 1976, the U.S. Supreme Court ruled in *Gregg v. Georgia*[35] that the use of the death penalty was not a violation of the Eighth Amendment's protection against cruel and unusual punishment. However, the court ruled that all circumstances of the crime, including age, must be considered before opting for the death penalty. In *Eddings v. Oklahoma* (1982)[36] the court did not specifically address the constitutionality of executing juveniles, but it did continue to assert the importance of considering mitigating circumstances, such as age, when sanctioning death. In 1989, the court upheld the constitutionality of a death sentence for 17-year-old Kevin Stanford in *Stanford v. Kentucky*, but in 1988, it ruled unconstitutional the execution of 15-year-old Wayne Thompson in *Thompson v. Oklahoma*,[37] due to his age.

More recent Supreme Court decisions emphasized the importance of the legal culpability of juveniles. In *Atkins v. Virginia* (2002)[38] the court ruled that it was unconstitutional to execute mentally retarded juveniles, adding another important mitigating factor. Atkins abducted, robbed, and murdered his victim and was sentenced to death, but the court reversed that decision. Then in *Roper v. Simmons* (2005)[39] the court ruled in a 5-to-4 decision that juveniles who committed their crimes when they were under age 18 could not be sentenced to death. Before this decision, 24 states allowed the execution of juveniles. Georgia had the highest number of juvenile executions at 41, followed by North Carolina and Ohio with 19 each. ●

SUMMARY

» LO 5.1   Describe the juvenile court system, including some of the personnel who work in the system.

The structure of a juvenile court varies depending on the size of the jurisdiction involved. For instance, larger jurisdictions will have employees dedicated to the operation of the juvenile court, while smaller locales will have judges who try both adult and juvenile cases. Smaller jurisdictions have limited resources available for the processing and management of juveniles. Personnel associated with the juvenile are similar to stakeholders seen in adult court, such as a prosecutor, defense attorney, and probation officer.

» LO 5.2   Show how pretrial procedures impact the handling of delinquency cases.

The juvenile court system handles almost 1 million status and criminal offense cases per year. However, before a youth goes to an adjudicatory hearing, the court must determine if he or she requires detention prior to the hearing. Youths who are a danger to the community, or who have safety needs of their own, are often candidates for preventive detention. Some juveniles will be released prior to trial but will be required to return for court proceedings as the case progresses. During the intake process, which is the initial juvenile court process, the court determines if the juvenile court or another social service agency is best suited to handle the case. To avoid unnecessary stigmatization, the juvenile court will often handle cases informally, if possible, with some form of nonjudicial adjustment or informal intervention. Last, as with the majority of adult criminal cases, juveniles are often afforded the option of a plea bargain to avoid the adjudication and disposition process. A plea generally allows defendants to admit guilt to a lesser charge and serve a more lenient sentence than they otherwise would.

Key Terms

bail 71	intake process 72	preventive detention 70
consent decrees 73	nonjudicial adjustment 72	release on
detention hearing 70	petition 73	recognizance 72
informal probation 72	plea bargain 74	

» LO 5.3   Describe adjudicatory and dispositional hearings in the juvenile justice system.

An adjudicatory hearing is equivalent to the trial stage in the adult system. This is the fact-finding stage that includes evidence presented by both sides and a decision by the judge. All due process and procedural requirements must be followed. The disposition hearing is equivalent to an adult sentencing hearing, where the judge has the option to order a combination of different punitive and treatment sanctions. These two hearings can occur together or as separate events.

Key Terms

adjudicatory hearing 73

bifurcated system 73

determinate
    sentencing 75

dispositional hearing 73

indeterminate
    sentencing 74

predisposition report 73

>> **LO 5.4** **Identify the constitutional protections applicable to juvenile proceedings.**

It was not until the mid-20th century that the U.S. Supreme Court addressed the constitutional rights of juveniles as they were processed through juvenile and adult court in landmark cases including *Kent v. United States* and *In re Gault*. These cases addressed the rights afforded to juveniles at the time of arrest, as well as during court processing in regard to notification of charges, the availability of legal counsel, and the use of evidence. Other court cases held that juveniles do not have the right to a jury trial.

>> **LO 5.5** **Explain judicial transfer procedures as they apply to juvenile court.**

Some jurisdictions are now transferring violent juveniles to adult court for prosecution and sentencing. There are several methods of transfer, including via judicial waiver (a decision made by judicial staff) or prosecutorial discretion. The management of juvenile offenders in adult court generally means more severe sentences and the mixing of young people with serious adult offenders.

Key Terms

blended sentence 79

concurrent
    jurisdiction 79

judicial waiver 79

presumptive diminished
    responsibility 78

prosecutorial
    discretion 79

reverse waiver 79

statutory exclusion 79

youthful offender
    programs 87

>> **LO 5.6** **Define status offenders and offer recommendations on their management.**

Status offenders are juveniles who participate in behaviors illegal only for non-adults, such as truancy and consumption of tobacco products. While these youths are not considered dangerous offenders, a large amount of time and resources is dedicated to their management within the juvenile justice system. There has been a systematic push for the deinstitutionalization of status offenders and alternatively managing problematic behavior with social services and community agencies—rather than stigmatic processing through the justice system.

Key Terms

1974 Juvenile Justice
    and Delinquency
    Prevention (JJDP)
    Act 86

crossover youths 86

deinstitutionalization
    of status offenders
    (DSO) 86

deinstitutionalize 86

DISCUSSION QUESTIONS

1. Based on its current operation, does the juvenile court system meet its rehabilitative goals, or does it tend to be punitive like the adult court system?

2. What kind of disposition is appropriate for a chronic shoplifter? Why?

3. At what age do individuals have a clear understanding of right and wrong, and the ability to understand the consequences of their actions? Might it vary from person to person?

EXPLORING JUVENILE JUSTICE FURTHER

1. Interview a juvenile court employee. Ask him or her questions regarding the efficiency and effectiveness of the system in your jurisdiction.

2. Investigate the availability of youthful offender programs in your area. Create a chart comparing the components of the programs. What types of programs do you feel are lacking?

⑤SAGE edge™

Give your students the SAGE edge!

SAGE edge offers a robust online environment featuring an impressive array of free tools and resources for review, study, and further exploration, keeping both instructors and students on the cutting edge of teaching and learning. Learn more at **edge.sagepub.com/schmallegerjj**.

PRACTICE AND APPLY WHAT YOU'VE LEARNED

▶ edge.sagepub.com/schmallegerjj

WANT A BETTER GRADE ON YOUR NEXT TEST?

Head to the study site, where you'll find:

- **eFlashcards** to strengthen your understanding of key terms

- **Practice quizzes** to test your comprehension of key concepts

- **Videos and multimedia content** to enhance your exploration of key topics

SAGE edge™

RJ Sangosti/Denver Post/Getty Images

The Juvenile Corrections System

After reading this chapter you should be able to

1. Define juvenile probation and know when it should be used

2. Describe some of the correctional options available to juvenile court judges that are less severe than institutionalization but more severe than probation

3. List some of the options that juvenile court judges have for the institutionalization of delinquents

4. Describe the legal rights of institutionalized youths

5. Explain the role of aftercare in juvenile justice

Key Terms in Chapter 6

aftercare

attention homes

boot camps

casework management

community corrections

community service

continuum of sanctions

detention centers

direct service

electronic monitoring

house arrest

institutionalization

intensive aftercare supervision (IAS)

intensive supervision programs (ISPs)

interstate compact

jail

parole

probation

ranches and forestry camps

reception and diagnostic centers

restitution

shelter care facilities

social study report

supervision

training schools

INTRODUCTION

In 1904, a Pennsylvania boy whom today we know only as Fisher was sent to a school for delinquent boys after a juvenile court at the county level found him guilty of a minor crime. Fisher's commitment to the school came only a year after the Pennsylvania state legislature had established that juvenile proceedings in the state were to be separated from those for adults. Following the model of the nation's first juvenile court, which had been established in Chicago only a little over a decade prior to Fisher's hearing, the boy was given what many at the time regarded as a lengthy sentence. In fact, had Fisher's delinquent acts been committed by an adult, that adult would likely have received probation or only a short jail term. The Pennsylvania juvenile court, however, took its new mandate seriously—and that mandate was to provide care and direction to juvenile law violators with an eye toward rehabilitation. In Fisher's case the court learned that the boy's home life was likely to be conducive to further criminality. Accordingly, the lengthy sentence the boy received was for his own good and not intended to punish him. Due to its length, Fisher's case reached the Pennsylvania Supreme Court, which reasoned that the sentence was appropriate under the guiding legislation. In its written decision,[1] the Pennsylvania Supreme Court held that the purpose of the juvenile court "is not for punishment of offenders but for the salvation of children . . . whose salvation may become the duty of the state." The court's decision asserted the importance of using the juvenile court system to provide rehabilitative resources and care to juveniles, rather than punishing them like adults. The court also stated that juvenile authorities must take the parental role of protector when the juvenile's actual parents do not have his or her best interests at heart.

The historic Carbon County, Pennsylvania, jail. The facility was completed in 1870. Prior to the juvenile court era, youthful offenders would likely have been sent to places like this to serve criminal sentences.

Frank Schmalleger

JUVENILE PROBATION

>> **LO 6.1**   Define juvenile probation and know when it should be used.

There a variety of sanctions available to the juvenile justice system. The options vary in severity of punitiveness as well as in focus on rehabilitation. This continuum of sanctions is a range of correctional strategies based on the degree of control of the juvenile and intrusiveness into his or her life, with probation being the least severe option and institutionalization the most severe. At the time of disposition, a juvenile court judge can decide placement for the youth.

The National Center for Juvenile Justice examined a typical case flow for delinquency cases in 2015 (most recent data available at time of publication).[2] For every 1,000 cases, 554 were petitioned. Of those 554 cases, the delinquent was adjudicated in 295, placed in a facility in 77, and given probation in 186. Of the 255 cases that were petitioned but not adjudicated delinquent, 75 of the juveniles were given probation and 143 had their cases dismissed. If we consider the 446 cases that were not initially petitioned, 71 of those juveniles received probation, 199 received some form of other sanction, and 177 had their cases dismissed.

Dispositional alternatives to institutionalization allowing juveniles to serve in the community are known as **community corrections**, and the most typical form is **probation**. About 60% of offenders are placed on probation.[3] It is also less costly than other options, allowing an offender to remain in the community while being supervised by a probation officer. The term *probation* can refer to the status of the offender, the actual disposition, and the activities involved. A juvenile on probation has an individualized set of requirements to be met, and the job of the probation officer is to make sure that the juvenile stays out of trouble. Probation is meant to have a rehabilitative function, making it possible for the youth to maintain his or her liberties, including school and community activities, with the aim of reintegrating back into society.

Juvenile probation is organized in a variety of ways, depending on the jurisdiction. Some states make probation a local responsibility, with the local jurisdiction providing financial support, standards, and training. Advocates of this method say it allows for community involvement and flexibility in decision making, while critics argue that a uniform method of juvenile probation is more efficient and less costly.

Most states administer juvenile probation through their departments of state, which allows for standardized policies, personnel management, and training, and the state's department of corrections can facilitate activities. Some states combine the two approaches, trying to use the best aspects of each one. Other states hire private contractors to assist with probation needs such as aftercare services and supervision for special offenders.

Stages of Probation

Juvenile probation involves four basic stages or functions: intake, caseload management, supervision and investigation, and reporting to court. In the intake stage, discussed in Chapter 5, the probation officer serves multiple functions. The probation officer screens all referrals to the juvenile court, which involves interviewing the juvenile and the parents or guardians. The probation officer also informs everyone involved in the case on the status of the juvenile and his or her legal rights throughout the process. The intake stage may also involve interviews with all important persons in a juvenile's life, such as friends, family, neighbors, and school officials, to determine if detention is necessary.[4]

Probation officers are also responsible for **casework management**, which involves maintaining a file on every juvenile they are responsible for. The file includes requirements and restrictions of probation, contact information of relevant individuals, and reports to the court. The number of required contacts between a probation officer and a juvenile is dependent on the security risk. Offenders categorized as minimum security may meet with their officer once a month or less, while maximum security–level offenders meet several times a month. Unfortunately, much like adult probation officers, juvenile probation officers have large caseloads, making it difficult to effectively monitor each one.

A probation officer has multiple roles, ranging from acting like a law enforcement officer to acting like a social worker. See Figure 6.1 for a list of these roles. **Supervision** not only includes casework and counseling, as mentioned above, but also surveillance of the juvenile in the community. Probation officers monitor school attendance and progress, adherence to supervisory guidelines, and whether the juvenile is breaking the law. They also assess the therapeutic needs of a juvenile, such as drug or alcohol treatment, counseling, and anger management. To cover all the bases, some probation offices oversee teams of officers, each of whom specializes in an area of supervision.[5]

A risk and needs assessment tool is often used to classify a juvenile and then provide a treatment plan. Indicators of recidivism—risk of being a repeat offender—are examined, such as prior arrest record, nature of behaviors, and school and employment record. This assessment also includes indicators of emotional well-being, such as family relationships, mental health, and patterns of romantic relationships. One of the most prevalent assessment tools is the Problem Severity Index, which helps probation officers predict warning signs of future behavior.[6]

A juvenile probation officer has a responsibility to report to the court after disposition, as well as during probation. First, a **social study report** is provided to the judge after a youth is adjudicated delinquent. As with a presentence investigation report for adults, probation officers investigate all facets of the youth's life and recommend appropriate disposition. The report includes a personal history, mental and physical

Bethany Mollenkof/Los Angeles Times/Getty Images

Juveniles are frequently required to meet with case mangers while under correctional supervision. What might such meetings accomplish?

FIGURE 6.1

Supervising Juveniles on Probation

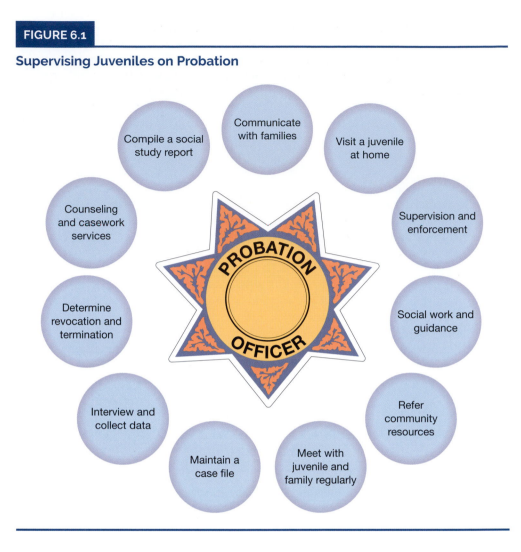

health, education, past and present criminal history, and a family history, including neighborhood interactions and parental history. The report then recommends whether the youth should serve his or her disposition in the community or needs to be institutionalized. After probation is initiated, the juvenile probation officer may make reports to the court regarding the progress of the juvenile, especially if probation has been violated and revocation is considered.

Applying the Sixth Amendment to Juveniles on Probation

In most jurisdictions, juveniles have the same rights as adults that protect them against revocation of probation, based on two Supreme Court rulings involving adults. In *Mempa v. Rhay*,[7] the court held that the Sixth Amendment right to counsel should extend to the sentencing hearings, as well as other steps in prosecution, including probation revocation hearings. The Mempa ruling inferred that the standard of "innocent until proven guilty" should also hold when someone is accused of violating probation requirements.

The second case, *Gagnon v. Scarpelli*,[8] involved the revocation of Scarpelli's probation without a hearing, after he was arrested for burglary while on probation for armed robbery. Scarpelli appealed the revocation, stating due process rights guaranteeing a hearing and right to counsel had been violated. The court ruled that offenders do not have a unilateral right to counsel if they are arrested on new charges within the probation period. Rather, counsel should be provided on a case-by-case basis.

As a result of these decisions, many jurisdictions now afford juveniles the same basic rights as adults, including the right to a hearing, 5-day notification of the probation revocation hearing, and the right to counsel. In addition, many jurisdictions allow juveniles the right to confront their accuser and examine reports on the violation. Most juvenile court judges adhere to the "reasonable efforts" standard, which holds that a judge can revoke probation if the court has made a reasonable effort to provide all the necessary resources to help the juvenile.

INTERMEDIATE CORRECTIONAL OPTIONS FOR JUVENILES

>> LO 6.2 **Describe some of the correctional options available to juvenile court judges that are less severe than institutionalization but more severe than probation.**

Authorities have a few options for disposition of juveniles, ranging in severity from probation to institutionalization. **Restitution** requires a juvenile to reimburse the victim of the crime, either through money or community service. Restitution became popular in the late 20th century, and it is now an option in most states. The Office of Juvenile Justice and Delinquency Prevention (OJJDP) has spent more than $30 million promoting the use of restitution in juvenile courts across the nation.[9]

Restitution can be ordered by the juvenile court in three ways: **Community service**, the most popular way, involves improving or repairing a site, such as cleaning up an area, removing graffiti, or washing cars. This is easy and economical to administer. **Direct service** involves working directly with the victim, which is used least frequently, because juveniles generally do not want to interact with their victims. Last, straight financial restitution involves paying the victim a sum of money, covering the damage caused by the crime. For instance, if a mailbox or a car was damaged, the juvenile would pay for repairs or a replacement.

Probation officers may be responsible for deciding the appropriate amount and determining how an offender can pay for the damage. They also handle much of the scheduling and implementation of the restitution and make sure the juvenile completes restitution. The juvenile may have to take a job to earn the money, which could be at a nonprofit company or government agency, such as a nursing home, shelter, youth agency, or park.

Intensive supervision programs (ISPs), formerly known as intensive probation supervision, are similar to probation but involve increased contacts with the court and stricter supervisory requirements.[10] ISPs originated in adult probation practices and became quite popular in the juvenile justice system in the late 20th century. States like Georgia and Oregon have instituted statewide ISPs for youths. The city of Baton Rouge has an ISP called Operation Elger that specifically targets high-risk youths, including violent and sex offenders.[11] Authorities offer treatment programs for substance abusers and sex offenders, providing a last chance for rehabilitation before institutionalization.

Another option for juveniles is **house arrest**, in which juveniles are confined to their homes on evenings and weekends. Youths must be preapproved to go to school, jobs, medical appointments, or religious services. They wear an **electronic monitoring** device on the ankle or wrist to detect their movement and even to alert probation officers of their whereabouts. Offenders may also be monitored for drug or alcohol abuse.

AP Photo/Jae C. Hong

An ankle bracelet used in electronic monitoring. Electronic monitoring is a form of community corrections that allow juvenile offenders to live in the community, yet still be supervised. What types of offenders are most likely to benefit from electronic monitoring?

INSTITUTIONALIZATION

>> **LO 6.3**   **List some of the options that juvenile court judges have for the institutionalization of delinquents.**

Once a youth has been adjudicated for a crime, a judge must decide the best way to handle the case by examining the entire picture. Is institutionalization necessary for the safety of the community and the juvenile? Would removing the youth from the community harm his or her chances of success after release? Or might that juvenile be in need of the resources that a juvenile confinement facility can provide? Might some form of community corrections be the answer? Today's juvenile justice system offers a **continuum of sanctions**, or a variety of correctional options ranging widely in severity and intrusiveness. Our current continuum of sanctions can be seen in Figure 6.2. This chapter will examine the various sanctions and treatments available for juveniles in the United States. We will examine the purpose of each correctional option and see whether they have been successful.

The United States has incarcerated more adults than any other nation in the world. Our juvenile justice system aims to rehabilitate and deter youths from an adult life of crime, yet **institutionalization** (or confinement in some form of residential facility) is a frequent choice. Judges have several short-term and long-term options to serve the needs of different categories of youths, and they will consider a multitude of factors (as discussed in Chapter 5) when determining which sanction is most appropriate.

FIGURE 6.2

Continuum of Severity of Juvenile Sanctions

Most Intrusive

↓

Institutionalization

↓

House arrest/electronic monitoring

↓

Intensive probation

↓

Day treatment programs

↓

Restitution

↓

Community service

↓

Probation

↓

Least Intrusive

Short-Term Institutionalization Options

There are various options for the short-term institutionalization of delinquents, including detention centers, shelter care facilities, diagnostic centers, group homes, wilderness camps, training schools, and residential treatment. Table 6.1 lists each type of available facility and the percentage of sentenced youths residing in it. Table 6.2 shows the allocation of juveniles in public and private facilities.

Detention centers, often referred to as juvenile halls, are temporary housing centers for juveniles.

Juveniles can be held in a detention center while waiting for adjudicatory hearings or placed there as a result of a disposition. Depending on the jurisdiction, these

TABLE 6.1

Juvenile Facilities in the United States in 2014

FACILITY OPERATION	TOTAL	FACILITY TYPE						
		DETENTION CENTER	SHELTER	RECEPTION OR DIAGNOSTIC CENTER	GROUP HOME	RANCH OR WILDERNESS CAMP	TRAINING SCHOOL	RESIDENTIAL TREATMENT CENTER
Number of facilities	1,852	664	143	61	360	37	176	726
Operations profile								
All facilities	100%	100%	100%	100%	100%	100%	100%	100%
Public	54	92	38	72	19	76	91	33
State	21	21	3	56	7	22	68	19
Local	33	71	35	16	12	54	24	14
Facility profile	100%	36%	8%	3%	19%	2%	10%	39%
Public	100	61	5	4	7	3	16	24
State	100	36	1	9	6	2	31	36
Local	100	76	8	2	7	3	7	16
Private	100	6	11	2	35	1	2	57

Source: Sarah Hockenberry, Andrew Wachter, and Anthony Sladky, *Juvenile Residential Facility Census, 2014: Selected Findings* (Washington, DC: U.S. Department of Justice, September 2016), https://www.ojjdp.gov/pubs/250123.pdf.

Note: Most recent data available at the time of publication

TABLE 6.2

Juveniles in Public Versus Private Institutions in the United States in 2014

	FACILITIES NUMBER	PERCENTAGE	JUSTICE-INVOLVED YOUTHS NUMBER	PERCENTAGE
Total	1,852	100	50,821	100
Public	1,008	54	36,110	71
State	390	21	17,200	34
Local	618	33	18,910	37
Private	844	36	14,711	29

Source: Sarah Hockenberry, Andrew Wachter, and Anthony Sladky, *Juvenile Residential Facility Census, 2014: Selected Findings* (Washington, DC: U.S. Department of Justice, September 2016), https://www.ojjdp.gov/pubs/250123.pdf.

Note: Most recent data available at the time of publication

centers can be administered by the court, state agencies, county governments, or welfare departments. Detention centers don't have treatment programs, use physical restraints as a sanction for bad behavior, and are often overcrowded.[12]

Attention homes (as opposed to detention homes) were created in Colorado to provide extensive programs and encouragement rather than punishment. These facilities have no fences or locks, giving juveniles the opportunity to make good

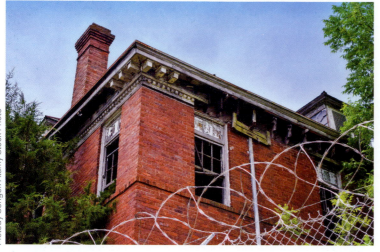

Melody Songer/Alamy Stock Photo

The Stonewall Jackson Juvenile Detention Center in Concord, NC. What purpose do such facilities serve?

choices. Another alternative, home detention, allows a youth to live at home and follow a set of conditions during a certain period of time, much like home confinement for adults.[13]

Shelter care facilities, another typical option for juveniles, were created in the 1970s to provide housing for status offenders, neglected children, and dependent minors. The Juvenile Justice and Delinquency Prevention Act (JJDPA) passed in 1974 provided funding for shelter care facilities as an alternative to placing youths in adult jails, which drastically increased the number of these facilities. A juvenile can stay in these facilities for a few days until suitable housing is found or for several weeks in the case of court delays. Shelter care may also be a reward for good behavior in a detention center.[14]

Shelter care facilities are nonsecure; that is, they don't have locked doors, giving residents the ability to choose activities. Residents can go back home on the weekends and take field trips during the week. However, the more open atmosphere makes it difficult to manage runaways and contraband drug use. Because of the relatively nonsecure aspect of shelter care facilities, staff members may find it more difficult to deal with youths who have disciplinary problems and negative attitudes toward authority.

A **jail** is the least appropriate short-term care option for juveniles because it is a transitional facility that offers very few, if any, resources to help a juvenile, such as supervision, mental and physical care, and educational programming. Jails also tend to be overcrowded, exposing youths to victimization. A jail holds three types of adults: (1) offenders who are given a minimal sentence of incarceration, generally less than 1 year; (2) individuals who have been accused of a crime and are waiting for trial procedures; and (3) individuals who have been transferred from another facility to testify in court in that jurisdiction.

The JJDPA set restrictions on confining juveniles in adult jails and prisons, and when it was amended in 1980, it called for the removal of juveniles from jails by 1985, or else federal funding would be denied. As a result, the number of youths held in adult jails fell dramatically. However, some states were slow to comply, and the law still allowed for waivers (discussed in Chapter 5), which meant that the percentage of the inmate population under age 18 actually increased.

States such as California and Utah have totally stopped housing juveniles in adult jails, while states such as Illinois, North Carolina, and Tennessee restrict minors in adult jails. States that still house juveniles in adult jails often cite a lack of resources. Some jurisdictions deal with the problem by holding juveniles in a separate location in the same jail.[15]

Long-Term Institutionalization Options

Juveniles who are sent to confinement are usually moved first to **reception and diagnostic centers**. These facilities determine which treatment plan and placement is most appropriate for the juvenile. Large states have their own reception and diagnostic centers, but most states evaluate youths in a training school. At the centers, youths are evaluated by a variety of professionals during their stay of 4 to 6 weeks. Clinical psychologists test for intelligence, maturity, and emotional problems while a social worker investigates family background. Educational staff identify learning disorders and proper grade placement while physicians and dentists perform physical exams for health. Staff running the dormitory may comment on peer relationships and adjustment. All staff then compile the reports and participate in a case conference to determine a juvenile's needs and decide placement.[16] After leaving the reception and diagnostic center, delinquent children usually enter one of three types

Miller v. Alabama, 567 U.S. 460 (2012)

This case includes two separate state court cases. Case 1 involved Kuntrell Jackson (age 14) and two other teenagers who went to a video store in Arkansas with the intention of robbing it. Jackson stayed outside while the other two youths first went inside the store. Jackson went into the store right before one of the other youths shot and killed the store clerk. Jackson was charged as an adult and given life in prison without the possibility of parole.

Case 2 involved Evan Miller (age 14) of Alabama, who was convicted of murder after he and another minor (Colby Smith) set fire to a trailer where they often bought drugs. Miller and Smith used alcohol and marijuana with the inhabitant of the trailer, Cole Cannon. Cannon fell asleep, and Miller stole the contents of his wallet. When Cannon woke up, Smith hit him over the head with a baseball bat and Miller beat him severely with the bat. Smith and Miller then set fire to the trailer and Cannon died. Miller was tried as an adult and given life without parole.

Jackson filed a petition seeking writ of habeas corpus on the basis of violation of the Eighth Amendment. The circuit court dismissed the petition, and the Supreme Court of Arkansas affirmed the lower court's decision.

Miller filed a post-trial motion for a new trial with the argument that a sentence of life without parole for a minor was a violation of the Eighth Amendment. The motion was denied, and the Alabama Court of Criminal Appeals affirmed the lower court's decision.

In 2012, the U.S. Supreme Court reversed and remanded the state supreme courts' decisions in Alabama and Arkansas. With the opinion written by Justice Elena Kagan, the court ruled that the Eighth Amendment protection against cruel and unusual punishment did not permit the mandatory sentencing of life in prison without parole for juvenile homicide offenders.

1. **Do you agree with the ruling?**

2. **If the defendant was closer to the age of 18 rather than 14, would you still have this opinion?**

3. **In your opinion, would this ruling be the same today?**

Online Case Opinion

https://caselaw.findlaw.com/us-supreme-court/10-9646.html ●

---

of facilities: boot camps, ranches and forestry camps, and training schools. Each type of facility is discussed briefly in the sections that follow.

Boot Camps

Boot camps, originally introduced in 1985, are based on the boot camps for newly enlisted recruits in the military. Using military discipline, they are supposed to shock juveniles back into law-abiding behavior. Juveniles go to these camps for 30 to 120 days. Generally, these youths have not responded to less severe sanctions but are not serious delinquents involved in violent or sex offenses.[17]

Boot camps appear to be a good way to put a juvenile delinquent back on track. They involve drill sergeants and a platoon structure but still provide a rehabilitative environment with education and job training. One part of the day is spent on work detail and strenuous exercise while the other part involves educational classes, therapy, and drug and alcohol treatment, where necessary. Youths who generally come from unstructured, criminal subcultures get mentorship and training to lead a law-abiding life.

Research shows that juveniles found boot camps to provide a more positive and structured environment than traditional detention centers, and they became less antisocial and more emotionally stable. However, recidivism rates for these juveniles are the same as or higher than rates for those in detention centers. The research shows that the strict regimen of the boot camp did not help youths after they were released and had to deal with the disorganized environment in their home communities. In addition, some boot camps have been linked to extensive abuse. States such as Maryland and Georgia have reevaluated the get-tough standards in their juvenile boot camps, and Florida shut down all its boot camps in 2006 after a juvenile was beaten to death in one of them.

Ranches and Forestry Camps

Ranches and forestry camps are another residential option that entails a minimum-security placement for first-time or minor juvenile offenders. Juvenile residents do conservation work in a local state park or similar area. They may also get visits from social workers and participate in group therapy, and they may regularly go on trips to nearby towns or cities for shopping and community events.[18]

These camps have a more relaxed atmosphere than other kinds of camps. While the sleeping quarters are locked at night, most facilities do not have other kinds of confinement. Residents appreciate frequent community contacts and better relations with staff members. The Hennepin County Home School near Minneapolis is a model of this kind of camp. This coeducational facility accepts juveniles who have committed several personal and property offenses, including violent and sex offenses. It provides educational and therapeutic programs, as well as recreational activities.

Training Schools

Training schools are residential facilities that have a specific organizational goal to target the needs of a certain classification of juveniles. The most punitive model focuses on obedience and conformity, keeping residents under constant surveillance without forming relationships with them. Facilities with reeducation and development, on the other hand, focus on hard work and intellectual growth. Residents can form relationships and get rewarded for success. Last, in treatment-oriented training schools, staff get emotionally involved with residents, with an emphasis on positive mental health and building relationships.[19]

While training schools try to focus on the *parens patriae* philosophy, they have security measures in place to provide a safe environment that can enhance rehabilitation. Facilities provide minimum, medium, or maximum security, but states with one training school provide all levels of security in the one facility. Some facilities lock all residents into sleeping quarters at night, while others do so only when a youth is out of control.[20]

Maximum-security training schools have high fences and walls topped with wire, and interior hallways have locked doors and cells, limiting movement during the day. Medium-security facilities are like dormitories, and residents can move more freely but they are enclosed by a fence. Minimum-security facilities are even more relaxed, with unrestricted movement.

Until the past decade and a half, training schools employed "cottage parents" to stay with juveniles and act as parental figures. These were often retired couples who provided a homelike atmosphere. However, due to the increased need for discipline, many of these facilities have replaced the cottage parents with regular staff, and the one-on-one nurturing has been replaced by structured responsibilities of parenting. For instance, youth supervisors ensure that chores are performed and juveniles participate in all their academic, vocational, and work programs. Staff members work 8 to 10 hours, meaning that residents deal with several shifts of caregivers. Staff on the night shift have to deal with illness and make sure juveniles do not escape while others are sleeping.

CMN/EyePress/CMN EyePress/Newscom

Youth being held in a detention center are still required to attend educational courses. Why?

The goal of all levels of training school is to produce citizens with life skills, academic achievement, and improved mental health. Remedial classes, educational programs for granting high school diplomas, and GED testing are offered. Classes are kept small, allowing for interaction between the instructors and students. Males also have access to a variety of vocational programs in areas such as auto repair, carpentry, woodworking, and food services, while females generally have programs in cosmetology, typing, and food service.

The training schools emphasize therapy in areas like peer interactions, drug and alcohol use, and gangs. They also get religious instruction, including services, choir, and community groups. Residents also get involved in a variety of sports, games, and artistic activities, where they learn team skills, self-respect, and peer cooperation.

The minimum-security facilities also provide reentry programs to help the released residents integrate into the community and avoid further deviancy. They may be transferred to step-down cottages or placed back in their community in home furloughs or working in jobs. They may also be allowed to see their parents for a few hours off campus. This freedom has a positive impact, but it does produce a higher percentage of runaways than in other programs

IIN THE MEDIA 6.1

Training Schools

Training schools bear a resemblance to adult prisons, although most facilities designed to confine juveniles are relatively new, clean, and well-staffed. In addition, training schools generally separate individual offenders, with each adolescent having his or her own room. Training schools are not without their problems, of course, some of which are due to the fact that youthful offenders tend to represent a greater risk to staff's physical safety than do older prisoners.

Putting It Into Action

To complete this active learning exercise you should arrange to visit a training school in your area. Call the facility, and explain to them that you are studying juvenile justice and would like to tour the facility (this might work better if you visit with a group of your fellow students and/or with the instructor).

Once there, interview staff members about their work experiences inside the facility; include questions about the nature of the job and daily activities, its rewards and dangers, and their thoughts about the likely future of the adolescents they oversee.

Gather your findings into a document that can be submitted to your instructor when you are asked to do so. ●

LEGAL RIGHTS OF INSTITUTIONALIZED YOUTHS

>> **LO 6.4**   Describe the legal rights of institutionalized youths.

The rights of juveniles during institutionalization have been challenged in regard to sufficient legal protection during confinement. The Children's Rights Movement asserts that confined juveniles should be guaranteed the right to treatment, have a right to deny treatment, and be protected from cruel and unusual punishment. Juveniles also have the right to access the courts, as was discussed in Chapter 5.

Multiple court decisions have ruled in favor of the right to treatment during commitment to training school. The court's decision on *White v. Reid* (1954),[21] a case in the District of Columbia, held that juveniles could not be held in institutions without rehabilitation programs, which was supported by later decisions in Rhode Island (*Inmates of the Boys' Training School v. Affleck* [1972][22]) and Indiana (*Nelson v. Neyne*

[1974][23]). In addition, the U.S. District Court for the Eastern District of Texas ruled in *Morales v. Turman* (1973)[24] that certain educational, psychological, and medical assessments and treatments must be provided to juveniles in confinement. Originally overruled by the Fifth Circuit Court of Appeals on the grounds that a three-judge court should have heard the case, that decision was reversed and remanded by the U.S. Supreme Court.

Juveniles also have the right to deny treatment as long as it is not legally required or does not affect the safety and health of the juvenile and community. For example, juveniles cannot refuse educational services. In addition, they cannot refuse services to prevent harm to physical health. A juvenile can refuse medication for a headache but cannot refuse an asthma inhaler or EpiPen if medical necessity arises.

The Eighth Amendment, barring cruel and unusual punishment, has also been applied to institutionalization of juveniles. The ruling on *Pena v. New York State Division for Youth* (1976)[25] found that use of tranquilizing drugs, restraints, and isolation was too punitive for juveniles and violated the Eighth Amendment. Other court decisions, including *Morales v. Turman* in Texas and *Morgan v. Sproat* (1977),[26] ruled against the use of solitary confinement, brutality, and other abusive behaviors.

AFTERCARE

>> LO 6.5   **Explain the role of aftercare in juvenile justice.**

The primary goal of the juvenile justice system is successful release without another occurrence of criminal behavior. About 100,000 juveniles are released from confinement each year. Many of these youths have physical and mental health problems, drug or alcohol addiction, educational deficiencies, and a history of family discord.[27] Unfortunately, residential facilities do not have enough resources to fully address these issues for the youths, and many are unprepared for the challenges of the outside world. Figure 6.3 portrays the typical characteristics of juveniles in aftercare.[28]

Youths are often sent back to the crime-ridden communities where they first got in trouble, making it extremely difficult to refrain from further crime. Those who came from abusive homes are especially vulnerable and need extra services to protect them. **Aftercare** programs, also known as **parole** in some jurisdictions, provide resources, treatment, and supervision necessary to successfully reenter society. Effective aftercare should begin at sentencing and continue throughout the youth's journey through the juvenile justice system.[29] During aftercare (or parole), a youth is required to follow a set of conditions and is monitored by a caseworker (or parole officer). Figure 6.4 depicts the goals of juvenile aftercare.

FIGURE 6.3

Average Picture of Juveniles Released From Detention Centers

GENDER	RACE/ ETHNICITY	OFFENSE	AGE	FAMILY BACKGROUND	EDUCATIONAL BACKGROUND	MENTAL HEALTH	ECONOMIC STATUS	CUSTODIAL EXPERIENCE
Male	Minority	Nonviolent	Older juvenile	Single-parent household (with the father incarcerated in about one quarter of cases)	Did not complete the eighth grade and is learning-disabled	Some form of disorder	From low-income family and neighborhood	Involves most of childhood

Sources: Abrams, L. & Snyder, S. (2010). Youth offender re-entry: Models for intervention and directions for future inquiry. *Children and Youth Services Review, 12,* 1787–1795; Snyder, H. (2004). An empirical portrait of the youth re-entry population. *Youth Violence and Juvenile Justice,* 39–55.

FIGURE 6.4

Goals of Juvenile Aftercare

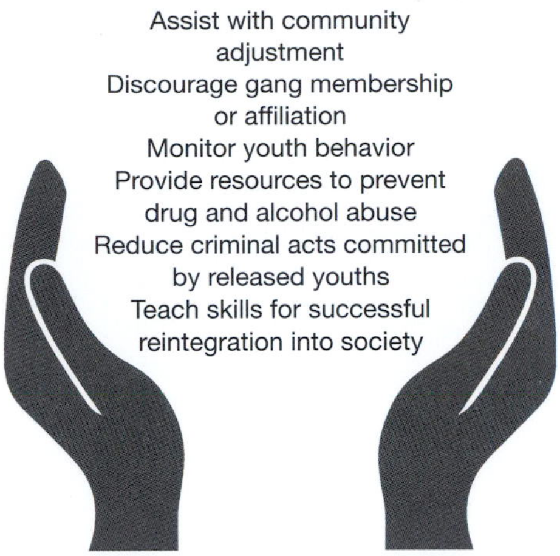

Assist with community
adjustment
Discourage gang membership
or affiliation
Monitor youth behavior
Provide resources to prevent
drug and alcohol abuse
Reduce criminal acts committed
by released youths
Teach skills for successful
reintegration into society

Assessment of Risk

Methods of determining institutional release of a juvenile vary by jurisdiction. Most state governments use the executive branch to make the release decision, but four states allow a probation or parole officer to make the decision and three states elicit advice from boards. Once the juvenile is released, an aftercare program must be created, and experts disagree on which entity should do this. Some argue that aftercare decisions should be made by staff at the institution where the juvenile was confined, because they have spent the most time with the juvenile and are familiar with his or her behaviors, needs, and risks. Others, however, say these staff could make prejudicial decisions based on personal interactions, and therefore the work should be assigned to independent agencies with expertise in juvenile psychology and behaviors.

If juveniles live in a state with determinate or mandatory sentencing, a decision on institutional release is made once they enter a training school. Some states, such as Ohio, refer to a guideline on structured sentencing to determine release. Authorities consider such factors as the severity of the offense and history of juvenile delinquency (see Figure 6.5). Factors that show less severe behavior are called mitigating factors, which may result in milder sentences. Factors that point to more severe behavior are called aggravating factors, which may result in stricter sentences.

This kind of structured assessment is also used to measure the risk of placing juveniles in aftercare and their supervision and treatment needs. A popular assessment tool is the Level of Service Inventory-Revised (LSI-R), which was developed in the late 1970s by frontline professionals in Canada for offenders age 16 and older. It helps predict success of an offender in a variety of correctional reentry situations, such as parole, halfway houses, or treatment programs, based on the following areas:

- Accommodation
- Alcohol or drug problems
- Attitudes
- Companions
- Criminal history

- Education
- Emotional health
- Employment
- Family and marital life
- Financial behavior
- Recreational activities

Since the LSI-R is a lengthy survey, authorities can use a shorter instrument called the LSI-R:SV when resources and time are short.[30]

Example Disposition Matrix for Youths Adjudicated Delinquent

MOST SERIOUS CURRENT ADJUDICATED OFFENSE	HISTORY 2+ PRIOR FELONY ADJUDICATIONS?	RISK OF REOFFENDING			
		VERY HIGH	HIGH	MEDIUM	LOW
CLASS I: Most serious violent felony offenses (murder, rape, armed robbery, etc.)	Yes	A	A	A	A
	No	A	A	A/B	A/B
CLASS II: Other felony offenses against the person; felony weapon and felony drug distribution	Yes	A/B	A/B	A/B	B/C
	No	D/E	D/E	E	E
CLASS III: Felony property and public order offenses	Yes	B/C	B/C	C/D	C/D
	No	D/E	D/E	E	E
CLASS IV: Misdemeanor offenses against the person	Yes	C/D	C/D	D/E	D/E
	No	E	E	E	E
CLASS V: All other misdemeanors; all status offenses	Yes	C/D	C/D	C/D	D/E
	No	E	E	E	E

PROGRAM LEVELS

A.   Secure correctional facilities, secure psychiatric hospitals

B.   Staff-secure correctional facilities, residential treatment programs, boot camp

C.   Community residential facilities: group homes, proctor homes

D.   Day treatment, intensive probation supervision, specialized programming (e.g., sex offenders, drug dealers)

E.   Probation—minimum, medium, or high supervision levels

MANDATORY OVERRIDES

1.   Any C, D, E designation overridden to B when clinical diagnosis indicates youth requires inpatient drug/alcohol or mental health treatment

2.   Other (as specified by adopting agency)

Source: National Council of Juvenile and Family Court Judges, *Graduated Sanctions for Juvenile Offenders*, vol. II, https://www.ncjfcj.org/sites/default/files/vol.2planning guidejsc18_0.pdf.

NAVIGATING THE FIELD 6.1

Big Brothers Big Sisters of America

Big Brothers Big Sisters of America is a mentoring program that targets youths between the ages of 6 and 18 years old, often from single-parent households and impoverished neighborhoods. Many of these youths are coping with the stress of parental incarceration. The mentoring program is based on social control theory, enforcing the importance of prosocial bonds to supportive adults.

Putting It Into Action

Using your Internet search engine, research this program and its implementation.

Explain how this program has reduced juvenile delinquency in at-risk areas.

Submit your explanation to your instructor when asked to do so. ●

Intervention Strategies in Aftercare

The goal of aftercare is to control behavior in the short term through various programs. **Intensive aftercare supervision (IAS)** involves high levels of supervision of a juvenile after release. Dozens of IAS programs were created in the 1980s and 1990s, and the more recent programs follow the integrated theoretical framework of social control, social learning, and strain theories. These programs are designed using the Intensive Aftercare Program (IAP) model, which is based on the premise that chronic delinquency is a result of weak social controls when a child grows up in disorganized communities. Youths are thought to learn that committing crime is acceptable and supported in the community, resulting in a negative view of their neighborhoods and no motivation to act within the law. The IAP model provides youths with resources so they can learn to deal with freedom, act responsibly, and make good choices. IAP programs showed great success in the first 5 years of implementation, from 1995 to 2000. Evaluations showed an improved level of communication and collaboration between agencies, allowing the juvenile to access aftercare and get assistance almost immediately after release.[31]

Dozens of intervention programs attempt to change the behavior of delinquent youths by focusing on jobs, school, mental health, and substance use. Successful programs try to change attitudes about delinquent behavior, in effect rewiring the brain so prosocial choices are made to pursue crime-free pathways through life. This involves using cognitive-behavioral therapies that are very structured and teach skills. To be effective, programs need to have dedicated staff who have frequent contacts with offenders.

Many youths released into aftercare do not have functional home lives and supportive parents. An option for these youths is the **interstate compact**, placement with a relative outside the jurisdiction of the juvenile court. Interstate compacts are also used for juveniles wanted in more than one state for various offenses. Under the compact, the jurisdictions agree to cooperate on supervision in aftercare and share the cost of services. If youths run away to the other jurisdiction, they can be sent back to the original jurisdiction for a revocation hearing and potential confinement.

Responsibilities of Aftercare Officers

The duties of aftercare officers are similar to those of probation officers. They have supervisory and investigatory responsibilities, and provide social services. They also have large caseloads and limited resources. Aftercare officers tend to be more experienced than probation officers, because the needs of institutionalized youths can be more serious. Their chief goal is to help juvenile delinquents transition back into the community by giving them the tools to do so. Leaving confinement can be

TABLE 6.3

Case Precedents for Aftercare Revocation

U.S. SUPREME COURT CASE	DECISION
Mempa v. Rhay (1967)	Probationers have the right to counsel and a hearing when accused of violation.
People ex rel. Gallo v. Warden of Greenhaven State Prison (1969)	Inmates have the right to counsel during hearings.
Murray v. Page (1970)	Parolees have due process rights and cannot be deprived freedom without following those rights
Morrissey v. Brewer (1972)	Hearings to determine parole revocation must be before an objective party.
Gagnon v. Scarpelli (1973)	The Morrissey ruling was applied to probationers.

a shock, and when one returns to one's old territory, it can be difficult to refrain from crime.[32]

Unlike probation officers, aftercare officers have a law enforcement function, in that they can return youths to confinement if conditions are violated. Released youths may resume their old attitudes and behaviors, such as truancy, disrespecting parents, and other minor infractions. While these are not criminal acts, they may cause aftercare officers to revoke aftercare if they feel the behavior will lead to recidivism. And if youths commit criminal acts or engage in substance abuse, they can be sent back to confinement to protect the community and themselves.

When the youth violates the program and aftercare is revoked, there are several actions that can be taken, including more intensive supervision, home confinement with electronic monitoring, or a return to confinement. However, revoking aftercare is not as simple as revocation of adult parole, because the juvenile has due process protections guaranteed by the U.S. Supreme Court. The court's rulings are presented in Table 6.3. Some aftercare officers, however, disregard these protections and make arbitrary decisions.

LOOKING INTO THE FUTURE OF JUVENILE CORRECTIONAL REFORM

Clear, Reisig, and Cole say that the nature of juvenile corrections has notably shifted over the past 20 years.[33] Juvenile arrest rates have decreased by two-thirds, and incarceration rates are down significantly. The rate at which youths are housed in adult prisons has dropped by more than 80% during the past two decades. Juvenile justice stakeholders are applying research on adolescent development to debunk myths about the capabilities of juveniles, as well as their lack of understanding of ramifications of violent behaviors. As the juvenile justice system continues to develop, a team of experts suggests four main areas in which reform can improve the system as a whole:[34]

1. Reduce the school-to-prison pipeline through the amendment of legal statutes that define which youths and which crimes are eligible for juvenile placement.

2. Desist the use of juvenile prisons and implement the use of homelike residential facilities that teach prosocial skills and leadership.

3. Reform the correctional culture from punitive control on juveniles to a focus on positive change for juveniles, families, and their communities.

4. Divert resources to finance community improvements and cultural environments.

By continuing to change the philosophy of the juvenile justice system and diverting resources toward more prosocial change, the expectation is that our reliance on the juvenile justice system as a crime control model will decrease. ●

SUMMARY

>> LO 6.1   Define juvenile probation and know when it should be used.

As in the adult criminal justice system, probation is the most typical form of adjudication for juveniles. Probation permits juveniles to serve their sentences in the community, allowing youths to remain with their families and drastically reducing the cost to the justice system. Generally, probation is used for nonviolent and/or first-time juvenile offenders. A probation officer is responsible for the assessment and supervision of a juvenile, reporting progress to the court, and making determinations in the management of the youth.

Key Terms

casework management   95
community
   corrections   94

probation   94
social study report   96
supervision   95

>> LO 6.2   Describe some of the correctional options available to juvenile court judges that are less severe than institutionalization but more severe than probation.

Institutionalization and probation are not the only options available to juvenile court judges. Less intrusive sanctions, such as community service and restitution, are available for use with low-level property offenders. For juveniles requiring more supervision, a juvenile court judge may place him or her on house arrest and monitor movement with electronic monitoring devices.

Key Terms

community service   97
direct service   97
electronic monitoring   98

house arrest   98
intensive supervision
   programs (ISPs)   97

restitution   97

>> LO 6.3   List some of the options that juvenile court judges have for the institutionalization of delinquents.

If juvenile court judges decide that institutionalization is appropriate for the treatment and safety of a juvenile, then there are many options available to them. One of the main goals of the juvenile court is family and community reunification, but institutionalization may be necessary for the safety of the community or for the protection of the juvenile. Some juveniles are placed in institutional settings, which can include detention centers, shelter care facilities, or group homes. Wilderness camps and training schools are other options. Juveniles deemed to have serious behavior problems and/or those who are violent are often placed in long-term institutionalization options, such as training schools. Boot camps that last between 30 and 90 days or diagnostic centers that entail a stay of at least a month are an alternative for these types of offenders.

Key Terms

attention homes   99
boot camps   101
continuum of sanctions   98
detention centers   98

institutionalization   98
jail   100
ranches and forestry
   camps   102

reception and diagnostic
   centers   100
shelter care facilities   100
training schools   102

>> LO 6.4   Describe the legal rights of institutionalized youths.

As the juvenile court system is designed to focus on the rehabilitation of youths, the legal rights of juveniles processed through the system revolve around treatment. Multiple court decisions have identified the necessity of medical and psychological treatment in juvenile facilities, as well as the availability of educational programming. While juveniles have the right to deny medical treatment that is not required for their personal safety, they cannot refuse educational services. Courts have also ruled that some measures violate the Eighth Amendment when applied to juveniles, such as use of solitary confinement and use of tranquilizing drugs.

›› LO 6.5   Explain the role of aftercare in juvenile justice.

About 100,000 juveniles are released from confinement every year, the majority of whom have mental health problems, addiction issues, and a history of abuse or family trauma. The presence of one or more of these issues can make successful societal reentry difficult. Aftercare programs provide resources, treatment, and supervision for youths to increase the likelihood of successful reentry experiences. Youths are given a risk and needs assessment prior to release, allowing a probation/parole officer to develop the best plan to intervene when the juvenile is met with challenging circumstances.

Key Terms

aftercare 104	intensive aftercare supervision (IAS) 107	interstate compact 107 parole 104

DISCUSSION QUESTIONS

1. Confinement options can be extremely restrictive and not therapeutic when a juvenile is deemed a security risk. What is your opinion on the use of solitary confinement for juveniles? Should there be a minimum age for its use?

2. Much like in the adult system, there are far fewer females than males in the juvenile justice system, and fewer resources are allocated specifically for females. Should programs for female juvenile offenders be enhanced?

3. It can be a challenge for states to provide effective aftercare, in part due to funding requirements. And yet recidivism rates for juvenile offenders, particularly those with more serious behaviors, are high. Are there cost-effective methods of aftercare that are not being used?

EXPLORING JUVENILE JUSTICE FURTHER

1. Interview an employee of a juvenile aftercare program (or probation/parole officer). Ask him or her about the most rewarding parts of the job, as well as the most frustrating.

2. Investigate the components of an Alcoholics Anonymous or Narcotics Anonymous in your jurisdiction. Do you feel as if this program is appropriate for juveniles, or should it be altered to better assist the addiction issues of this age group?

$SAGE edge™

Give your students the SAGE edge!

SAGE edge offers a robust online environment featuring an impressive array of free tools and resources for review, study, and further exploration, keeping both instructors and students on the cutting edge of teaching and learning. Learn more at **edge.sagepub.com/schmallegerjj**.

PART III

Juvenile Behaviors

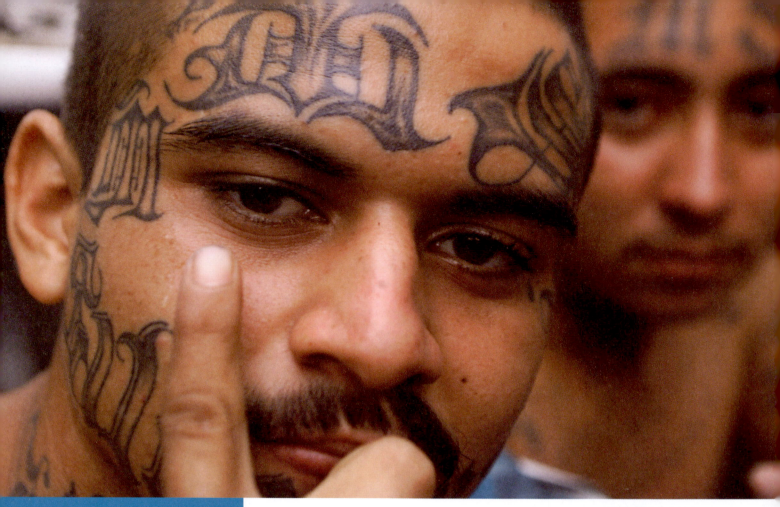

7

Juveniles and Gangs

After reading this chapter you should be able to

1. Describe how gangs developed in the United States

2. Define the term *gang*, and describe today's gang activities

3. Explain what an urban street gang is, and give examples of types of gangs

4. Show how race and ethnicity relate to gang involvement and gang activity

5. Describe some of the illegal activities that gangs engage in

6. Provide an overview of gangs in schools

7. Describe gang prevention efforts

8. Describe problems involved in leaving a gang

Key Terms in Chapter 7

corporate gangs
cross-border gangs
gang
G.R.E.A.T.
hedonistic gangs

horizontal/commission
    structure
influential structure
instrumental gangs
predatory gangs
scavenger gangs

supergang
territorial gangs
turf
urban gangs
vertical/hierarchical
    structure

INTRODUCTION

Gangs are a very big problem in the United States, especially in urban environments. They can be attractive to juveniles in poor communities because they appear to offer a lifestyle of physical protection, camaraderie, wealth, and power. Some of the names of the largest **urban gangs** are emblazoned in our culture's language—including Bloods, Crips, Gangster Disciples, and Vice Lords. Gangs provide respite and protection for young people who have no family or are victims of violence. This appeal encourages the continuous growth of gang membership across the United States, making it difficult for prosocial alternatives to persuade members to abandon the gang lifestyle.

In one heartwarming story, Los Angeles, California, Catholic priest Gregory J. Boyle, S. J., founded and established Homeboy Industries in 1988 as an alternative to gang participation. Homeboy Industries, which Boyle initially called Jobs for a Future, offers an alternative to youths entrenched in neighborhoods where violence is encouraged and gang membership can be very attractive. Homeboy Industries got its start by refurbishing an abandoned Los Angeles bakery following the 1992 Los Angeles riots, calling it the Homeboy Bakery. Soon

Father Gregory J. Boyle, S. J., is founder of Homeboy Industries. What does Homeboy Industries offer gang members that might help them abandon a gang lifestyle?

CIRO CESAR/LA OPINION/Newscom

Homeboy Industries expanded to include numerous other employment options, including solar panel installation and refurbishment. It continues to offer an avenue of escape for young men who would otherwise be swayed by the pull of street gangs. Father Boyle still heads Homeboy Industries and today is also known for his *New York Times* best seller *Tattoos on the Heart: The Power of Boundless Compassion*. Boyle, who has been widely recognized for his work, was the subject of the Academy Award–winning 2012 documentary *G-Dog*. In 2016, he received the Humanitarian of the Year Award from the James Beard Foundation—a national culinary-arts group.

Today Homeboy Industries employs around 220 trainers, most of whom are former gang members, and continues its work to build marketable skills in those seeking to escape gang life. It has grown to serve more than 15,000 men and women annually.

This chapter examines the development of gangs in the United States and the extent of juvenile gang involvement. In addition, the various types of gangs present in the United States will be discussed. As you delve into the chapter, consider what type of programming, if any, can help with this pertinent issue.

A HISTORY OF AMERICAN GANGS

» LO 7.1   Describe how gangs developed in the United States.

Juvenile gangs existed in the United States as far back as the American Revolution, according to some accounts. In any case, there are clear records that youth gangs existed in the southwestern states after the Mexican War of Independence in 1810, and there were gangs in New England at about the same time. More juvenile gangs began to show up during the immigration boom of the late 1800s, in cities such as New York, Chicago, and Philadelphia. These early gangs mainly involved youths of Italian, Irish, and Jewish descent, but the makeup began to change in the 20th century.[1]

Gang development in urban areas was normal in ethnic neighborhoods in the 1920s,[2] according to Frederick Thrasher, a pioneer in the field (see Figure 7.1). Youths who grew up in the same neighborhood and went to school together formed their own sense of community, naturally gravitating toward each other for play. These groups formed what would now be called a gang, run by a leader and lieutenants. While each group promoted different ideals, they all had one common goal: protection of **turf**, or a geographic region perceived to be "owned" by the gang.

In the 1940s and 1950s, a more formalized version of juvenile gangs appeared in Boston, New York City, and Philadelphia.[3] Members spent most of their time just hanging out, and they fought other gangs only when necessary. These groups were capable of violence but did not resort to the level of aggressiveness we see in gangs today. Still, the growing presence of gangs was concerning to policymakers. Millions of dollars in federal and state money were spent on prevention programs and diversionary efforts for current gang members. The most widely funded effort was the detached workers' program, which sent professionals into the community to work with gang youths, but rather than diverting behaviors, it actually increased gang membership.

The supergang started in Chicago in the 1960s, a time of great upheaval, and became a prevalent force in political activism and social betterment. A **supergang** is a large and powerful gang in a neighborhood, often absorbing smaller gangs in the area. Parts of Chicago were dominated by three gangs: the Vice Lords, Blackstone Rangers, and Disciples. Leaders of the Vice Lords met with representatives of Western Electric and Sears to form committees for education, recreation, and justice. In February 1967, the Rockefeller Foundation awarded a grant to the Vice Lords to help them start a variety of ventures. In addition, this supergang worked with Jesse Jackson on Operation Breadbasket and with the Coalition for United Community Action to protest racial bias in hiring practices at construction sites.

The rest of the 20th century involved many changes in gang life. Adults began to account for a large proportion of gang membership. Juvenile members were more likely to move on to more legitimate pathways, while adults in prison gangs became more prominent.[4]

Street gangs began committing most urban crime, and violence increased. Two supergangs in Los Angeles, the Bloods and Crips, began turf wars involving murder

FIGURE 7.1

Timeline History of American Gangs

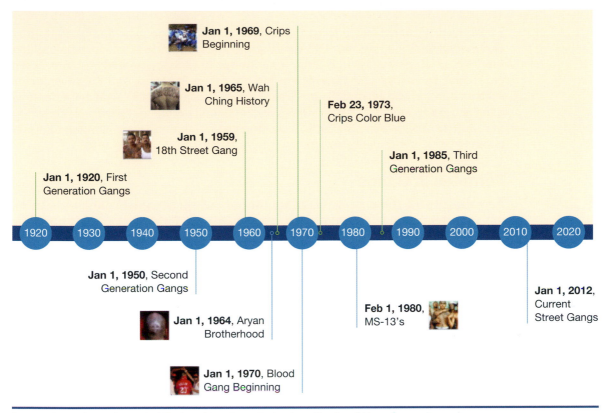

Source: "History of Gangs in America," *Timetoast*, https://www.timetoast.com/timelines/history-of-gangs-in-america.

and other violence. Urban gangs were credited with a large proportion of muggings, extortions, and robberies in cities. In addition, gangs became entrenched in the sale of crack cocaine in the 1980s and eventually other drugs. Los Angeles gangs had connections to Colombian drug smugglers, and in Chicago drugs were openly sold on the streets by heavily armed gang members.

CONTEMPORARY GANGS IN THE UNITED STATES

>> **LO 7.2** Define the term *gang*, and describe today's gang activities.

Currently, the U.S. Department of Justice defines a **gang** using the following criteria:[5]

1. Three or more people identify themselves as members of the group.

2. Members use intimidation or fear as part of a group identity that uses symbols such as tattoos, styles or colors of clothing, hand signs, graffiti, or other markings, as seen in Figure 7.2.

3. The group engages in criminal activity or juvenile delinquency, and intimidation through violence.

4. The goal is to maintain and enhance the reputation and power of the group.

The group may also operate in the following manner:

a. Implement rules for joining

b. Meet on a regular basis

c.   Provide physical protection from other gangs

d.   Attempt to exercise control over a particular area

e.   Possess an identifiable structure

Currently, membership in gangs and the number of gangs overall has slightly declined since the mid-1990s. However, ethnic gang membership is increasing and reported in cities worldwide. Gang activity has been documented in large Asian cities such as Beijing and Hong Kong, Melbourne in Australia, and European cities such as London and Madrid. South America and Russia have also seen an increase in gang presence. The most recent survey of gang membership in the United States—by the National Youth Gang Survey in 2012—indicated that there were 30,700 gangs and about 850,000 gang members, which represented a 10% drop since 2010.[6]

Females in Gangs

According to the National Gang Center, the presence of females in gangs is not new, but attention on female gang members has increased. From the late 1990s to 2010, law enforcement agencies reported that a national total of 6.1% to 7.7% of gang members were females. However, recent research by the National Gang Center indicated that up to 30% of gang members are female.

Of those females who are involved with a gang, many are fully active members and not just associates of male gang members. The National Council for Crime & Delinquency found that 72% of female gang members had been asked, forced, or volunteered to commit an act of violence. Sixty-six percent of female gang members had dealt drugs.[7]

Female gang members often experience a high rate of abuse, either from family or other gang members.[8] Compared with male gang members, they are more likely to internalize this abuse and then become involved in self-harm. However, female gang members are likely to phase out of gang membership, especially if they are pregnant or already have children. As only a small percentage of funding for juvenile justice is directed toward young females, progressive organizations are now beginning to provide time and resources to help at-risk females. For instance, Working on Womanhood in Chicago, Illinois, provides small-group therapy sessions for young women in violent areas, including education, resources, and conflict resolution training.[9]

GANG ORGANIZATION

>> LO 7.3   Explain what an urban street gang is and give examples of types of gangs.

Based on the research of several criminologists, urban street gangs fall into several categories depending on their intent, goals, and behaviors. Carl Taylor analyzed gangs in Detroit, Michigan, and identified three main categories of gangs. **Scavenger gangs** are quite disorganized, lacking goals and consistent leadership. They generally prey on people unable to defend themselves. **Territorial gangs** often promote narcotics within their territory and defend their "turf" from other gangs. **Corporate gangs**, or organized criminal groups, are focused on economic success and participate in various illegal ventures, including the sale of drugs. These gangs have divisions like a legitimate company, including those that handle sales, marketing, distribution, and enforcement of rules.[10]

C. Ronald Huff categorized gangs based on research in the Cleveland and Columbus, Ohio, areas. He found that **hedonistic gangs** focused on getting high on drugs or alcohol and having a good time. These types of gangs committed more property crimes and few violent crimes. Huff's **instrumental gangs** aimed at economic success by committing property crimes. While many gang members in instrumental gangs used drugs recreationally or even sold drugs, this was not an organized activity. Last, Huff's **predatory gangs** committed muggings, robberies, and crimes of opportunity. Gang members were likely to use crack cocaine and sell drugs to buy weapons.[11]

Jeffrey Fagan also identified four types of gang typologies based on his work in multiple urban areas, but he focused on gangs who have only drug involvement. Type 1 gangs use only alcohol and marijuana, and participate in few other activities. Type 2 gangs are heavily involved in vandalism and drug sales, generally to support their individual habits. Type 3 gangs are involved in a variety of serious and nonviolent crimes but have less involvement in drug sales and use. Last, Type 4 gangs are at the highest risk of becoming a formal criminal organization. Members commit both serious and nonviolent offenses and are heavily involved in drug sales and drug use.[12]

Gangs can have a formal organization, even though they appear to be haphazard street-based groups and their members do not work in an office environment. Leadership can be structured in three different ways: A **horizontal/commission structure** involves several leaders who share duties and equal powers over members. The Bloods and the Crips are examples of this type of structure. The **vertical/hierarchical structure** divides leadership into different levels. The Gangster Disciples and the Vice Lords are organized in this fashion. Last, gangs having an **influential structure** have no easily identifiable leadership positions, and authority is based on the personality and abilities of each member.[13]

Recruiting can be informal or formal. Some individuals join simply because it is expected of them, based on the involvement of other family members, or because their entire community is involved. Gangs may also have recruiting parties for new "soldiers," advertising gang life as glamorous or lucrative. The 2015 *National Gang Report* found that gang membership increased in about 49% of the jurisdictions polled during the year and stayed the same in 43% of the jurisdictions.[14] In summary, the gang lifestyle continues to remain an attractive option for many young people and is not showing signs of decreasing anytime soon.

Gangs are also using social media to recruit new members. Facebook, YouTube, and Instagram are a few of the social media platforms used to recruit new members.[15] Gangs also use these platforms to communicate with current members, including incarcerated members who use the Internet through smuggled phones or paid computer use in prison. Figure 7.3 outlines the frequency and type of social media used by gang members.

Gang members are initiated in at least one of the following ways:

1. *Blessed-in*: entrants mentored by older family members or others already in the gang

2. *Jumped-in*: entrants who have to take a beating from other members and often are expected to fight back

3. *Blood-in*: entrants expected to commit a gang-assigned murder

FIGURE 7.2

Social Media Use by Gangs

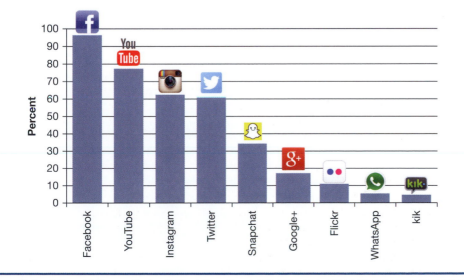

Source: National Gang Intelligence Center, *National Gang Report 2015*, https://www.fbi.gov/file-repository/stats-services-publications-national-gang-report-2015.pdf/view.https://www.fbi.gov/file-repository/national-gang-report-2015.pdf/view.

A young man shows off his tattoos. What purpose do tattoos serve among gang members?

Entrants may also be expected to participate in illegal acts, such as theft, drug trafficking, or shootings. Some members may be expected to play Russian roulette with a partly loaded pistol or perform sexual acts on other gang members.[16]

GANG DEMOGRAPHICS

>> LO 7.4   **Show how race and ethnicity relate to gang involvement and gang activity.**

The first dimension of a gang profile is age. Research has indicated that 14% to 30% of juveniles join a gang at some point in their lives.[17] However, the percentage of juveniles in gangs has decreased. In 1996, 50% of gang members were under age 18, and that figure fell to 33% by 2001. Juvenile membership is higher than average in smaller communities and lower than average in large urban areas. Juveniles as young as 8 years old are used for a variety of tasks by gangs, including delivering messages and weapons or running errands. Youths are also used as lookouts or to sell drugs in "rock houses," which are small, steel-reinforced homes.

The category of a gang is determined by its size. A traditional gang that focuses on territory and has a long history typically has about 150 members. Supergangs in urban areas such as Chicago and Los Angeles may have thousands of members. But newer gangs or those that traffic drugs may have as few as 25 members.

The attraction of the gang lifestyle, the final dimension of the gang profile, is multifaceted. Many gang members originate from dysfunctional homes, often lacking in parental guidance or care. Gangs offer a surrogate family that gives juveniles without a home access to mentoring by an adult, which helps them feel accepted and builds their self-esteem. Gang life provides power and security from outside threats. Members can earn money and receive an alternative education to that of the school system, where they received poor grades. They have opportunities to prove "adult" status. Last, gang life offers a lifestyle that members find more exciting than everyday life.

Criminologists have several theories to explain the allure of gang membership, which are briefly summarized in Table 7.1.[18] As can be seen, these theories stress the ability of gangs to provide a sense of community. Respect and masculinity are also extremely important factors for gang members, with a push to demonstrate these qualities through violent behaviors if ever disrespected by a rival gang member.

Gangs are generally organized in racial or ethnic groups.[19] The majority of gangs are identified as African American or Hispanic/Latino, but they can also be Asian or Caucasian. This section will explores these racial and ethnic categories.

TABLE 7.1

Criminological Theories Explaining Juvenile Gang Membership

THEORY	THEORISTS	DESCRIPTION
Normalcy of male adolescence	Block and Niederhoffer	Joining a gang is a normal part of adolescence that can be a path to manhood.
Social disorganization	Yablonsky	The discord of urban slums breeds violent juvenile gangs.
Strain	Cloward and Ohlin	Gangs provide illegitimate means for youths to achieve desired success.
Subcultural affiliation	Miller	Gang behavior is embraced and expected in a lower-class culture.
Subcultural affiliation and strain theory	Cohen	Gang membership helps lower-class boys deal with the strains they face.
Underclass	Fagan	Gangs provide economic stability for youths who are excluded from many occupations.

Bloch, H. & Niederhoffer, A. (1958). *The gang: A study in adolescent behavior.* New York: Philosophical Library.

Bob Chamberlin/Los Angeles Times/Getty Images

The Comprehensive Gang Model

The National Gang Center (NGC) is jointly funded by the federal Office of Juvenile Justice and Delinquency Prevention and the Bureau of Justice Assistance (which is a part of the U.S. Department of Justice). The NGC is regarded as an integral component of the Justice Department's mission to provide innovative leadership in coordination with federal, state, and local justice systems to prevent and reduce crime. The NGC disseminates information about outcome-driven practices that engage and empower those in local communities with chronic and emerging gang problems to create comprehensive solutions to prevent gang violence, reduce gang involvement, and suppress gang-related crime.

Putting It Into Action

This active learning activity asks you to visit the NGC on the web at https://www.nationalgangcenter.gov.

Once there, read about the NGC's Comprehensive Gang Model. Then create a Word document describing the model; include its historical development, major components, and present-day applicability.

Submit your completed document to your instructor when asked to do so. ●

African American Gangs

Many of the large, urban-based African American gangs have received a lot of attention because they are major drug traffickers. The most well-known gangs are infamous rivals, the Bloods and the Crips, who are based in the Los Angeles area but are found all over the United States. People Nation and Folk Nation are rival alliances of gangs in the Chicago area. The Black Gangster Disciples (otherwise known as the Gangster Disciples) are also found in Chicago and are allied with the Folk Nation. These gangs identify themselves by the colors of their clothing or by hand signals.

Asian Gangs

Asian gangs—including Chinese, Filipino, Japanese, Vietnamese, and Korean organizations—are present in some large cities, especially in California. They have identifiable leadership and are involved in severe violence and heroin trafficking. Examples of Asian gangs are the Asian Boyz, Asian Street Walkers, and Tiny Oriental Crips.

Caucasian Gangs

Until the late 1900s, adolescents were the most common members of Caucasian gangs, but now they make up only 10% of membership. Caucasian gangs are often affiliated with white supremacy and neo-Nazi causes that may be involved in drug trafficking and hate crimes. Other Caucasian groups participate in Satanism and support a "stoner" culture of drug and alcohol use. Examples of Caucasian gangs are the Aryan Brotherhood and Nazi Lowriders.

Hispanic/Latino Gangs

These gangs are divided into Mexican American, Cuban, Puerto Rican, and Central American organizations. Membership is expressed through dress, colors, graffiti, and tattoos. The most prominent gangs are Sur 13, Latin Kings, Norteños,

Robert Nickelsberg/Archive Photos/Getty Images

The Bloods and the Crips have common identifying tattoos. Can you identify any?

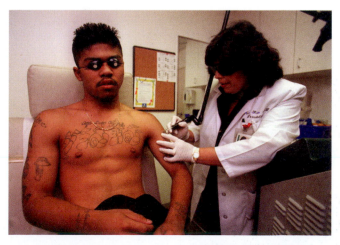

Bob Carey/Los Angeles Times/Getty Images

A member of the Asian Boyz gang getting a tatoo. How common are youth gangs?

An Aryan Brotherhood tatoo. What kinds of illegal activities do gang members engage in?

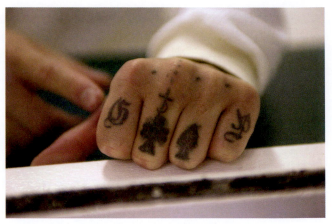

MS-13 tattoos. How prevalent are gangs in schools?

18th Street, and MS-13 (Mara Salvatrucha). MS-13, in particular, can be extremely violent. Originating as a Salvadoran gang and infiltrating the United States in California, MS-13 members can now be found in large urban areas across the United States.

ILLEGAL GANG ACTIVITIES

≫ LO 7.5   Describe some of the illegal activities that gangs engage in.

In the 2015 *National Gang Report*, about half of jurisdictions showed an increase in illegal gang activity. Gang activity can vary but includes a variety of personal, property, and drug crimes.[20] Jurisdictions with gang presence have reported a high occurrence of motor vehicle theft, assault, street-level drug sales, and robberies. Figure 7.4 shows the extent of gang activity in the 2015 *National Gang Report*.

Cross-border gangs, gangs that pursue illegal activities in more than one country, are especially prominent on both sides of the Mexico–U.S. border. Gangs such as the Sureños and Barrio Azteca are involved in a variety of drug- and weapon-based crimes, such as drug manufacturing and distribution, as well as smuggling of firearms. In addition, they can be active participants in human smuggling, human

CASE STUDY

Graham v. Florida, 560 U.S. 48 (2010)

In July 2003, Terrance Graham attempted to rob a barbeque restaurant in Jacksonville, Florida. He was 16 years old at the time and was charged and convicted as an adult with armed burglary and attempted armed robbery. He served a year and was released, but he was arrested 6 months later for armed home robbery. He was then convicted and sentenced to life imprisonment without the possibility of parole. He appealed to the District Court of Appeal of Florida, stating that the imposition of life without parole for a juvenile convicted of a nonhomicidal crime was unconstitutional on its face and was cruel and unusual punishment under the Eighth Amendment.

In 2010, the U.S. Supreme Court agreed with Graham's claim. Written by Justice Anthony Kennedy, the decision indicated it was a violation of the Eighth Amendment to sentence a juvenile to life imprisonment without parole

if convicted of a crime other than homicide. At that time, the majority of states had legislation allowing for life sentences without parole for nonhomicidal crimes. In February 2012, Graham was resentenced to a 25-year term in prison.

1. **Do you agree with the ruling?**

2. **Are there certain crimes in addition to homicide that you would consider as justified in receiving a sentence of life imprisonment without parole?**

3. **In your opinion, would this ruling be the same today?**

Online Case Opinion

https://www.supremecourt.gov/opinions/09pdf/08-7412.pdf ●

FIGURE 7.3

National Gang Activity in 2015

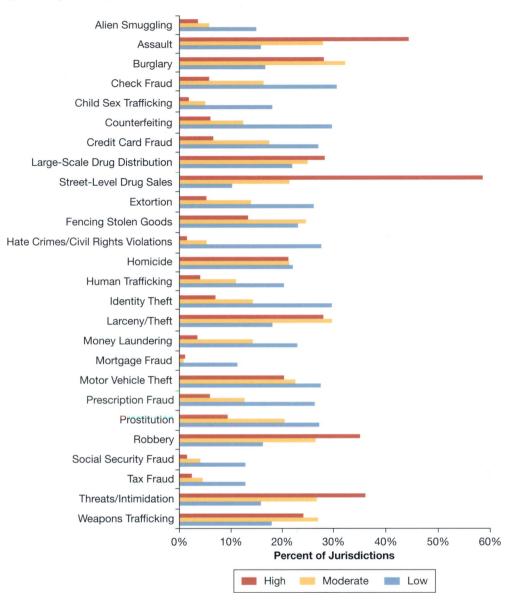

Source: National Gang Intelligence Center, *National Gang Report 2015*, https://www.fbi.gov/file-repository/stats-services-publications-national-gang-report-2015.pdf/view.

Note: Most recent data available at time of publication.

trafficking, and the child sex trade. Figure 7.5 outlines the extent of cross-border gang activity as indicated by the 2015 *National Gang Report*.

GANG PRESENCE IN OUR SCHOOLS

>> LO 7.6   Provide an overview of gangs in schools.

Gangs are having an increasing presence in schools, especially in urban areas. They bring weapons and drugs into the school, and members of opposing gangs may battle on the premises. Recruiters may react violently against students who refuse to join. While it is difficult to know exactly how many students are gang members, Table 7.2 shows the percentage of students age 12 to 18 who reported a gang presence in their schools.

FIGURE 7.4

Cross-Border Gang Activity in 2015

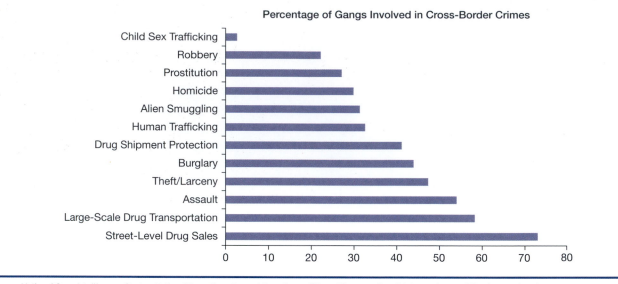

Percentage of Gangs Involved in Cross-Border Crimes

Source: National Gang Intelligence Center, *National Gang Report 2015*, https://www.fbi.gov/file-repository/stats-services-publications-national-gang-report-2015.pdf/view.

Note: Most recent data available at time of publication.

A significant presence of gang members in a school creates a chaotic and unpredictable environment. Gang members feel free to "raise hell" at school and generally do not want to study, contributing to higher rates of absences, suspensions, and dropouts. Getting an education in an academic setting is often not encouraged by gang leadership, who instead promote acquiring a "street" education and hustling to earn money.

TABLE 7.2

Percentage of Students Age 12 to 18 Reporting Gangs Were Present at School by Location, 2011 to 2015

YEAR	TOTAL	MALE	FEMALE	PUBLIC SCHOOL	PRIVATE SCHOOL
2011					
Urban	22.8	23.0	22.6	25.7	—
Rural	16.1	16.5	15.6	17.1	2.9
Suburban	12.1	10.2	14.1	12.5	—
2013					
Urban	18.3	18.6	18.0	19.9	4.6
Rural	10.8	11.7	9.8	11.7	—
Suburban	6.8	5.7	7.9	6.8	—
2015					
Urban	15.3	14.8	15.8	16.4	4.4
Rural	10.2	10.7	9.6	10.7	—
Suburban	3.9	4.2	3.7	4.1	—

Source: National Center for Education Statistics, "Percentage of Students Ages 12–18 Who Reported That Gangs Were Present at School During the School Year, by Selected Student and School Characteristics and Location; Selected Years 2001 Through 2015," *Digest of Education Statistics* (2016), https://nces.ed.gov/programs/digest/d16/tables/dt16_230.20.asp.

Note: Most recent data available at time of publication

GANG PREVENTION

>> **LO 7.7**   **Describe gang prevention efforts.**

Law enforcement and social agencies have tried to combat the presence of gangs. Reaching into neighborhoods, many programs try to stop at-risk youths from joining gangs, helping them learn skills to make better decisions. The most popular antigang program is Gang Resistance Education and Training (**G.R.E.A.T.**), which started at the Phoenix, Arizona, Police Department in 1991. Using federal funds, G.R.E.A.T. sent law enforcement officers into classrooms to teach life skills to middle school students and help them choose life options other than joining a gang. Based on the success of the program, the Phoenix Police Department; the Bureau of Alcohol, Tobacco, and Firearms; and the Federal Law Enforcement Training Center joined forces to expand the program nationally. By 1995, more than 500,000 middle school students nationwide had completed the G.R.E.A.T. curriculum. While the program demonstrated some effectiveness at combating the allure of gangs, it was still unclear if it was successful in deterring gang membership.[21]

Young members of a G.R.E.A.T. program. How do such pro-social programs provide positive alternatives for youth?

After a lengthy evaluation in 2000, a new G.R.E.A.T. curriculum was introduced in 14 cities in 2003. The program has continued to evolve in cities nationwide, with the hopes of deterring gang membership. Currently, the federal Office of Juvenile Justice and Delinquency Prevention has become an active partner, and the Bureau of Justice Administration provides financial support for G.R.E.A.T. instructors. The program also works with other organizations such as the Boys and Girls Clubs of America and Families and Schools Together.

A recent evaluation of G.R.E.A.T. compared students who had completed the G.R.E.A.T. program and students who had not completed the program. As students complete the program in middle school, researchers wanted to know if the positive results achieved by the program persisted into high school for these participants. Students were questioned in the 10th and 11th grades, generally 3 years after completion of G.R.E.A.T. programming. Participants were found to have more positive attitudes about the police and less positive attitudes about gangs after completion of the program. In addition, students used more prosocial behaviors in addressing conflict, and lower rates of gang membership were reported.[22]

NAVIGATING THE FIELD 7.1

Project BUILD

Project BUILD (Broader Urban Involvement and Leadership Development) is a Chicago-based violence prevention curriculum for youths in detention who come from a community with gang presence. Using several popular gang prevention strategies, the program provides sports and recreational activities, field trips, leadership, and civic engagement for youths in some of Chicago's most crime-ridden and economically depressed neighborhoods.

Putting It Into Action

Using your Internet search engine, research this program and its implementation. In your opinion, why has this program been so successful? Could it be implemented in other urban areas? Record your conclusions in a Word document, and submit that document to your instructor when asked to do so. ●

LEAVING A GANG

>> **LO 7.8**   **Describe the problems involved in leaving a gang.**

It is a common myth that gang membership is based on a "blood-in, blood-out" process, meaning that it is not easy to leave a gang and that any attempts to do so may leave the "quitter" either dead or seriously injured. However, this is often untrue for youth gang members. The majority of youths who join a gang do not stay in it for an extended amount of time, on average remaining active for 1 to 2 years. Only 1 out of 10 gang members actually stays in a gang for 4 years or more. A youth who is more embedded in a gang and derives his or her identity from gang membership is more likely to maintain ties to the group.[23]

Leaving a gang, often termed *desistance* by gang scholars, is generally a gradual process. This departure can simply be a matter of aging out of the gang life or becoming disillusioned with its culture. Former members have gotten stable jobs, married and/or had children, and moved into a different life phase. Sometimes desisters have witnessed violence against a friend or loved one by a gang and want to leave the lifestyle before more harm occurs. ●

SUMMARY

›› LO 7.1   Describe how gangs developed in the United States.

Juvenile gangs in the United States have origins that can be traced as far back as the American Revolution. As the rate of immigration dramatically increased in the late 1800s and early 1900s, gangs associated with various ethnicities began to develop in urban areas. The gangs of the mid-1900s focused more on the protection of turf and frequently resorted to violence. However, as the 21st century began, supergangs like the Bloods and Crips were formed, and these groups became heavily involved in violence, drug activity, and other criminal enterprises.

Key Terms

supergang   114   turf   114   urban gangs   113

›› LO 7.2   Define the term *gang* and describe today's gang activities.

The U.S. Department of Justice has provided clear criteria for identifying a gang, including the requirement of at least three persons who represent the gang with symbols, clothing, or other markings. The goal of a gang is to maintain its reputation and power, often through intimidation and criminality. Gang life can be very appealing to youths, especially young men, as it provides protection, financial stability, and a quasi-family unit that replaces home life.

Key Terms

gang   115

›› LO 7.3   Explain what an urban street gang is and give examples of types of gangs.

There are different types of urban street gangs. Some gangs are extremely organized and participate in a variety of lucrative criminal behaviors, while others are disorganized and not very successful. In addition, gangs can be organized in different ways based on leadership style. Gang members can be initiated through simple methods, such as verbal alliances, or with more involved and even violent methods.

Key Terms

corporate gangs   117   influential structure   117   territorial gangs   117
hedonistic gangs   117   instrumental gangs   117   vertical/hierarchical
horizontal/commission   predatory gangs   117   structure   117
    structure   117   scavenger gangs   117

›› LO 7.4   Show how race and ethnicity relate to gang involvement and gang activity.

Gangs are generally organized based on race. African American and Asian gangs are often immersed in drug enterprises. While Caucasian gangs can also be involved with drug trafficking, they are better known for hate crimes against minority groups. Hispanic gangs are also known for drug trafficking and often severe violence.

>> LO 7.5   Describe some of the illegal activities that gangs engage in.

Gang members engage in a variety of activity, ranging from non-violent behaviors to violent homicides. Distribution and possession of drugs is a frequent criminal enterprise by gangs. In addition, gangs participate in a variety of property crimes, financial scams, and crimes against persons.

Key Term

cross-border gangs   120

>> LO 7.6   Provide an overview of gangs in schools.

Gangs are a prominent presence in many high schools, especially in low-income, urban areas. As violence can often infiltrate schools as a result of gang presence, the G.R.E.A.T. program has become a mainstay in many of these schools. This program, taught by law enforcement officers, provides prosocial alternatives and resources to at-risk youth.

>> LO 7.7   Describe gang prevention efforts.

The key to gang prevention is providing alternative, prosocial options and resources for at-risk youth. One of the most effective programs is G.R.E.A.T., a law enforcement-guided programed that provides youth with life skills and legal alternatives to the gang lifestyle.

Key Term

G.R.E.A.T.   123

>> LO 7.8   Describe the problems involved in leaving a gang.

Leaving a gang can be a difficult process, as loyalty is key to many gangs. However, an aging process often occurs where members merge into a more legitimate lifestyle.

DISCUSSION QUESTIONS

1. This chapter focuses mainly on urban gangs, but there are also gangs located in suburban and rural areas. How do these gangs differ in purpose and behaviors?

2. Gang membership and identity are often rooted in a dislike for other races and ethnic groups. Can this attitude be traced back to the historical time periods of immigration and the civil rights movements?

EXPLORING JUVENILE JUSTICE FURTHER

1. Read the report in Appendix C "Gangs in Schools," then interview a school administrator and ask which of the three strategies they use (prevention, intervention, and/or suppression) and which has been most effective.

2. Interview an employee of a public school in your jurisdiction where the G.R.E.A.T. program has been implemented. Ask him or her about the opinion of the program and its effectiveness.

$SAGE edge™

Give your students the SAGE edge!

SAGE edge offers a robust online environment featuring an impressive array of free tools and resources for review, study, and further exploration, keeping both instructors and students on the cutting edge of teaching and learning. Learn more at **edge.sagepub.com/schmallegerjj**.

8

Juveniles and Violence

After reading this chapter you should be able to

1. Identify some of the risk and protective factors for juvenile violence
2. Describe some of the risk factors associated with youth gun violence
3. Describe school violence in elementary and secondary schools
4. Explain teen dating violence within the context of intimate partner violence
5. Explain the relationship between juvenile violence and violence in the media

Key Terms in Chapter 8

bullying
homicide
intimate partner violence

Olweus Bullying
    Questionnaire (OBQ)
physical dating violence
protective factors

risk factors
sexual dating violence
violence
youth gun violence

INTRODUCTION

Charles "Andy" Williams is now 33 years old but vividly remembers the day in 2001 when he stole his father's .22 revolver and took it to school. He brought with him plenty of ammunition, hid in a bathroom stall, and jumped out shooting when the halls of California's Santana High School were filled with students. Two people died, and 13 others were injured.[1]

Williams is one of around 40 people who have taken firearms into American schools and opened fire. Most are male, teenagers, white, and from a rural or suburban neighborhood. Most attacked the school they attended, and they obtained guns from their own homes or from family members.

In June of 2018, 17 years after Williams's crime, *The Wall Street Journal* sent a reporter to California's Ironwood State Prison, where Williams is serving a 50-year-to-life sentence for first-degree murder. The purpose of the trip was to interview Williams and find out why he and others like him committed the crimes they did. During the interview Williams told of bullying at school. Although he was only 5 feet 4 inches tall at the time of the shooting, he's grown a foot taller and now stands at nearly 6 feet 5 inches.

Williams lived with his father after the age of 3, when divorce broke apart his family. His mother and half brother moved away, but all reports show that his father, who continues to visit him regularly in prison, doted on him. By the age of 12 he was using narcotics and started taking pills and snorting cocaine. It wasn't long before he surrounded himself with other young people who were into drugs. Left unattended during the day by his working father, he often skipped school and hung out with

Charles "Andy" Williams (left) at an arraignment on March 7, 2001. Williams shot two of his fellow students to death at Santana High School in Santee, California. Thirteen others were wounded when Williams jumped from a bathroom stall and fired 40 shots at classmates. What motivates school shooters like Williams?

NANCEE E. LEWIS/AFP/Getty Images

friends, smoking weed or downing opiates obtained from a friend whose mother had been diagnosed with Lyme disease. Soon his grades began to fall, and before long he was labeled a problem student. The bullying, he said, was constant. "In high school," he told the interviewer, "if they see a kid not fighting back, they think he's an easy target. I was little and easy, I guess."

Soon Williams became the target of an adult sexual predator who was the live-in boyfriend of one of his friends. The man bought alcohol and drugs and provided them to the teenagers, who repaid him with sexual favors. Williams, embarrassed by what was taking place, thought about killing himself. Before the shooting, a teacher embarrassed Williams further in front of his class by telling everyone he was failing. That was when Williams resolved to shoot the teacher and took the .22 caliber pistol from his father's gun case. After he started shooting he reloaded three or four times, using up most of the bullets he had brought. Then the police arrived and ordered him to the ground, and he surrendered without resisting. Today Williams is held in protective custody, fearing for his life after refusing to stab another inmate as he was ordered to do by a prison gang leader.

JUVENILE VIOLENCE

>> LO 8.1   Identify some of the risk and protective factors for juvenile violence.

Juvenile delinquents are not all the same. They vary in shape and size, race and gender, and of course, criminality. Some juveniles participate in delinquent behaviors for only a few months, while others stretch it into adulthood and become offenders who are more proficient in their criminality. Furthermore, the method of criminality can differ greatly between youths, especially when it comes to violence.

According to the Violence Prevention Alliance, **violence** is the "intentional use of physical force or power, threatened or actual, against oneself, another person, or against a group or community, that either results in or has a high likelihood of resulting in injury, death, psychological harm, maldevelopment, or deprivation."[2] Youths can experience violence as victims, offenders, or bystanders. They can be the direct recipients of violence or hear about violence on television or social media. No matter the level of intensity or duration of the exposure to violence, the concept of violence is becoming further immersed in the lives of young people. This chapter will explore the different facets of violence that are a part of the lives of juveniles in the United States.

Risks and Protective Factors

While it may seem easy to label all juvenile offenders as delinquents, many of these youths are quite distinguishable by certain characteristics or **risk factors**. These risk factors can be found at various levels, such as individual factors or factors associated with the community where a youth resides. Youths who demonstrate patterns of chronic violence generally exhibit behaviors and personality traits that separate

Weapons are often smuggled into schools, hidden in backpacks and bags. How can such smuggling be prevented?

A teenager aims a handgun. What are the causes of juvenile violence?

them from other, less serious delinquents.[3] Violent youths participate in high frequencies of delinquent behaviors, including violent acts, and have had interventions with the juvenile justice system throughout childhood. In addition, they have a difficult time meeting expectations at school and with family. Figure 8.1 provides a full list of risk factors associated with violent juvenile behavior.

FIGURE 8.1

Risk Factors of Youth Violence

Source: Centers for Disease Control and Prevention. (2017). *Youth violence: Risk and protective factors.*

Conversely, there are also behaviors that decrease the likelihood that a youth will participate in violent behaviors. These are called **protective factors**. Much like risk factors, protective factors can be found at different levels surrounding a youth, including family characteristics and peer factors. While none of these protective factors is a foolproof buffer against participating in violent behavior, they definitely help dissuade a young person from veering toward a life of juvenile violence. Figure 8.2 provides a full list of protective factors associated with violent juvenile behavior.

FIGURE 8.2

Protective Factors of Youth Violence

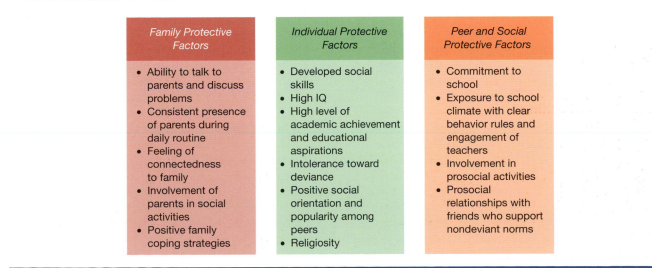

Source: Centers for Disease Control and Prevention. (2017). *Youth violence: Risk and protective factors.*

There is no guarantee that youths who experience one or more of these factors will absolutely commit violent acts or vice versa. However, what can be certain is that the more risk factors present in the life of a juvenile, the higher the likelihood that he or she will participate in violent behavior. These factors can strongly influence the decision to be aggressive and use other forms of violence.

YOUTH GUN VIOLENCE

>> **LO 8.2** **Describe some of the risk factors associated with youth gun violence.**

While atrocious mass shootings such as Sandy Hook Elementary and Parkland High School are the focus of media coverage for weeks after the event, these occurrences actually account for less than 1% of gun deaths each year.[4] Deaths attributed to gun violence are more often single-victim events and targeted at a particular individual. However, these statistics are not to diminish how prevalent gun violence has become in the lives of American youths.

The Office of Juvenile Justice and Delinquency Prevention defined **youth gun violence** as intentional use of a firearm to threaten or harm others, by a person age 10 to 24 years.[5] Almost 70% of youth **homicide** (aka commission of murderous acts) offenders are African Americans, and 27% are Caucasian, with 90% of known homicide offenders being male. The rate of firearm-related homicides caused by juveniles has fluctuated over the years, most recently decreasing by 39% between 2007 and 2014.

If a young person is the victim of gun violence, he or she has been injured or killed as a result of the use of a firearm by a person of any age who intended to threaten or harm someone (even if the youth was not the original target). About 20% of the 33,000 gun-related deaths each year in the United States involve victims under the age of 25, and gun violence is the third leading cause of homicide among young people.[6] Of those youths killed by a firearm, 68% of victims are African Americans and 19% are Hispanics. Furthermore, almost 90% of homicide victims between ages 10 and 24 years are male, and the majority live in urban areas. Of the 5,504 youths between the ages of 10 and 24 years who committed suicide in 2014, about half involved a firearm.[7] The majority of youths who use a firearm to commit suicide are white, and males are highly more likely than women to use a firearm.

While there is not one single risk factor or specific combination of factors that can accurately predict youth gun violence, increased exposure to multiple risk factors can have a significant effect on participation in this form of violence. The following risk factors have the most significant effect on youth gun violence, as can be

Breed v. Jones, 421 U.S. 519 (1975)

Gary Jones was 17 years old when he was charged with robbery. He was detained and then adjudicated in juvenile court for robbery. Later, he was tried as an adult and convicted of robbery in criminal court. Jones filed a writ of habeas corpus under the violation of the double jeopardy clause. His writ was denied by the trial court, court of appeal, and Supreme Court of California. He then filed for a writ of habeas corpus with the federal district court, but it was denied on the ground that the juvenile proceedings and adult proceedings were so different, it did not qualify as double jeopardy. The U.S. Court of Appeals of the Ninth Circuit reversed the decision, reasoning that protection against double jeopardy would not impede the juvenile courts.

In May 1975, the U.S. Supreme Court ruled unanimously in favor of Jones. Written by Justice Anthony Kennedy, the decision remanded the lower court decision, stating that the criminal trial in adult court had put Jones in double jeopardy. The court stated that juvenile courts should make the decision to transfer a youth to adult court before adjudication, rather than holding with two separate proceedings.

1. **Do you agree with the ruling?**

2. **Based on his age and the crime, do you feel Gary Jones should have been tried in adult court originally or only in juvenile court?**

3. **In your opinion, would this ruling be the same today?**

Online Case Opinion

https://caselaw.findlaw.com/us-supreme-court/421/519.html •

seen in Figure 8.3: exposure to violence, access to firearms, emotional distress, peer delinquency, and alcohol use.

There have been numerous federal gun laws passed to regulate the sale and use of firearms, including the Brady Handgun Violence Prevention Act of 1993. The Brady Act required new standards for selling and purchasing firearms, including a 5-day waiting period before a licensed seller can transfer a gun to a buyer and mandatory background checks for individuals purchasing firearms. Over 3,200 laws passed by states have either loosened or tightened gun restrictions,[8] but some of those laws have actually made stricter requirements than what Brady originally set. Some states have adopted stricter background requirements,[9] and other states, such as Massachusetts, require citizens to report not only sales but also transfers and inheritances of firearms.[10]

FIGURE 8.3

Risk Factors of Youth Gun Violence

Access to firearms	Residing in homes with firearms not safely stored
	Peers with homes with firearms not safely stored
Alcohol use	Alcohol in the home and unhealthy use by parents
	Unhealthy use of alcohol by peers
	Use of alcohol at an early age
Emotional distress	Anxiety
	Depression
	Posttraumatic stress syndrome
Exposure to violence	Personal victimization by violence
	Witnessing victimization of others
Peer delinquency	Participation of peers in violence
	Pressure from peers to participate in violence

Other federal acts have specifically addressed juvenile use and possession of handguns. The Youth Handgun Safety Act, part of the Violent Crime Control and Law Enforcement Act of 1994, changed the legal age of handgun possession to 18 years old. Under the Gun-Free Schools Act, passed in 1994, students who bring a firearm to school must be expelled for at least a year.[11]

SCHOOL VIOLENCE AND VICTIMIZATION IN ELEMENTARY AND SECONDARY EDUCATION SETTINGS

≫ LO 8.3 **Describe school violence in elementary and secondary schools.**

It is not unusual for the term *school violence* to be associated with school shootings. However, school violence and victimization actually reference a range of behaviors. They can include theft of possessions, vandalism, and physical and verbal bullying. They can also include physical and sexual assault, as well as homicide. Furthermore, school violence and victimization do not include just incidences between students. Violence and victimization at school can involve teachers and staff members as victims or offenders.[12]

School violence and victimization can occur at any geographical location related to school events. Not surprisingly, violent events can occur in classrooms, gymnasiums, and cafeterias. They can also occur on athletic fields at a home institution or during an away game. In addition, violence and victimization can occur on a school bus or a school-sponsored field trip.

FREDERIC J. BROWN/AFP/Getty Images

A mother and daughter hug following a school shooting. Why have school shootings become so commonplace in the U.S.?

One of the most comprehensive projects on violence and victimization in schools is Crime and Safety Surveys, produced by the National Center for Education Statistics, which collects data on crime and safety measures in elementary and secondary schools in the United States.[13] Data were compiled from the following sources: the National Crime Victimization Survey, the School Crime Supplement to the National Crime Victimization Survey, the Youth Risk Behavior Survey, the School Survey on Crime and Safety, the Schools and Staffing Survey, EDFacts, and the Campus Safety and Security Survey. These surveys were completed by either principals, teachers, or students. Figure 8.4 highlights some of the key findings from the most recent report of 2016 data.

Bullying

School **bullying** is commonly defined as the victimization of a student with targeted aggression by one or more other students.[14] This can include physical assault, deliberately ignoring that student, spreading rumors, and other hurtful behaviors. To be considered an act of bullying, the behavior should be a repeated occurrence and not just a solitary event. In other words, an offender has to commit an act of aggression or harassment (e.g., physical assault, name-calling, or theft of personal belongings) on more than one occasion for it to be considered bullying.

The **Olweus Bullying Questionnaire (OBQ)** is administered every year to measure bullying and antisocial behaviors in school. Students in the third through twelfth grades are questioned on their own experiences with school bullying. During the 2013–2014 school year, more than 150,000 surveys were collected from 629 schools in the United States. Findings from this most recent administration of the OBQ

FIGURE 8.4

Highlights of Violence and Victimization Events in Elementary and Secondary Schools

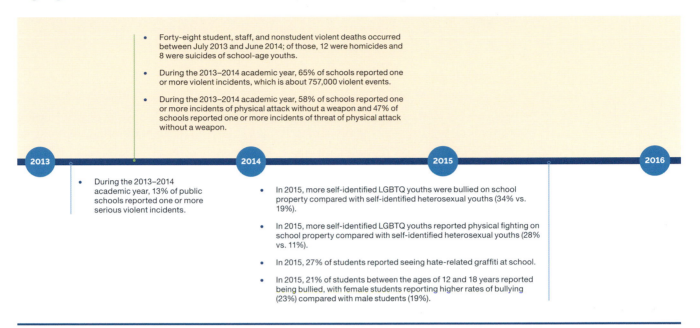

- Forty-eight student, staff, and nonstudent violent deaths occurred between July 2013 and June 2014; of those, 12 were homicides and 8 were suicides of school-age youths.

- During the 2013–2014 academic year, 65% of schools reported one or more violent incidents, which is about 757,000 violent events.

- During the 2013–2014 academic year, 58% of schools reported one or more incidents of physical attack without a weapon and 47% of schools reported one or more incidents of threat of physical attack without a weapon.

2013   **2014**   **2015**   **2016**

- During the 2013–2014 academic year, 13% of public schools reported one or more serious violent incidents.

- In 2015, more self-identified LGBTQ youths were bullied on school property compared with self-identified heterosexual youths (34% vs. 19%).

- In 2015, more self-identified LGBTQ youths reported physical fighting on school property compared with self-identified heterosexual youths (28% vs. 11%).

- In 2015, 27% of students reported seeing hate-related graffiti at school.

- In 2015, 21% of students between the ages of 12 and 18 years reported being bullied, with female students reporting higher rates of bullying (23%) compared with male students (19%).

Source: National Center for Education Statistics, U.S. Department of Education.

indicated that an average of 14% of students reported being victims of bullying, while only 5% of students admitted to bullying another student. The percentage of juveniles who reported being bullied slowly decreased as youths got older. About 22% of third graders reported bullying, with this figure decreasing to 15% in the eighth grade. Those juveniles who self-reported bullying offending behaviors remained stable as age increased, generally ranging from 4% to 6% of youths between third and twelfth grade.

The OBQ also examined the findings comparing boys and girls. Girls are more likely to be the victims of physical bullying, and boys are more likely to be the offending bullies. In addition, the frequency of students who are bullied and also bully others varies between the sexes. The rate of girls who bully and are bullied stays relatively constant between third and twelfth grade, ranging from 10% to 12% of respondents. However, the rate of boys who both bully and are bullied rose from 14% of respondents in third grade to 23% of respondents in twelfth grade.

There are also differences in the types of bullying directed at each sex. While many types of behaviors can be considered bullying, the OBQ categorized these bullying behaviors in 10 different ways:

An adolescent uses a computer to interact with friends in a social network. How does the Internet influence attitudes among young people today?

©iStockphoto.com/Marta Ortiz

1. Cyber—via mobile phone, computer, or electronic device

2. Damage—personal property damaged or taken

3. Exclusion—left out or completely ignored on purpose

4. Physical—hit, kicked, or punched

5. Racial—prejudicial behavior based on race
6. Rumors—spreading false rumors or lies
7. Sexual—words, gestures, or other behaviors with sexual innuendo
8. Threat—threatened or forced to do things undesired
9. Verbal—called mean names or teased hurtfully
10. Other—all other bullying behaviors

As can be seen in Figure 8.5, verbal bullying occurs for both boys and girls at very similar rates. However, the remaining forms of bullying occur at different frequencies for both sexes.

Deaths at School

The Centers for Disease Control (CDC) defined school-associated violent death as a fatal injury (homicide, suicide, or legal intervention) on school property, on the way to or from school, or on the way to or from or during a school-sponsored event.[15] Since 1992, the CDC has been collecting data on school-associated violent deaths, most recently with the School-Associated Violent Death Study (SAVD). The SAVD presents the most recent data on deaths, common features of these events, and potential risks for perpetration and victimization. Based on data that were collected from 1992 to 2010, the CDC was able to determine that the majority of school-associated violent deaths occur before or after the school day or during lunch (i.e., transition times). In addition, they are more likely to occur at the beginning of each semester. About 50% of perpetrators of school-associated deaths gave a warning signal, such as making threats or leaving a note before the event. In the school-associated deaths that involved a firearm, the firearm generally came from the perpetrator's home or from a friend/relative.

FIGURE 8.5

Victimization by Bullying: Comparison of the Sexes

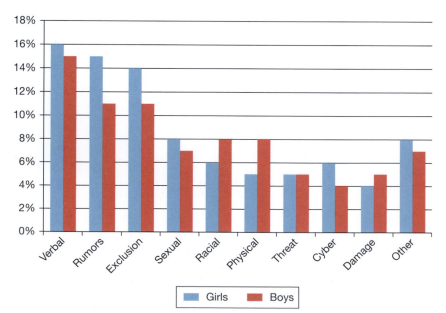

Source: Luxenberg, H., Limber, S., & Olweus, D. (2015). *Bullying in U.S. Schools: 2014 Status Report.* Hazelden Publishing.

It is also important to note that the SAVD revealed that homicide is the second leading cause of death in youths between the ages of 5 and 18 years. However, only 2% of these deaths occurred on school property or going to or from school. While it is extremely important to stress school safety and working toward prevention of school violence, these findings indicate the necessity of education and efforts in the community as well.

TEEN DATING VIOLENCE

>> LO 8.4   Explain teen dating violence within the context of intimate partner violence.

The adolescent years should include developing a sense of independence and creating a sense of identity, which includes figuring out what traits are attractive in a potential romantic partner. While dating can be a fun and exciting part of the middle and high school years, it can also be a tumultuous and dangerous time should a teen become involved in a violent relationship. Physical and sexual dating violence is a growing and prominent problem for middle and high school students in the United States.[16] Many teenagers are becoming involved in relationships that are based on fear, intimidation, and assaultive behavior. This type of relationship behavior, often called **intimate partner violence**, can include physical, sexual, emotional, and psychological aggression.[17]

According to the 2015 National Youth Risk Behavior Survey, about 10% of 11- to 17-year-old students experienced some form of **physical dating violence**, which includes pinching, hitting, slapping, kicking, punching, and shoving. In addition, 10% of this same age group experienced **sexual dating violence**, including forcing a partner to participate in any sex act without consent. When comparing dating violence experiences by sex, 21% of female high school students and 10% of male high school students reported physical and/or sexual dating violence.[18] The following factors and behaviors have been linked to both forms of dating violence:

- Older juveniles
- Drug and alcohol abuse
- Participation in risky sexual behaviors
- Sexual minorities (homosexual or bisexual)

While there is educational programming on healthy relationships available for middle and high school students, some of these programs are limited in their audience. It is important to note that victims of intimate partner violence are not just women, as the rate of victimization against males is growing. In addition, sexual minorities are experiencing dating violence at alarming rates, so assuming that violence occurs only in a male–female relationship is incorrect.

JUVENILE VIOLENCE AND THE MEDIA

>> LO 8.5   Explain the relationship between juvenile violence and violence in the media.

There has been much debate about the potential criminogenic effects of violent television, movies, and games. Extensive psychological research has linked exposure to violent media to aggressive behaviors and antisocial conditions.[19] In other words, juveniles who watch violent movies and TV, as well as those who play violent video games, are more likely to participate in violent behaviors themselves. The release of video games such as *Mortal Kombat* in the 1990s triggered parental concern that youths were becoming exposed to too much violence, and the continued

Children playing a video game. Why do some people think that violent video games can lead to real-world violence?

release of violent game series such as *Grand Theft Auto* and *Resident Evil* has increased the verbal outcry against these kinds of games. The General Aggression Model asserted that violent media exposure desensitizes youths. After repeated exposure to that behavior in media, youths become less fearful of it and it becomes normal, even acceptable behavior. These youths become less empathetic when violent events occur and may even participate in more violent behaviors.[20]

Not surprisingly, there are definitely arguments against the assertion that violent media is causing our youths to be more violent. Multiple studies have found no relationship between violent media and violent behavior. Critics have argued that exposure to these violent forms of media is simply part of growing up and does not have an influential effect on everyday behavior.[21] Even the U.S. Supreme Court weighed in on this controversy in *Brown v. Entertainment Merchants Association* (2011).[22] The court ruled that California's law restricting minors' access to violent video games was unconstitutional. Justice Antonin Scalia wrote in the majority opinion:

> The State's evidence is not compelling. California relies primarily on the research of Dr. Craig Anderson and a few other research psychologists whose studies purport to show a connection between exposure to violent video games and harmful effects on children. These studies have been rejected by every court to consider them, and with good reason: They do not prove that violent video games *cause* minors to *act* aggressively.

In other words, the court did not believe that sufficient evidence existed to prove that exposure to violent video games could cause juveniles to commit aggressive acts. ●

NAVIGATING THE FIELD 8.1

Operation Ceasefire

Operation Ceasefire (aka the Boston Gun Project and the Boston Miracle) is a problem-oriented policing program that was initiated in Boston, Massachusetts, in 1996. Based on deterrence theory, it involves combatting interstate gun traffickers who provide firearms to minors. When able, the program works in collaboration with street gangs to build a no-tolerance culture toward gun violence. Studies have shown a 63% reduction in youth homicide attributable to the program, and it has become a federally funded initiative that has spread nationwide.

Putting It Into Action

Use the web to research this program and its implementation (one site to visit is https://operationceasefire.com).

Create a Word document that details your opinion of whether the program can bring about long-lasting change in the area of gun control.

Submit that document to your instructor when asked to do so. ●

>> LO. 8.1   Identify some of the risk and protective factors for juvenile violence.

It is impossible to pinpoint a factor or factors that always cause juvenile violence, but there are many factors that increase the risk of it occurring. For example, youths who are chronically violent and delinquent, as well as those with antisocial beliefs and a history of violent victimization, are more likely to commit violence. Conversely, protective factors such as strong family and community bonds, prosocial attitudes, and high academic achievement decrease the likelihood of violence.

Key Terms

protective factors   129   risk factors   128   violence   128

>> LO. 8.2   Describe some of the risk factors associated with youth gun violence.

Youth gun violence is defined as the use of a firearm to threaten or harm others, by a person age 10 to 24 years. The majority of offenders are African American, and about 40% of firearm-related homicides are caused by juveniles. Risk factors associated with youth gun violence include access to firearms, alcohol use, emotional distress, exposure to violence, and peer delinquency. Numerous federal and state laws have been passed to curb the sale and use of firearms by youths in the hope of decreasing firearm violence and death.

Key Terms

homicide   130   youth gun violence   130

>> LO. 8.3   Describe school violence in elementary and secondary schools.

The term *school violence* does not mean just school shootings but also applies to assault and bullying behaviors. School violence can involve teachers, staff, and students. In addition, school violence is not limited to events on school property but includes violence at athletic events (home or away), on school buses, and during school-sponsored field trips.

Key Terms

bullying   132   Olweus Bullying Questionnaire (OBQ)   132

>> LO 8.4   Explain teen dating violence within the context of intimate partner violence.

Physical and sexual dating violence are continuing to increase in frequency for middle and high school students. Often called intimate partner violence, this behavior can include physical, sexual, emotional, and psychological aggression. The following characteristics and behaviors of juveniles are more likely to be linked to these forms of violence: older, sexual minorities, drug and alcohol use, and risky sexual behavior.

Key Terms

intimate partner violence   135   physical dating violence   135   sexual dating violence   135

>> LO 8.5   Explain the relationship between juvenile violence and violence in the media.

Not surprisingly, there is a lack of societal agreement on the effects of violent video games, television, and other media on the incidence of juvenile violence. Some individuals argue that consistent viewing of such material desensitizes youths, increasing the likelihood that they will find such behavior acceptable and will be less empathetic when violence occurs. However, critics of this argument suggest that exposure to violent media does not influence behavior. Even the U.S. Supreme Court has ruled it unconstitutional to deny minors access to violent video games.

DISCUSSION QUESTIONS

1. How have preventive and reactive measures toward school violence changed since you were in middle and high school? What did your school do to address the issue?

2. Do you feel that some recent school shootings could have been prevented? Why or why not?

3. How can schools better educate youths on healthy relationship behaviors? When should this kind of program be implemented?

EXPLORING JUVENILE JUSTICE FURTHER

1. Compare and contrast two video games considered violent by their ratings. In your opinion, what components make them risky for juvenile use?

2. Choose a private school and a public school in your state of origin. How do their policies on addressing physical and sexual violence between students compare?

$SAGE edge™

Give your students the SAGE edge!

SAGE edge offers a robust online environment featuring an impressive array of free tools and resources for review, study, and further exploration, keeping both instructors and students on the cutting edge of teaching and learning. Learn more at **edge.sagepub.com/schmallegerjj**.

9 Juveniles and Cybercrime

After reading this chapter you should be able to

1. Explain the emergence of cybercrime

2. Define digital piracy and discuss the perception of many juveniles that it is an acceptable form of behavior

3. Define cyberbullying and describe its categories

4. Define cyberstalking and cyberharrassment

5. Identify various forms of online sexual exploitation

6. Describe the behaviors and values of the hacking community

Key Terms in Chapter 9

black hats	digital piracy	revenge porn
cyberbullying	hackers	sexting
cybercrime	hacking	sextortion
cyberstalking	Internet	white hats

INTRODUCTION

In 2008, Jonathan Joseph James shot himself in the head in the shower of his home. He was 24 years old. James, however, will always hold a not-so-enviable record: He was the first juvenile incarcerated for cybercrime in the United States. Born in South Florida, James was 15 when he committed his first offense—a hack of the Miami-Dade school system's computers. After that, he became a prolific hacker. He was brought down a year later when he attacked computers of the federal Defense Threat Reduction Agency, a part of the U.S. Defense Department (DOD).[1] In the attack, James obtained mission-critical NASA files, including software used to control the living habitat inside the International Space Station. The news caused NASA to disconnect its computers from the Internet for 3 weeks while an investigation was underway. Federal agents were able to identify James as the source of the DOD attacks, and his house was raided in January of 2000. A few months later, he entered into a plea agreement under which he admitted to two counts of juvenile delinquency. He was sentenced to 7 months of house arrest and placed on probation until his 18th birthday. Under the terms of the agreement, he was banned from the recreational use of computers. He soon violated the probationary terms when he tested positive for drugs. Following the failed drug test James was arrested and sent to a federal correctional facility, where he served a 6-month sentence.

Jonathan James, the first American juvenile incarcerated for cybercrimes. Could his case have been handled some other way?

The prison experience appeared to have a huge impact on James, and he vowed never to return. Not long after his release, however, some of his cyber associates carried out a massive data breach of numerous department stores' computers, and authorities began to investigate James's possible involvement in the scheme. While credible evidence linking James to the crimes was never found, he apparently believed that he would soon be arrested again—a belief that led to his suicide. He left a note in which he wrote: "I honestly, honestly had nothing to do with [these crimes, but] I have no faith in the 'justice' system."

THE INTERNET

>> LO 9.1   Explain the emergence of cybercrime.

The Internet has dramatically changed the lives of many youths, but it has also opened up a variety of new possibilities for crime—much of it involving young people. The Internet can be traced back to the early 1960s, when J. C. R. Licklider of the Massachusetts Institute of Technology (MIT) proposed the idea of an internationally connected set of computers, known as the Intergalactic Computer Network. Working with MIT colleagues, Licklider pressed for improvements in networking capabilities and efficiency. Licklider and colleagues eventually created a set of interconnected computers called the ARPANET, which evolved into the Internet. While large corporations were active in the early days of Internet, using computer systems that took up entire rooms, Internet did not become popular in homes and businesses until the 1990s.

The **Internet** we know today is a global network of interconnected networks using standardized protocols, allowing people to share information, pictures, and other data. We have become dependent on it for shopping, paying bills, researching, maintaining relationships, and even getting an education. Because the Internet contributes to many different types of activities, it has also provided a new nexus for criminality—and it often does not take a degree from MIT to commit crime online, known as cybercrime. **Cybercrime** is the "destruction, theft, or unauthorized or illegal use, modification or copy of information, programs, services, equipment or communication networks."[2] In other words, cybercrime is any crime that uses technology, including computers, smartphones, and the Internet itself.

Cybercrime can range from the smallest online credit card theft to the biggest Ponzi scheme. Someone can request a mail-order bride and get scammed out of a lot of money or become the victim of a nasty malware infection. Similarly, terrorist groups can recruit and raise funds online. This chapter will review common forms of cybercrime, especially those often committed or experienced by juveniles.

Digital piracy of music and movies has been economically detrimental o the entertainment industry. How can it be prevented?

DIGITAL PIRACY

>> LO 9.2   Define digital piracy and discuss the perception of many juveniles that it is an acceptable form of behavior.

For years, a popular target for young shoplifters was cassette tapes, and later music CDs. Today, music and other digital material are often stolen on the Internet. This material can be downloaded onto smartphones, iPods, and other electronic devices.

Digital piracy is the act of illegally copying music, movies, software, and other digital materials without permission from or payment to the copyright holder. Piracy behaviors are quite simple to carry out, possibly explaining why a great many such pirates are under age 21. Youths enjoy listening to music and watching movies, and the temptation to access them for free (albeit illegally) can be extremely alluring.[3] Juveniles generally pirate movies or music for convenience and not for the thrill of stealing. Several studies have estimated that digital music worth $14 billion has been stolen over the past decade or so. According to the Recording Industry Association of America, only 37% of music owned in the United States was legally purchased, and legitimate music sales have dropped by 50% since 1999, when file sharing was introduced. Even with all the free music available on apps and Internet radio, about 70% of Internet users admit to supporting the idea of digital piracy.[4]

The question is, how can someone justify stealing this material? Many people who would find it unfathomable to walk into a music store and steal a CD think nothing of illegally downloading music online. One potential explanation comes from social learning theory (discussed in Chapter 3), which asserts that criminal behavior is learned, much like tying your shoes or using a fork. Offenders learn these behaviors from people close to them. According to this theory, if your friends are illegally downloading online material and find it completely acceptable, you will mimic that behavior. After all, everyone is doing it!

Another view is found in Sykes and Matza's techniques of neutralization (see Chapter 3), under which offenders rationalize behaviors. They justify their behavior by denying that it causes any injury, or by telling themselves that everyone does it. For instance, offenders can justify that illegally downloading Beyoncé's newest song and not paying the $1.49 charge (on iTunes or Amazon Music) won't affect Beyoncé or her record company. However, if 100,000 Internet users steal the song, that's a loss of $149,000.[5]

Digital piracy is often overlooked by the juvenile court system because the system is overloaded with more serious cases, such as burglary, auto theft, and sexual assault. While legislation such as the Copyright Felony Act and the No Electronic Theft Act introduces higher fines and even prison sentences for adults who commit digital piracy, courts have generally taken a milder stance with juveniles. Antipiracy advertising campaigns on TV are often directed at juveniles, and if digital piracy is committed in a school, it could result in loss of computer privileges for the whole school.

CYBERBULLYING

>> **LO 9.3** **Define cyberbullying and describe its categories.**

Bullying is repeated, intentional, and aggressive behavior that is intended to establish dominance and intimidate.[6] The Internet version of bullying is called **cyberbullying**, which is the "willful and repeated harm inflicted through the use of computers, cell phones, and electronic devices."[7] Unlike physical bullying, just one act of cyberbullying can be repeated again and again virtually when one nasty and untrue post is passed on to others.

Cyberbullying can occur in many ways via electronic means, as described in Table 9.1.

TABLE 9.1

Categories of Cyberbullying

CATEGORY OF CYBERBULLYING	DEFINITION
Harassment	Insulting or taunting the victim through repetitive messages, such as e-mails, instant messages, or texts
Outing	Sharing of the victim's personal information with others without permission, such as telling others that a person who has not "come out" publicly is gay
Flaming	Hostile and insulting interaction in a chat room or on a discussion board, often involving the use of profanity
Denigration	Posting untrue and insulting information
Exclusion	Ostracizing a person

©iStockphoto.com/Spmemory

Cybercrimes can be committed with a variety of technological devices. Are they as serious as more traditional forms of criminal activity?

In many cases, cyberbullies have dominant personalities and short tempers.[8] Many youths who say their friends are cyberbullies are also cyberbullies themselves.[9] And cyberbullies are less likely to be caught than are bullies on the playground, because they can act anonymously on the Internet.[10]

Victims of cyberbullying, especially juveniles, often have a difficult time coping with the harassment, gossip, and humiliation that results from cyberbullying. They may not be physically abused, but they face many of the same outcomes as victims of physical bullying, such as dropping out of school, drug use, and even displaying aggression toward others.[11] They may experience anxiety, depression, loneliness, and suicidal thoughts, and may even attempt suicide.[12]

The Cyberbullying Research Center surveyed middle school and high school students in the United States regarding what would help block or reduce the impact of cyberbullying. More than 30% of these students reported that blocking a cyberbully online stopped the behavior, and 18.9% ignored the behavior. While 16.5% informed the cyberbully's parent, only 7.6% reported the perpetrator to the website, but those students who did said this was an effective strategy. Faced with losing privileges on Twitter, Facebook, or other social media, cyberbullies often end their behavior.[13] However, victims may also refrain from reporting cyberbullying for fear that their parents or guardians will take away their cell phones, laptops, or social media, not as a punishment but as a protective measure.

CYBERSTALKING

» LO 9.4   Define cyberstalking and cyberharrassment.

Most stalkers in physical space are familiar to their victims, such as would be the case with past romantic partners or shunned acquaintances. But online stalkers, known as cyberstalkers, may victimize complete strangers. **Cyberstalking** is the monitoring or harassment of another person on the Internet.[14] Cyberstalkers may access their victims' e-mail and social networking accounts without permission. They may then pretend to be the victim in posts and other communication. For instance, a female high school student (Girl 1) could log into the Instagram page of another student (Girl 2) and post nasty remarks about a male friend, making it seem as though Girl 2 was the writer. Cyberstalkers may also threaten to release personal information about their victims, continually send them unwanted instant messages, or post humiliating photographs of them.

Cyberstalking can be a part of cyber dating abuse. Current or former romantic partners, many of whom are juveniles or young adults, monitor the online behaviors, locations, and other activities of their victims. This is called "low-tech" cyberstalking. Cyberstalkers are often very open about their activities, location, and helpers, so their movements can usually be tracked by officials. In addition, there are "high-tech" methods, such as computer spyware apps, listening devices and bugs, and video or digital cameras, that allow some to stalk victims online without their knowledge.[15] GPS locators can be downloaded on a person's cell phone without their knowledge so the victim's movements can be tracked. Since most young people depend on the Internet to form and maintain relationships, they often find these forms of cyberstalking more acceptable as a way of checking up on what partners are doing.[16]

Cyberstalking is becoming a growing trend among young people as a way to monitor romantic partners. New federal and state laws are addressing cyberstalking as a serious criminal offense and have designated appropriate punishments. The National Conference of State Legislatures (NCSL) reports that many states have passed laws against cyberstalking or cyberharassment, often by adding new language to existing antistalking laws.[17] The NCSL defines these two activities this way:

> *Cyberstalking* is the use of the Internet, email or other electronic communications to stalk, and [it] generally refers to a pattern of threatening or malicious behaviors. Cyberstalking may be considered the most dangerous of the types of Internet harassment, based on posing a credible threat of harm. Sanctions range from misdemeanors to felonies.

> *Cyberharassment* differs from cyberstalking in that it is generally defined as not involving a credible threat. This behavior usually pertains to threatening or harassing email messages, instant messages, or blog entries or websites dedicated solely to tormenting an individual. Some states approach cyberharassment by including language addressing electronic communications in general harassment statutes, while others have created stand-alone cyberharassment statutes.

ONLINE SEXUAL OFFENSES BETWEEN ROMANTIC PARTNERS

>> **LO 9.5**   **Identify various forms of online sexual exploitation.**

Using the Internet, intimate partners can share personal and sexual material. If the relationship ends, one of the former partners may share this material online in a degrading way and without the other's permission. This can be extremely humiliating, demeaning, and disturbing for victims, their families, and friends. This section will discuss a few of the more prominent methods of online sexual exploitation experienced by juveniles, such as sexting, revenge porn, and sextortion.

IN THE MEDIA 9.1

Child Pornography and Sexting

A Florida news outlet reported that Phillip Alpert, age 18, and Jane Doe, age 16, had been dating for 2 years when Jane sent Alpert a nude picture of herself. Afterward the couple had an argument. As revenge, Alpert forwarded the picture to Jane's family and friends. Alpert was subsequently charged with possession and distribution of child pornography, as well as lewd and lascivious battery. He pled no contest and was sentenced to a year of probation. Under Florida law, Alpert also had to register as a sex offender and will remain on the list for at least 25 years. Being listed as a sex offender harmed his reputation, destroyed employment opportunities, and led to his expulsion from community college.

Putting It Into Action

To complete this active learning assignment, you should pair up with a friend (whether a classmate or not) and discuss the following questions:

How do you both feel about Alpert's punishment? Was it appropriate for his crime? Should Jane have also been punished (if so, how)? Should sexting offenders be required to register as sex offenders? Why should age matter?

Summarize the conclusions that you and your friend arrive at, and describe any differences in opinion.

Submit your work to your instructor when asked to do so. ●

Source: Renée Lamphere and K. Pikciunas, "Sexting, Sextortion, and Other Internet Sexual Offenses," in *The Intersection Between Intimate Partner Abuse, Technology and Cybercrime: Examining the Virtual Enemy,* eds. Jordana N. Navarro, Shelly Clevenger, and Catherine D. Marcum (Durham, NC: Carolina Academic Press, 2016), 141–165.

Tinker v. Des Moines Independent School District, 393 U.S. 503 (1969)

In December 1965, Mary Beth Tinker was 13 years old when she and a group of friends wore black armbands to protest the Vietnam War. The school board heard about the protest and passed a preemptive ban. Four other students were suspended, including Mary Beth's brother, John, and his friend Chris Eckhardt. They were not allowed to return to school until the armbands were removed. The suspended students returned after Christmas break without the armbands but wore black the rest of the year in protest.

Via their parents, the students sued the school district for violating their right to expression, claiming that the students should not have been disciplined. The district court dismissed the case, and the U.S. Court of Appeals of the Eighth Circuit confirmed that ruling. In February 1969, the U.S. Supreme Court ruled in favor of the students, stating they do not "shed their constitutional rights to freedom of speech or expression at the schoolhouse gate." In the ruling, written by Justice Abe Fortas, the court held that wearing the armbands was freedom of speech and if schools wished to suppress the speech of the students, they must verify that it would "materially and substantially interfere" with the school's operation.

1. Do you agree with the ruling?

2. How does a juvenile's right to freedom of speech apply to what can be posted online?

3. In your opinion, would this ruling be the same today?

Online Case Opinion

https://caselaw.findlaw.com/us-supreme-court/393/503.html ●

Sexting

Sexting is the use of a cell phone, tablet, or other electronic device to share sexually explicit content.[18] Pictures or videos often show at least one person nude or partially nude, and sometimes performing sexual acts. Sexting may also include sexually suggestive or aggressive text.[19] Past research shows that 5% to 35% of young people participate in sexting.[20] Females are often more likely to admit to creating and sending the material than are males.

Although the activity is socially discouraged, sexting is permissible between two consenting adults, but not when it is unwanted, harmful, or involves an adult and a minor.

Sexual material can easily be forwarded to other parties without the permission of the victim. Let's say John, age 17, and Hailey, age 16, are high school students consensually dating. Hailey sends a topless picture of herself to John. Rather than keeping it to himself, John sends the picture to a few friends, and they post it on social media sites, where it can be viewed by thousands of people within a few hours, potentially traumatizing Hailey and destroying her reputation.

While most sexting is a protected form of free speech under the First Amendment, the age of the people sending and receiving the material can lead to serious federal and state criminal offenses. In our example, if John sent the photo of Hailey to Henry, a high school senior who is 18 years old and thus legally an adult, Henry could be criminally prosecuted for possession of child pornography, because Hailey is a minor. And if Henry forwarded the photo to his friends, he could also be charged with distribution of

Youth experience stress, anxiety, and depression as a result of online harassment. Can children be taught to use online services without feeling intimated by the actions of others?

child pornography.[21] Child pornography statutes protect individuals under the age of 18 from violation and abuse.[22] Although Hailey originally sent the picture of her own volition, child pornography statutes protect her from what transpired after that point.

Revenge Porn and Sextortion

Angry ex-lovers can seek revenge against their ex-partners on thousands of websites by posting **revenge porn**, which is sexually explicit material posted without the consent of the subject.[23] Some argue that this is a form of sexual assault, because it is demeaning to the subject. Many of these photos are selfies taken by the subject, usually a woman, and only meant for her partner. The subject did not give permission to share the photo with others.

Victims of revenge porn are sometimes harassed or stalked by strangers who saw the pornographic material online. Laws against this behavior are slowly going on the books. As of May 2017, 35 states and the District of Columbia had passed bills criminalizing revenge porn.[24] However, penalties vary. For instance, while California considers revenge porn a misdemeanor disorderly conduct, North Carolina considers it a Class H felony for adults over age 18. Initiatives to pass legislation in more states are gaining prominence, such as EndRevengePorn.org, headed by Dr. Holly Jacobs, a victim of revenge porn.

A fairly new online crime, often linked with revenge porn, is sextortion. **Sextortion** is the acquisition of sexually explicit photographs or videos that are then used to blackmail the victim.[25] The material is often obtained by hacking into the victim's computer or cell phone, but the victim may also have provided it willingly. Offenders may use the photographs to get money from the victim in exchange for not posting the sexually explicit material online, or even request more photographs or videos of sexual acts as a kind of ransom.

The Crimes Against Children Research Center at the University of New Hampshire found that about 60% of sextortion victims knew the offenders in some way and 40% met them online.[26] Most offenders were male and most victims were female, and almost half of victims were under the age of 18.

The Federal Bureau of Investigation has warned Internet users about the dangers of extortion, citing fake identities and other schemes to prey on users of social networks. Predators also use instant messaging and other apps to lure victims. For example, Christopher Gunn, an adult, created fake Facebook pages that cast him as a boy moving into the neighborhood or the singer Justin Bieber. Gunn befriended 9- to 16-year-old girls and obtained sexually explicit photographs from them, and then acquired more photographs and videos by threatening to inform parents or school officials. After his arrest, he was sentenced to 35 years in prison for creating child pornography.[27]

Since sextortion is still not illegal in some states, criminal courts in many states handle these offenses using current laws against bribery, extortion, corruption, child pornography, computer hacking, and sexual exploitation or assault. State and federal law enforcement agencies have been proactively combatting these crimes with sting operations and other targeting methods.

HACKING

>> **LO 9.6**   **Describe the behaviors and values of the hacking community.**

While some delinquents commit burglary or larceny to gain access to physical property without permission, the analogous activity in the cyberworld is hacking. **Hacking** is usually seen as unauthorized intrusion into a computer or network for illegal purposes.[28] Some **hackers** argue that hacking requires a great deal of skill and knowledge of the technology.[29] Hackers also argue that information on the Internet should be freely available. Furthermore, not all hacking is malicious. Some hackers are hired by legitimate parties to try to break into government or corporate computer systems to check security.

Anonymous is an infamous hacking group, commonly identified with the Guy Fawkes mask. **What is the purpose of the group?**

The following activities are categorized as illegal computer hacking:

1. Accessing a computer system without permission

2. Development or use of viruses

3. Destruction or alteration of a computer file without permission

4. Theft of services

5. Fraudulent use of credit cards

6. Infiltration of software[30]

Hackers as a group pride themselves on mastering technology.[31] They communicate in online forums and on discussion boards, as well as on social media. Hackers who overcome challenging security win high respect from their colleagues. Hackers are distinguished as white hats or black hats (see Figure 9.1). **White hats** are ethical hackers who try to improve security systems by successfully hacking them, while being careful not to harm anyone. The goal of **black hats**, however, is to exploit and destroy, sometimes for revenge.

Research on juvenile hackers is still rare. Hackers tend to be male and white or Asian.[32] They also tend to be highly intelligent and are often college age. Youths with high academic achievement are more likely to be involved in hacking. Researchers have found that 5% to 15% of high school students admitted gaining unauthorized access to a website, e-mail address, or social networking page.[33]

FIGURE 9.1

White Hats Versus Black Hats

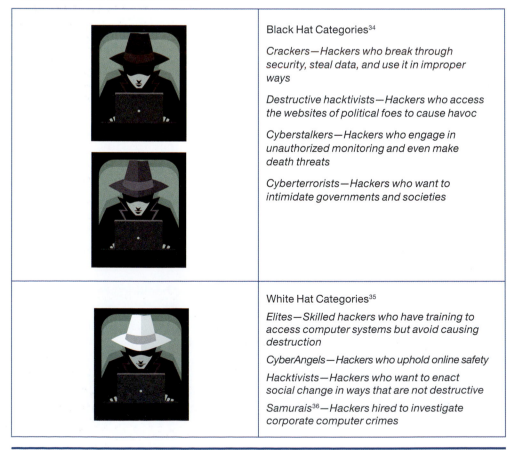

Black Hat Categories[34]

Crackers—Hackers who break through security, steal data, and use it in improper ways

Destructive hacktivists—Hackers who access the websites of political foes to cause havoc

Cyberstalkers—Hackers who engage in unauthorized monitoring and even make death threats

Cyberterrorists—Hackers who want to intimidate governments and societies

White Hat Categories[35]

Elites—Skilled hackers who have training to access computer systems but avoid causing destruction

CyberAngels—Hackers who uphold online safety

Hacktivists—Hackers who want to enact social change in ways that are not destructive

Samurais[36]—Hackers hired to investigate corporate computer crimes

Furnell, S. (2002). *Cybercrime: Vandalizing the information society.* Boston: Addison-Wesley; Holt, T.J. (2007). Subcultural evolution? Examining the influence of on- and off-line experiences on deviant subcultures. *Deviant Behavior, 28,* 171-198.

Federal and state legislation to combat hacking started in the late 1970s and continues today. The Federal Computer System Protection Act of 1977 defined hacking behaviors as a federal crime and was adopted as model legislation by almost all states by 1986. The Counterfeit Access Device and Computer Fraud and Abuse Act of 1984 identifies certain behaviors as hacking. The Identity Theft Enforcement and Restitution Act of 2008 revised previous legislation and identified malware and denial-of-service attacks as hacking crimes.[37] ●

NAVIGATING THE FIELD 9.1

District of Columbia v. Cleveland (2014)

In September 2014, Washington, D.C., Superior Court judge Juliet McKenna dismissed all criminal charges against Christopher Cleveland. Cleveland had been arrested in 2013 for taking pictures up the skirts of women sitting on the steps of the Lincoln Memorial, an activity known as "upskirting." McKenna ruled that women have no reasonable expectation of privacy when "clothed and positioned" in a public place, regardless of the posture they assume. Upskirting, downblousing, and other forms of similar activity are deemed "nonconsensual pornography" and are handled differently by each state.

Putting It Into Action

Use the web to determine how your state classifies and handles nonconsensual pornography.

Include a description of your state's laws in a written file, and add to it whether or not you agree with the law.

Submit your paper to your instructor when requested to do so. ●

SUMMARY

›› LO 9.1 Explain the emergence of cybercrime.

Although the average college student cannot remember a world without the Internet, many people still remember a time when they did not rely on computers or use the Internet. The Internet was introduced in the 1960s and became a prominent feature in most people's lives in the 1990s, when a new form of criminality—cybercrime—began to develop and grow. While cybercrime can occur in many ways, there are a few main categories that involve juvenile offenders and victims.

Key Terms

cybercrime 142   Internet 142

›› LO 9.2 Define digital piracy and discuss the perception of many juveniles that it is an acceptable form of behavior.

Digital piracy is the act of illegally copying music, movies, software, and other digital materials without the permission of or compensation to the copyright holder. Pirating behaviors can be extremely simple to perform, possibly explaining why a large amount of such pirates are under the age of 21. Music piracy is a common crime among juveniles, often perceived as a victimless one that doesn't really affect a wealthy music artist. The perception that "everyone does it" diminishes deterrence.

Key Terms

digital piracy   142

>> LO 9.3   Define cyberbullying and describe its categories.

Cyberbullying is purposeful and repeated harm inflicted through the use of technology, and can be performed in multiple ways. Cyberstalking is monitoring or harassing another person through the Internet. Some cyberbullying behaviors are also considered cyberstalking. State legislatures have enacted new statutes that criminalize the offenses or have added language on them to existing statutes.

Key Terms

cyberbullying   143   cyberstalking   144

>> LO 9.4   Define cyberstalking and cyberharrassment.

>> LO 9.5   Identify various forms of online sexual exploitation.

The Internet can easily be used for sexting, which involves consensually sharing sexual material, such as nude or partially nude photographs. But it can also be used to share this material for revenge and humiliation, without the consent of the subject. Revenge porn is sexually explicit material that is posted online, often by a former sex partner, as a form of revenge for perceived wrongdoing. Sextortion, often used in conjunction with revenge porn, is a form of blackmail with the intention of gaining more sexually explicit material, money, or other demands.

Key Terms

revenge porn   147   sexting   145   sextortion   147

>> LO 9.6   Describe the behaviors and values of the hacking community.

Hackers are often intelligent and proud of their work. They think free access to information is a basic right. Hackers have different levels of expertise and different intentions. Hacking usually involves unauthorized access to computer systems and files, but it can sometimes be altruistic. White hat hackers try to improve security, while black hat hackers have malicious intent.

Key Terms

black hats   148   hacking   147
hackers   147   white hats   148

DISCUSSION QUESTIONS

1. Why do so many juveniles commit some forms of cybercrime?

2. What types of punitive measures should the juvenile court system take to combat this type of criminality?

3. How should public and private school systems address juvenile cybercriminality?

EXPLORING JUVENILE JUSTICE FURTHER

1. Investigate and outline the legal ramifications in your state of origin for a juvenile who participates in the distribution of child pornography. Do you believe the sanctions are too harsh or too lenient?

2. Interview a law enforcement officer in your area, and ask him or her about the jurisdiction's experience with juvenile cybercrimes, as well as his or her perception of the jurisdiction's preparedness for investigation of these crimes.

$SAGE edge™

Give your students the SAGE edge!

SAGE edge offers a robust online environment featuring an impressive array of free tools and resources for review, study, and further exploration, keeping both instructors and students on the cutting edge of teaching and learning. Learn more at **edge.sagepub.com/schmallegerjj**.

10

Juvenile Drug Use

After reading this chapter you should be able to

1. Identify the various schedules of controlled substances under federal law and explain the differences between them

2. Explain the importance of the juvenile drug court as a method of diversion

3. Discuss various methods used to combat juvenile drug use in the United States

Key Terms in Chapter 10

alcohol	hallucinogens	marijuana
amphetamines	heroin	methamphetamine
cocaine	illicit drugs	opioids
controlled substances	inhalants	prescription drug abuse
crack cocaine	juvenile drug treatment	stimulants
depressants	court (JDTC)	synthetic marijuana
drug addiction	licit drugs	vapes

INTRODUCTION

James Eslick had done hard drugs for years but got clean and moved to New Jersey. However, when his 3-year-old son, Joseph, drowned, he and his wife, Desiree, started using drugs to cope with their grief. After a move to northern Pennsylvania, he and Desiree quit their drug use and moved forward with raising their daughter, Grace. The family later moved to Wyoming, and Grace began experimenting with opioids. Grace went to short-term rehabilitation facilities to get help with her addiction. In October 2017, Grace, then age 16, succumbed to her addiction and fatally overdosed. A few weeks later, Desiree fatally overdosed as well, and James believes she died from a broken heart.[1]

Luzerne County, Wyoming, experienced a record number of fatal opioid overdoses in 2017, with 150 overdose deaths, a 60% increase since 2015. This trend is not unusual for many regions in the country. Thousands of individuals are overdosing every year, many of whom do not survive the overdose. Billions of dollars are spent in rural, suburban, and urban areas to provide resources for individuals struggling with drug addiction, as well as their families and friends, who are indirectly victimized by this raging phenomenon. Juveniles and adults are falling victim to drug use and, often, severe addiction to these substances.

The societal perception of juvenile drug use is generally about the harder illegal drugs, like opioids, cocaine, and heroin. But juvenile drug use is actually more encompassing, involving a wide range of legal and illegal substances. This chapter will explore in depth the

©iStockphoto.com/South_agency

Grace Eslick succumbed to a drug overdose at age 16; her mother Desiree overdosed and died a few weeks later. What is the attraction of drugs?

various drugs juveniles use. A definition of the term *drug* will be provided, as well as explanations of the various methods of administering drugs. Drugs are known by many names, which will be further explored, as will the potential effects of each drug. To better understand the current state of drug use among juveniles, Table 10.1 provides a breakdown of drug use in 2016 by juveniles in the eighth, tenth, and twelfth grades in the United States, as reported by the Monitoring the Future Survey, sponsored by a grant from the National Institute on Drug Abuse.

Addiction comes in many forms, including cigarettes, alcohol, and drugs. How would you define *addiction*?

TABLE 10.1

Monitoring the Future 2016 Survey Results: Trends in Drug Use Among High School Students

DRUG	TIME PERIOD	EIGHTH GRADE	TENTH GRADE	TWELFTH GRADE
Alcohol	Any lifetime use	22.80	43.40	61.20
	Past year use	17.60	38.30	55.60
	Past month use	7.30	19.9	33.20
Cigarettes	Lifetime	9.80	17.50	28.30
	Past year	—	—	—
	Past month	2.60	4.90	10.50
Smokeless tobacco	Lifetime	6.90	10.20	14.20
	Past year	—	—	—
	Past month	2.50	3.50	6.60
Cocaine	Lifetime	1.40	2.10	3.70
	Past year	0.80	1.30	2.30
	Past month	0.30	0.40	1.40
Crack cocaine	Lifetime	0.80	0.80	1.40
	Past year	0.50	0.40	0.80
	Past month	0.20	0.20	0.50
Hallucinogens	Lifetime	1.90	4.40	6.70
	Past year	1.20	2.90	4.30
	Past month	0.20	0.20	0.50
Heroin	Lifetime	0.50	0.60	0.70
	Past year	0.30	0.30	0.30
	Past month	0.20	0.20	0.20
Inhalants	Lifetime	7.70	6.60	5.00
	Past year	3.80	2.40	1.70

DRUG	TIME PERIOD	EIGHTH GRADE	TENTH GRADE	TWELFTH GRADE
	Past month	1.80	1.00	0.80
K2/spice	Lifetime	—	—	—
	Past year	2.70	3.30	3.50
	Past month	—	—	—
Marijuana	Lifetime	12.80	29.70	44.50
	Past year	10.10	23.90	35.60
	Past month	5.40	14.00	22.50
MDMA	Lifetime	1.70	2.80	4.90
	Past year	1.00	1.80	2.70
	Past month	0.30	0.50	0.90
Methamphetamine	Lifetime	0.60	1.30	1.20
	Past year	0.40	0.40	0.60
	Past month	0.30	0.20	0.30
Adderall	Lifetime	—	—	—
	Past year	1.50	4.20	6.20
	Past month	—	—	—
Amphetamine	Lifetime	5.70	8.80	10.00
	Past year	3.50	6.10	6.70
	Past month	1.70	2.70	3.00
OxyContin	Lifetime	—	—	—
	Past year	0.90	2.10	3.40
	Past month			
Ritalin	Lifetime	—	—	—
	Past year	0.80	1.20	1.20
	Past month	—	—	—
Vicodin	Lifetime	—	—	—
	Past year	0.80	1.70	2.90
	Past month	—	—	—

Source: National Institute on Drug Abuse, *Monitoring the Future Study: Trends in Prevalence of Various Drugs*, https://www.drugabuse.gov/trends-statistics/monitoring-future/monitoring-future-study-trends-in-prevalence-various-drugs.

Note: All figures are percentages.

TYPES OF DRUGS

>> **LO 10.1**   **Identify the various schedules of controlled substances under federal law and explain the differences between them.**

The Controlled Substances Act (CSA) divides drugs that are considered controlled substances into different schedules, or categories (see Table 10.2). The schedules can be found in Title 21 Code of Federal Regulations (C.F.R.) §§ 1308.11 through

1308.15. **Controlled substances** are categorized based on whether each drug has an accepted medical use and what its potential abuse and likelihood of dependence are. Substances in Schedule I have no current accepted medical use for treatment in the United States and cannot be legally prescribed or administered for medical use. In contrast, substances in Schedules II through V have some form of accepted medical use and may be legally prescribed or administered.

All substances listed in Table 10.2, as well as alcohol and tobacco, are used by many juveniles. Alcohol and tobacco are considered **licit drugs**, meaning that they are legal substances for users of a certain age—18 for tobacco products and 21 for alcohol. In addition, certain states allow recreational use of marijuana. Juveniles use alcohol, tobacco, and marijuana more than any other substance. In contrast, **illicit drugs** are illegal to use except when they are prescribed. Juveniles can often become addicted to illicit drugs. **Drug addiction** is the craving of, and physical dependence on, a drug—which leads to more frequent use as the body develops a tolerance. Use of certain illicit drugs can produce identifiable physical and psychological symptoms that can harm one's health and personal relationships, and it can lead to other criminal behaviors. This section will explore the different types of drugs used by juveniles.

TABLE 10.2

Controlled Substance Schedules According to the CSA

SCHEDULE NUMBER	DEFINITION	EXAMPLES
I	These substances have high potential for abuse and have no accepted medical use.	Heroin, lysergic acid diethylamide (LSD), marijuana (cannabis), peyote, methaqualone, and 3, 4-methylenedioxymethamphetamine (ecstasy)
II	These substances have high potential for abuse, which can lead to severe psychological or physical dependence.	hydromorphone (Dilaudid), methadone (Dolophine), meperidine (Demerol), oxycodone (OxyContin, Percocet), fentanyl (Sublimaze, Duragesic), morphine, opium, codeine, hydrocodone, amphetamine (Dexedrine, Adderall), methamphetamine (Desoxyn), methylphenidate (Ritalin), amobarbital, glutethimide, and pentobarbital
III	These substances' potential for abuse is lower than those in Schedules I or II. Abuse may lead to moderate or low physical dependence or high psychological dependence.	Products containing not more than 90 milligrams of codeine per dosage unit (Tylenol with Codeine), buprenorphine (Suboxone), benzphetamine (Didrex), phendimetrazine, ketamine, and anabolic steroids such as Depo-Testosterone
IV	These substances have low potential for abuse compared with substances in Schedule III.	Alprazolam (Xanax), carisoprodol (Soma), clonazepam (Klonopin), clorazepate (Tranxene), diazepam (Valium), lorazepam (Ativan), midazolam (Versed), temazepam (Restoril), and triazolam (Halcion)
V	These substances have lower potential for abuse than other categories. They primarily consist of limited quantities of certain narcotics.	Cough preparations containing not more than 200 milligrams of codeine per 100 milliliters or per 100 grams (Robitussin AC, Phenergan with Codeine), and ezogabine

Alcohol and Tobacco

Alcohol is a liquid that is produced by a fermentation of various sugars and that causes intoxication.

It is found in the form of beer, wine, and spirits (e.g., vodka, scotch, brandy, and other liquors). Alcohol can reduce inhibitions, making juveniles become more emotional and at times aggressive. In a 2016 study of more than 45,000 high school students, about 33% of twelfth graders, 20% of tenth graders, and 7% of eighth graders had consumed alcohol in the past month. However, alcohol use has declined in all juvenile age groups since 1996.[2]

©iStockphoto.com/Mixmike

Cigarette smoking often begins at a young age. Can it lead to other "problem" behaviors?

While tobacco is not considered a mind-altering substance, it can have a range of negative health consequences. Cigarette smoking causes more than 480,000 deaths each year, more than all the deaths from HIV, motor vehicle accidents, alcohol use, and illegal drug use.[3] The Monitoring the Future Survey found that 10.5% of twelfth graders, 4.9% of tenth graders, and 2.6% of eighth graders said they had smoked cigarettes in the past month. Meanwhile, smokeless tobacco had been used by 6.6% of twelfth graders, 3.5% of tenth graders, and 2.5% of eighth graders within the past month, according to the survey. Like alcohol use, use of cigarettes and smokeless tobacco has steadily declined since 1996. However, more of today's juveniles are using e-cigarettes, or **vapes**. The survey showed that almost 13% of twelfth graders, 11% of tenth graders, and 6% of eighth graders had used e-cigarettes during the past month.

Marijuana

Marijuana is the most frequently used illicit drug for juveniles. It is derived from dried hemp leaves and buds and is usually smoked. There are currently more than 1,000 slang terms for marijuana (see Table 10.3). The Monitoring the Future Survey found that within the past month, over 22% of twelfth graders, 14% of tenth graders, and 5.4% of eighth graders had used marijuana. Frequency of use has been steady

IN THE MEDIA 10.1

Hope for the Future?

The U.S. Centers for Disease Control and Prevention recently released a report showing that many risky teenage behaviors have been declining over the past decade, including pregnancy, cigarette smoking, and alcohol consumption.

Putting It Into Action

Give one reason why you think the decline has occurred, and either

1. write it on a sticky note or
2. post it to a website designated by your instructor for such postings.

Once all the students in the class have posted their notes, create a document in which you do the following: Arrange the notes in order from what appears to be the best answer to the worst (notes with similar answers can be combined into one).

Then submit your document to your instructor when asked to do so. ●

Source: Lenny Bernstein, "Fewer Teens Are Having Sex as Declines in Risky Behaviors Continue," *Washington Post*, January 4, 2018, https://www.washingtonpost.com/national/health-science/fewer-teens-having-sex-as-decline-in-risky-behaviors-continue/2018/01/04/a868bf84-f15c-11e7-97bf-bba379b809ab_story.html?utm_term=.efec37bf3c26.

TABLE 10.3

Popular Pseudonyms for Marijuana[5]

Asparagus
Blunt
Chronic
Dank
Doobie
Ganja
Grass
Mary Jane
Pot
Reefer

Steinmetz, K. (2017, April 20). 420 day: Why there are so many different names for weed. *Time.com*.

since 1996. Almost 70% of high school seniors did not believe regular marijuana smoking was harmful, but the same percentage of seniors said they did not approve of regular marijuana smoking.[4]

The medical benefits of marijuana use are subject to debate, but support for legalization has grown. Over the past few years, there has been a dramatic shift in legalized use of marijuana, both medically and recreationally, for individuals over age 21. More than a dozen states have legalized marijuana for medical use, including Montana, Florida, Louisiana, and Vermont (Figure 10.1). While fewer states have legalized marijuana for recreational use, this trend is expected to grow. States like Colorado, California, and Maine have been the forerunners in this change, but states in the South and Midwest have held back.

Legalization of marijuana is limited to its pure form. Synthetic forms, which can be very dangerous, are not included in marijuana legalization efforts. **Synthetic marijuana** is a substance that produces a high that resembles that of natural marijuana. It is made by spraying chemicals onto dry herbs and other plants. Until recently, such synthetic substances were not on the Drug Enforcement Administration's list of scheduled substances, making them completely legal to sell in convenience stores, gas stations, or marijuana paraphernalia shops under names like K2, Spice, and Moon Rocks. In 2016, about 3.5% of high school seniors admitted to using some form of synthetic marijuana. After a continued pattern of overdoses, debilitating behaviors, and other negative reactions, the Drug

FIGURE 10.1

Marijuana Laws by State, 2018

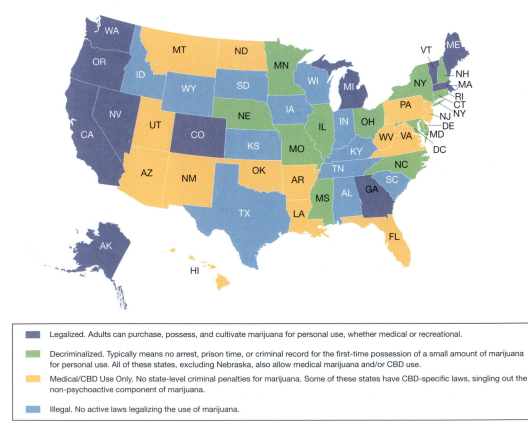

- **Legalized.** Adults can purchase, possess, and cultivate marijuana for personal use, whether medical or recreational.
- **Decriminalized.** Typically means no arrest, prison time, or criminal record for the first-time possession of a small amount of marijuana for personal use. All of these states, excluding Nebraska, also allow medical marijuana and/or CBD use.
- **Medical/CBD Use Only.** No state-level criminal penalties for marijuana. Some of these states have CBD-specific laws, singling out the non-psychoactive component of marijuana.
- **Illegal.** No active laws legalizing the use of marijuana.

Source: Norml.com.

Enforcement Administration declared a number of chemicals in these synthetic drugs unsafe, with no legitimate use. More than 20 states have banned known forms of synthetic marijuana, and more are working to pass legislation to attempt to curb further production and sale of these substances.[6] Because the molecules that compose synthetic cannabinoids can differ vastly from one another, however, many jurisdictions find it difficult to make them illegal without creating laws that are unconstitutionally overbroad in their reach.

Cocaine

Cocaine, a powder-based drug originating from the coca plant grown in South America, became the center of media attention during the war on drugs in the 1980s. Addiction rates of this destructive, illicit drug soared and impacted men, women, and children in America. Cocaine is snorted, injected, or smoked in a glass pipe, which is called freebasing. Freebase cocaine is created by crystalizing pure cocaine, then crushing it. Smoking or injecting cocaine provides a quicker and more powerful high than snorting. Pure cocaine is also snorted and is mainly used by higher income groups.

Crack cocaine is a less expensive, yet more potent, version of cocaine that gained popularity in inner-city, low-income neighborhoods in the 1980s and 1990s. It is often smoked in glass pipes but can also be found laced with marijuana in cigarette form. Crack addiction is especially prominent among impoverished minority men and women, and it has contributed to high rates of criminal behavior and abusive relationships. There has been a significant racial disparity in the severity of sentencing between cocaine and crack cocaine users.

"Crack babies," whose mothers used crack in pregnancy, became an epidemic in the 1980s. When pregnant women use crack, the placenta can separate early from the uterus, causing stillbirth, premature birth, and withdrawal symptoms in surviving infants. They often experience learning disabilities and emotional problems.

Use of cocaine causes multiple problems for juveniles, including abusive behavior toward family and friends, but abuse of both cocaine and crack cocaine among juveniles has decreased in the past 10 years. The Monitoring the Future Survey shows that 0.3% of eighth graders, 0.4% of tenth graders, and 0.9% of twelfth graders admitted to cocaine use. For crack cocaine, the rate was 0.2% for both eighth graders and tenth graders and 0.5% for twelfth graders.

TABLE 10.4

Popular Pseudonyms for Cocaine and Crack Cocaine

COCAINE	CRACK COCAINE
Coke	Bricks
Lady snow	Doo-wap
Nose candy	Eight balls
Toot	White

Heroin

Heroin is related to drugs that are used for legitimate purposes. Opium, which comes from certain forms of the poppy plant, can be used to create morphine and codeine, which are used for medical purposes today. **Heroin**, an illicit drug introduced in the early 20th century, is a refined form of morphine but not used for any legitimate medical purpose. Though heroin is extremely addictive and lethal, the drug itself creates only minor permanent physiological damage. The more severe damage derives from users' neglect of their own bodies. Heroin abusers often suffer from heart and lung abnormalities, vein scarring, malnutrition, hepatitis, and skin infections.

Other names for heroin include black tar, H, horse, junk, and smack. It can be in pure form or mixed with other substances, making it look white, black, or brown, and it can feel sticky. Heroin is often mixed with water and injected but can be snorted or smoked. It can also be "speedballed," when it is combined with another drug such as cocaine or alcohol, which increases the likelihood of overdose. Fortunately, heroin use in juveniles is fairly low, with 0.2% of eighth, tenth, and twelfth graders admitting to its use in the Monitoring the Future Survey.[7]

CASE STUDY

Vernonia School District v. Acton, 515 U.S. 646 (1995)

James Acton was 12 years old and in the seventh grade in Vernonia, Oregon, when he asked to try out for the football team at Washington Grade School. Prior to Acton's request, the Vernonia School District of Oregon had passed the Student Athlete Drug Policy, which required all potential student athletes to have their urine tested before participation in sports, as well as random testing of urine throughout the season. Acton's parents refused to allow him to be tested, insisting there was no evidence of alcohol or drug use and the test was unwarranted. The school suspended him from athletics, and Acton's parents sued the school district.

The case was heard by the U.S. Supreme Court, with the consideration of whether required drug testing for students violated the Fourth Amendment protection against unreasonable search and seizure. The court ruled in favor of the school district. The majority opinion written by Justice Antonin Scalia stated that the consideration of

reasonableness of a search is judged by "balancing the intrusion of the individual's Fourth Amendment interests against the promotion of legitimate governmental interests." The governmental concern for the student's safety overrides protections against intrusions, and students who participate in school athletics should expect to surrender some privacy rights.

1. **Do you agree with the ruling?**

2. **How much privacy intrusion into the life of a student is justified by a school district?**

3. **In your opinion, would this ruling be the same today?**

Online Case Opinion

https://caselaw.findlaw.com/us-supreme-court/515/646.html ●

Methamphetamine

Methamphetamine originally started in Western states and slowly moved across the country, concentrating in the South and Midwest. **Methamphetamine** is a highly addictive, synthetic stimulant that can be injected, smoked, or snorted, and its effect can last up to 8 hours, with a very intense rush within the first few minutes. Methamphetamine provides a new type of high. Many users take it up when the high from other drugs becomes less intense. This drug helps users stay awake for long periods of time and makes them extremely aware, but also causes anxiety and paranoia.[8]

Although making methamphetamine requires an advanced understanding of chemistry, it can be made using familiar household products. Also known as crystal meth, glass, ice, and meth, it can be created with cold medicine, drain cleaner, or antifreeze. It can be made in sophisticated laboratories or even in a soda bottle. Exposure to the drug is extremely dangerous. When it is being made, people can become severely ill or die from inhaling the chemicals being used.

Fortunately, only a small percentage of youths use methamphetamine compared with other drugs. In 2016, 0.3% of eighth graders, 0.2% of tenth graders, and 0.3% of twelfth graders had used methamphetamine, according to the Monitoring the Future Survey.[9] Youths who do use it, however, have a higher likelihood of depression and suicidal ideation compared with those who use other substances. Some studies have even indicated that female juveniles are more likely to use methamphetamine than are males.[10]

Inhalants

Inhalants are substances generally sold for household use or other legitimate purposes that are inhaled to get high. They can be solvents (paint thinners, electronic cleaners, or lighter fluid), aerosols (spray paints, hair spray, or vegetable oil sprays), gases (propane fuel or whipped cream aerosols), and nitrites (room odorizers or leather cleaners). Abusers can inhale these products from a chemical-soaked rag, from chemicals sprayed inside a plastic bag (known as "huffing"), or they can inhale balloons filled with nitrous oxide, also known as laughing gas.[11]

Inhalants can cause organ damage, loss of coordination, and delays in brain development in juveniles. They can also cause deaths from sudden sniffing. Juvenile's use of inhalants decreases with age. The Monitoring the Future Survey showed that eighth graders are much more likely to use inhalants than are twelfth graders.[12]

Inhalants are another method of getting high. How are they obtained?

Art Directors & TRIP/Alamy Stock Photo

Club Drugs

Amphetamines and hallucinogens were part of the club and party scene in the late 20th century. Their popularity diminished with the emergence of other drugs, but recently these substances have been gaining popularity with adolescents because they provide a new type of high.

Amphetamines are stimulant drugs that come in several forms. They were originally used by American soldiers to relieve fatigue and anxiety, and then became popular with truck drivers and other workers who needed to stay awake for long periods of time. Benzedrine and Dexedrine, which are common forms, have street names like bennies, black beauties, and pinks. Ecstasy (MDMA), another amphetamine, was popular with juveniles and college students in the 1990s due to its euphoric effects. As of 2016, 0.3% of eighth graders, 0.5% of tenth graders, and 0.9% of twelfth graders had used these drugs, according to the Monitoring the Future Survey.[13]

Hallucinogens, including PCP and LSD, became popular for their effects on the nervous system, creating relaxed feelings and hallucinations. These drugs have street names like angel dust, elephant juice, rocket fuel, and THC.[14] The dangerous effects of PCP became apparent in the 1970s and 1980s. Use of these drugs is becoming more popular than use of amphetamines. In the Monitoring the Future Survey, 0.6% of eighth graders, 0.9% of tenth graders, and 1.4% of twelfth graders admitted to using them.

Prescription Drugs

Prescription drug abuse is the improper use of prescribed medication, either by overuse or unauthorized use. According to the National Institute on Drug Abuse, prescription drugs have one of the highest rates of use among juveniles 14 years or older, behind alcohol and marijuana use. Juvenile users get prescription drugs from friends or relatives. They use them to get high, decrease pain, or concentrate on schoolwork. Female juveniles in particular use prescription medications to lose weight or stay awake longer.

The most commonly misused prescription drugs by juveniles are opioids, depressants, and stimulants. **Opioids** are similar to endorphins, natural pain relievers in the body, and they originate from the poppy plant.[15] The common varieties are oxycodone (OxyContin, Percocet), hydrocodone (Vicodin, Lortab), and methadone. Prescription opioids are most commonly prescribed to treat chronic pain, but they can also cause nausea, confusion, and shallow breathing. Almost 23,000 people died from overdoses of prescription pain medications in 2015, including a sharp increase in overdoses among individuals ages 15 to 24.

Depressants slow down brain activity and are often prescribed for anxiety or insomnia.[16] While appropriate dosages of these drugs can be helpful, they can lead to addiction when taken in excess. Users of sleep medications like Ambien or Lunesta can build a physical tolerance, prompting them to take even higher doses. Combination of depressants with alcohol or other drugs can cause overdose and even death. In 2015, more than 8,500 people died from an overdose of benzodiazepine, found in Valium or Xanax. About 0.70% of eighth graders, 1.50% of tenth graders, and 2.0% of twelfth graders had used depressants according to the Monitoring the Future Survey.

Stimulants boost energy and attention by accelerating the body's physical processes, which raises blood pressure and increases the heart rate. They are generally safe and effective under doctors' supervision but are dangerous when improperly used. Overuse can lead to seizures, heart problems, and even death. Juveniles' interest in stimulants has grown because they are commonly prescribed for attention deficit hyperactivity disorder (ADHD) and depression in children. Medicines like Adderall and Ritalin can be accessed through friends, or even their own prescriptions. For instance, according to the Monitoring the Future Survey, almost 5.5% of twelfth graders had tried Adderall in the past year and 1.3% had tried Ritalin.[17]

JUVENILE DRUG COURTS

>> LO 10.2   **Explain the importance of the juvenile drug court as a method of diversion.**

The number of juveniles who have substance abuse issues is growing at rapid rates, indicating not only delinquency issues but also an addiction problem for individuals under the age of 18. A disposition of punishment for a juvenile will not address the long-term issues associated with addiction. These issues can be addressed by targeting the physical and psychological issues of addiction while not assigning a stigma to the juvenile. Juvenile court systems have become a leading source of referrals of youths into treatment programs for substance abuse.[18] Similarly, specialized drug treatment courts have had success with adult and juvenile offenders.

Juvenile justice stakeholders adopted the adult drug court model for juveniles in the 1990s. A **juvenile drug treatment court (JDTC)** is a docket designated for youths with substance abuse issues who have a medium to high risk of further offenses.[19] It is a diversionary alternative that allows participants to get specialized treatment for addiction rather than just being punished. Juvenile drug courts are a family-based model appropriate for youths, who differ from adults in cognitive and physical development.[20] Juveniles are not fully able to make mature decisions, are more susceptible to peer pressure, and have relatively low physical tolerances for drugs and alcohol.[21]

Within 10 years of implementation of the first JDTCs, most juvenile drug courts started undergoing improvements, including better staff training on adolescent needs and development, greater involvement of families, and greater use of community resources. Drug court staff also called for more understanding of assessment and treatment processes and more responsiveness to gender and cultural issues.[22]

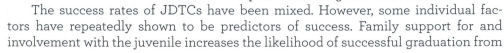

AP Photo/Amanda Myers

Youth can be placed in drug courts as a method of individualized treatment for addiction issues. How did drug courts develop?

The success rates of JDTCs have been mixed. However, some individual factors have repeatedly shown to be predictors of success. Family support for and involvement with the juvenile increases the likelihood of successful graduation from

JDTCs.[23] School cooperation and collaboration are key, because youths likely won't succeed if they simply return to the same environment that fostered the original drug use.[24] Programs with strict eligibility requirements tend to have higher success rates.[25] To ensure continued improvement and success, the Office of Juvenile Justice and Delinquency Prevention advocates collection of the following data from participants in each JDTC:

- Family-related factors
- Recidivism rates, including substance use and other delinquent behavior
- Educational attainment and employment patterns
- Involvement in prosocial activities and groups

SUBSTANCE ABUSE TREATMENT FOR JUVENILES

>> **LO 10.3** **Discuss various methods used to combat juvenile drug use in the United States.**

In 2014, about 1.3 million juveniles ages 12 to 17 (5% of all juveniles in this age group) met the criteria to be diagnosed with substance abuse disorder.[26] Most of them listed marijuana as the primary abused substance. Juveniles experience substance use disorders differently than adults do because their body size and tolerance levels are lower, and the substances affect a developing juvenile brain differently.[27] This means treatment modalities for them have to be different. Figure 10.2 shows various methods of treatment that have been used to address juvenile substance abuse.

Several research studies have indicated that family therapy programs are the most effective way to treat juvenile substance abuse. General counseling programs and cognitive-behavioral therapy programs can also be effective. ●

TABLE 10.5

Categories of Juvenile Substance Abuse Treatment Programs[28]

Assertive continuing care programs—integrated and coordinated case management after discharge from outpatient or inpatient treatment, including home visits and social support services
Behavioral or contingency management programs—involving operant conditioning, which provides penalties and incentives, such as gift certificates, to help juveniles end substance use
Cognitive-behavioral therapy (CBT)—use of classical conditioning, which employs a stimulus or reward for a desired response, so that the juvenile learns skills in coping and problem solving, and dealing with stimuli that trigger substance use
Family therapy—programs in which family members play an active role, addressing issues such as functioning, parenting skills, and communication skills
Motivational enhancement therapy (MET)—nonconfrontational therapeutic techniques used to motivate change based on a juvenile's readiness for behavior change
MET/CBT—combines techniques used in MET and CBT
Pharmacological therapy—pharmaceutical drugs designed to reduce substance use cravings used in combination with other therapies
Psychoeducational therapy—teaching methods used to show the harms and consequences of substance abuse
Group/mixed counseling—individual or group counseling sessions that provide a variety of therapeutic behavior-changing techniques
Multiservice package—a combination of many of the therapies already listed

Tanner-Smith, E. E., Steinka-Fry, K. T., Hensman Kettrey, H., & Lipsey, M. W. (2016). *Adolescent substance use treatment effectiveness: A systematic review and meta-analysis.* Nashville, TN: Peabody Research Institute, Vanderbilt University.

FIGURE 10.2

Methods of Treatment for Juvenile Substance Abuse

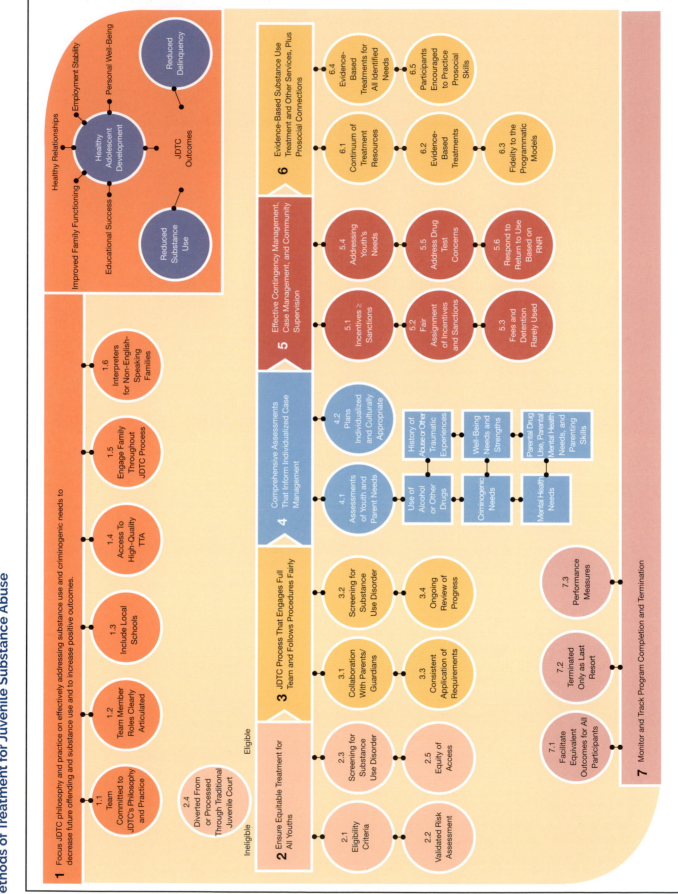

The D.A.R.E. Program

PJF Military Collection/Alamy Stock Photo

The D.A.R.E. program is a popular program targeting drug avoidance by young people. Has the program been successful?

The Drug Abuse Resistance Education (D.A.R.E.) program, formed in 1983, aimed to teach students about the dangers of drug use. Initially promoted by then-First Lady Nancy Reagan, millions of dollars were invested in the program's implementation in schools across the country. Under the program, law enforcement officers provide instruction to elementary and middle school students about the dangers of drug use. Although the D.A.R.E. program is still active, some studies have shown that it has had little impact in reducing juvenile drug use. The D.A.R.E. website, however, continues to tout the success of the program.

Putting It Into Action

Visit the D.A.R.E. website at dare.org, and learn more about the program.

Write a document that expresses your opinion as to why studies have shown D.A.R.E.'s failure but it continues to be used. How could it be improved?

Submit your written document to your instructor when asked to do so. ●

>> **LO 10.1**   **Identify the various schedules of controlled substances under federal law and explain the differences between them.**

Controlled substances are categorized based on their use in medicine, their relative potential for abuse, and the likelihood of dependence. Schedule I substances cannot be prescribed because they have no accepted medical use, while substances in Schedules II through V have some form of accepted medical use and may be legally prescribed.

Key Terms

controlled substances   156   illicit drugs   156
drug addiction   156   licit drugs   156

>> **LO 10.2**   **Explain the importance of the juvenile drug court as a method of diversion.**

There are multiple forms of licit, or legal, drugs and illicit, or illegal, drugs used by juveniles. Alcohol, tobacco, and marijuana are the three most frequently used drugs. Harder drugs such as heroin and cocaine are used much less frequently, but they are extremely dangerous and very addictive. Youths are also abusing prescription medications that have detrimental psychological and physical effects.

Key Terms

alcohol   157   heroin   159   prescription drug
amphetamines   161   inhalants   161   abuse   161
cocaine   159   marijuana   157   stimulants   162
crack cocaine   159   methamphetamine   160   synthetic marijuana   158
depressants   162   opioids   161   vapes   157
hallucinogens   161

>> **LO 10.3**   **Discuss various methods used to combat juvenile drug use in the United States.**

Juvenile drug treatment courts are diversionary courts that are used to remove the punitive stigma from drug crimes and provide better treatment resources for youths. In addition, substance abuse treatment programs can improve recovery from drug addiction.

Key Terms

juvenile drug treatment
    court (JDTC)   162

DISCUSSION QUESTIONS

1. What was the prevalence of drug use when you were in high school, and how was it handled by the administration?

2. Do you believe the opioid epidemic is going to become as problematic for juveniles as it is for adults?

3. In your opinion, what is the best strategy to decrease drug use in juveniles?

EXPLORING JUVENILE JUSTICE FURTHER

1. Interview a law enforcement officer or school resource officer in your area about the prevalence of juvenile drug use. What does he or she feel is the biggest problem?

2. Explore the policies of vape shops in your area in regard to sale of nicotine and marijuana vapes to juveniles. Do you agree with the current rules and regulations? Why or why not?

⑤SAGE edge™

Give your students the SAGE edge!

SAGE edge offers a robust online environment featuring an impressive array of free tools and resources for review, study, and further exploration, keeping both instructors and students on the cutting edge of teaching and learning. Learn more at **edge.sagepub.com/schmallegerjj**.

PART IV

Moving Forward

CHAPTER 11.
Effective Programs for Juveniles

11

Effective Programs for Juveniles

After reading this chapter you should be able to

1. Explain the importance of evidence-based strategies
2. Identify some effective and promising programs to combat juvenile delinquency

Key Terms in Chapter 11

Blueprints for Healthy Youth Development	Office of Juvenile Justice and Delinquency Prevention (OJJDP)	randomized controlled trials
evidence-based strategies		Youth.gov

INTRODUCTION

A few years ago, Scott Earnest of Lewistown, Pennsylvania, earned an Associate of Arts degree from the Pennsylvania State University.[1] His parents and 88-year-old grandmother attended the commencement ceremony to watch Earnest become the first member of their family to graduate with a college degree. You could literally see his relatives swell with pride as Earnest took the stage to give the commencement address. Only a few years earlier, however, few would have predicted Earnest's success. Earnest is one of 13 grandchildren, and his home life was admittedly strict—which led him to rebel at the age of 14. After numerous run-ins with the law, he landed in reform school, with court authorities telling his parents he would be sure to end up in prison.

While confined, however, Earnest came to believe that gangsta rap had instilled in him a bad attitude, which he needed to change. At commencement, he told the audience, "With determination, anything is possible." It wasn't easy, though, Earnest said. When he was first confined, he asked some of the police officers he knew to work with him on a project about the dangers of certain forms of rap music, but they refused because they thought of him as a seriously troubled kid, not worth the effort. "With a juvenile delinquent label," he noted, "a stigma is attached to you, and you don't get support." After release from confinement, Earnest found a position working at a facility that serves autistic children. He says that the determination he saw in those children gave him the strength he needed to finish college. His plan is to work on a bachelor's degree while continuing to help autistic kids. "If I can turn around just one kid on the cusp of making bad choices," he said, "it will be worth it."

©iStockphoto.com/Wittayayut

Scott Earnest went from juvenile confinement to college graduate by following his personal motto, "Decisions determine destiny." Why do some juvenile delinquents become successful later in life while others don't?

EVIDENCE-BASED STRATEGIES IN JUVENILE JUSTICE

>> **LO 11.1**   Explain the importance of evidence-based strategies.

Until around the turn of the century, programs and policies to reduce criminality and dysfunctional behaviors in youths and adults were consistently ineffective.[2] Since then, however, many crime prevention programs and evaluation practices have proven their worth.

How did this change take place? Due to increasingly tight budgets in the past 20 years, federal and state governments have forced programs designed to curb violence, drug abuse, truancy, and delinquency to prove their effectiveness. Rigorous studies have demonstrated that some programs can effectively prevent delinquent behaviors, intervene with active criminals, and even improve physical and mental health, academic achievement, employment, and family life.[3] The root of many of these changes was a White House decision in 2002 to support **evidence-based programs**, or programs whose effectiveness has been demonstrated through empirical research.[4]

The most rigorous evaluations are based on experiments where subjects are randomly assigned to an experimental group. Some agencies will accept only programs that have been evaluated with a **randomized controlled trial**, where participants are randomly assigned to several interventions, including control groups that undergo the standard practice or no intervention at all.[5] Evidence-based prevention programs are now standard for federal and state agencies, and programs that prove to be ineffective may be discontinued.

This chapter will discuss some of the entities that provide information on evidence-based strategies to federal and state governments when officials are deciding which programs to use to combat juvenile delinquency. The chapter will also evaluate a variety of programs found to be effective or promising in combating juvenile delinquency, and it will examine programming that were found ineffective. Each review will include a brief discussion of the program's purpose and implementation and an explanation of the evaluation technique and findings. While there are dozens more programming options, this overview provides a representative summary of what works and what doesn't.

Databanks of Evidence-Based Programs

Multiple agencies and consortiums provide information and evaluations of programs for at-risk youths and juvenile delinquents. The **Office of Juvenile Justice and Delinquency Prevention (OJJDP)**, part of the Department of Justice, sponsors research, programs, and training initiatives through grant funding to states and localities. OJJDP is a resource for enforcement agencies, academics, and political figures looking to improve the lives of juveniles in crisis.[6] It disseminates information on juvenile justice issues and assists with goal setting and policy planning in the federal government.

OJJDP has historically advocated for early intervention programs that provide treatment and resources to at-risk and delinquent youths. These programs are more successful if they are introduced immediately after symptoms or behaviors arise. OJJDP recommended the following programs or curriculums to prevent or decrease juvenile delinquency:

The OJJDP is a government entity that provides resources and recommendations to juvenile programs and courts. What does "OJJDP" stand for?

- After-school recreation

- Bullying prevention

- Classroom and behavior management

- Comprehensive community interventions

- Conflict resolution and violence prevention

- Mentoring

- Multicomponent and classroom-based programs

- Social competence promotion

These categories have consistently shown success in providing resources for at-risk youths and decreasing juvenile delinquency.

Blueprints for Healthy Youth Development (formerly Blueprints for Violence Prevention) is a way to evaluate programs that address delinquency. Evaluations focus on programs to prevent delinquency, youth violence, and substance abuse, as well as emotional and physical health, relationships, and academic success.[7]

Blueprints was created in 1996 by the Center for the Study and Prevention of Violence at the University of Colorado Boulder using several small grants. The OJJDP has funded it since 1997, and in 2010 the Annie E. Casey Foundation provided funding for an expansion in types of assessed programs.

Blueprints identifies effective programming for children based on rigorous evaluations. Programs found to be effective are classified as "promising," meaning that they meet the minimum standard; "model," meaning they meet a higher standard; or "model plus," which is a still higher rating. Blueprints considers model or model plus programs the most effective in addressing juvenile delinquency and risky behaviors. For example, the Lifeskills Training program, rated model plus, is a classroom-based program for middle school students that focuses on prevention of drug and alcohol abuse, violence, and other risky behaviors. It is taught for 3 years, using instruction, reinforcement, and practice. Evaluations of the program have demonstrated its short- and long-term effectiveness. Alcohol, tobacco, and illicit drug use decreased for the intervention group, as did violent behaviors, risky sexual behaviors, and risky driving.[8]

One program that Blueprints ranks as "model" is called Functional Family Therapy (FFT), short-term family therapeutic intervention that targets at-risk children and delinquent youths who are exhibiting conduct disorders, behavioral issues, and substance abuse. The goal is to improve family communication and decrease dysfunctional behavior patterns. Instruction includes lessons in parenting skills and compliance. Studies show that families participating in FFT show significant improvement in behavior and that recidivism among delinquent youths decreased.[9]

Another source for evaluating programs that aim to protect youths from the risks of delinquency is **Youth.gov**, a federal website providing up-to-date information on effective programs. The website is operated by the Interagency Working Group on Youth Programs, a group of 20 federal agencies, including the Department of Education, Social Security Administration, Department of Homeland Security, and Department of Agriculture. Youth.gov evaluates programs, deeming them "effective" or "promising," based on robust empirical findings. Programs that don't meet these criteria receive a "no effects" designation.[10]

JUVENILE PROGRAMMING

>> **LO 11.2**   Identify some effective and promising programs to combat juvenile delinquency.

This section will explore a small sample of juvenile programs that are aimed at providing services for at-risk youths or at reducing juvenile delinquency. Table 11.1 provides an overview of the programs, as well as the rating given to each of them based on rigorous evaluations. These ratings were determined by Youth.gov. Programs are rated as effective, promising, and no effects (not demonstrating effectiveness).

Evidence-Based Practice

In 2017, the National Institute of Corrections, an office of the U.S. Department of Justice, released a 90-page annotated bibliography on evaluation of programs in multiple areas of the justice system. Several of the featured evaluations were on juvenile programming.

Putting It Into Action

You can find the paper online at http://www.justice studies.com/pubs/evidence-based-practices.pdf.

Skim through the paper, then select and closely read one of the highlighted evaluations that you find especially interesting.

Create a document that provides a brief description of the program, including how it was implemented and why it was deemed effective by the National Institute of Corrections.

Submit your paper to your instructor when asked to do so. ●

Source: National Institute of Corrections, *Evidence-Based Practices in the Criminal Justice System* (August 2017), https://nicic.gov/evidence-based-practices-criminal-justice-system-annotated-bibliography.

TABLE 11.1

Effective and Ineffective Juvenile Programming

NAME OF PROGRAM	CURRENT STATUS	GENDER	RACE/ ETHNICITY	SETTING	PROGRAM TYPE	EFFECTIVENESS RATING
All Stars	Active	Both	All races	School	Academic skills enhancement, conflict resolution, violence prevention, alcohol and drug prevention	No effects
Behavior Intervention at Cook County, Illinois, Juvenile Temporary Detention Center	Not active	Male	All races	Correctional	CBT, conflict resolution	Promising
Big Brothers Big Sisters Community-Based Mentoring Program	Active	Both	All races	Other community setting	Mentoring, children exposed to violence, alcohol and drug prevention	Effective
Boys and Girls Clubs of America	Active	Both	All races	Other community setting	Academic skills enhancement, after school, truancy prevention	Promising
CASASTART	Active	Both	All races	Home, school, community	After school, CBT, parent training, truancy prevention	No effects
Drug Abuse Resistance Education (D.A.R.E.)	Not active	Both	All races	School	Classroom, alcohol and drug prevention	No effects
Gang Reduction Program	Active	Both	All races	Community, high-crime neighborhoods	Aftercare, gang prevention, violence prevention	No effects

NAME OF PROGRAM	CURRENT STATUS	GENDER	RACE/ ETHNICITY	SETTING	PROGRAM TYPE	EFFECTIVENESS RATING
Gang Resistance Education and Training	Active	Both	All races	School	Classroom, conflict resolutions, gang prevention	Promising
The GREAT School Program	Active	Both	All races	School	Classroom curriculum	No effects
HOMEBUILDERS	Active	Both	All races	Home, community setting	CBT, crisis intervention, family therapy	Effective
Moving to Opportunity Demonstration Program	Active	Both	All races	Community, high-crime neighborhoods	Community crime prevention, violence prevention	No effects
Perry Preschool Project	Active	Both	Black	Home, school	Academic skills enhancement, parent training	Effective
SAM (Solution, Action, Mentorship) Program for Adolescent Girls	Active	Female	All races	School	Classroom, CBT, alcohol and drug prevention	Promising
STARS for Families	Active	Both	All races	School, community	Alcohol and drug prevention	No effects
Serious and Violent Offender Reentry Initiative	Not active	Both	All races	Correctional, community	Academic skills enhancement, CBT, probation, violence prevention	No effects

Effective and Promising Juvenile Programming

FEATURED EFFECTIVE AND PROMISING JUVENILE PROGRAMMING
• **Behavior Intervention at Cook County, Illinois, Juvenile Temporary Detention Center**
• **Big Brothers Big Sisters Community-Based Mentoring Program**
• **Boys and Girls Clubs of America**
• **Gang Resistance Education and Training**
• **HOMEBUILDERS**
• **Perry Preschool Project**
• **SAM (Solution, Action, Mentorship) Program for Adolescent Girls**

Behavior Intervention at Cook County, Illinois, Juvenile Temporary Detention Center

The Cook County, Illinois, Juvenile Temporary Detention Center (JTDC) is a 500-bed facility, the largest of its type in the country, where high-risk juvenile arrestees are placed before their cases are adjudicated. The Behavior Intervention program at JTDC is focused on reduction of reactive behavior, especially anger, which is triggered by feeling threatened or disrespected, getting frustrated, or experiencing a sense of loss. Using a curriculum that is based on cognitive-behavioral therapy (CBT)

The first juvenile court, Cook County, is still in operation today. What is its guiding principle?

and conflict resolution, the JTDC encourages deep breathing and relaxation techniques when the juvenile encounters a trigger. Juveniles are asked to weigh situations as if they were an outside spectator, and they complete "thinking reports" when they are placed in a "time-out" for misbehavior.

Evaluation of the JTDC indicated promising results for participants, who are male and mainly in minority races. Almost 2,700 male residents who entered the JTDC between 2009 and 2011 were randomly assigned either to a CBT residential unit or to a "status quo" unit where they did not receive treatment. Juveniles who received the behavior intervention were 16% less likely to be readmitted to the JDTC, compared with those who received no treatment.[11]

Big Brothers Big Sisters Community-Based Mentoring Program

The Big Brothers Big Sisters (BBBS) community-based mentoring (CBM) program uses prosocial adult contact to influence juvenile development. The target population is juveniles ages 6 to 18, generally from low-income or single-parent households. They generally have had high exposure to violence and trauma, and they reside in communities that are disorganized and crime-ridden. An adult mentor is assigned to a juvenile mentee to form supportive relationships. These pairs meet several times a month during one year.

Big Brothers, Big Sisters is one of the many programs that provide mentorship to at-risk youth. Why is mentorship important in preventing delinquency?

A randomized study of eight BBBS sites revealed that mentored juveniles were 46% less likely to use drugs and 27% less likely to use alcohol compared with nonparticipants. Mentored youths were more interested in academics, earning better grades, and skipping fewer classes, and they had more confidence with schoolwork. In addition, mentored juveniles had better relationships with their parents and scored higher with communication techniques.[12]

Boys and Girls Clubs of America

The Clubs recognize that many young people live in impoverished areas, which degrades their ability to access educational, social, and employment opportunities. They provide a safe and positive place for youths to go after school and in the summer—the points when youths are most likely to participate in illegal and unsafe activities. The Clubs provide tutoring, indoor activities, and field trips.

About 73% of low-income members of the Clubs between ages 12 and 17 earned mostly As and Bs, compared with 69% of a national sample of low-income youths.[13] Almost 70% of twelfth graders who attend the Clubs volunteer at least once a month, compared with 40% of high school seniors nationally. Almost 90% of the ninth graders who attend the Clubs reported that they avoided alcohol use, compared with 77% of ninth graders not in the program.

The Supreme Court of You

Every chapter has featured a U.S. Supreme Court opinion that has affected the way we process and protect juveniles who are accused and convicted of delinquent and criminal acts. There has been a recent influx of cases filed on the basis of constitutional rights violations in the LGBTQ community. For this particular case study, *you* are charged with finding a case that is currently in one of the stages of the court process (e.g., adjudication, trial, appeal) involving an LGBTQ juvenile. If you were a justice on the U.S. Supreme Court and this case were argued in front of you, how would you rule and why?

Discussion Questions

1. Explain the importance of evidence-based strategies in reducing juvenile delinquency rates.

2. What are some key components in unsuccessful programs? Why are these components so crucial to success?

3. Could ineffective programs become successful with some changes? Choose one of the ineffective programs noted in the chapter and discuss how you would change it. ●

Gang Resistance Education and Training

This program is a school-based intervention that targets middle school students. Gang Resistance Education and Training (G.R.E.A.T.) has three primary goals: (1) avoidance of gang membership, (2) prevention of violence and criminal behavior, and (3) development of positive relationships with law enforcement. Programming is implemented with a cognitive-based curriculum that teaches conflict resolution, responsibility, and goal setting in 13 lessons. Generally, law enforcement officers teach this program to cultivate trust between juveniles and officers. The program has also expanded to include lessons for elementary schools, a summer program, and a parent-and-child program.

A recent evaluation of the program used an experimental, multisite, and longitudinal panel design in seven cities. About 3,800 students participated in the evaluation, with more than half representing a minority race. Results of the evaluation were promising but should be viewed with caution due to the measurements used. The program had a moderately positive effect on gang membership, with the odds of joining a gang 39% lower compared with the control group. Students who participated had a slight increase in prosocial attitudes toward police and were better able to resist peer pressure. There was no significant difference between groups on rates of delinquency or violence.[14]

HOMEBUILDERS

This is an in-home program that works with youths ranging from newborn to age 17. It is involved in the child welfare, mental health, and juvenile justice systems. Youths who are in a residential facility, foster care, or a psychiatric hospital or who are returning from one are eligible for the program. The purpose is to improve parenting skills, family communication, and family safety to preserve or reunify families. Families are in intensive therapy and can access other resources in the community or schools. A family can have access to crisis intervention on a 24/7 basis.

An evaluation of participants in two states was performed by randomly selecting participants in the program and comparing them to a group participating in an out-of-home care program. Results indicated that participating children were reunified with family in a shorter amount of time, and more children were reunified at home compared with an out-of-home care group. These children were also less likely to be removed from the home and placed in a facility or foster care.[15]

Perry Preschool Project

The project is meant to provide high-quality education for African American children ages 3 and 4 who live in urban areas. It has a 30-week school year involving a 2½-hour classroom session and a weekly home visit. Visiting the home allows parents—generally single mothers—to get involved in their child's education and provides them with support. The curriculum involves active learning, role-playing, and decision making. Children are taught language skills, music, and other preschool topics.

The program was originally evaluated in the 1960s and then more recently in 1993. Children with low IQs and high risk for school failure were divided into two random groups. The children in the treatment group significantly outperformed the control group throughout their academic careers and also had a higher graduation rate. As adults, participants had lower rates of delinquency and repeat arrests and significantly higher earnings and employment rates.[16]

SAM (Solution, Action, Mentorship) Program for Adolescent Girls

This is a school-based program aimed at preventing substance abuse. Targeting middle school girls, it aims to reduce drug-using behaviors through group therapy and community and peer mentorship. It features 16-week group sessions, meeting 1 hour a week and consisting of action-learning lessons, discussion, and guest speakers who are community or peer mentors. Students also have individual meetings with school counselors. The focus is on drug education, decision making, goal setting, and relationships. Parents are asked to participate in two meetings with the school counselor, one at the beginning and one at the end of the program.

SAM was evaluated by randomly assigning a group of 40 girls to a program group and 40 girls to a control group. A little more than half of the girls in each group were Mexican American, and about 40% were Caucasian. About half the students in each group were on the free or reduced-price lunch program. Results indicated that participation produced successful outcomes compared with the control group. Participants had lower self-reported drug use and higher social competence behaviors as measured by parents and teachers. Participants also had greater knowledge of the physical effects of drug use.[17]

Ineffective Juvenile Programming

FEATURED INEFFECTIVE JUVENILE PROGRAMMING
• **All Stars**
• **CASASTART**
• **Drug Abuse Resistance Education (D.A.R.E.)**
• **Gang Reduction Program**
• **The GREAT School Program**
• **Moving to Opportunity Demonstration Program**
• **STARS for Families**
• **Serious and Violent Offender Reentry Initiative**

All Stars

The program tries to prevent risky behaviors, such as premature sexual activity, violence, and substance abuse, among juveniles ages 11 to 15. The premise is to strengthen character by learning positive norms, promoting parental and community bonds, and establishing commitments. A program specialist or classroom teacher leads classwide small-group sessions and one-on-one sessions, which involve debates, games, and discussion. It can also be an after-school program at community centers.

All Stars was evaluated with a single-cohort longitudinal design, including a pretest, posttest, and 1-year follow-up. Middle school students from 14 schools participated. Rates of violence, drug use, and sexual activity rose over time for both the treatment and control groups. All Stars had no significant positive effects on participants.[18]

CASASTART

Originally named Children at Risk, the current name is short for Striving Together to Achieve Rewarding Tomorrows. It is a community-based program meant to decrease substance abuse and delinquent behaviors and promote school attendance and performance in children ages 11 to 13. Case managers provide services to high-risk youths and their families by collaborating with schools, community organizations, and criminal justice agencies. Every program has eight core components: after-school and summer activities, community-oriented policing, criminal justice intervention, education services, family services, incentives, and mentoring. A case manager serves 13 to 18 children at one time.

A recent evaluation of the program, modeled after the first evaluation in 1999, used random assignment to evaluate seven sites across the country. Results indicated harmful programmatic effects in regard to prevalence and frequency of delinquency. Juveniles who participated in the program had higher rates of disciplinary incidents. While male youths who participated had less serious delinquency offenses than the control group, females had higher amounts of drug use, sexual activity, arrest, and truancy incidences. Furthermore, youths who stayed in the program longer had higher measures of serious delinquency.[19]

Drug Abuse Resistance Education (D.A.R.E.)

This school-based drug use prevention program, whose slogan was "Just say no" to drugs, became a media sensation in the 1980s due to the support of First Lady Nancy Reagan. The school-based drug use prevention arm of the D.A.R.E. program ended in 2009. It was originally taught by police officers and targeted fifth and sixth graders. It later expanded to include high school students. The curriculum was 17 weeks long, involving education on drug use and effects, resistance techniques, and self-esteem building.

A quasi-experimental design compared the effectiveness of the D.A.R.E. program with a similar drug education program in Kentucky over 5 years. Participants in both groups showed an increase in drug and cigarette use and a decline in negative attitudes toward alcohol, marijuana, and cigarette use.[20]

A police officer provides drug education training to school students. How effective is such training likely to be?

Mikael Karlsson/Alamy Stock Photo

Gang Reduction Program

The OJJDP funded this program from 2003 to 2008 to reduce delinquency and violence among juvenile street gangs in urban areas. The Gang Reduction Program (GRP) used a multidisciplinary intervention team and outreach workers from federal and local agencies to provide services focusing on child welfare, education, employment, health, and interactions with the criminal justice system. The particular GRP evaluated in this study was operated by the Richmond, Virginia, Police Department, which created a citywide gang unit, added patrols to the area, and provided a variety of prevention and intervention services, such as physical and mental health care, reentry services, tattoo removal, and dropout prevention services.

The evaluation of GRP was based on police incident reports over 5 years and hospital admission data. Results indicated that the Richmond GRP had no effect on gang-related crimes. There was an increase in drug-related, violent, and gang-related incidents. There was a slight decrease in the amount of patients admitted to the hospital for gunshot injuries related to gang violence, along with a slight increase in stabbing and other injuries.

The GREAT School Program

This school-based program, whose acronym stands for Guiding Responsibility and Expectations for Adolescents for Today and Tomorrow, was created to promote nonviolence among juveniles. Youths participate in 20 weekly sessions involving a social-cognitive, problem-solving curriculum. Students are instructed on how to avoid dangerous situations, respond to negative behaviors in nonviolent ways, and use manners to defuse tense situations. A program is also provided for teachers to improve classroom management and address aggressive juveniles.

A quasi-experimental study analyzing outcome measures of aggression and nonviolent behaviors in eighth graders at 37 schools was used to evaluate the usefulness of GREAT. Schools were randomized into four treatment conditions: universal intervention, selective intervention, a combination, or no intervention. The majority of students who participated were minority and from low-income backgrounds. After measuring 2-year follow-up points on participants, results indicated that participants' behavior was not significantly different from that of nonparticipants. Measured behaviors included support of fighting, nonviolent response, and aggression.

Moving to Opportunity Demonstration Program

The Department of Housing and Urban Development (HUD) created the Moving to Opportunity (MTO) housing mobility experiment in five cities in the early 1990s. The purpose was to help families living in high-poverty public housing move to low-poverty private housing to improve their lives. A lottery system was used to select families with children under age 18 to be relocated. HUD provided families with Section 8 or MTO vouchers to pay the rent, and they received mobility counseling for leasing and relocation issues.

Long-term effects of the program were evaluated with a randomized controlled trial, examining families who were placed in either the MTO group, Section 8 group, or a control group. Most families were racial minorities and female led. Adult and juvenile arrest histories were collected on the residents for 10 to 15 years after enrollment. There were no significant differences for total arrests, violent crime arrests, and drug crime arrests. Juveniles in the MTO group had significantly fewer arrests for property crimes, but there were no significant differences between grown children in the groups.[21]

STARS for Families

This program, whose acronym stands for Start Taking Alcohol Risks Seriously, promotes avoidance of alcohol for at-risk middle school students until they reach adulthood. They learn about the risks of alcohol use and situational and peer influences that can lead to alcohol consumption. The program has three phases: (1) consultation with health care providers on avoiding alcohol use and other risk factors; (2) mailing of key-facts postcards to parents or guardians, with instructions on communicating with their children about alcohol avoidance; and (3) take-home lessons, with prevention activities to be completed on a weekly basis.

The evaluation of the program compared two randomly distributed groups, one that received the intervention and one that received a minimal intervention. Most participants were African American and male, and more than half qualified for a free lunch program. Results found no significant differences between the two groups on rates of alcohol use or susceptibility to others who use alcohol.[22]

Serious and Violent Offender Reentry Initiative

This federal initiative is meant to improve the quality of life for juvenile and adult offenders returning to the community. It especially targets serious and violent offenders who have a higher risk of recidivism. The purpose is to decrease recidivism through goal-initiative programming. Services and resources focus on employment, education, housing, substance use, and physical and mental health.

Researchers evaluated programs in 14 states, comparing offenders receiving the services with those who received normal services provided in their states. Interviews of the offenders were conducted 30 days before release and then multiple times after release. Male juvenile offenders in the Serious and Violent Offender Reentry Initiative group were significantly less likely than nonparticipants to achieve housing independence at the 15-month interview. There were no significant differences between groups on drug testing. In fact, both groups had increased levels of drug use over time. And there were no significant differences between the two groups on self-reported recidivism.[23] ●

NAVIGATING THE FIELD 11.1

NPR's Podcast Series *Caught*

All kids make mistakes. But depending on your zip code, race, or just bad luck, those mistakes can have a lasting impact. Mass incarceration starts young. In *Caught: The Lives of Juvenile Justice,* you can hear from kids about the moment they collided with law and order, and how it changed them forever.[24]

Putting It Into Action

Visit the NPR podcast series *Caught* at https://www.npr.org/podcasts/589480586/caught.

Listen to the podcast episodes you find there. Then decide which is your favorite and write a description of that episode.

Create a document explaining why it is your favorite, and show how it relates to the ideas and concepts discussed in this textbook.

Submit the document to your professor when asked to do so. ●

SUMMARY

>> LO 11.1   Explain the importance of evidence-based strategies.

Due to tight budgets in federal and state governments over the past 20 years, states and localities are encouraged to use evidence-based strategies that have been deemed effective for juveniles, rather than waste money on programs that do not work. It is now regular practice for federal and state agencies to implement prevention programs that are evidence based and to discontinue programs that are ineffective. Evidence-based programs receive rigorous evaluations, generally using randomized experiments or randomized controlled trials.

Key Terms

Blueprints for Healthy Youth Development 171	Office of Juvenile Justice and Delinquency Prevention (OJJDP) 170	randomized controlled trial 170
evidence-based strategies 170		Youth.gov 171

>> **LO 11.2** Identify some effective and promising programs to combat juvenile delinquency.

No one type of juvenile programming has been found successful, but many use cognitive-behavioral therapy and instruction, as well as mentoring programs and prosocial resources for children in impoverished communities. This provides children with an alternative to a life of crime and opportunities they might otherwise not have access to.

EXPLORING JUVENILE JUSTICE FURTHER

1. Interview an employee of any juvenile-related agency in your area. Ask him or her questions about the most effective programs compared with the least effective programs.

2. As you've seen from this chapter, it is important to use evidence-based practices to evaluate effective and promising juvenile programs. Read Appendix D "Juvenile Justice Model Data Project," then interview an employee of any juvenile-related agency in your area and ask the questions included in Appendix D. Write a summary of your findings.

$SAGE edge™

Give your students the SAGE edge!

SAGE edge offers a robust online environment featuring an impressive array of free tools and resources for review, study, and further exploration, keeping both instructors and students on the cutting edge of teaching and learning. Learn more at **edge.sagepub.com/schmallegerjj**.

U.S. Department of Justice

Office of Justice Programs

Office of Juvenile Justice and Delinquency Prevention

JUVENILE JUSTICE STATISTICS
NATIONAL REPORT SERIES BULLETIN

Caren Harp, Administrator

April 2019

Girls in the Juvenile Justice System

Samantha Ehrmann, Nina Hyland, and Charles Puzzanchera

Highlights

This bulletin presents statistics on girls in the juvenile justice system from three national data collections, covering their involvement from arrest through residential placement. It also provides an analysis of trends and case processing in addition to characteristics of the youth studied and their offenses.

In recent years, the involvement of girls in the juvenile justice system declined at a rate similar to that for boys

As a result, the proportion of females at various stages of the juvenile justice system has changed very little since the mid-2000s

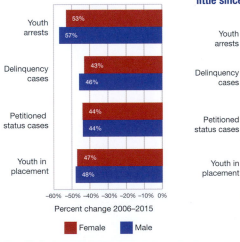

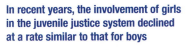

- Arrests involving girls decreased by more than half (53%) between 2006 and 2015, reaching their lowest point in three decades.

- Delinquency cases and petitioned status cases involving girls also reached their lowest points since the early 1990s, decreasing 43% and 44%, respectively, from 2006 through 2015.

- After falling 47% since 2006, the number of females in placement in 2015 was at its lowest level since at least 1997.

- Since 2006, the proportion of females remained relatively constant for arrests, delinquency cases, petitioned status cases, and youth in placement.

- Larceny-theft, simple assault, and disorderly conduct accounted for 50% of arrests and 56% of delinquency cases involving girls in 2015. Truancy offenses accounted for more than half (55%) of petitioned status offense cases involving females.

- In 2015, delinquency cases involving girls were less likely to be petitioned, adjudicated, or result in out-of-home placement than cases involving boys.

OJJDP
Access OJJDP publications online at *ojjdp.gov*

Source: Girls in the Juvenile Justice System. (2019). Juvenile Justice Statistics: National Report Series Bulletin. Office of Juvenile Justice and Delinquency Prevention. U.S. Department of Justice.

A Message From OJJDP

The Office of Juvenile Justice and Delinquency Prevention (OJJDP) supported the statistical analyses reported in this bulletin to help the field better understand the nature of girls' offending and how the justice system handles cases involving girls. The authors drew upon three national data collections—the Federal Bureau of Investigation's Uniform Crime Reporting Program and OJJDP's National Juvenile Court Data Archive and Census of Juveniles in Residential Placement—to create a statistical portrait of girls in the juvenile justice system, including trends in the demographics of this population, the offenses they committed, and how they move through the system.

Both genders' involvement in the juvenile justice system has declined at similar rates over the past decade. However, focusing on the overall trend may obscure important details. For example, although girls accounted for less than one-third of youth arrests in 2015, they made up a relatively large share for certain types of offenses, such as larceny-theft and liquor law violations. Additionally, 2015 data reveal that the offense profiles of petitioned status offense and delinquency cases involving younger girls differ from those of older girls.

The examination of these types of trends and characteristics of girls in the juvenile justice system is critical to assessing needs, identifying potential service gaps, and directing interventions for this population. OJJDP prepared this bulletin to help states, communities, and tribal jurisdictions understand the national trends and consider how they may use their own data to identify and target effective and cost-efficient strategies for girls.

Caren Harp
Administrator

The latest data highlight trends and characteristics of girls in the juvenile justice system and the system's response to them

Boys have always accounted for the majority of youth involved in the juvenile justice system. Consequently, advancements in policy and practice tended to focus on males. As the number of female youth entering the juvenile justice system grew throughout the 1990s, policymakers and researchers shifted their attention to girls to better understand the reasons behind this increase.[1]

In 2004, the Office of Juvenile Justice and Delinquency Prevention (OJJDP) established the Girls Study Group to examine what influences delinquent behavior among girls and how the juvenile justice system should respond. The group disseminated knowledge acquired from literature reviews, studies, and assessments through its bulletin series Understanding and Responding to Girls' Delinquency. Today, OJJDP provides funds to support comprehensive, community-based services for girls in an effort to reduce violence and victimization and to promote public safety.

Research has revealed the various adversities many girls face as well as their unique responses to trauma that place them at risk for entering the system. This statistical bulletin presents a national portrait of girls involved with the juvenile justice system as assessed through three national data collections: the Federal Bureau of Investigation's (FBI's) Uniform Crime Reporting (UCR) Program, OJJDP's National Juvenile Court Data Archive, and OJJDP's Census of Juveniles in Residential Placement. The bulletin examines recent trends of girls involved in the system and addresses their demographics, the offenses that led to their involvement, and how they move through the system.

---

[1] Zahn, M.A., Hawkins, S.R., Chiancone, J., and Whitworth, A. 2008. *The Girls Study Group—Charting the Way to Delinquency Prevention for Girls.* Girls Study Group series. Washington, DC: U.S. Department of Justice, Office of Justice Programs, Office of Juvenile Justice and Delinquency Prevention. Available at www.ncjrs.gov/pdffiles1/ojjdp/223434.pdf.

©iStockphoto.com/Linda Raymond

Arrests of girls accounted for less than one-third of all youth arrests

In 2015, law enforcement agencies in the United States made an estimated 921,600 arrests of persons younger than age 18. Girls accounted for 269,900 of those arrests, or less than one-third; however, their involvement varied by offense.

Females accounted for a relatively large share of youth arrests[2] involving larceny-theft (40%), liquor law violations (40%), simple assault (37%), and disorderly conduct (35%). In comparison, females accounted for a small share of murder (6%) and robbery (11%) arrests. While the male proportion of youth arrests exceeded the female proportion across most offenses, arrests for prostitution-related offenses were an exception. Of the 600 estimated youth arrests for prostitution-related offenses, more than three-fourths (76%) involved girls.

[2]In the arrest section of this bulletin (pages 3–5), "youth" refers to persons younger than age 18. In 2015, this definition was at odds with the legal definition of youth involved in the justice system where 16- and 17-year-olds in some states are defined as adults.

About the data

Findings in the arrest section of this bulletin are from data that local law enforcement agencies across the country report to the Federal Bureau of Investigation's (FBI's) Uniform Crime Reporting (UCR) Program. These statistics report the number of arrests that law enforcement agencies made in a given year—not the number of youth arrested nor the number of crimes committed. Under the UCR Program, the FBI requires law enforcement agencies to classify an arrest by the most serious offense charged in that arrest. More information on arrest data is available in the "Data Sources" section of this bulletin (p. 23).

Females accounted for a small proportion of youth arrests for violent offenses in 2015

Most serious offense	Female youth arrests, 2015	Female proportion	Percent change 2006–2015
Total*	269,900	29%	−53%
Violent Crime Index[†]	–	–	–
Murder	100	6	−30
Rape[†]	–	–	–
Robbery	2,000	11	−40
Aggravated assault	7,300	26	−48
Property Crime Index	70,700	34	−45
Burglary	4,800	13	−48
Larceny-theft	63,000	40	−44
Motor vehicle theft	2,600	18	−55
Arson	400	16	−61
Simple assault	48,200	37	−42
Fraud	1,500	33	−41
Stolen property	1,700	16	−45
Vandalism	7,000	17	−55
Weapons violations	2,100	11	−56
Prostitution and commercialized vice	400	76	−61
Sex offenses[†]	–	–	–
Drug abuse violations	21,100	21	−33
Offenses against child and family	1,300	37	−39
Driving under the influence	1,600	25	−65
Liquor law violations	17,200	40	−66
Drunkenness	1,600	29	−62
Disorderly conduct	25,100	35	−64
All other offenses except traffic	46,200	28	−55
Curfew	12,700	28	−73
Runaway	NA	NA	NA

■ Females accounted for 26% of youth arrests for aggravated assault and 40% of arrests for larceny-theft.

■ Across offenses, arrests involving females declined 30% or more since 2006.

*Includes offenses not shown.
[†]Beginning in 2013, the FBI broadened the definition of rape, removing the phrase "forcible" from the offense name and description. Law enforcement agencies may submit data on rape arrests based on either the new or legacy definition of rape. Due to differences in agency reporting practices, national estimates for the offenses of "rape" and "sex offenses" are no longer available. Additionally, estimates for the Violent Crime Index (which included "forcible rape") are not shown.
NA = National estimates for runaway arrests are no longer available.

In 2015, arrests involving girls reached the lowest level since at least 1980

Half of arrests involving girls in 2015 were for larceny-theft, simple assault, or disorderly conduct offenses

Among arrests involving girls, larceny-theft was the most common offense, accounting for about one-fourth (23%) of their arrests in 2015. Simple assault accounted for nearly one-fifth (18%) of arrests involving girls, while disorderly conduct accounted for 9%. In contrast, more serious violent offenses (murder, robbery, and aggravated assault) accounted for 3% of arrests of girls.

In comparison, larceny-theft (14%), drug abuse violations (12%), and simple assault (13%) were the most common offenses for arrests involving boys. While these offenses accounted for 39% of arrests involving boys, the three most common offenses for girls accounted for half of their arrests. Across most other offenses, the offense profiles for females and males were about the same. For example, stolen property offenses, driving under the influence, and drunkenness each accounted for 1% of arrests for boys and girls, and aggravated assault accounted for 3% for both.

Arrests involving girls declined more than 50% since 2006

Overall, arrests involving youth peaked in 1996 at nearly 2.7 million. By 2015, the number of arrests involving youth reached its lowest point in three decades, 65% less than the 1996 peak. Between 1996 and 2015, arrests declined substantially for males (68%) and females (56%), but the patterns of decline were different.

Arrests of male youth decreased gradually from their peak through the mid-2000s and then fell more sharply through 2015 (down

Arrest trends differed between girls and boys

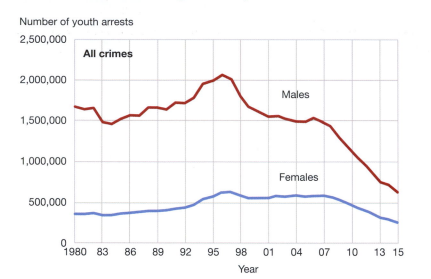

Number of youth arrests

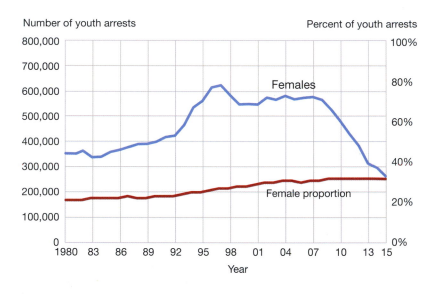

Number of youth arrests   Percent of youth arrests

57% since 2006). In contrast, arrests of female youth peaked in 1997, declined from their peak through 1999, and then increased slightly through the late 2000s. As a result of the decline in male arrests, coupled with an increase in female arrests through the late 2000s, the female proportion of youth arrests increased from 23% in 1996 to 29% in 2009.

More recently, from 2009 through 2015, the relative decline in arrests for boys and girls was the same (down 49%). As a result, the female proportion of youth arrests remained stable at 29% each year since 2009.

Select offenses influenced changes in female arrest patterns

Larceny-theft, simple assault, and disorderly conduct accounted for half of all arrests involving girls. Combined, these offenses accounted for 42% of the decline in arrests of females in the past 10 years (2006–15). As a result, changes in the volume of these offenses have influenced the overall trend of arrests involving females.

Larceny-theft

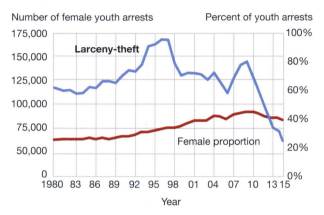

- Larceny-theft arrests involving girls decreased 33% from 1996 to 2006 before rising through 2009. After 6 years of steady decline (56% since 2009), the number of arrests of females in 2015 was at its lowest level in more than three decades.

- From 1996 through 2006, arrests for larceny-theft involving female youth did not fall as sharply as those involving male youth. As a result, the female proportion grew from 33% to 40%. Given the larger relative decline in female arrests than male arrests since 2009 (down 56% and 46%, respectively), the female share fell from 45% to 40%.

Simple assault

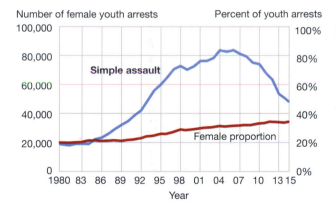

- Arrests for simple assault offenses involving female youth more than quadrupled between 1980 and 2006. In comparison, arrests of males for simple assault more than doubled (increasing 140%) during the same period, leading to an increase in the female share of arrests from 21% in 1980 to 34% in 2006.

- Since the 2006 peak, arrests of girls for simple assault decreased 42%, compared with a 50% decrease for boys. Given the larger relative decline in male arrests, the female share grew, averaging 36% in the past 5 years.

Disorderly conduct

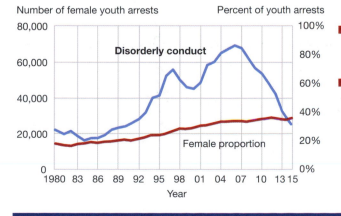

- After declining from 1997 through 2000, arrests for disorderly conduct involving female youth peaked in 2006. Since 2006, arrests of females fell 64%, reaching their lowest level since the early 1990s.

- While male arrests for disorderly conduct followed a similar pattern as female arrests, they increased relatively less and decreased relatively more than female arrests. As a result, the female proportion of arrests gradually increased from 26% in 1997 to 35% in 2015.

The female delinquency caseload in 2015 was at its lowest level since the early 1990s

Overall, delinquency cases referred to juvenile court grew substantially from 1985 to 1997, when the caseload peaked at an estimated 1.9 million cases. Since 1997, the number of delinquency cases fell 53% through 2015 and dropped below 900,000 for the first time since the mid-1970s.

The caseload for females also increased between 1985 and 1997, but the increase outpaced the overall caseload. In a little more than a decade, the female caseload doubled (up 99%), while the overall caseload increased 62%. Consequently, the female share of the delinquency caseload increased from 19% in 1985 to 24% in 1997.

After 1997, the female caseload increased slightly, peaking in 2005 (up 4%). Since the peak, the female caseload declined through 2015 (down 47%), reaching its lowest level since the late 1980s. In comparison, the male caseload declined slightly between 1997 and 2005 before also declining 47% through 2015, reaching its lowest level since at least 1985. As a result of the similar trends, the female proportion of the delinquency caseload remained fairly stable at 27% to 28%.

About the data

Findings in this section are based on national estimates of delinquency cases and petitioned status offense cases handled in juvenile court developed by the National Juvenile Court Data Archive project, which is funded by the Office of Juvenile Justice and Delinquency Prevention. Each case represents the initial disposition of a new referral to juvenile court for one or more offenses. As with the arrest data, if a case has more than one offense, the most serious offense is selected. Similarly, cases with multiple dispositions are categorized by their most severe or restrictive disposition. More information on juvenile court data is available in the "Data Sources" section of this bulletin (p. 23).

In 2015, juvenile courts handled 244,000 cases involving girls, 9% more than in 1985

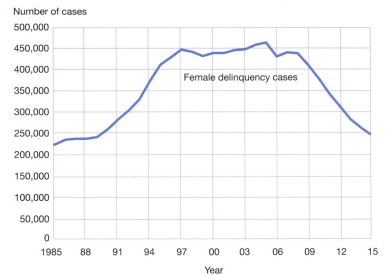

■ Between 2010 and 2015, the female caseload decreased an average of 8% per year.

From 1985 to 2009, the female share of delinquency cases grew from 19% to 28% and remained stable through 2015

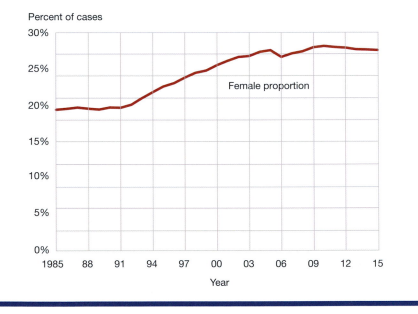

Many delinquency cases involving girls were for nonviolent offenses

Less than one-third of delinquency cases involved girls in 2015

Of the estimated 884,900 delinquency cases that juvenile courts handled in 2015, 28% involved girls. Among the general offense categories, females accounted for 31% of all person offense cases, 28% of public order offense cases, 27% of property offense cases, and 22% of drug offense cases.

Girls accounted for a relatively large share of certain offenses in 2015. For example, they accounted for more than one-third of all cases involving larceny-theft (39%), simple assault (36%), and disorderly conduct (37%) offenses. In comparison, the female proportion of violent offenses was relatively small—in 2015, girls accounted for less than one-fifth (16%) of all Violent Crime Index offense cases (i.e., criminal homicide, rape, robbery, and aggravated assault).

Overall, the caseload involving females fell 43% between 2006 and 2015. Public order offense cases had the largest relative decline since 2006, largely influenced by reductions in disorderly conduct (a 51% decrease) and obstruction of justice (a 44% decrease) cases. Property offenses closely followed, driven by a 44% decrease in larceny-theft cases. The declines in larceny-theft, disorderly conduct, and obstruction of justice cases accounted for nearly half of the decrease in the female caseload between 2006 and 2015.

Nearly half of the female delinquency caseload in 2015 involved simple assault or larceny-theft offenses

The majority of female cases involved nonviolent offenses. In 2015, less than one-third of female delinquency cases involved person offenses, with simple assault accounting for 24% and Violent Crime Index offenses accounting for 4% overall. Property offenses accounted for the largest share of the female caseload (33%), with larceny-theft contributing to nearly one-fourth (23%) of the overall volume.

Across offenses, girls accounted for fewer than 4 of every 10 delinquency cases in 2015

Most serious offense	Female cases, 2015	Female proportion	Percent change 2006–2015
Total delinquency*	244,000	28%	−43%
Person offenses	75,400	31	−39
Violent Crime Index	8,600	16	−44
Criminal homicide	100	16	NA
Rape	300	4	NA
Robbery	2,200	11	−29
Aggravated assault	6,000	23	−49
Simple assault	59,100	36	−35
Property offenses	81,200	27	−47
Property Crime Index	64,800	30	−45
Burglary	5,800	11	−45
Larceny-theft	55,800	39	−44
Motor vehicle theft	2,800	21	−56
Arson	500	15	−54
Vandalism	7,600	17	−54
Trespassing	5,500	21	−45
Stolen property offenses	1,400	16	−56
Drug law violations	24,600	22	−27
Public order offenses	62,700	28	−48
Obstruction of justice	30,800	27	−44
Disorderly conduct	21,400	37	−51
Weapons offenses	2,100	11	−59
Liquor law violations	2,000	32	−64
Nonviolent sex offenses	2,400	21	−4

■ Girls accounted for a smaller share of cases involving aggravated assault (23%) than simple assault (36%).

■ Female cases involving motor vehicle theft, arson, vandalism, stolen property, disorderly conduct, weapons offenses, and liquor law violations fell by at least 50% since 2005.

*Includes offenses not shown.

NA = Too few cases to develop a reliable estimate.

Offense profile of female delinquency cases, 2015

Most serious offense	Percent
Total delinquency	100%
Person offenses	31
Violent Crime Index	4
Criminal homicide	<1
Rape	<1
Robbery	1
Aggravated assault	2
Simple assault	24
Other violent sex offenses	<1
Other person offenses	3
Property offenses	33
Property Crime Index	27
Burglary	2
Larceny-theft	23
Motor vehicle theft	1
Arson	<1
Vandalism	3
Trespassing	2
Stolen property offenses	1
Other property offenses	1
Drug law violations	10
Public order offenses	26
Obstruction of justice	13
Disorderly conduct	9
Weapons offenses	1
Liquor law violations	1
Nonviolent sex offenses	1
Other public order offenses	2

The typical female delinquency case involved an older girl and over half involved black or Hispanic youth

Most female delinquency cases involved youth age 15 or older

Two-thirds (67%) of the female caseload in 2015 involved girls age 15 or older at the time of referral. Older girls accounted for at least 60% of all cases across the four major offense categories. For example, females age 15 or older accounted for 76% of all female drug offense cases and 71% of all female property offense cases.

The offense profile of cases involving younger girls differed from that of older girls. Cases involving younger girls, those younger than age 15, included a larger proportion of person offenses (38%) compared with older youth (28%). Conversely, cases involving older females involved a larger proportion of property offenses (35% vs. 29%) and drug offenses (11% vs. 7%) than cases involving younger females.

More than half of all female delinquency cases involved black or Hispanic youth

Fifty-four percent of female cases handled in 2015 involved minority youth (i.e., black, Hispanic, American Indian, and Asian).[3] Cases involving black girls accounted for more than one-third of all female delinquency cases (35%), while cases involving Hispanic girls accounted for another 17%.

---

[3]Throughout this bulletin, the racial classification American Indian includes American Indian and Alaska Native. The racial classification Asian includes Asian, Native Hawaiian, and Other Pacific Islander.

About one-third of female delinquency cases involved youth younger than 15 and 1 in 10 involved a drug offense

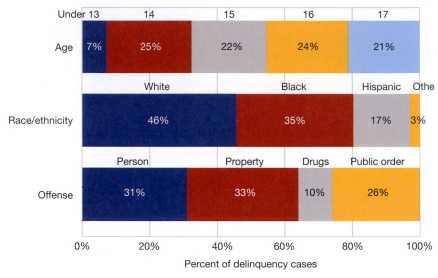

Percent of delinquency cases

■ Other race includes American Indian, Asian, and youth of unknown race.

Offense profiles varied by race in 2015. Overall, property offense cases accounted for the largest share of the 2015 female caseload (33%). White female and Hispanic female caseloads followed this general pattern; however, the caseload involving black females differed. Person offenses accounted for a larger share of the black female caseload (37%) than did property offenses (31%). The black female caseload was also unique in terms of the relatively small proportion of drug offense cases (3%) compared with the Hispanic (12%) and white (14%) female caseloads.

Offense profile of female delinquency cases, by race/ethnicity, 2015

Offense	White*	Black*	Hispanic
Total	100%	100%	100%
Person	27	37	30
Property	35	31	32
Drugs	14	3	12
Public order	24	28	26

*Excludes persons of Hispanic ethnicity.

In 2015, three of every four delinquency cases involving girls did not receive formal sanctions

An intake department first screens cases referred to juvenile court to determine if the matter will be handled formally, with the filing of a petition, or informally. Of the estimated 244,000 delinquency cases involving girls in 2015, more than half (53%) were handled informally without the filing of a petition.

If the intake department decides that a case should be handled formally, a petition is filed and the case is placed on the court calendar (or docket) for an adjudicatory or waiver hearing. Half of all formally handled delinquency cases involving females did not result in a delinquency adjudication, and less than half of 1% were judicially waived to criminal court.

At the disposition hearing, the juvenile court judge determines the most appropriate sanction, generally after reviewing a predisposition report. One-fifth (21%) of adjudicated delinquency cases involving girls resulted in out-of-home placement and two-thirds (66%) resulted in formal probation.

Case dispositions can be grouped into three general categories: dismissed, informal sanctions, and formal sanctions. Formal sanctions include cases judicially waived to criminal court and dispositions of adjudicated cases. Informal sanctions include all remaining outcomes except for dismissals. Overall, 33% of delinquency cases involving females were dismissed, 44% received informal sanctions, and 23% were adjudicated delinquent and received formal sanctions.

Few female delinquency cases involved detention

Juvenile courts may hold youth charged with an offense in a secure juvenile detention facility if it is in the best interest of the community and/or the youth. A youth may be detained at different points as a case proceeds through the juvenile justice system. In this section, "detention" refers to being placed in a restrictive facility under court authority at some point after referral to court and prior to disposition.

Overall, one-fourth (24%) of all delinquency cases handled in 2015 involved the youth being securely detained. Courts detained a smaller proportion (20%) of cases involving females. For females, person (27%) and public order (23%) offense cases were most likely to result in detention in 2015. Across the four general offense categories, cases involving girls were less likely to be detained than cases involving boys.

Many delinquency cases involving girls were redirected away from deeper involvement in the juvenile justice system

Female delinquency cases, 2015
244,000

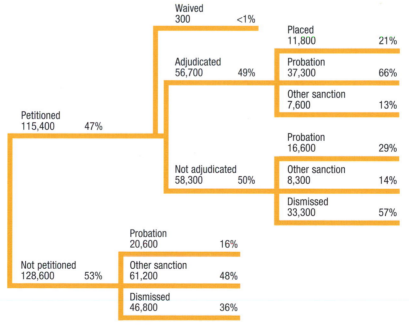

Note: Detail may not sum to total due to rounding.

In 2015, delinquency cases involving girls were less likely to receive formal sanctions than cases involving boys

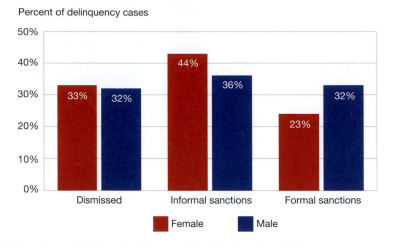

Percent of delinquency cases

- Overall, courts dismissed a similar proportion of female and male delinquency cases.

Percent of cases detained, by offense and gender, 2015

	Female	Male
Total	20%	26%
Person	27	32
Property	14	22
Drugs	14	18
Public order	23	30

More than half of female delinquency cases were handled informally

When a case is referred to court, decisionmakers first determine if sufficient evidence exists to prove the allegation brought against the youth. If evidence does not exist, an intake officer or prosecutor dismisses the case; otherwise, intake officials decide if the case should be handled formally. Decisionmakers may consider informal case handling if they believe that accountability and rehabilitation can be achieved without formal court intervention.

In 2015, more than half (53%) of all delinquency cases involving girls were handled informally, compared with 42% of cases involving boys. Informal handling was more likely for less serious offenses among cases involving girls. For example, 58% of all property offense cases involving females were handled informally, compared with 50% of person offense cases involving females. Similarly, a greater proportion (53%) of simple assault cases involving females were handled informally than were aggravated assault (29%) cases.

More than one-third of nonpetitioned delinquency cases involving females were dismissed

Most nonpetitioned cases received some type of informal sanction in 2015. In some instances, the youth agreed to informal probation, restitution, school attendance, drug counseling, or community service, or the court referred them to another agency for services. These informal sanctions generally involve little or no continuing supervision. Although specific information about diversion decisions is not available,

In 2015, cases involving females were more likely to be handled informally than those involving males

	Percent of cases not petitioned	
	Female	Male
Total delinquency	53%	42%
Person offenses	50	40
Violent Crime Index	25	21
Criminal homicide	NA	24
Forcible rape	NA	25
Robbery	14	13
Aggravated assault	29	26
Simple assault	53	48
Property offenses	58	42
Property Crime Index	60	39
Burglary	43	25
Larceny-theft	63	49
Motor vehicle theft	31	24
Arson	35	30
Vandalism	49	48
Trespassing	63	54
Drug law violations	58	49
Public order offenses	46	38
Obstruction of justice	30	26
Disorderly conduct	61	55
Weapons offenses	52	39

- For some offenses, the likelihood of informal handling was similar between female and male cases. For example, 49% of female cases involving vandalism were handled informally, as were 48% of male cases.

NA = Too few cases to develop a reliable estimate.

the data on informal handling mentioned above provide a rough gauge of how often officials use diversion-like sanctions.

In 2015, 64% of all nonpetitioned delinquency cases involving females received an informal sanction or were otherwise diverted, compared with 59% of nonpetitioned cases involving males. Conversely, nonpetitioned cases involving boys were more likely to be dismissed at intake than were nonpetitioned cases involving girls (41% vs. 36%).

Courts refrained from adjudicating half of the petitioned cases involving girls

Formal case handling involves filing a petition requesting that the court hold an adjudicatory or waiver hearing. At the adjudicatory hearing, the judge, or in some instances a jury, determines if a youth is responsible for the offense(s) and may adjudicate (i.e., judge, similar to a conviction in criminal court) the youth a delinquent or status offender.

In 2015, courts adjudicated half (49%) of the 115,400 petitioned delinquency cases that involved females. The likelihood of adjudication varied slightly across the general offense categories, ranging from 47% of person offenses to 53% of public order offenses. Courts judicially waived to criminal court an estimated 300 cases involving girls, or less than half of 1% of petitioned cases.

One-fifth of all petitioned delinquency cases involving females received an informal sanction

Overall, more than one-fourth (29%) of petitioned delinquency cases involving girls were dismissed and one-fifth (22%) received an informal sanction. Informal sanctions are associated with cases that did not result in a finding of delinquency (i.e., not adjudicated) and can include a range of disposition options, such as informal probation, community service, and restitution. If the youth complies with the informal sanctions, the case may be dismissed, preventing an adjudication on the youth's record. Formally handled cases involving girls were somewhat more likely than cases involving boys to receive informal sanctions (22% vs 20%); however, female cases were less likely to receive formal sanctions (49%) than male cases (55%).

Outcome of formally handled (petitioned) delinquency cases, by gender, 2015

Result	Female	Male
Total	100%	100%
Dismissed	29	25
Informal sanction	22	20
Formal sanction	49	55

Note: Detail may not sum to total due to rounding.

Formal sanctions include out-of-home placement and probation as well as other sanctions. Placement options vary, ranging from commitment to a secure institution (prison-like environment) to placement in a less secure, home-like setting, such as a group home or treatment foster care home. The majority (66%) of adjudicated cases involving females were ordered to probation and one-fifth (21%) received a placement disposition. In comparison, 62% of adjudicated cases involving males received probation and 28% were placed.

Adjudicated public order offenses involving females were more likely to result in placement (25%) than cases adjudicated for other general offense categories. The majority of those public order cases (83%) involved obstruction of justice offenses, such as violating probation and escaping from custody.

© iStockphoto.com/onebluelight

Case processing for females varied by offense in 2015

Cases proceed through the juvenile court system contingent on a variety of factors, including legal factors such as the seriousness of the offense and prior offending. This section looks more closely at case processing for two high-volume offenses, larceny-theft and simple assault, which combined to account for nearly half of all delinquency cases involving females in 2015.

Larceny-theft cases involving females, 2015
55,800

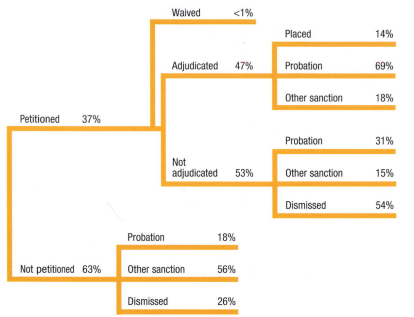

■ Almost two-thirds (63%) of larceny-theft cases involving females were handled informally, with 74% of these cases receiving informal sanctions.

■ More than half (53%) of petitioned larceny-theft cases did not result in an adjudication of delinquency.

■ Of the larceny-theft cases that resulted in adjudication, the majority (86%) received a disposition other than placement.

■ Of the estimated 55,800 larceny-theft cases involving females in 2015, 27% were dismissed, 56% received informal sanctions, and 17% received formal sanctions.

Note: Detail may not sum to total due to rounding.

Simple assault cases involving females, 2015
59,100

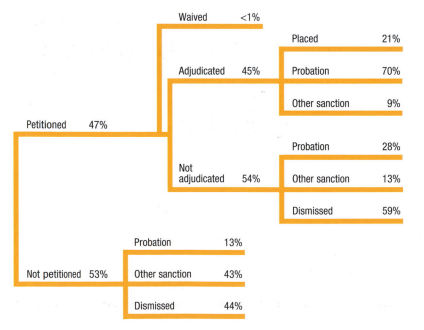

■ More than half (53%) of the simple assault cases involving females were handled informally and 44% of these cases were dismissed.

■ Most (54%) petitioned simple assault cases involving girls were not adjudicated, and 59% of these cases were dismissed.

■ More than two-thirds of adjudicated simple assault cases involving females received formal probation (70%) and 21% received a placement sanction.

■ Of the estimated 59,100 simple assault cases involving girls in 2015, 39% were dismissed, 40% received informal sanctions, and 22% received formal sanctions.

Note: Detail may not sum to total due to rounding.

Case processing differences occurred in juvenile court cases involving females of different races

Black girls accounted for a large share of delinquency cases

In 2015, black females accounted for 15% of the female youth population, but their share of the female delinquency caseload was higher (35%). The proportion of female delinquency cases involving black girls ranged from 12% of drug law violations to 42% of person offenses. Conversely, white, Hispanic, and Asian female youth each accounted for a smaller share of the female delinquency caseload than their share of the general population.

Race profile of the female youth population and delinquency caseload, 2015

Race/ethnicity	Population	Delinquency caseload
Total	100%	100%
White*	55	46
Black*	15	35
Hispanic	23	17
American Indian	2	2
Asian*	6	1

*Excludes persons of Hispanic ethnicity.
Note: Detail may not sum to 100% due to rounding.

Case processing differences can occur at various decision points among races

Delinquency cases involving black girls in 2015 were about three times more likely to be referred to juvenile court than cases involving their white and Hispanic peers. Once referred, more than half of delinquency cases involving black girls were petitioned for formal processing, compared with about 44% of cases involving either white or Hispanic girls. Conversely, petitioned cases involving black girls were less likely to result in an adjudication of delinquency than were cases involving white or Hispanic girls.

Detention rates for delinquency cases involving black girls and Hispanic girls were higher than the rate for cases involving white girls

Case processing rate, 2015

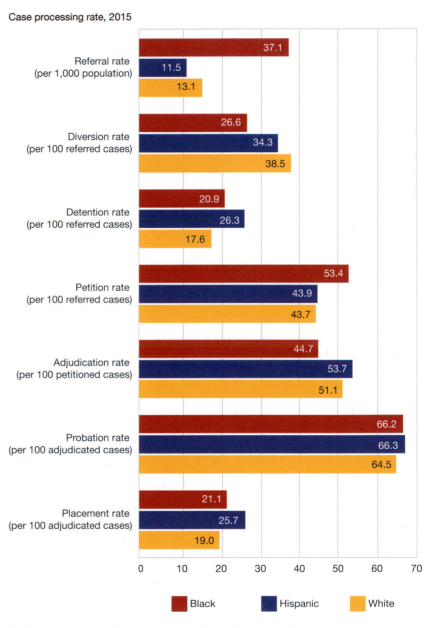

■ Diversion rates were higher for cases involving white girls and Hispanic girls than for cases involving black girls.

■ Adjudicated cases involving Hispanic girls were more likely to result in a disposition of placement than cases involving white girls or black girls.

The 2015 petitioned status offense caseload involving females was at its lowest level since 1995

Status offenses are acts that are illegal only when juveniles commit them (see sidebar, "What are status offenses?"). Overall, the number of petitioned status offense cases handled in juvenile courts increased steadily between 1995 and 2002. In less than a decade, the caseload increased 61%, reaching its peak at nearly 199,900 cases. Since 2002, the caseload has declined 50%, reaching its lowest level in 2015 since at least 1995.

Trends in the petitioned status offense caseload were similar for girls and boys. Both caseloads peaked in the early 2000s—2000 for boys and 2002 for girls. Between 1995 and the peak in 2000, the male caseload increased 64%. Between 1995 and the peak in 2002, the female caseload grew 65%. Over the past 10 years, the relative decline for boys and girls was the same (each down 44%).

Given the similar trends for girls and boys, the female share of the status offense caseload has remained fairly constant. Since 1995, the female share varied from a low of 39% in 1996 to a high of 43% in 2003. Between 2003 and 2015, the proportion averaged 43%.

Among status offenses in 2015, girls had the largest relative share of runaway cases (56%) followed by truancy cases (46%). Liquor offense cases had the largest relative decline from 2006 through 2015 (66%), while truancy decreased 21%. In comparison, cases involving runaway offenses declined 56%.

After peaking in 2002, the female petitioned status offense caseload declined 49% through 2015

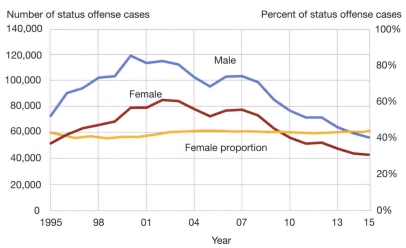

- Declines in truancy and liquor law violations accounted for 45% of the overall decrease in female cases since 2002.
- Females accounted for a larger proportion of the status offense caseload (43%) than the delinquency caseload (28%) in 2015.

Females were involved in 4 of 10 petitioned status offense cases in 2015

	Female cases, 2015	Female proportion	Percent change 2006–2015
All status	43,100	43%	−44%
Runaway	4,500	56	−56
Truancy	25,100	46	−21
Curfew	2,100	29	−63
Ungovernability	4,200	43	−55
Liquor	4,800	40	−66

- Less than one-third of all petitioned curfew cases involved females.
- The relative decline in truancy offenses since 2005 was less than the decline for other offenses.

Note: Detail may not sum to total due to rounding.

What are status offenses?

Status offenses are acts that are illegal only because the persons committing them are juveniles. These include events such as running away, truancy, curfew law violations, ungovernability (i.e., beyond the control of one's parents), and underage liquor law violations.

In many jurisdictions, agencies other than juvenile courts (e.g., family crisis units, county attorneys, and social service agencies) process these cases. In others, youth charged with a status offense are referred to juvenile court. These cases may be diverted away from

the formal justice system or may be handled formally with the filing of a petition. The analyses in this section are limited to petitioned cases. For ease of reading, the terms "petitioned status offense" and "status offense" are used interchangeably in this section.

Status offense profiles vary across age and race groups

In 2015, juvenile courts handled an estimated 43,100 petitioned status offense cases involving girls. The majority of these cases involved truancy offenses (58%). Runaway cases accounted for 10%, while curfew violations accounted for the smallest share (5%) of the caseload. Compared with males, the status offense caseload for females included larger proportions of truancy and runaway offenses, and fewer curfew offenses.

Offense profile of petitioned status offense cases, by gender, 2015

	Female	Male
All status	100%	100%
Runaway	10	6
Truancy	58	52
Curfew	5	9
Ungovernability	10	10
Liquor	11	13
Other status	6	10

Similar to the delinquency caseload, most female status offense cases involve youth age 15 and older

In 2015, two-thirds (67%) of all female petitioned status offense cases involved youth age 15 and older. This proportion was identical to the proportion of the female delinquency caseload (67%). Older girls, those age 15 or older, accounted for more than half of all cases across the five status offense categories: liquor law violations (88%), curfew (75%), runaway (73%), truancy (62%), and ungovernability (61%).

The offense profile of cases involving younger girls differed from that of older girls. Cases involving younger girls, those younger than age 15, included a larger proportion of truancy offenses (66%) compared with older girls (54%). Conversely, cases involving older females involved a larger proportion of liquor law violations (15%) than cases involving younger females (4%).

Minority youth accounted for a small share of the female status offense caseload

Compared with the delinquency caseload, minority youth accounted for a smaller proportion of the petitioned status offense

caseload involving females in 2015 (54% vs. 36%). Cases involving black girls accounted for 22% of all female status offense cases, and cases involving Hispanic girls accounted for 9%. Combined, cases involving American Indian and Asian girls made up 5% of the caseload.

Truancy offenses accounted for the largest share of the status caseload for each race/ethnicity group. Liquor law violations accounted for 14% of the caseload for white females, but 3% of the caseload for black females. Running away was the second most common offense for black females (19%), yet this accounted for 8% for white females. In comparison, runaway and liquor law violations accounted for 9% and 10%, respectively, of the caseload involving Hispanic females.

Truancy offenses accounted for more than half of the status caseload across demographics

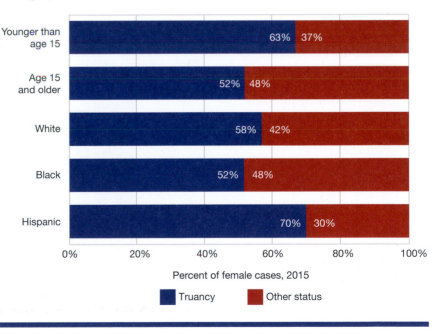

Percent of female cases, 2015

Truancy   Other status

Courts dismissed or ordered informal sanctions for three-fifths of petitioned status offense cases involving females

In 2015, 39% of all petitioned status cases involving females resulted in an adjudication. Compared with the female delinquency caseload, status cases were less likely to be adjudicated (49% vs. 39%). The likelihood of adjudication varied by offense, ranging from 33% of truancy cases to 52% of curfew and liquor law violation cases.

Once adjudicated, more than half (59%) of the status cases involving females received a probation disposition and 35% resulted in other sanctions, such as fines, community service, restitution, or referrals to other agencies for services. Courts ordered out-of-home placement for the remaining 6% of cases. Of the cases that were not adjudicated, 76% were dismissed and a smaller proportion received informal probation (18%) or other informal sanctions (7%). The disposition pattern for status offense cases involving males aligned with the pattern for females.

As with delinquency cases, dispositions for status cases can be grouped into three general categories: dismissed, formal sanctions, and informal sanctions. Overall, almost half (46%) of petitioned status offense cases involving girls were dismissed and 15% received an informal sanction.

Less than half of all female petitioned status offense cases resulted in an adjudication and few subsequently resulted in placement

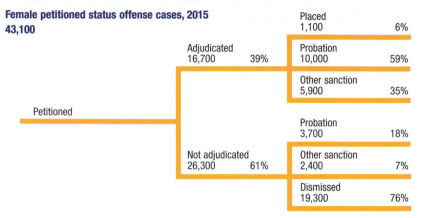

Note: Detail may not sum to total due to rounding.

In 2015, courts ordered informal sanctions for a similar share of petitioned status offense cases involving girls as for those involving boys

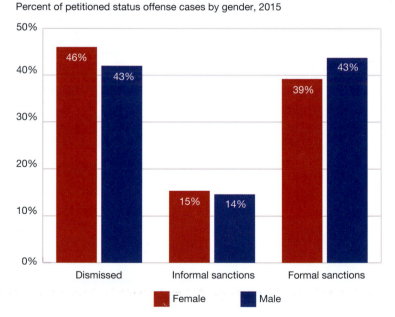

Percent of petitioned status offense cases by gender, 2015

Cases involving females were more likely to be dismissed and less likely to receive formal sanctions than cases involving males.

Overall, more than half of petitioned truancy and runaway cases were dismissed

In 2015, the highest volume of status offense cases for females involved truancy offenses. Of all offenses (both delinquency and status), running away was the offense with the greatest proportion of females. This section looks more closely at case processing for these two offenses.

Truancy cases involving females, 2015
25,100

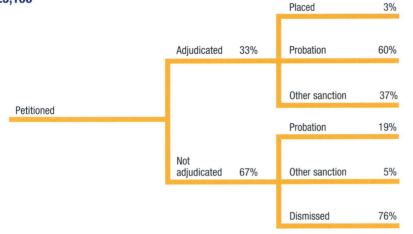

- Two-thirds (67%) of truancy cases involving girls did not result in an adjudication.

- Three-fourths (76%) of the cases not adjudicated were dismissed.

- Formal probation was the most severe disposition for 60% of adjudicated truancy cases.

- Overall, more than half of the petitioned truancy cases were dismissed (52%), a small share received informal sanctions (16%), and one-third (33%) received formal sanctions.

Note: Detail may not sum to total due to rounding.

Runaway cases involving females, 2015
4,500

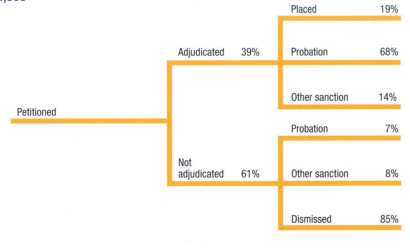

- The majority (61%) of runaway cases involving females did not result in adjudication.

- More than 8 of every 10 (85%) cases not adjudicated were dismissed without further sanction.

- The majority of runaway cases involving girls who were adjudicated received probation (68%).

- Compared to other status offenses, a higher proportion of adjudicated runaway cases received placement (19%) and a smaller proportion received other sanctions (14%).

- Overall, 51% of petitioned runaway cases were dismissed, 9% received informal sanctions, and 39% received formal sanctions.

Note: Detail may not sum to total due to rounding.

Girls accounted for a small share of youth in residential placement

CJRP provides detailed data on girls in placement

Juvenile residential facilities held approximately 48,000 youth offenders on October 28, 2015, the reference date for the 2015 OJJDP Census of Juveniles in Residential Placement (CJRP). Girls accounted for 15% of those youth. Since the first CJRP in 1997, the proportion of female youth in placement stayed within a narrow range (between 13% and 15%). Since 2006, the number of girls and boys in residential placement has declined at similar rates, 47% and 48%, respectively.

In general, males outnumbered females in most offense categories in 2015. However, females in placement accounted for larger proportions of the less serious offenses, particularly status offenses. Girls accounted for 14% of youth held for delinquency offenses, but 38% of those held for status offenses. Specifically, females accounted for 52% of youth held for running away, 38% for ungovernability, 35% for truancy, and 25% for liquor law violations. However, females constituted relatively smaller proportions of youth held for serious offenses, such as criminal homicide (13%), sexual assault (1%), and robbery (8%).

The majority of females were held for a nonviolent offense in 2015

While person offenses accounted for the largest share (34%) of the female offense

Females accounted for more than one-third of youth held for status offenses in 2015

Most serious offense	Females in placement, 2015	Female proportion	Percent change 2006–2015
Total*	7,293	15%	−47%
Delinquency	6,415	14	−46
Person	2,445	13	−38
Violent Crime Index	1,090	8	−36
Criminal homicide	96	13	−1
Sexual assault	45	1	−57
Robbery	380	8	0
Aggravated assault	569	15	−49
Simple assault	1,125	29	−39
Property	1,250	12	−53
Burglary	242	6	−53
Theft	412	18	−52
Auto theft	276	15	−58
Drugs	447	17	−55
Possession	300	17	−59
Other drug	147	17	−42
Public order	547	9	−56
Weapons	74	3	−60
Technical violations	1,726	20	−41
Status offense	878	38	−54
Ungovernable	286	38	−62
Running away	237	52	−50
Truancy	222	35	−40
Liquor law	65	25	−65

■ Among delinquency offenses, females accounted for a relatively large share of youth held for simple assault (29%).

■ Across most offenses, the number of females in placement fell 36% or more between 2006 and 2015.

*Includes offenses not shown.

About the data

The Census of Juveniles in Residential Placement (CJRP) is a 1-day population count of youth held in residential placement facilities on the census date. This count is substantially different from annual admission and release data, which measure the flow of a facility's population. The CJRP 1-day count encompasses both status offenses and delinquency offenses, and includes youth who are either temporarily *detained* while the court processes their case or *committed* by the court after adjudication. In addition, a small proportion of youth may be admitted voluntarily in lieu of adjudication as part of a *diversion* agreement. CJRP does not capture data from adult prisons or jails. More information on CJRP data is available in the "Data sources" section of this bulletin (p. 23).

profile, the majority of females in placement were held for nonviolent offenses. Status offenses (12%) and technical violations (24%) made up more than one-third of these placements. In comparison, person, property, and public order offenses accounted for larger shares of the male offense profile, while status offenses constituted a much smaller share.

Offense profile of youth in placement, by gender, 2015

Offense	Female	Male
Total	100%	100%
Person	34	38
Property	17	22
Drugs	6	5
Public order	8	13
Technical violation	24	17
Status offense	12	4

Note: Detail may not sum to 100% due to rounding.

Most females in placement were age 15 or older

In 2015, less than one-fifth (17%) of females in residential placement were younger than age 15 at the time of admission. More than half (52%) of females in placement were age 16 or 17. Age profiles differed among girls and boys. Compared with males (30%), a larger proportion of females were younger than age 16 (37%) and a smaller proportion of females were age 18 or older (11% for females and 15% for males).

Offense profiles of younger (under age 15) and older (age 15 and older) girls were similar. For both age groups, person offenses accounted for the largest share, followed by technical violations. However, person offenses accounted for a larger share among girls younger than age 15 (37%) than older girls (33%), and technical violations accounted for a smaller share (21% and 24%, respectively).

More than half of girls in placement were minority youth

Similar to the delinquency caseload, most females in placement were minority youth. In 2015, more than 6 of every 10 females in residential placement were minority youth, a pattern that held for each general offense category except drug (45%) and status (47%) offenses. More than three-fourths (81%) of females held for Violent Crime Index offenses were minority youth.

Together, black (34%) and Hispanic (22%) youth accounted for more than half of females in placement. Black females accounted for 55% of the female minority caseload and Hispanic females accounted for 35%.

Race profile of females in placement, 2015

Total	100%
White	37
Minority	63
Black	34
Hispanic	22
American Indian	3
Asian	1
Two or more	3

Most females were in placement as the result of a court-ordered disposition

More than half (61%) of females in placement were committed by court adjudication, 37% were detained while awaiting court processing, and a small proportion were held as part of a diversion agreement (2%). In general, the offense profiles for committed and detained girls were similar. However, compared with the profile for detained girls, the profile for committed girls included a larger proportion of females held for status offenses and a smaller proportion held for delinquency offenses, most notably technical violations.

Offense profile of females in placement, by commitment status, 2015

	Committed	Detained
Total	100%	100%
Person	34	32
Property	18	17
Drugs	6	5
Public order	7	9
Technical violation	20	30
Status offense	14	7

Note: Detail may not sum to 100% due to rounding.

Nearly half of all juvenile females committed were held in private facilities

State or local government agencies operate public facilities. Private facilities include nonprofit and for-profit corporations and organizations. In general, private facilities are smaller than public facilities and tend to hold youth with less serious offenses. Therefore, private facilities house slightly different populations than public facilities.

Nearly half (46%) of committed females were placed in a private facility as part of their court-ordered disposition in 2015. More than one-fifth (21%) of girls were held in a local facility as part of their commitment, and one-third (33%) were placed in a state-operated facility. Compared with girls, a smaller proportion of boys were held in a private facility (40%), while a greater proportion were held in a state-operated facility (40%).

Youth in placement can be held in various settings, including but not limited to long-term secure facilities, detention centers, treatment centers, group homes, and shelters. Overall, more than one-third (37%) of girls committed were held in a residential treatment center, 31% were held in a long-term secure facility, 15% were in a detention center, and 10% were placed in a group home. A relatively small proportion of committed females were in shelters (4%).

Private facilities held the overwhelming majority of girls committed for a status offense (78%) in 2015. In fact, residential treatment centers, group homes, or shelters housed 90% of these females. Private facilities also held a relatively large proportion of females committed for a drug offense (51%). Conversely, females committed for a person offense—a group of offenses generally more serious than drug or status offenses—were more likely to be held in a state-operated facility. Of the girls committed to a state-operated facility for a person offense, 84% were in a long-term secure facility.

Females were held in smaller facilities

Facilities report the number of residents held in their facility on the census date. The total number of residents indicates the facility's size and how many residents it can accommodate.

Overall, small facilities (50 or fewer residents) held more than half (54%) of committed females in 2015, and large facilities (more than 150 residents) housed 15%. As noted previously, private facilities held slightly less than half of all committed females in 2015. The majority (62%) of these private commitments were in facilities that housed 50 or fewer residents. In comparison, the majority (61%) of females committed to a state-operated facility were held in facilities housing more than 50 residents.

In 2015, at least 50% of committed girls (across most offenses) were placed in state or local facilities

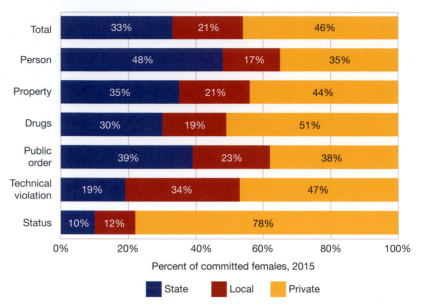

Percent of committed females, 2015

■ State   ■ Local   ■ Private

■ Placements in private facilities were most common for girls committed for status offenses and least likely for those committed for person offenses.

Most committed females in placement were in small or medium facilities in 2015

Facility size	Facility size profile for committed females, 2015			
	Total	State	Local	Private
Total	100%	100%	100%	100%
Small (50 or fewer residents)	54	40	59	62
Medium (51 to 150 residents)	31	31	32	31
Large (more than 150 residents)	15	30	9	8

Note: Detail may not sum to 100% due to rounding.

Overall, time in placement was shorter for females than for males

More than three-fourths of committed females had been in placement for at least 1 month

CJRP captures the number of days each youth had spent in placement from admission to the census referral date. Among committed youth in 2015, the majority (78%) of females had been in placement for at least 1 month, almost two-thirds (64%) for at least 2 months, and more than half (52%) for at least 3 months. After a year, fewer than 1 in 10 committed females (7%) remained in placement. Females were in placement for a shorter time than males, with the median time in placement for committed males (117 days) exceeding that for females (93 days).

Time in placement varied by offense

Females held for more serious offenses remained in placement longer than those held for less serious offenses. Committed females held for person offenses were held the longest: 81% had been in placement for at least 1 month, 59% for at least 3 months, and 12% remained after 1 year. In contrast, females committed for less serious offenses were in placement for a shorter time. For example, 74% of females held for a status offense or technical violation had been in placement for at least 1 month. After 3 months, one-half (50%) of females committed for a status offense remained in placement, as did 45% of females held for a technical violation. The median time in placement for females committed for a person offense (113 days) exceeded that for females held for a status offense (89 days) and for a technical violation (77 days).

In 2015, committed females remained in placement for a shorter time than males

Percent of committed residents remaining in placement by gender, 2015

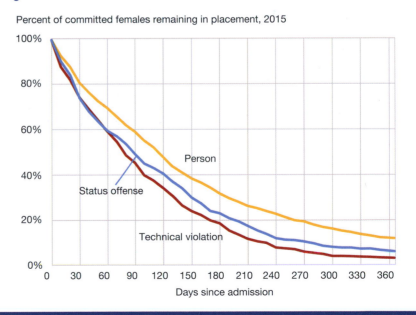

In 2015, females committed for a person offense remained in placement longer than females committed for other offenses

Percent of committed females remaining in placement, 2015

Understanding how the juvenile justice system responds to girls can improve policy and practice

Most girls enter the juvenile justice system for a nonviolent offense and, typically, the system response aligns with the nature of the offense. Three-fourths of nonviolent delinquency cases involving females were either dismissed or received informal sanctions, such as probation or referral for service.

The data show that the number of girls at various stages of the juvenile justice system has declined considerably. Female arrests are at two-fifths of their 1997 peak, and delinquency cases are half of their 2005

peak. Similarly, the petitioned status caseload for females and the number of girls in residential placement are half of what they were in the early 2000s. In the past 10 years, the relative decline across the system (arrests, delinquency and petitioned status cases, and youth in residential placement) has been about the same for girls and boys. As a result, the female proportion at each stage of the system has changed little during this period.

The national data presented in this bulletin provide an example of how states, local

communities, and tribal jurisdictions can examine trends and characteristics of girls in their juvenile justice systems. These data can help identify how girls move through the

system and, when linked to other information sources, assess girls' needs, uncover gaps in services and treatment, and inform strategies to address offending behavior in an effective and cost-efficient manner.

Data sources

National arrest estimates for 1980–2014 were developed by the Bureau of Justice Statistics and are available from the Arrest Data Analysis Tool (www.bjs.gov/index.cfm?ty=datool&surl=/arrests/index.cfm). The National Center for Juvenile Justice developed the national arrest estimates for 2015 based on data published in the FBI's *Crime in the United States 2015* report (www.ojjdp.gov/ojstatbb/crime/faqs.asp). More information on arrest data is available in the OJJDP bulletin *Juvenile Arrests 2012* (www.ojjdp.gov/pubs/248513.pdf).

The National Center for Juvenile Justice developed national estimates of juvenile court caseloads for OJJDP's National Juvenile Court Data Archive. More information on juvenile court data is available in the *Juvenile Court Statistics 2015* report (www.ncjj.org/pdf/jcsreports/jcs2015report.pdf). The information about delinquency cases presented in this bulletin is available from Easy Access to Juvenile Court Statistics (www.ojjdp.gov/ojstatbb/ezajcs) and the National Disproportionate Minority Contact Databook (www.ojjdp.gov/ojstatbb/dmcdb).

Data about youth in residential placement are from OJJDP's Census of Juveniles in Residential Placement. More information on these data is available in the OJJDP bulletin *Juveniles in Residential Placement, 2015* and from Easy Access to the Census of Juveniles in Residential Placement (www.ojjdp.gov/ojstatbb/ezacjrp).

Visit OJJDP's Statistical Briefing Book for more information on girls in the juvenile justice system

OJJDP's online Statistical Briefing Book (SBB), available at www.ojjdp.gov/ojstatbb, is a comprehensive online resource that describes various topics related to juveniles and the justice system, including the latest information on juvenile victims of crime, juvenile arrests, juvenile court cases, and youth in residential placement facilities. SBB also includes several data analysis and dissemination tools that give users quick and easy access to statistics on a variety of juvenile justice topics, including population, arrests, homicide victims and offenders, delinquency cases handled in juvenile court, youth in residential placement, and disproportionate minority contact.

The Office of Juvenile Justice and Delinquency Prevention is a component of the Office of Justice Programs, which also includes the Bureau of Justice Assistance; the Bureau of Justice Statistics; the National Institute of Justice; the Office for Victims of Crime; and the Office of Sex Offender Sentencing, Monitoring, Apprehending, Registering, and Tracking.

Acknowledgments

This bulletin was written by Samantha Ehrmann and Nina Hyland, Research Assistants, and Charles Puzzanchera, Senior Research Associate, at the National Center for Juvenile Justice, with funds provided by OJJDP to support the National Juvenile Court Data Archive and the National Juvenile Justice Data Analysis Program.

This bulletin was prepared under grant numbers 2015–JF–FX–0061 and 2016–JF–FX–K001 from the Office of Juvenile Justice and Delinquency Prevention, U.S. Department of Justice.

Points of view or opinions expressed in this document are those of the authors and do not necessarily represent the official position or policies of OJJDP or the U.S. Department of Justice.

APPENDIX B

OFFICE OF JUVENILE JUSTICE AND DELINQUENCY PREVENTION
JUVENILE JUSTICE MODEL DATA BRIEF

5 Ways Law Enforcement Agencies Can Use Data on Juveniles

Law enforcement agencies are a valuable, and often overlooked, partner in the juvenile justice system. Law enforcement officers have an important job in keeping the public safe, which involves exercising discretion in how they deal with youth alleged to have committed a crime. Law enforcement officers weigh factors such as community safety, offense seriousness, and a prior offense record to decide whether to arrest or if diversion is suitable. Data summarizing crimes that come to the attention of law enforcement and law enforcement responses to criminal behavior can help plan operations, monitor performance of our justice system, and provide a starting place for understanding the front door of the juvenile justice process. Here are five important ways that law enforcement agencies can use data on juveniles.

01 Understand juvenile crime in the community

Law enforcement officers collect data on specific crimes in the community for investigative and prosecution purposes by the very nature of their job; however, law enforcement agencies are increasingly embracing a data-informed approach in their overall crime-reduction strategy (Bahney, et al., 2014). There is a movement to become more rigorous about using data to identify crime trends and neighborhood hot-spots (Roberts & Lissey, 2013). Advances in automation have supported law enforcement's ability to understand crime in their communities by demographics such as age and offense (Roberts, 2013). Understanding patterns of juvenile crime in a community can support the law enforcement agency's strategic plan and tactics and also help community partners develop and support targeted prevention strategies.

02 Improve information sharing

Collaboration between law enforcement and juvenile justice agencies is critical to successfully address the risk level and criminogenic needs of justice-involved youth. Information sharing is one of the primary ways that law enforcement contributes to public safety and efficient use of community resources (OJJDP & IACP, 2008). Formal information sharing agreements that allow for a two-way exchange of information between law enforcement and the juvenile justice system support both the primary responsibilities of law enforcement and the mission of juvenile justice. Juvenile justice agencies can share information with law enforcement to inform charging decisions and investigations while law enforcement can provide information that assists juvenile justice system case planning (OJJDP & IACP, 2008).

03 Manage deployment of scarce resources

Law enforcement officers want to respond to youth law violating behavior in a timely and efficient manner, and data is integral to informing responses. In recent years, some communities have developed structured decision making tools to inform officer discretion when addressing a juvenile's behavior. The officer enters data, such as offense and prior arrests, and the tool provides guidance on the most appropriate response. Some jurisdictions have developed assessment centers where law enforcement can take juveniles alleged to have committed an offense to be assessed by juvenile justice professionals. The data collected through those assessments helps the juvenile justice professional match the juvenile to the appropriate response or service. Such processes are examples of coordinated methods to address juvenile crime and strategically invest resources.

Source: National Center for Juvenile Justice. (2018). 5 Ways Law Enforcement Agencies Can Use Juvenile Data. Pittsburgh, PA: National Center for Juvenile Justice.

04 ▶ Identify risk factors for youth victimization

There is evidence that exposure to traumatizing experiences, like community and domestic violence, can have negative lifelong effects on a child. Police are often the first responders to family conflicts or intra-familial violence, and protecting youth from victimization is a fundamental obligation of law enforcement agencies (IACP, 2015). The federal government is investing in improving systems for law enforcement data collections and allowing for more details related to the elements of reported crime, victims, and social context of the crime (Roberts, 2013). Understanding this information and how it relates to youth as victims, offenders, and bystanders can assist law enforcement agencies in identifying training issues relevant to preventing and addressing juvenile victimization in their communities.

"The Scottsdale Police Department is a proponent for supporting safe communities through the use of data collection and analysis. We are rich in data and have highly skilled staff that provide information allowing us to make evidence-based decisions, enabling us to be responsible to our community. A year ago we implemented a pre-arrest and court record diversion program, Restorative Justice Intervention Program, as an alternative to arrest for first-time offenders who met the program criteria. Our intention is to reduce recidivism through this early intervention away from the juvenile justice system and offer a lasting positive impact to our young people. Data allow us to be intentional in how we intervene with youth based on trending patterns of juvenile offenses. As this program grows we plan to evaluate recidivism of those youth that participate in the program, using analysis to determine the impact this has had as they move into adulthood."

HELEN GÁNDARA
ASSISTANT CHIEF, SCOTTSDALE POLICE DEPARTMENT

PROJECT DESCRIPTION

The OJJDP Juvenile Justice Model Data Project aims to enhance the quality and consistency of juvenile justice information and to increase its appropriate use in policy and practice decisions by providing guidance to states and jurisdictions on data improvements. The Model Data Project is a collaboration between the Office of Juvenile Justice and Delinquency Prevention, the National Council of Juvenile and Family Court Judges, the National Center for Juvenile Justice, the International Association of Chiefs of Police (IACP), the American Probation and Parole Association (APPA), the Council of Juvenile Correctional Administrators (CJCA), the Performance-based Standards Learning Institute (PbS), and researchers from the Florida Department of Juvenile Justice (FLDJJ).

05 ▶ Inform public opinion on crime and safety

When law enforcement agencies demonstrate transparency and accountability by making their data public, either in annual reports or online, it enhances relationships with the public (www.policedatainitiative. org). Seeing the volume and types of crime law enforcement handles in the community contributes to increasing community confidence in their police. Data on juvenile crime specifically can help community organizations identify and address emerging local needs. The impact of transparent law enforcement data is not limited to the local community. Data collected by local law enforcement agencies contributes to the nation's understanding of juvenile crime and helps policymakers evaluate the needs of their community and guide government policy and investments (Roberts & Lissy, 2013).

"The Metropolitan Nashville Police Department supports a specialized Youth Services Division (YSD) that works with communities to identify what works in preventing youth crime and diverting youth from the juvenile justice system. The YSD uses data to foster trust through transparency and by leading with principles that value diversity. The YSD contributes to addressing public safety and better outcomes for youth by regularly collaborating with a variety of community stakeholders and metro-government agencies to identify underserved populations, promote school engagement, support prevention and police-led diversion strategies and to use crime data to identify community needs."

DHANA K. JONES
CAPTAIN, METROPOLITAN NASHVILLE POLICE DEPARTMENT

CONTACT

Teri Deal, Senior Research Associate
Email: tdeal@ncjfcj.org, Phone: 412-246-0846

SUGGESTED CITATION

National Center for Juvenile Justice. (2018). *5 Ways Law Enforcement Agencies Can Use Juvenile Data*. Pittsburgh, PA: National Center for Juvenile Justice

This project was supported by Grant No. 2015-JF-FX-K003 awarded by the Office of Juvenile Justice and Delinquency Prevention, Office of Justice Programs, U.S. Department of Justice. Points of view expressed in this document are those of the author(s) and do not necessarily represent the official position or policies of OJJDP or the U.S. Department of Justice.

REFERENCES

Bahney, A., Daugirda, R., Firman, J., Kurash, A., & Rhudy, K. (2014). Law Enforcement Leadership Role in Juvenile Justice Reform: Actionable Recommendations for Policy and Practice. Alexandria, VA: IACP

Roberts, D.J. (2013). Advances in law enforcement information technology will enable more accurate, actionable analysis. Technology Talk. The Police Chief (80), 58-59.

Roberts, D.J., & Lissy, K. (2013). Incident-based reporting – The foundation of effective police operations and management. Technology Talk. The Police Chief (80), 64-65.

The International Association of Chiefs of Police. (2015). Youth Focused Policing Agency Self-Assessment Tool. http://www.theiacp.org/Portals/0/documents/pdfs/ IACPYouthFocusedPolicingAgencySelfAssessmentToolMarch2015.pdf

U.S. Department of Justice, Office of Justice Programs, Office of Juvenile Justice and Delinquency Prevention & The International Association of Chiefs of Police. (2008). Serious Habitual Offender Comprehensive Action Program Facilitator Guide. http://www.theiacp.org/portals/0/pdfs/SHOCAP_ FacilitatorGuide.pdf

APPENDIX C

NATIONAL GANG CENTER

Gangs in Schools

RESPONDING TO GANGS IN SCHOOLS: A COLLABORATIVE APPROACH TO SCHOOL SAFETY

A guide designed to provide schools and law enforcement with sound practices and collaborative techniques to identify, assess, and address gang activity in the school setting.

iStockphoto.com/Lincoln Beddoe

Office of Juvenile Justice and Delinquency Prevention
Office of Justice Programs • U.S. Department of Justice

Source: Responding to Gangs in Schools: A Collaborative Approach to School Safety. (2019). National Gang Center. Office of Juvenile Justice and Delinquency Prevention. U.S. Department of Justice.

Table of Contents

Impact to Schools

Gang affiliation is not something that students leave behind when they come to school. Gang members do not leave their behaviors, attitudes, and conflicts outside the school environment. Gangs, unchecked and unidentified in a school setting, often engage in threat and intimidation; physical and cyber bullying; fighting; recruiting; and criminal activities such as the introduction and use of weapons, assault, sex trafficking, vandalism, and illegal drug sales. The absence of a well-developed, strategic, collaborative, and effective school safety plan can lead to violence and other unsafe and disruptive activities within a school setting.

It is not solely the responsibility of schools to create and maintain a safe learning environment, free from the disruption gangs can cause, for students, faculty, and staff. To develop a comprehensive plan that identifies effective, evidence-based strategies to address gang issues in the school environment requires the involvement of law enforcement, school administrators and staff, and other key sectors of the community. The **OJJDP Comprehensive Gang Model** highlights such a holistic approach by coordinating the roles of all agencies and organizations within a community that are responsible for addressing gang-related crime and violence. Schools are part of the larger community.

PREVENTION

Gang prevention is based on early identification of occurrences and trends within the school and community and the provision of evidence-based services and activities designed to discourage a youth's decision to join a gang.

THREE-PRONGED RESPONSE

The best strategies are proactive rather than simply reactive. An effective response begins with the coordination of prevention, intervention, and suppression efforts guided by appropriate information sharing protocols. This establishes shared responsibility for tackling gang-related problems in schools.

INTERVENTION

Gang intervention strategies focus on youth who exhibit some level of engagement in a gang and are provided with evidence-based services to facilitate gang disengagement.

SUPPRESSION

Gang suppression strategies related to the school environment focus on proactive measures to mitigate many of the factors that can contribute to disruptive, gang-related behaviors that pose a threat to the learning environment and to the safety and well-being of others.

What Does Gang Activity Look Like?

Distinctive indications of gang activity present themselves in many forms. Determining the presence of gangs, the level of gang activity, and possible threats within a community or school starts with intelligence gathering. Law enforcement agencies use these techniques to gather specific facts that are designed to ascertain and understand the level of gang activity within a community or school and are critical to accurately identifying specific individuals involved in delinquent and criminal activity associated with gangs. Coordination of information sharing between law enforcement and school administrators is essential in answering the following questions:

- Are just a few students creating problems? Who are they? What is the level of these students' gang association or affiliation?

- Are there rival gangs on campus fighting among themselves?

- Are there outside influences or circumstances entering the school grounds and driving the gang activity?

- Are the incidents in question actually gang-related?

Depending on the community, gang identifiers among young people can shift over time, in the same manner that fads and trends change among mainstream youth. However, common gang identifiers can include, but are not limited to, the following:

- Cliques of students wearing the same colors in clothes, bandanas, specific types of belts/buckles, jewelry, charms, or team sports clothing.

- Tattoos, graffiti, and drawings/sketches on folders, notebooks, or school assignments, including area codes and geographical locations represented numerically.

- Hand signs, handshakes, and other expressions of gang association or affiliation.

The reliability of gang identification depends on the sharing and validation of information between school personnel and local law enforcement. Taken together, this authentication of information establishes a more **accurate** picture of the level of disruption and threat to school safety posed by gang activity. It protects individual students from unsubstantiated labels. It equips school administrators with the ability to develop data-driven policies.

Creating a Collaborative Process Between Schools and Law Enforcement

The ultimate goal of a collaborative process to abate gang activity is to:

- Ensure school and community safety.

- Coordinate resources for gang-involved youth to promote successful gang disengagement.

The best way to identify, document, and respond to gangs within the school environment is to create a process that:

- Begins with awareness, understanding, and documentation of the gang issue.

- Develops active collaborations among agencies and organizations that can reduce gang activity within the school environment.

- Identifies students involved in or susceptible to gang activity.

- Provides a range of prevention measures.

- Addresses specific gang behaviors with consistent consequences and offers youth avenues to reduce or disengage from gang involvement.

- Establishes school safety and crisis planning.

- Includes ongoing staff training.

iStockphoto.com/alacatr

The Role of Law Enforcement

Law enforcement is an integral component in the development and implementation of any collaborative and comprehensive safety plan to address gang activity within a school setting and surrounding community. Law enforcement can assist school administrators in identifying problems occurring at school as gang-related. There are a number of steps that a law enforcement agency can take to proactively contribute to the safety of a school/school district that is in its jurisdictional area of responsibility.

It is the responsibility of law enforcement and the criminal justice system to verify and document gang members under state statute; conduct investigations; and work with prosecutors to ensure accountability for criminal gang behavior, incarceration, and probation.

- Provide training delivered by subject experts to school resource officers, campus security personnel, and other law enforcement personnel. The training should focus on current gang-related trends within their areas of jurisdictional responsibility.

- Provide annual gang awareness training to all school personnel as well as to parents/guardians. The training/education should focus on gangs and gang-related activity specific to the community in which the school is located.

- Regularly communicate with school resource officers and other school safety personnel whose responsibilities include campus security and student engagement. The exchange of situational awareness can head off potential gang-related disruptions on campus and within the community.

- Understand the role of school administrators and the various disciplinary options available to them to help mitigate gang violence. When arrest is not the only option, law enforcement officers, including school resource officers, should work in collaboration with school administrators to determine a best path forward.

- When an arrest is appropriate, leverage the criminal justice system and various criminal justice programs to mitigate potential violence or other disruptions as a result of the arrest.

- Work with school districts to develop and implement well-written safety plans. Safety plans in place should encompass all hazards but have a specific section outlined to address gang-related hazards. The plan should be exercised three to four times per year. The exercises should include local law enforcement personnel and school safety officers, as well as school administrators and school staff.

- Develop a trusted relationship in which law enforcement officers, school administrators, and school staff can openly share concerns about suspected gang-related activities in the school setting. Trust is vital. **The timely sharing of information is essential to the mitigation of a potential threat.**

- It is not uncommon for a school district's boundaries to encompass more than one law enforcement agency. Law enforcement agencies need to have agreements in place that allow for the timely sharing of critical information and actionable intelligence among themselves. Disparate criminal intelligence databases and lack of information sharing protocols are barriers that can raise the risk of potential gang-related threats. Connecting criminal/gang databases to RISSIntel™ or RISSGang™ is a valuable way to share information within the law enforcement community.

The Role of School Administration

Gang-related crime and violence in the community can spill over into the schools. School administrators can take an active role in providing a safe school environment by collaborating with law enforcement to assess gang-related threats; document gang-related incidents; address gang-related conduct; and implement a continuum of prevention, intervention, and suppression practices. Steps should include the following:

One of the biggest challenges for school administrators is finding ways to foster safe and positive learning environments that promote success for all students. Working closely with law enforcement agencies and school resource officers will help foster a collaborative approach to success.

- Develop juvenile and criminal justice partnerships—it is imperative to know what is happening with gang-involved students outside of the school setting. This knowledge and coordination will be beneficial if a gang-related violent incident occurs that requires a law enforcement response to the school.

- Conduct an assessment of what the problem really looks like within a specific school and its feeder schools. It is also helpful to review data of gang experience from the previous school year. Become informed of the larger picture by learning about the gang history in the community:
  - What are the current gang alliances and rivals?
  - What gang violence is currently taking place in the community?
  - What gang issues are trending in the community?

Law enforcement can provide detailed, accurate, and current information that may have an effect on the safety of a school. Collaborating with local law enforcement is essential to understand specific gang-related issues within the school environment. This information may include specific gangs and their affiliations, as well as the students involved in gang activity. Ensure that communication among partners is timely; otherwise, information may not be relevant by the time it is transmitted.

- Recognize signs of gang activity and identify those involved. Monitor behaviors for gang affiliation and look for gang identifiers. Things to monitor closely include the following:

  ▸ Social media outlets, to include identification of social media sites and trends specific to the community and school. Gang-involved youth often will highlight their activities via social media outlets, thus providing school personnel, law enforcement, and other adults with supervisory responsibility over these youth with a direct means for gathering information about them. In addition, social media is beneficial for anonymous reporting of gang involvement and/or activity by concerned parents, students, and staff.

  ▸ Students who assume leadership roles on campus may have influence over groups of gang-involved students and their activities. Creating a relationship with those students and monitoring their behavior can help reduce or prevent violence.

  ▸ Behaviors and activities of students in spaces such as lunchrooms, hallways, bathrooms, the schoolyard, the bus stop, the bus, extracurricular school-sponsored events, and other spaces where students can freely congregate before, during, and after school.

  ▸ Apartment complexes, stores, restaurants, parks, or other establishments near the school. These places can be used for gang-related activity.

  ▸ Repeated incidents of disrespect, threat, and intimidation by students (verbal and nonverbal).

  ▸ Reports of delinquent and criminal activity at school.

  ▸ Registrations of students coming from probation, detention, or other schools with known gang issues.

  ▸ Rumors of gang activity in the schools and community; for example, rumors of fights or drive-by shootings.

- Work with local law enforcement agencies to keep an accurate and current record to account for all gang-related incidents and associated behaviors. Accurate documentation of both gang-related activity on the school campus and a student's level of gang involvement is dependent on the corroboration of sources that paints a complete picture. This documentation will be beneficial to law enforcement and prosecutors in the event that criminal activity is identified and prosecution is necessary.

- Make a commitment to staff training; empower all school personnel with the knowledge of what to look for and how to safely respond.

- Encourage timely information sharing by school personnel. Teachers and school staff often receive valuable information about gang activities that otherwise may never be shared with law enforcement. They should report this information no matter how small or insignificant the information may seem.

- Develop/foster partnerships with other state, county, local, and private (nonprofit) agencies/ organizations that may be able to aid in gang prevention, intervention, and mitigation strategies.

Responding to Gangs Within the School Setting

Contain the spread of gang activity

Mitigate risks that foster gang activity

Protect those who are most suspectible

School Prevention Strategies to Consider

Gang prevention is based on early identification of occurrences and trends within the school and community and the provision of evidence-based services and activities designed to discourage a youth's decision to join a gang. Prevention practices can include the following:

- Consult with local law enforcement to bring in subject matter experts to provide ongoing gang awareness and education for teachers, school personnel, and parents and guardians. This training, to include gang identifiers, should be constantly updated and reinforced.

- Provide opportunities to develop relationships between law enforcement officers and students as early as possible, preferably in elementary schools. Bonding and positive relationships with law enforcement officers can influence student choices in the future.

- Implement the evidence-based Gang Resistance Education And Training (**G.R.E.A.T.**) Program, taught by law enforcement officers in the communities and schools they serve, for fourth through seventh grades. The G.R.E.A.T. Summer Program builds stronger bonds with students and their communities, and the G.R.E.A.T. Families component aims to strengthen the resiliency of individual families susceptible to gang influences.

- Refer parents to the **Parents' Guide to Gangs** brochure found on the National Gang Center Website. It provides tips on what to look for and how to respond.

- Utilize mentors who are experienced in working with this population as an added support for students who are at risk for gang joining.

- Provide alternative activities and after-school programing; include law enforcement programs such as the **Police Athletic League** (PAL).

- Develop a **safe-passage-to-school program** for students who have to traverse rival gang territories to get to school.

- Develop community partnerships to support prevention activities.

A key to success is trusted communication and collaboration among school administrators and law enforcement, juvenile probation, and children and youth system providers. The ability to work though challenges is very important. Everyone's role is integral to developing a solid process.

School Intervention Strategies to Consider

Gang intervention strategies focus on youth who exhibit some level of engagement in a gang and are provided with evidence-based services to facilitate gang disengagement. School-based activities can include the following:

- Convene a team of school administrators, teachers, school-based counselors, mental health specialists, school resource officers, outside law enforcement, vetted gang intervention specialists, and representatives from agencies that have responsibilities for gang-involved youth (e.g., probation and parole). Everyone has a different perspective and can contribute his or her own professional expertise. The team can focus on the most difficult gang-involved students by collectively monitoring their behaviors and by providing case management, referral to services in and out of the school environment, and constant follow-up.

- Have a plan for confronting/addressing students involved in gang-related activities. Always consider the safety of students and staff in developing this plan.

- Get to know those students who are suspected of gang involvement. Determine each student's level of involvement and commitment as a member or associate. (Is the student deep in the gang, or does the student have a loose affiliation with gang members?) This will assist in determining the best individual approach to use.

- Establish a rapport with these students; sometimes this is as simple as providing intervention techniques such as mentoring, academic support, and a system of wraparound support services to help students disengage from gang involvement. At other times, it may require justice system intervention.

> **Research has shown that race is not a risk factor for joining a gang. Instead, recruitment into a gang is influenced by compounding factors such as where youth live, family issues, under-resourced school systems, a youth's mind-set, and other individual characteristics, especially peers with whom a youth associates.***

* Howell, J. C. and Egley, A., Jr. (2005). Moving risk factors into developmental theories of gang membership. Youth Violence and Juvenile Justice, 3(4), 334–354.

- For those students suspected of gang affiliation or association, track and document behaviors and progress in school (e.g., regularly monitor attendance and grades). Address concerns of behavior, grades, and attendance. Utilize existing school supports for academic and behavioral issues.

- Be consistent with discipline; hold youth accountable for infractions. Balance consistent discipline and accountability with positive support.

- Use graduated sanctions based on school discipline policies.

- Use conflict-resolution strategies and other restorative justice practices demonstrated to be effective with gang-involved youth.

- Involve these students' parents/guardians early and consistently. Be proactive with parents, and allow them to be a part of the solution instead of the problem. Notify a parent of possible gang identifiers that the school is noticing with his or her child. Parents appreciate your attempts to inform and help them instead of contacting them when their children are already in trouble. A parent who feels that you are being proactive, rather than simply labeling or picking on his or her child, is more apt to help instead of becoming combative.

School Suppression Strategies to Consider

Gang suppression strategies related to the school environment focus on proactive measures to mitigate many of the factors that can contribute to disruptive gang-related behaviors posing a threat to the learning environment and the safety and well-being of others. As a part of a school safety plan, implement suppression practices to end gang-related incidents on school campuses, on school buses, and at school-sponsored events. Suppression practices can include the following:

- Review district policy and ensure that there is sound policy specific to addressing gang-related incidents.

- Ensure that law enforcement is notified and aware once a student is identified as gang-involved (as a member or associate).

- Document and follow up on gang-related incidents.

- All school personnel should be consistent with all students in enforcing discipline and consequences for school infractions.

- Use random safety checks by police and school administration to prevent drugs and weapons from coming onto the campus.

- Practice site security drills to include lockdown procedures.

- Document graffiti, notify law enforcement, and remove immediately. Graffiti tells a story, which can help law enforcement determine whether a threat or incident is about to occur.

- Confiscate gang paraphernalia, and address the matter with students and parents.

Creating a collaborative process to abate gang activity provides law enforcement and school administrators with a powerful tool to stem the escalation of gang-related situations, as well as a means to hold youth suspected of gang affiliation accountable for their behaviors within a disciplined, supportive structure.

Making Schools

S — Share gang intelligence/information

A — Accountability of key stakeholders

F — Foster an environment of trust

E — Educate key stakeholders

R — Response strategies aimed at suppression gang activity

www.nationalgangcenter.gov

MANAGED BY

Institute for Intergovernmental Research

This project was supported by Cooperative Agreement No. 2014-MU-MU-K011, awarded by the Office of Juvenile Justice and Delinquency Prevention, Office of Justice Programs. The opinions, findings, and conclusions or recommendations expressed in this publication are those of the author(s) and do not necessarily reflect the views of the U.S. Department of Justice

Version 1, March 2019

Infrastructure	Data Use and Dissemination	Indicators of Juvenile Justice System Involvement

Juvenile Justice Model Data Project
3D DATA CAPACITY ASSESSMENT

03 ▸ INDICATORS OF JUVENILE JUSTICE SYSTEM INVOLVEMENT

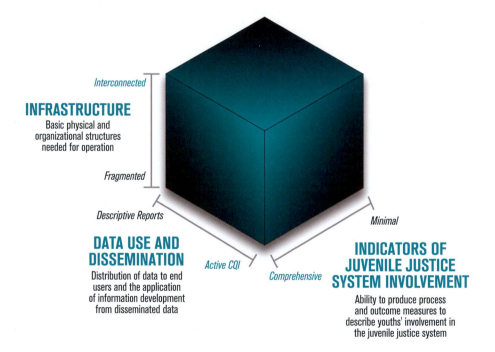

Interconnected

INFRASTRUCTURE
Basic physical and organizational structures needed for operation

Fragmented

Descriptive Reports

DATA USE AND DISSEMINATION
Distribution of data to end users and the application of information development from disseminated data

Active CQI

Comprehensive

Minimal

INDICATORS OF JUVENILE JUSTICE SYSTEM INVOLVEMENT
Ability to produce process and outcome measures to describe youths' involvement in the juvenile justice system

The Juvenile Justice Model Data Project 3D Data Capacity Assessment is a tool for juvenile justice practitioners to strategically examine the data capacity of their juvenile justice system and reflect on their own use of data to inform decisions and drive improvements. The assessment indicates areas where system-wide, agency-level, and staff-level improvements can be made, and the responses listed inform improvement plans. The assessment has three sections: **Infrastructure**, **Data Use and Dissemination**, and **Indicators of Juvenile Justice System Involvement**.

This section, Indicators of Juvenile Justice System Involvement, is intended to help juvenile justice practitioners understand the extent to which their agency and juvenile justice system have the data elements available to them to generate the model measures of juvenile justice recommended by the Juvenile Justice Model Data Project.

INDICATORS OF JUVENILE JUSTICE SYSTEM INVOLVEMENT

The Office of Juvenile Justice and Delinquency Prevention (OJJDP) "envisions a nation where our children are free from crime and violence. If they come into contact with the justice system, the contact should be both just and beneficial to them." It is incumbent on juvenile justice systems to effectively monitor whether or not policies and practices lead to fair and beneficial treatment of youth who come in contact with the system by collecting data and using those data to inform decisions.

It is beneficial to think about system involvement in three inter-related ways:

1. **Counting** – The number of youth involved at various points of the system as well as the number of key system processing events including arrests, admissions to detention, juvenile referrals to court, and dispositions

2. **Responses** – Describing the timeliness and equity with which the system responds to youth behavior

3. **Results** – Identifying the ways in which youth change both while involved with the system and after their involvement

The following 26 questions allow juvenile justice system practitioners to determine the extent to which they have access to the data elements required to apply recommended model measures of juvenile justice system involvement. Items represent two levels (System and Agency), and each item is scored along a four-point scale (No Capacity, Minimal, Moderate, and Optimal). The scale itself illustrates recommended practice. For example the following instances, taken from the assessment, highlight "optimal" practice at the system and agency level:

-   **System: Systemwide Mission Statement** – There is a documented measurable mission statement, and it is measured regularly.

-   **Agency: Risk/Needs Assessment Data** – There is a policy to use a specific risk/needs assessment, and data are captured in data system and able to be analyzed.

Optimal practice and the approaches used to get there may look different depending on a jurisdiction's structure, policies, and resources; however, the responses provided are intended to illustrate one example of how a jurisdiction can improve data capacity. In practice, this means that juvenile justice administrators and/or agency leadership, have rated *Agency: Does your agency consistently use a standardized risk/ needs assessment?* as "No Capacity" will be able to implement optimal practice by formalizing the use of standardized risk/needs assessment and modifying the data system to store assessment scores.

1. creating a list of assessments currently in use across all agencies, as well as throughout the state;

2. working as a multi-stakeholder group to determine where gaps, differences, and/or similarities in use of a risk/need assessment;

3. determining if there is a possibility to make a statewide change in practice regarding the implementation of a single standardized assessment; and

4. following with policy or legislative changes that are needed to achieve a uniform statewide process.

INSTRUCTIONS

The 3D Data Capacity Assessment is most effective when a group of individuals from different juvenile justice-related agencies and different departments within each agency who have diverse perspectives and roles completes it. Juvenile justice-related agencies may vary across jurisdictions, but usually include the juvenile court; probation, detention, corrections and parole agencies; legal representatives; law enforcement; and community service providers. We recommend convening a group to complete the assessment together or to complete the assessment individually and then meet to compare and discuss responses. Some items on the assessment may not be relevant to all juvenile justice-related agencies; however, it can still be beneficial for everyone to hear and learn from their partners.

Please carefully review each item. Respond to each item taking into account current activities and procedures of the system, agency, and practitioners.

SYSTEM QUESTIONS

Does your state's juvenile justice system stakeholder group have a measurable mission statement?

UNSURE	NO CAPACITY	MINIMAL	MODERATE	OPTIMAL
I do not know/ Unsure	No mission statement exists	There is a mission statement, but no way of measuring it	There is a documented measureable mission statement, but it is not currently being measured	There is a documented measurable mission statement, and it is measured regularly

Can your state's juvenile justice system access data to determine how many youth are arrested each year in your jurisdiction?

UNSURE	NO CAPACITY	MINIMAL	MODERATE	OPTIMAL
I do not know/ Unsure	No, I cannot access that information	Yes, but there are some subsets of arrests that are not accounted for in the number	Yes, we have to request this information from another agency	Yes, we have immediate or routine access to this information

Can your state's juvenile justice system access data to determine how many youth or cases are referred to court each year?

UNSURE	NO CAPACITY	MINIMAL	MODERATE	OPTIMAL
I do not know/ Unsure	No, I cannot access that information	Yes, but there are some petitions that are not accounted for in the number	Yes, we have to request this information from another agency	Yes, we have immediate or routine access to this information

Can your state's juvenile justice system access data to determine how many youth or cases are petitioned to juvenile court each year?

UNSURE	NO CAPACITY	MINIMAL	MODERATE	OPTIMAL
I do not know/ Unsure	No, I cannot access that information	Yes, but there are some referrals that are not accounted for in the number	Yes, we have to request this information from another agency	Yes, we have immediate or routine access to this information

Can your state's juvenile justice system access data to determine how many youth or cases are adjudicated each year?				
UNSURE	**NO CAPACITY**	**MINIMAL**	**MODERATE**	**OPTIMAL**
I do not know/ Unsure	No, I cannot access that information	Yes, but there are some adjudications that are not accounted for in the number	Yes, we have to request this information from another agency	Yes, we have immediate or routine access to this information

Can your state's juvenile justice system access data to determine how many youth are admitted to detention each year both pre-disposition and post-disposition?				
UNSURE	**NO CAPACITY**	**MINIMAL**	**MODERATE**	**OPTIMAL**
I do not know/ Unsure	No, I cannot access that information	Yes, but there are some detentions that are not accounted for in the number	Yes, we have to request this information from another agency	Yes, we have immediate or routine access to this information

Can your state's juvenile justice system access data to determine how many youth are under community supervision each year?				
UNSURE	**NO CAPACITY**	**MINIMAL**	**MODERATE**	**OPTIMAL**
I do not know/ Unsure	No, I cannot access that information	Yes, but there is not enough detail to describe the type or level of supervision	Yes, we have to request this information from another agency	Yes, we have immediate or routine access to this information

Can your state's juvenile justice system access data to determine how many youth are admitted to an out-of-home placement each year?				
UNSURE	**NO CAPACITY**	**MINIMAL**	**MODERATE**	**OPTIMAL**
I do not know/ Unsure	No, I cannot access that information	Yes, but there are some placements that are not accounted for in the number	Yes, we have to request this information from another agency	Yes, we have immediate or routine access to this information

Are there efforts to understand the financial cost of system involvement?				
UNSURE	**NO CAPACITY**	**MINIMAL**	**MODERATE**	**OPTIMAL**
I do not know/ Unsure	No, we have not engaged in efforts to understand the financial costs of the system	Yes, we have an understanding of the budget for each sector of the juvenile justice system	Yes, we understand the marginal costs related to residential placements and supervision	Yes, we conduct cost analyses and/or have been involved with cost-benefit evaluations

AGENCY QUESTIONS

To what extent is your agency able to report on these key demographic characteristics?
- Age
- Sex
- Race/Ethnicity
- Residence
- Prior involvement in justice system
- Involvement with other systems
- Current living situation
- Academic performance
- Employment status

UNSURE	NO CAPACITY	MINIMAL	MODERATE	OPTIMAL
I do not know/ Unsure	We do not collect the data elements necessary to report measures based on demographics	We report measures by age, gender, and race/ethnicity	We regularly report measures by at least five of the characteristics listed	We regularly report measures by all characteristics listed

Do all data systems used by your agency share a common method for coding race and ethnicity categories?

UNSURE	NO CAPACITY	MINIMAL	MODERATE	OPTIMAL
I do not know/ Unsure	No, all systems use different terminology for race and ethnicity coding	No, but we have agreed on one coding structure that is preferred	Yes, we have agreed to use the same terminology, but there is no specific strategy that is outlined in a document accessible to everyone	Yes, we have a standardized coding strategy that is outlined in a document accessible to everyone

How consistent is the coding of offense types in similar agencies in your state?

UNSURE	NO CAPACITY	MINIMAL	MODERATE	OPTIMAL
I do not know/ Unsure	Every jurisdiction or agency has its own method of coding offense types	There is no statewide crosswalk, but our agency has a structure for rolling statutes or offense detail up into general offense types	A statewide crosswalk exists that matches statutes to offense codes, but it is outdated or cumbersome to implement	All agencies apply a statewide offense crosswalk where statutes are matched to offense codes and offense detail can be rolled up to general offense types

Does your agency collect information on source of court referral (i.e., the manner in which a youth entered the juvenile justice system) such as law enforcement, school or public agency, etc.?				
UNSURE	NO CAPACITY	MINIMAL	MODERATE	OPTIMAL
I do not know/ Unsure	We do not collect this information	We have access to this information in paper files, but it is not in our primary data system	We have access to source of referral in our primary data system, but there is either not enough detail or too much detail for the information to be useful	We have access to source of referral in our primary data system and have a method for rolling multiple detailed categories into broader categories for reporting purposes

Does your agency collect information on legal representation?				
UNSURE	NO CAPACITY	MINIMAL	MODERATE	OPTIMAL
I do not know/ Unsure	Our agency does not collect this information	Information on whether or not youth have representation is contained in paper files and not stored electronically	Information on whether or not youth have representation is collected and stored electronically and we can report this information, but it either lacks detail on type of representation OR the information isn't specific to type of hearing	We regularly report on the number of youth represented by type (retained, appointed, public defender) and those unrepresented (waived), and which hearings the youth was represented

Does your agency collect information on youth diverted from further juvenile justice system involvement?				
UNSURE	NO CAPACITY	MINIMAL	MODERATE	OPTIMAL
I do not know/ Unsure	We do not collect this information	We can calculate or determine the number of youth diverted for at least one possible point of diversion	We regularly report on the number of youth diverted, but do not collect information on whether or not diversions are completed (if applicable)	We regularly report on not only how many youth are diverted, but also whether they completed their diversion (if applicable), and if they returned to court within a specified period of time

Does your agency's data system track start and end dates for programming?				
UNSURE	**NO CAPACITY**	**MINIMAL**	**MODERATE**	**OPTIMAL**
I do not know/ Unsure	No, we may track some dates related to events, like hearings or home visits, but not start and end dates	Yes, we have start and/ or end dates for their involvement with our agency	Yes, we have start and end dates for their involvement with our agency as well as for supervision levels	Yes, we have start and end dates for their involvement with our agency, supervision levels, and specific interventions

Does your agency consistently use a standardized risk/needs assessment?				
UNSURE	**NO CAPACITY**	**MINIMAL**	**MODERATE**	**OPTIMAL**
I do not know/ Unsure	No, there is no use of a standardized risk/needs assessment	No, there is not a risk/ needs assessment specified by policy, but there are some are used in practice	Yes, there is a policy to use a specific risk/ needs assessment, but data are not contained in our data system	Yes, there is a policy to use a specific risk/ needs assessment; data are contained in our data system and able to be analyzed

Does your agency consistently use behavioral health screenings?				
UNSURE	**NO CAPACITY**	**MINIMAL**	**MODERATE**	**OPTIMAL**
I do not know/ Unsure	No, there is no consistent use of behavioral health screenings	No, there is not a behavioral health screening specified by policy, but there are some used in practice	Yes, there is a policy to use specific behavioral health screenings, but data are not contained in our data system	Yes, there is a policy to use specific behavioral health screenings and data are in the database when youth are flagged for further assessment

Does your agency systematically collect information on a youth's family's presenting issues?				
UNSURE	**NO CAPACITY**	**MINIMAL**	**MODERATE**	**OPTIMAL**
I do not know/ Unsure	No, the information may be captured in case notes, but it is not systemic	Yes, family presenting issues are identified, but the information is stored in paper files	Yes, strengths and protective factors are systematically assessed and the information is entered into a database, and is used primarily for individual case planning	Yes, family presenting issues are systematically assessed and the information is entered into a database and used for both individual case planning and aggregate reporting

Does your agency systematically collect information on a youth's strengths and protective factors?				
UNSURE	**NO CAPACITY**	**MINIMAL**	**MODERATE**	**OPTIMAL**
I do not know/ Unsure	No, the information may be captured in case notes, but it is not systemic	Yes, strengths and protective factors are assessed, but the information is stored in paper files	Yes, strengths and protective factors are systematically assessed and the information is entered into a database, and is used primarily for individual case planning	Yes, strengths and protective factors are systematically assessed and the information is entered into a database and used for both individual case planning and aggregate reporting

Does your agency systematically collect information on incentives provided to youth for compliance or progress?				
UNSURE	**NO CAPACITY**	**MINIMAL**	**MODERATE**	**OPTIMAL**
I do not know/ Unsure	No, the information may be captured in case notes, but it is not systemic	Yes, but the information is stored in paper files	Yes, we document these events in the database, but not in a way that is easily aggregated	Yes, incentives are systematically documented in a database and reports on their use are reviewed regularly

Does your agency systematically collect information on the use of detention, isolation, and/or restraints as sanctions?				
UNSURE	**NO CAPACITY**	**MINIMAL**	**MODERATE**	**OPTIMAL**
I do not know/ Unsure	No, the information may be captured in case notes, but it is not systemic	Yes, some of this information is collected but it is stored in paper files	Yes, we document these events in the database, but not in a way that is easily aggregated	Yes, information on the use of detention, isolation, and/or restraints as sanctions is systematically documented in a database and reports on their use are reviewed regularly

Does your agency collect information on the reason why a case was closed?				
UNSURE	**NO CAPACITY**	**MINIMAL**	**MODERATE**	**OPTIMAL**
I do not know/ Unsure	We do not collect this information	The information may be captured in case notes or an open text field in the primary data system, but it is not able to be analyzed	This information is collected and has specific codes in our data system; however, we do not use it for aggregate reporting	We regularly report on the number of case closures by reason and have benchmarks associated with the measure

Has your agency documented measurable short-term outcomes (i.e., events or changes expected prior to case closure)? For example, completion of community service hours, restitution collected, or treatment completion.				
UNSURE	NO CAPACITY	MINIMAL	MODERATE	OPTIMAL
I do not know/ Unsure	We have not documented short-term outcomes	We have documented short-term outcomes, but do not or cannot currently measure them	We have documented measureable short-term outcomes and can measure them, but have not determined benchmarks or a plan for how the information will be used	We have documented measureable short-term outcomes, set benchmarks, and report regularly on short-term outcome measures
Has your agency documented measureable long-term outcomes (i.e., events or changes expected a specified time after case closure)? For example, recidivism, progression in education, or obtaining employment.				
UNSURE	NO CAPACITY	MINIMAL	MODERATE	OPTIMAL
I do not know/ Unsure	We have not documented long-term outcomes	We have documented long-term outcomes, but do not or cannot currently measure them	We have documented measureable long-term outcomes and can measure them, but have not determined benchmarks or a plan for how the information will be used	We have documented measureable long-term outcomes, set benchmarks, and report regularly on long-term outcome measures
Does your agency collect information on victim services?				
UNSURE	NO CAPACITY	MINIMAL	MODERATE	OPTIMAL
I do not know/ Unsure	We do not collect this information	We have access to information on what services victims received on paper, but is it not in our primary data system	We have access to what services victims were offered in our primary data system, but do not know if the services were completed	We have access to what services victims were offered in our primary data system and whether services were completed as well as other outputs

THE JUVENILE JUSTICE MODEL DATA PROJECT

The Office of Juvenile Justice and Delinquency Prevention (OJJDP) invested in improving juvenile justice data and increasing its consistency across states and localities through the Juvenile Justice Model Data Project (MDP). The MDP developed model measures and analyses to monitor trends and assess the efficiency and effectiveness of juvenile justice systems and provided guidance to the field on the data elements and coding categories required to calculate the model measures. Organizations representing all sectors of juvenile justice—from law enforcement through the court process and juvenile corrections—contributed to the measures. This assessment is one of the products from the MDP. Please see https://www.ojjdp.gov/research/juvenile-justice-model-data-project.html for more information.

SUGGESTED CITATION

Deal, T., Schiller, W., Taylor, M., & Boc, J. (2018). *Model Data Project 3D Data Capacity Assessment: Indicators of Juvenile Justice System Involvement*. Pittsburgh, PA: National Center for Juvenile Justice.

This project was supported by Grant No. 2015-JF-FX-K003 awarded by the Office of Juvenile Justice and Delinquency Prevention, Office of Justice Programs, U.S. Department of Justice. The opinions, findings, and conclusions or recommendations expressed in this publication are those of the author(s) and do not necessarily reflect those of the Department of Justice.

GLOSSARY

1974 Juvenile Justice and Delinquency Prevention Act (JJDPA): A federal law providing funds to states that follow a series of federal protections, known as the "core protections," on the care and treatment of youth in the justice system

adjudicatory hearing: The court process that determines if a juvenile committed the act with which he or she is charged

aftercare: Follow-up processes within the juvenile justice system that target the successful release of offenders without future occurrences of criminal behavior

age of onset: Age at which a juvenile first begins committing offending behaviors

age–crime curve: A trend in which the prevalence of committing delinquent acts increases during late childhood, generally peaking between the ages of 15 and 19 years old

alcohol: Beer, wine, and spirits, which cause intoxication

amphetamines: Stimulant drugs that come in several forms

anomie: Social instability, or normlessness, often resulting from a disjuncture in obtaining socially approved goals and legitimate means to obtain them

antisocial personality disorder: A disorder that is characterized by the person violating the rights of others while exhibiting no remorse for those behaviors

atavistic: The label for physical characteristics, as a result of evolutionary throwback, that indicate likelihood toward criminality

attention homes: Group homes that were created in Colorado to provide extensive programs and encouragement rather than punishment for juvenile offenders

bail: A method of pretrial release that allows temporary release of an accused person awaiting adjudication after the person posts valuables with the court, to help ensure that person will return for trial proceedings

bifurcated system: A judicial system that includes the ability to separate a trial into two parts: an adjudicatory hearing and disposition hearing

biological school: School of thought that used scientific testing to support or debunk theoretical assertions, looking for possible biological and genetic components of criminality

biosocial theory: A new approach to criminology that merged the original idea of genetic predisposition as a predictor of crime with environmental factors, to create a modern explanation of criminality

black hats: Unethical hackers whose purpose is to exploit and destroy, sometimes for revenge

blended sentence: A juvenile sentence combined with an adult sentence; often used for serious juvenile offenders

Blueprints for Healthy Youth Development: Databank sponsored by the Office of Juvenile Justice and Delinquency Prevention that provides information on effective evidence-based strategies targeting juveniles

boot camps: Juvenile rehabilitation facilities that employ quasi-military-style discipline and are intended to shock juveniles back into law-abiding behavior

bridewells: Facilities founded in England in the mid-16th century to house impoverished and delinquent youths and that also offered skills training

bullying: The victimization of a student with targeted aggression by one or more students

casework management: A responsibility of probation officers that involves working with juvenile clients and maintaining files on every juvenile they are responsible for

causation: The relationship between cause and effect

Chicago school: A theory of criminology that says that criminal behavior does not result from individualistic characteristics but, rather, from environmental conditions

child savers: A movement that began during the Progressive Era in America and that proposed restoring the values of the American family by rescuing delinquents from the streets. It emphasized respect for parental authority, and domesticating young women to make them ready to become wives and mothers.

Children in Custody Survey (CIC): A twice-yearly survey administered to public and private correctional facilities by the U.S. Census Bureau

classical school: The first modern criminological school of thought that emerged in the mid-1700s that asserted that human beings are rational and make choices based on their own free will

clearances by arrest: Arrests made because an offender confessed to a crime or was implicated by evidence or by witnesses

cocaine: A powder-based drug originating from the coca plant grown in South America that became a target of the war on drugs in the 1980s

collective efficacy: The ability of members in a community to control the behaviors of other individuals and groups in the same community

Commonwealth v. Fisher: A 1905 Pennsylvania Supreme Court case that settled the issue of child and parental rights in that state by citing the positive intent of juvenile court intervention

community corrections: The use of a variety of officially ordered program-based sanctions that permit adjudicated offenders to remain in the community under conditional supervision

community policing: The system of allocating police officers to particular areas so they become familiar with the local inhabitants and earn trust from them

community service: A juvenile sentencing alternative that requires participation in public programs intended to help the community

community-based interventions: Efforts to control juvenile crime by forming positive relationships with organizations that serve juveniles, as well as police trying to help parents and youths feel comfortable working with law enforcement

concentric zones: Five varying environments mapped by Park and Burgess in the city of Chicago

concordance: In criminality, a similarity between adopted children and their offending parents

concurrent jurisdiction: A condition that allows more than one court to exercise judicial review of a case at the same time

confession: A formal statement that admits one's guilt of a crime

consent decrees: Intermediate measures between probation and nonjudicial adjustment

containment theory: A theory that identifies two types of forces that can control behavior—outer containments and inner containments

continuum of sanctions: A range of correctional options available to juvenile court judges that vary in severity

controlled substances: Drugs that are regulated by the government because they could be dangerous; divided into six categories or "schedules"

corporate gangs: Organized crime groups that are focused on economic success and participate in illegal ventures such as selling crack cocaine

correlation: Demonstration of the fact that changes in the purported cause and effect occur in relation to each other

cottage reformatories: Small facilities created in response to overcrowding that mimicked houses of refuge

crack cocaine: A less expensive, yet more potent, version of cocaine that gained popularity in inner-city, low-income neighborhoods in the 1980s and 1990s

cross-border gangs: Gangs that pursue illegal activities in more than one country, especially prominent on both sides of the Mexico–U.S. border

crossover youths: Juveniles who are seen as victims when managed by the child welfare system and offenders when under the care of the juvenile justice system

cyberbullying: The act of humiliating others by transmitting demeaning comments and photos through electronic devices, often with the knowledge that the material will be sent on by others

cybercrime: The destruction, theft, or unauthorized or illegal use, modification, or copy of information, programs, services, equipment, or communication networks

cyberstalking: Monitoring or harassing others through the Internet with the use of computers, cell phones, and other devices

dark figure of crime: Crimes that are unknown to police

deinstitutionalization of status offenders (DSO): A movement in the juvenile justice system to eliminate laws and policies that had previously placed many status offenders in secure confinement

depressants: Drugs that slow brain activity and are often prescribed for anxiety or to aid sleep

desistance: Ceasing committing acts of crime

detention centers: Temporary housing facilities for juveniles

detention hearing: A judicial hearing that determines whether a juvenile will be detained or released on bail

determinate sentencing: A form of criminal sentencing that imposes a fixed term of confinement on an offender.

developmental theories: Perspectives that focus on an individual's conception of right and wrong as it develops over a period of time (particularly in childhood)

differential association: Interaction in intimate peer groups with others who support law violation and therefore influence others to violate the law

differential reinforcement: Selective reinforcement of a desired response

digital piracy: The illegal copying of music, movies, software, and other digital materials without getting needed permissions or providing compensation

direct service: A juvenile court-ordered form of restitution that requires juvenile offenders to work directly with victims

discretion: The ability of law enforcement to decide what action to take

dispositional hearing: The juvenile equivalent of a sentencing hearing in the adult criminal justice system

dopamine: A neurotransmitter that has been correlated with aggression

drug addiction: Craving of and physical dependence on a drug, causing more frequent use as the body develops a tolerance

due process: The constitutional right to fair treatment for all citizens during processing by the criminal justice system

ecological fallacy: A false belief resulting from the thought that when the crime rate is higher in low-income areas, everyone who lives in government housing and is on or below the poverty line will be delinquent.

electronic monitoring: Use of a device on the wrist or ankle to monitor the location of a juvenile with radio frequency or satellite signal

empirical research: Scientific research, or research that validates or invalidates theories in criminology

the Enlightenment: The time period that marked the end of the Dark Ages, sparking advances in philosophical thought and scientific innovation

evidence-based strategies: Coordinated services and activities that demonstrate effectiveness through empirical research

Ex parte Crouse: A Pennsylvania Supreme Court case that held that the state had the power to intervene in the lives of juveniles if it could provide help that a family could not

exclusionary rule: A rule established by the U.S. Supreme Court that says that evidence seized without a proper search warrant cannot be used in court against persons accused of criminal offenses

fingerprints: Identifiers that are unique to individuals, making them a useful form of evidence in criminal cases

focal concerns: A set of values and beliefs that are important to group members and may be different from those of other groups

free will: The ability to act according to one's own discretion

gang: Currently, the U.S. Department of Justice defines a gang by the following criteria:

1. Three or more people identify themselves as members of the group.
2. Members use intimidation or fear as part of a group identity that uses symbols such as tattoos, styles or colors of clothing, hand signs, graffiti, or other markings.
3. The group engages in criminal activity or juvenile delinquency, and intimidation through violence.
4. The group's goal is to maintain and enhance its reputation and power.

gang detail: Law enforcement detail requiring officers to focus professional efforts on proactive and reactive management of gang issues

gang unit: A permanent division in a police force that uses confidential information and intelligence, and works with gang members

gang-based interventions: Programs and actions performed by law enforcement to dispel the appeal of gang membership and activity

general strain theory: Robert Agnew's 1992 theory that asserted that individuals who commit crime use it as a coping mechanism to deal with strain

general theory of crime: A criminological theory that holds that self-control is developed at an early age through parental management and is the determining factor for participation in deviant behaviors

G.R.E.A.T.: Gang Resistance Education and Training; a 1991 program that used federal dollars to educate law enforcement officers on how to teach life skills to middle school students and help them choose life options other than joining a gang

hackers: Individuals who access computer systems without authorization and often with malicious intent

hacking: Intruding unauthorized into a computer or network for illegal purposes

hallucinogens: Drugs that affect a user's nervous system to create a relaxed feeling and hallucinations

hands-off doctrine: A philosophy adopted by the U.S. Supreme Court prior to the 1960s to allow correctional agencies to manage their charges without court intervention

hedonistic calculus: A mental (and perhaps less than fully conscious) calculation of the pleasure and pain associated with a particular behavior

hedonistic gangs: Gangs focused on getting high on drugs or alcohol and having a good time

heroin: A drug introduced in the early 1900s as a refined form of morphine that has no legitimate medical use

homicide: The unlawful and deliberate killing of another

horizontal/commission structure: Gang management structure involving several leaders who share duties and equal powers over members

house arrest: Confinement of a juvenile to his or her home, generally on evenings and weekends, allowing him or her to attend school and/or work with permission from the judge

houses of refuge: Living facilities that offered skills training, education, discipline, and religious teaching to juveniles in an attempt to change the direction of their lives

illicit drugs: Substances that are illegal except for certain prescribed uses or in certain states, in the case of marijuana

indeterminate sentencing: A form of criminal sentencing that imposes a range of time for a sentence involving detention, allowing for rehabilitation and early release

influential structure: Gang management structure involving no assigned duties to a handful of leadership positions and authority based on the personality and abilities of each person

informal probation: Release back into the community with certain supervisory conditions, such as curfew, employment, and community service

inhalants: Substances that are generally sold for household use and are misused via inhaling as a way to get high

inner containments: The values, beliefs, and level of self-control that an individual refers to when deciding on behavior

institutionalization: Juvenile confinement in a residential facility

instrumental gangs: Gangs aimed at economic success by committing property crimes

intake process: The first stage in juvenile court processing. It typically involves a juvenile probation officer who screens all referrals to the juvenile court using interviews with parents or guardians.

intensive aftercare supervision (IAS): A delinquency-prevention strategy that involves close supervision of juveniles after release

intensive supervision programs (ISPs): A delinquency-prevention strategy that is similar to probation but involves increased contacts with the court and stricter supervisory requirements

Internet: A global network of interconnected smaller networks and computers using standardized protocols, functioning as a highway of connectivity to share information, pictures, and other data

interrogation: The action of asking questions aggressively with the hope of obtaining relevant information in a criminal case

interstate compact: Juvenile placement, often with a relative, outside the geographic jurisdiction of the juvenile court

intimate partner violence: The type of relationship behavior that can include physical, sexual, emotional, and psychological aggression

jail: A detention center that holds three types of persons: (1) offenders who are given a minimal sentence of incarceration, generally less than 1 year; (2) individuals who have been accused of a crime and are waiting for trial procedures; and (3) individuals who have been transferred from another facility to testify in court in that jurisdiction

judicial waiver: The most common method of transferring juveniles to adult courts that is made by judicial staff during the intake process

juvenile bureau: A specialized agency assigned with the task of monitoring juvenile crime and maintaining organized efforts to work with youths

Juvenile Court Statistics **(JCS):** A publication that tracks children who appear before juvenile courts

juvenile drug treatment court (JDTC): A court docket designated for youths with substance abuse issues that have a medium to high risk of offending

Kent v. United States: The 1966 U.S. Supreme Court case that granted some protection for the rights of juveniles but still did not make their rights equal to those of adult offenders

labeling: A criminological perspective that holds that juveniles' self-perceptions are based on how they are thought of by others and how they are treated by people around them

licit drugs: Legal substances permitted for users of a certain age—18 for tobacco products and 21 for alcohol

lineup: A law enforcement technique involving witnesses or victims who are asked to identify suspects from a small group of individuals, including the suspect

marijuana: The illicit drug most frequently used by juveniles; derived from dried hemp leaves and buds and usually smoked

methamphetamine: A highly addictive synthetic stimulant that can be injected, smoked, or snorted

Minnesota Multiphasic Personality Inventory (MMPI): A standardized psychological test used to assess personality traits

modeling: Mimicking the behavior of another person; seen primarily in children, who copy the behaviors of people who are close to them

Monitoring the Future Survey: A survey that collects data on the behaviors, attitudes, and values of about 50,000 eighth-, tenth-, and twelfth-grade students

National Council on Crime and Delinquency (NCCD): An organization that collects data from juvenile justice agencies and assists them with policy development

National Crime Victimization Survey (NCVS): A national survey administered annually to a sample of households in the United States that collects data on victimization experiences of household members

National Juvenile Court Data Archives: A collection of data about offenders on the individual level, as reported by juvenile courts

National Survey of Youth in Custody: A survey that collects detailed data on the types of juveniles in facilities and personal factors that have influenced their behaviors; administered by Westat, a private professional services company

National Youth Survey: A survey that collects data on deviant behaviors from a representative sample of U.S. youths; sponsored by the National Institute of Mental Health

neoclassicism: School of criminology that places the blame for committing crimes solely on the individual and not environmental factors

neurotransmitters: Chemicals responsible for transmission of impulses in the nervous system that can alter the behavior of an individual by impacting the processing of information in the brain

nonjudicial adjustment: Interventions taken by court intake officers that exclude formal handling by the juvenile court

nonspurious: The quality of a relationship between two variables that cannot be attributed to a third variable

nullification: A refusal to enforce laws and sanctions against children because of lack of legislation and statutes geared specifically to children

Office of Juvenile Justice and Delinquency Prevention (OJJDP): An agency run by the Department of Justice that sponsors research, programs, and training initiatives through grant funding to states and localities

Olweus Bullying Questionnaire (OBQ): A test administered to measure bullying and antisocial behaviors in school

operant conditioning: A method of shaping behavior through the use of rewards and punishments that reinforce or discourage the repetition of particular behaviors

opioids: Drugs originating from a poppy plant that are similar to endorphins, a natural pain reliever in the body

outer containments: Direct controls over an individual's behavior, consisting of things such as family values and peer pressure

parens patriae: A Latin term that literally means "parent of the nation." It implies that the government can make decisions on behalf of people who are unable to make their own. *Parens patriae* became the guiding principle of the juvenile court, making the court a child's guardian.

parole: Early release of a juvenile from a detention center with the remainder of the sentence served under community supervision

People v. Turner: The 1870 Illinois Supreme Court ruling that upheld parents' rights to care for their children without excessive or unnecessary government intervention

persistence: The continuance of delinquent behaviors, potentially increasing in severity

petition: A document filed to send a youth to juvenile court

phrenology: The study of the shape of the skull to predict criminality

physical dating violence: Relationship behavior that includes pinching, hitting, slapping, kicking, punching, and shoving

plea bargain: An agreement made between the prosecutor and defense attorney that allows a defendant to plea to a lesser charge and serve a less severe sentence

police process: Interaction of a juvenile offender with law enforcement from initial contact to final disposition

positivism: School of criminality that believed that criminality did not result from individual choice but from factors beyond an individual's control

predatory gangs: Gangs that commit muggings, robberies, and other crimes of opportunity

predisposition report: A comprehensive document that provides a full background report on the juvenile for the judge to use during the disposition hearing

prescription drug abuse: The improper use of prescribed medication, whether it is overuse or unauthorized use

presumptive diminished responsibility: A judicial standard that states juveniles should not be held fully responsible for their actions due to a lack of cognitive development

preventive detention: A practice where serious offenders or status offenders with abusive or neglectful home situations are detained for the protection of society or for their own protection

primary deviance: The initial act of delinquency committed by a juvenile

probation: A judicial sanction that entails a sentence in the community under government supervision, to include specified conditions

problem-oriented policing: Policing efforts, policies, and actions focused on improving police relations in communities as a whole, rather than focusing on juveniles

Progressive Era: A period in America from 1880 to 1929 that saw widespread social activism and political reform

prosecutorial discretion: A lawful choice made by a prosecutor; often used to waive juveniles to adult court in states with concurrent jurisdiction

protective factors: Behaviors that decrease the likelihood that a youth will participate in violent behaviors

psychoanalysis: A psychological approach to uncovering the instinctual and subconscious factors that underlie an individual's personality, often in an effort to determine therapeutic methods for modifying thought and behavior

psychological school: A criminological school of thought that examines how the personality and functioning of the mind affect criminal behavior

ranches and forestry camps: A residential sentencing option that entails a minimum-security placement for first-time or minor juvenile offenders

randomized controlled trials: Experiments where participants are randomly assigned to several interventions, including a control group that receives a standard practice or no intervention at all

rational choice theory: A concept introduced in the late 20th century that assumes that offenders make a choice to commit crime based on the opportunities and threats that surround them

reasonable suspicion: A legal standard of proof in the United States that is less than probable cause and is based on suspicion that a crime has occurred and someone committed it

reception and diagnostic centers: Facilities that determine which treatment plan and placement is most appropriate for juveniles

reintegrative shaming: A strategy used in the juvenile justice system that shows disapproval of bad behavior but provides forgiveness and reintegrates offenders back into society

release on recognizance: Early release from detention with a verbal promise to return for proceedings

reliability: The consistency of a measurement

restitution: An order by the juvenile court that requires a juvenile to reimburse the victim of the crime, either through money or community service

revenge porn: Sexually explicit material posted without the consent of the subject

reverse waiver: The process of sending youths who are over the maximum age of jurisdiction back to juvenile court in certain cases

risk factors: Distinguishable characteristics that increase the likelihood for juvenile delinquency

routine activities theory: A criminological perspective that explains victimization through lifestyle choices, focusing on routines that may expose a person to victimization; also called lifestyle theory

scavenger gangs: Gangs that are quite disorganized and lack goals and consistent leadership

school resource officers (SROs): Officers assigned to schools to provide law enforcement services but also to act as problem solvers and community liaisons

search and seizure: Procedures used by law enforcement when investigating crime commission

secondary deviance: Deviant behaviors that occur after an initial act of deviance

self-report studies: Studies that collect data from juveniles reporting their own delinquent acts

serotonin: A neurotransmitter that has been correlated with aggression

sexting: The use of a cell phone, tablet, or other electronic device to share sexually explicit content

sextortion: The theft of sexually explicit photographs or videos, generally by hacking into the victim's computer or cell phone, and use of the material for blackmail

sexual dating violence: Behavior that involves forcing a partner to participate in any sex act without consent

shelter care facilities: Publically funded facilities for juveniles that function to provide housing for status offenders, neglected children, and dependent minors

social bond: A tie or attachment to the community, developed in early childhood, that encompasses four elements—attachment, belief, commitment, and involvement

social disorganization: A criminological perspective related to ecological theory that links crime rates to neighborhood characteristics

social ecology: A concept that involves the interaction of social groups competing for resources in the same area

social learning: A learning process that occurs through interaction and imitation of others

social study report: A report provided to the judge after a youth is adjudicated delinquent that details all facets of the youth's life and also recommends disposition

soft determinism: A criminological school of thought that posits individuals have a limited number of choices available to them and these choices determine how much free will is in play

somatotypes: Body types that Sheldon felt were related to deviant behavior

status offenses: Acts that are in violation of the law only when committed by a person under a certain age—for example, running away, being truant from school, buying cigarettes

statutory exclusion: A practice that some states use that automatically transfers juveniles to adult court for certain offenses

stimulants: Drugs that increase processes of the body and boost energy and attention

strain: Stress that occurs when individuals feel unable to reach norms through legitimate (legal) means

subculture: A smaller group within a larger culture that provides an identity for its members and has its own unique set of values and norms

supergang: A large and powerful gang in a neighborhood, often absorbing smaller gangs in the area

supervision: The oversight of a juvenile offender by a probation or parole officer that includes casework, counseling, and surveillance of the juvenile in the community

symbolic interaction: A criminological school of thought in which individuals are thought to create a self-image based on their reaction to the surrounding world

synthetic marijuana: A substance that produces a high that resembles the high from natural marijuana; a synthetic cannabinoid produced by spraying chemicals onto dry herbs and other plants

techniques of neutralization: Rationalizations used by people who commit crimes to justify their behavior

territorial gangs: Gangs that often promote the sale of narcotics within their territory and defend it from other gangs

theory: A system of ideas intended to explain a general principle or behavior

time sequence: The amount of time between a purported cause and its effect

training schools: Residential facilities that target the needs of institutionalized juveniles

turf: A geographic region perceived to be "owned" by a gang

Uniform Crime Report (UCR): An annual compilation of crime data from all U.S. law enforcement agencies

urban gang: A gang that appears to offer a lifestyle of protection, camaraderie, wealth, and power. Some of these gangs have become urban legends, including the Bloods, Crips, Gangster Disciples, and Vice Lords.

validity: The extent to which data accurately reflect what is being measured

vapes: Electronic cigarettes that use liquid nicotine or other substances but do not contain tar

vertical/hierarchical structure: Gang organizational structure that divides leadership into different levels

victimization studies: Studies that collect data on crime victims' experiences

violence: The intentional use of physical force or power, threatened or actual, against oneself, another person, or a group or community, that either results in or has a high likelihood of resulting in injury, death, psychological harm, maldevelopment, or deprivation

white hats: Ethical hackers who try to improve security systems information gained by hacking

youth gun violence: The intentional use of a firearm, by a person age 10 to 24 years, to threaten or harm others

youth service program: A temporary intervention to address a specific gang issue; not the primary responsibility of the police but of officers who are involved in a gang detail and gang unit

youthful offender programs: A strategy that imposes strict adult-level sanctions on violent youth offenders while still focused on rehabilitation

Youth.gov: A government website sponsored by 20 different government agencies that provides up-to-date information on effective programs to address risk and protective factors of juvenile delinquency

NOTES

CHAPTER 1

1. Sheryl Gay Stolberg, "Lee Boyd Malvo, Serving Life in 'Beltway Sniper' Case, Must Be Resentenced, Judge Says," *New York Times*, May 26, 2017, https://www.nytimes.com/2017/05/26/us/beltway-sniper-lee-boyd-malvo-resentencing.html (accessed July 5, 2017).

2. *Miller v. Alabama*, 132 S. Ct. 2455 (2012).

3. *Graham v. Florida*, 560 U.S. 48 (2010).

4. "The Execution of Children and Juveniles," *Capital Punishment U.K.*, http://www.capitalpunishmentuk.org/child.html (accessed June 20, 2017).

5. Malia Zimmerman, "74 Children Executed by ISIS for 'Crimes' That Include Refusal to Fast, Report Says," Fox News, July 2, 2015, http://www.foxnews.com/world/2015/07/02/isis-executioners-spare-no-one-killing-74-children-for-crimes-including-not.html (accessed October 1, 2017).

6. "Iran's Hypocrisy Exposed as Scores of Juvenile Offenders Condemned to Gallows," *Stop Child Executions*, January 27, 2016, http://www.stopchildexecutions.com/ (accessed October 5, 2017).

CHAPTER 2

1. Information for this story comes from Charles Webster, "Juvenile Identified as Wal-Mart Bomb Threat Caller," Office of the Monmouth Country Prosecutor press release, March 29, 2018, https://mcponj.org/2018/03/29/juvenile-identified-as-walmart-bomb-threat-caller (accessed July 25, 2018).

2. David P. Farrington, "Age and Crime," in *Crime and Justice: An Annual Review of Research*, vol. 7, eds. Michael Tonry and Norval Morris (Chicago, IL: University of Chicago Press, 1986), 189–250; Alex R. Piquero, David P. Farrington, and Alfred Blumstein, *Key Issues in Criminal Career Research: New Analyses of the Cambridge Study in Delinquent Development* (Cambridge, UK: Cambridge University Press, 2007).

3. Arjan A. J. Blokland and Hanneke Palmen, "Criminal Career Patterns," in *Persisters and Desisters in Crime From Adolescence Into Adulthood: Explanation, Prevention and Punishment*, eds. Rolf Loeber, Machteld Hoeve, N. Wim Slot, and Peter H. van der Laan (Aldershot, UK: Ashgate, 2012), 13–50; Alex R. Piquero, J. David Hawkins, and Lila Kazemian, "Criminal Career Patterns," in *From Juvenile Delinquency to Adult Crime: Criminal Careers, Justice Policy, and Prevention*, eds. Rolf Loeber and David P. Farrington (New York, NY: Oxford University Press, 2012), 14–46.

4. Blokland and Palmen, "Criminal Career Patterns"; Farrington, "Age and Crime"; Delbert S. Elliott, Fred Pampel, and David Huizinga, *Youth Violence: Continuity and Desistance. A Supplemental Report to Youth Violence: A Report of the Surgeon General* (Boulder, CO: Center for the Study and Prevention of Violence, Institute of Behavior Science, University of Colorado, 2004).

5. Anthony Fabio, Li-Chuan Tu, Rolf Loeber, and Jacqueline Cohen, "Neighborhood Socioeconomic Disadvantage and the Shape of the Age–Crime Curve," *American Journal of Public Health 101*, Suppl. 1 (July 2011): S325–332; Delbert, Pampel, and Huizinga, *Youth Violence: Continuity and Desistance*.

6. Rolf Loeber and David P. Farrington, *Young Homicide Offenders and Victims: Risk Factors, Prediction, and Prevention From Childhood* (New York, NY: Springer, 2011).

7. Richard Rosenfeld, Helene R. White, and Finn-Aage Esbensen, "Special Categories of Serious and Violent Offenders: Drug Dealers, Gang Members, Homicide Offenders, and Sex Offenders," in *From Juvenile Delinquency to Adult Crime: Criminal Careers, Justice Policy, and Prevention*, eds. Rolf Loeber and David P. Farrington (New York, NY: Oxford University Press, 2012), 118–149.

8. National Institute of Justice, "From Juvenile Delinquency to Young Adult Offending," last modified March 11, 2014, https://www.nij.gov/topics/crime/Pages/delinquency-to-adult-offending.aspx#note6.

9. Rosenfeld, White, and Esbensen, "Special Categories of Serious and Violent Offenders: Drug Dealers, Gang Members, Homicide Offenders, and Sex Offenders."

10. See, e.g., David P. Farrington, "Key Results From the First Forty Years of the Cambridge Study in Delinquent Development," in *Taking Stock of Delinquency: An Overview of Findings From Contemporary Longitudinal Studies, Longitudinal Research in the Social and Behavioral Sciences: An Interdisciplinary Series*, eds. Terrence P. Thornberry and Marvin D. Krohn (New York, NY: Kluwer-Plenum, 2003), 137–183; Marc Le Blanc and Marcel Fréchette, *Male Criminal Activity From Childhood Through Youth: Multilevel Developmental Perspectives; Research in Criminology* (New York, NY: Springer, 1989); Rolf Loeber and David P. Farrington, eds., *Serious and Violent Juvenile Offenders: Risk Factors and Successful Interventions* (Thousand Oaks, CA: Sage, 1998).

11. Federal Bureau of Investigation, *Uniform Crime Report, 2018*, https://ucr.fbi.gov/; Federal Bureau of Investigation, *Crime in the United States, 2017*, https://ucr.fbi.gov/crime-in-the-u.s/2016/crime-in-the-u.s.-2016.

12. Sarah Hockenberry and Charles Puzzanchera, *Juvenile Court Statistics 2014* (Pittsburgh, PA: National Center for Juvenile Justice, 2017), https://www.ojjdp.gov/ojstatbb/njcda/pdf/jcs2014.pdf.

13. Melissa Sickmund and Charles Puzzanchera, eds., *Juvenile Offenders and Victims: 2014 National Report* (Pittsburgh, PA: National Center for Juvenile Justice, 2014), https://www.ojjdp.gov/ojstatbb/nr2014/downloads/NR2014.pdf.

14. National Center for Juvenile Justice, *Juvenile Court Statistics, 2015*, https://www.ojjdp.gov/ojstatbb/njcda/pdf/jcs2015.pdf.

15. Bradford Smith, "Children in Custody: 20-Year Trends in Juvenile Detention, Correctional and Shelter Facilities," *Crime and Delinquency* 44, no. 4 (1998): 526–543.

16. U.S. Bureau of Justice Statistics, *National Survey of Youth in Custody, 2013* (Washington, DC: Author, 2013).

17. U.S. Department of Justice, Office of Justice Programs, Bureau of Justice Statistics, *PREA Data Collection Activities, 2013*, https://www.bjs.gov/content/pub/pdf/pdca13.pdf.

18. R. DeComo, S. Tunis, B. Krisberg, and N. Herrera, *Juveniles Taken Into Custody Research Program: FY 1992 Annual Report* (Washington, DC: U.S. Department of Justice, Office of Justice Programs, Office of Juvenile Justice and Delinquency Prevention, 1993).

19. Barry A. Krisberg, *Juvenile Justice and Delinquency* (New York, NY: Sage, 2018).

20. Ronald L. Akers, "Socioeconomic Status and Delinquent Behavior: A Retest," *Journal of Research in Crime and Delinquency* 1, no. 1 (1964): 38–46; Lamar T. Empey and Maynard L. Erickson, "Hidden Delinquency and Social Status," *Social Forces* 44, no. 4 (1966): 546–554.

21. David P. Farrington, Darrick Jolliffe, Rolf Loeber, and D. Lynn Homish, "How Many Offenses Are Really Committed per Juvenile Court Offender?" *Victims & Offenders* 2, no. 3 (2007): 227–249; Delphine Theobald, David P. Farrington, Rolf Loeber, Dustin A. Pardini, and Alex R. Piquero, "Scaling Up From Convictions to Self-Reported Offending," *Criminal Behaviour and Mental Health* 24, no. 4 (2014): 265–276.

22. Lia Ahonen, Rolf Loeber, David P. Farrington, Alison E. Hipwell, and Stephanie D. Stepp, "What Is the Hidden Figure of Delinquency in Girls? Scaling Up From Police Charges to Self-Reports," *Victims & Offenders* 12, no. 5 (2017): 761–776.

23. Krisberg, *Juvenile Justice and Delinquency*.

24. Nicholas Prieur, *National Adolescent Drug Trends in 2017: Findings Released*, December 14, 2017, http://www .monitoringthefuture.org/pressreleases/17drugpr.pdf.

25. Clemens Bartollas and Stuart J. Miller, *Juvenile Justice in America*, 8th ed. (Boston, MA: Pearson Education, 2017); Alex R. Piquero, Carol A. Schubert, and Robert Brame, "Comparing Official and Self-Report Records of Offending Across Gender and Race/Ethnicity in a Longitudinal Study of Serious Youthful Offenders," *Journal of Research in Crime and Delinquency* 51, no. 4 (2014): 526–556.

26. Rachel E. Morgan and Grace Kena, *Criminal Victimization, 2016* (U.S. Department of Justice, Office of Justice Programs, Bureau of Justice Statistics, 2017), https://www.bjs.gov/content/pub/ pdf/cv16.pdf.

CHAPTER 3

1. George B. Vold, Thomas J. Bernard, and Jeffrey B. Snipes, *Theoretical Criminology*, 5th ed. (New York, NY: Oxford University Press, 2002).

2. John T. Whitehead and Steven P. Lab, *Juvenile Justice: An Introduction,* 8th ed. (New York, NY: Routledge, 2015).

3. Cesare Beccaria, *On Crimes and Punishment*, trans. Henry Paolucci (Indianapolis: Bobbs-Merrill, 1963).

4. Jeremy Bentham, *An Introduction to the Principles of Morals and Legislation* (New York, NY: Hafner, 1948).

5. Derek B. Cornish and Ronald V. Clarke, *The Reasoning Criminal* (New York, NY: Springer-Verlag, 1986).

6. L. Cohen and M. Felson, "Social Changes and Crime Rate Trends: A Routine Activities Approach," *American Sociological Review* 44 (1979): 588–608.

7. Whitehead and Lab, *Juvenile Justice: An Introduction*.

8. Cesare Lombroso, *L'uomo Delinquent [The Criminal Man]*, 4th ed. (Torino: Bocca, 1889).

9. Cesare Lombroso, *Crimes, Its Causes and Remedies* (Montclair, NJ: Patterson Smith, 1912).

10. Charles Goring, *The English Convict: A Statistical Study* (Montclair, NJ: Patterson Smith, 1913).

11. William Herbert Sheldon, *Varieties of Human Physique* (New York, NY: Harper, 1940).

12. Sheldon Glueck and Eleanor Glueck, *Physique and Delinquency* (New York, NY: Harper, 1956).

13. K. Christiansen, "Seriousness of Criminality and Concordance Among Danish Twins," in *Crime, Criminology and Public Policy*, ed. Roger Hood (New York, NY: Free Press, 1974), 63–77; M. Lyons, "A Twin Study of Self-Reported Criminal Behavior," in *Genetics of Criminal and Antisocial Behavior*, eds. Gregory R. Bock and Jamie A. Goode (Chichester, UK: John Wiley and Sons, 1996), 61–69.

14. Glenn D. Walters, "A Meta-analysis of the Gene–Crime Relationship," *Criminology* 30 (1992): 595–613.

15. T. Owen, "The Biological and the Social in Criminological Theory," in *New Directions in Criminological Theory*, eds. Steve Hall and Simon Winslow (New York, NY: Routledge, 2012).

16. Paul Goldstein, "Drugs and Violent Crime," in *Pathways to Criminal Violence,* eds. Neil A. Weiner and Marvin E. Wolfgang (Newbury Park, CA: Sage, 1989), 16–48; Albert J. Reiss, Jr. and Jeffrey A. Roth, *Understanding and Preventing Violence*, vol. 1 (Washington, DC: National Academy Press, 1993).

17. A. Scerbo and A. Raine, *Neurotransmitters and Antisocial Behavior: A Meta-analysis*, unpublished manuscript, University of Southern California (1992).

18. Whitehead and Lab, *Juvenile Justice: An Introduction.*

19. Albert Bandura and Richard H. Walters, *Social Learning and Personality Development* (New York, NY: Holt, Rinehart, and Winston, 1963).

20. B. F. Skinner, *Science and Human Behavior* (New York, NY: Macmillan, 1953).

21. National Center for Biotechnology Information, *Antisocial Personality Disorder* (2010), http://www.ncbi.nlm.nih.gov/ pubmedhealth/PMH0001919/.

22. Mayo Clinic, *Antisocial Personality Disorder* (2010), https://www .mayoclinic.org/diseases-conditions/antisocial-personality-disorder/symptoms-causes/syc-20353928.

23. Ibid.

24. Edwin I. Megargee and Martin Bohn, *Classifying Criminal Offenders: A New System Based on the MMPI* (Beverly Hills, CA: Sage, 1979).

25. Richard J. Hernstein and Charles Murray, *The Bell Curve: Intelligence and Class Structure in American Life* (New York, NY: Free Press, 1994); Travis Hirschi and Michael J. Hindelang, "Intelligence and Delinquency: A Revisionist Review," *American Sociological Review* 42 (1977): 572–587.

26. Lawrence Kohlberg, *The Philosophy of Moral Development* (San Francisco, CA: Harper & Row, 1981).

27. Clyde Sullivan, Marguerite Q. Grant, and J. Douglas Grant, "The Development of Interpersonal Maturity: Applications to Delinquency," *Psychiatry* 20 (1957): 373–385.

28. E. Burgess, "The Growth of the City," in *The City*, eds. Robert E. Park, E. W. Burgess, and Roderick D. McKenzie (Chicago, IL: University of Chicago Press, 1925).

29. Clifford Shaw and Henry H. McKay, *Juvenile Delinquency and Urban Areas* (Chicago, IL: University of Chicago Press, 1942).

30. Robert K. Merton, "Social Structure and Anomie," *American Sociological Review* 3 (1938): 672–682.

31. Robert Agnew, "Foundation for a General Strain Theory of Crime and Delinquency," *Criminology* 30 (1992): 47–87.

32. Edwin H. Sutherland, *Principles of Criminology*, 3rd ed. (Philadelphia, PA: Lippincott, 1939).

33. Robert L. Burgess and Robert L. Akers, "A Differential Association-Reinforcement Theory of Criminal Behavior," *Social Problems* 14 (1966): 128–147.

34. Edwin M. Lemert, *Social Pathology: A Systematic Approach to the Theory of Sociopathic Behavior* (New York, NY: McGraw-Hill, 1951); Frank Tannenbaum, *Crime and the Community* (New York, NY: Columbia Press University, 1938).

35. Albert K. Cohen, *Delinquent Boys: The Culture of the Gang* (Glencoe, IL: Free Press, 1955).

36. Walter B. Miller, "Lower Class Culture as a Generating Milieu of Gang Delinquency," *Journal of Social Issues* 15 (1958): 5–19.

37. Gresham M. Sykes and David Matza, "Techniques of Neutralization: A Theory of Delinquency," *American Sociological Review* 22 (1957): 664–670.

38. Walter Cade Reckless, *The Crime Problem* (New York, NY: Appleton, Century, Crofts, 1967).

39. Travis Hirschi, *Causes of Delinquency* (Berkeley: University of California Press, 1969).

40. Michael R. Gottfredson and Travis Hirschi, *A General Theory of Crime* (Stanford, CA: Stanford University Press, 1990).

CHAPTER 4

1. Jason Hanna and Amanda Watts, "Tamir Rice Shooting Probe: 1 Officer Fired, 1 Suspended," *CNN*, May 20, 2017, http://www.cnn.com/2017/05/30/us/cleveland-tamir-rice-police-officers-disciplined/index.html.

2. Clemens Bartollas and Frank Schmalleger, *Juvenile Delinquency* (Upper Saddle River, NJ: Pearson Education, 2014); David Ralph Johnson, *Policing the Urban Underworld: The Impact of Crime on the Development of the American Police, 1800–1887* (Philadelphia, PA: Temple University Press, 1979).

3. Robert M. Fogelson, *Big-City Police* (Cambridge, MA: Harvard University Press, 1977).

4. Clemens Bartollas and Stuart J. Miller, *Juvenile Justice in America*, 8th ed. (Upper Saddle River, NJ: Pearson Education, 2017).

5. V. Bolden-Barrett, "Police Officer's Roles in the Juvenile Justice System," Chron.com, 2018, https://work.chron.com/police-officers-roles-juvenile-justice-system-24909.html.

6. Office of Juvenile Justice and Delinquency Prevention, "Interactions Between Youth and Law Enforcement," January 2018, https://www.ojjdp.gov/mpg/litreviews/Interactions-Youth-Law-Enforcement.pdf.

7. Joseph B. Sanborn and Anthony W. Salerno, *The Juvenile Justice System: Law and Process* (Los Angeles, CA: Roxbury, 2005).

8. Terrence T. Allen, "Taking a Juvenile Into Custody: Situational Factors That Influence Police Officers' Decisions," *Journal of Sociology and Social Welfare* 32 (2005): 121–129.

9. Lisa H. Thurau, Paige Pihl Buckley, Geneva Gann, and Johanna Wald, *If Not Now, When? A Survey of Juvenile Justice Training in America's Police Academies* (Cambridge, MA: Strategies for Youth, 2013).

10. Bartollas and Miller, *Juvenile Justice in America*.

11. *Mapp v. Ohio*, 367 U.S. 643 (1961).

12. *State v. Lowery*, 230 A. 2d 907 (1967).

13. *Terry v. Ohio*, 392 U.S. 1, 20 L 2d 889, 911 (1968).

14. See "Fourth Amendment—Search and Seizure," *Justia: US Law*, http://law.justia.com/constitution/us/amendment-04/20-plain-view.html.

15. See Kristin Henning, "The Fourth Amendment Rights of Children at Home: When Parental Authority Goes Too Far," *William & Mary Law Review* 53, no. 1 (2011), http://scholarship.law.wm.edu/cgi/viewcontent.cgi?article=3398&context=wmlr.

16. *New Jersey v. T.L.O.*, 469 U.S. 325 (1985).

17. *Safford Unified School District v. Redding* (no. 08-479) 557 U.S. (2009).

18. *Terry v. Ohio*, 392 U.S. 1, 20 L 2d 889, 911 (1968).

19. *In re Burrus*, 169 S.E.2d 879 (N.C. 1969).

20. *Haley v. Ohio*, 332 U.S. 596 (1948).

21. *Commonwealth v. Guyon*, 405 Mass. 497 (1989).

22. *In re Gault*, 387 U.S. 1 (1967).

23. *Brown v. Mississippi*, 297 U.S. 278 (1936).

24. E. Ferster and T. Courtless, "The Beginning of Juvenile Justice, Police Practices, and the Juvenile Offender," *Vanderbilt Law Review* 22 (1969): 598–601.

25. *In re Carl T.*, 81 Cal. Rptr. 655 (2d C.A., 1969).

26. *In re Holley*, 107 R. I. 615, 268 A. 2d 723 (1970).

27. See, for example, "2010 Tennessee Code Title 37, "Juveniles Chapter 1, Juvenile Courts and Proceedings." https://law.justia.com/codes/tennessee/2010/title-37/chapter-1/part-1/37-1-155.

28. Office of Juvenile Justice and Delinquency Prevention, *OJJDP Statistical Briefing Book*, March 27, 2017, https://www.ojjdp.gov/ojstatbb/crime/qa05104.asp?qaDate=2015.

29. Joshua Rovner, *Racial Disparities in Youth Commitments and Arrests* (Washington, DC: Sentencing Project, April 1, 2016), http://www.sentencingproject.org/publications/racial-disparities-in-youth-commitments-and-arrests/.

30. D. Black and A. Reiss, "Police Control of Juveniles," *American Sociological Review* 35 (1979): 63–77.

31. Gail Armstrong, "Females Under the Law—'Protected' but Unequal," *Crime & Delinquency* 23 (1977): 109–120; Meda Chesney-Lind, "Juvenile Delinquency: The Sexualization of Female Crime," *Psychology Today* 8 (1974): 43–46; Theodore N. Ferdinand and Elmer J. Luchterhand, "Inner-City Youth, the Police, the Juvenile Court, and Justice," *Social Problems* 17 (1970): 510–527; Merry Morash, "Establishment of Juvenile Police Record," *Criminology* 22 (1984): 97–111; Marvin E. Wolfgang, Robert M. Figlio, and Thorsten Sellin, *Delinquency in a Birth Cohort* (Chicago, IL: University of Chicago Press, 1972).

32. Jerald G. Bachman, Lloyd D. Johnson, and Patrick M. O'Malley, *Monitoring the Future: Questionnaire Responses From the Nation's High School Seniors* (Ann Arbor, MI: Institute for Social Research, 2007); Scott H. Decker, "Citizen Attitudes Toward the Police: A Review of Past Findings and Suggestions for Future Policy," *Journal of Police Science and Administration* 9 (1981): 80–87; Y. Hurst, "Juveniles Attitudes Toward the Police," *Criminal Justice Review* 32 (2007): 121–141; Michael J. Leiber, Mahesh K. Nalla, and Margaret Farnworth, "Explaining Juveniles' Attitudes Toward the Police," *Justice Quarterly* 15 (1998): 151–171; K. Murty, J. Roebuck, and J. Smith, "The Image of Police in Black Atlanta Communities," *Journal of Police Science and Administration* 17 (1990): 250–257; Terry Nihart, Kim Michelle Lersch, Christine S. Sellers, and Tom Mieczkowski, "Kids, Cops, Parents and Teachers: Exploring Juvenile Attitudes Toward Authority Figures," *Western Criminology Review* 6 (2005): 79–88.

33. Nancy LaVigne, Jocelyn Fontaine, and Anamika Dwivedi, *How Do People in High-Crime, Low-Income Communities View the Police?* (Washington, DC: Urban Institute, February 2017), https://www.urban.org/sites/default/files/publication/88476/how_do_people_in_high-crime_view_the_police.pdf.

34. Office of Justice Programs, "Frequently Asked Questions," *AMBER Alert: America's Missing: Broadcast Response*, https://www.amberalert.gov/faqs.htm.

35. Bartollas and Miller, *Juvenile Justice in America*.

36. Anthony A. Braga, David M. Kennedy, Elin J. Waring, and Anne Morrison Piehl, "Problem-Oriented Policing, Deterrence, and Youth Violence: An Evaluation of Boston's Operation Ceasefire," *Journal of Research in Crime and Delinquency* 38 (2001): 195–225; Anthony A. Braga and Glenn L. Pierce, "Disrupting Illegal Firearms Markets in Boston: The Effects of Operation Ceasefire on the Supply of New Handguns to Criminals," *Criminology & Public Policy* 4 (2005): 717–748.

37. Office of Juvenile Justice and Delinquency Prevention, "Interactions Between Youth and Law Enforcement."

38. Irving A. Spergel, Kwai Ming Wa, Susan F. Grossman, Ayad Jacob, Sungeun E. Choi, Rolando V. Sosa, Elisa M. Barrios, and Annot Spergel, *The Little Village Gang Violence Reduction Project in Chicago* (Chicago, IL: Illinois Criminal Justice Information Authority, 2003).

39. Bartollas and Miller, *Juvenile Justice in America*.

40. F. Esbensen and D. Osgood, "Gang Resistance Education and Training (G.R.E.A.T.): Results From the National Evaluation," *Journal of Research in Crime and Delinquency* 36 (1999): 194–225; F. Esbensen, D. Taylor, D. Peterson, and A. Frenger, "How Great Is G.R.E.A.T.: A School-Based Gang Prevention Program," *Criminology and Public Policy* 1 (2001): 87–118; "History," *G.R.E.A.T.*, https://www.great-online.org/Home/About/History.

41. J. Little and F. Haley, *Implementing Effective LRE Programs* (Boulder, CO: Social Science Education Consortium, 1982).

CHAPTER 5

1. *Kent v. United States*, 383 U.S. 541, 86 S. Ct. 1045, 16 L. Ed. 2d 84 (1966).

2. Ibid.

3. Sarah Hockenberry and Charles Puzzanchera, *Juvenile Court Statistics 2016* (Pittsburgh, PA: National Center for Juvenile Justice, 2018).

4. B. McCarthy, "An Analysis of Detention," *Juvenile and Family Court Journal* 36 (1985): 43–59.

5. Clemens Bartollas and Frank Schmalleger, *Juvenile Delinquency* (Upper Saddle River, NJ: Pearson Education, 2014).

6. Clemens Bartollas and Stuart J. Miller, *Juvenile Justice in America*, 8th ed. (Boston, MA: Pearson Education, 2017).

7. "Schall v. Martin," *United States Law Review* 52, no. 47 (1984), 4681–4696.

8. Patrick Griffin and Patricia Torbet, eds., *Desktop Guide to Good Juvenile Probation Practice* (Pittsburgh, PA: National Center for Juvenile Justice, 2002).

9. Bartollas and Miller, *Juvenile Justice in America*.

10. Patrick Griffin and Patricia Torbet, *Desktop to Good Juvenile Probation Practice: Mission-Driven, Performance-Based, and Outcome-Focused* (Washington, DC: National Center for Juvenile Justice, 2002).

11. Joyce Dougherty, "Negotiating Justice in the Juvenile Justice System: A Comparison of Adult Plea Bargaining and Juvenile Intake," *Federal Probation* 52 (1988): 72–80.

12. J. Rovner, *Juvenile Life Without Parole: An Overview* (Washington, DC: The Sentencing Project, 2018), https://www.sentencingproject.org/publications/juvenile-life-without-parole.

13. Bartollas and Miller, *Juvenile Justice in America*.

14. A. Nellis, *The Lives of Juvenile Lifers: Findings From a National Survey* (Washington, DC: The Sentencing Project, 2012).

15. *In re Gault*, 387 U.S. 1, 18 L. Ed. 527, 87 S. Ct. 1428 (1967).

16. *In re Winship*, 397 U.S. 358, 90 S. Ct. 1968, 25 L. Ed. 2d 368 (1970).

17. *McKeiver v. Pennsylvania*, 403 U.S. 528, 535 (1971).

18. *In re Terry*, 438 Pa. 339, 265 A. 2d 350 (1970).

19. *In re Barbara Burruss*, 275 N.C. 517, 169 S.E. 2d 879 (1969).

20. *Breed v. Jones*, 421 U.S. 519, 95 S. Ct. 1779 (1975).

21. Elizabeth S. Scott and Thomas Grisso, "The Evolution of Adolescence: A Developmental Perspective on Juvenile Justice Reform," *Journal of Criminology and Criminal Justice* 88 (1998): 137–174.

22. Todd D. Minton, *Jail Inmates at Midyear 2009* (Washington, DC: U.S. Department of Justice, Office of Juvenile Justice and Delinquency Prevention, June 2010).

23. Patrick Griffin, Sean Addie, Benjamin Adams, and Kathy Firestine, *Trying Juveniles as Adults: An Analysis of State Transfer Laws and Reporting* (Washington, DC: Juvenile Offenders and Victims, National Report Series, September 2011), 10.

24. Kent v. United States, 383 U.S. 541, 86 S. Ct. 1045, 16 L. Ed. 2d 84 (1966).

25. Bartollas and Miller, *Juvenile Justice in America*.

26. U.S. Congress, Senate Committee on the Judiciary, Subcommittee to Investigate Juvenile Delinquency, 1973, *The Juvenile Justice and Delinquency Prevention Act*, S. 3148 and S. 821. 92d Cong. 2d sess.; 93d Cong. 1st sess.; National Council on Juvenile Justice, *National Juvenile Court Case Records 1975–1992* (Pittsburgh, PA: National Center for Juvenile Justice, 1994).

27. Federal Advisory Committee on Juvenile Justice, *Annual Report 2008* (Washington, DC: Office of Juvenile Justice and Delinquency Prevention, 2008), 1.

28. Charles W. Thomas, "Are Status Offenders Really so Different?" *Crime and Delinquency* 22 (1976): 440–442.

29. Bartollas and Miller, *Juvenile Justice in America*; Federal Advisory Committee on Juvenile Justice, *Annual Report 2010* (Washington, DC: Office of Juvenile Justice and Delinquency Prevention, 2010), 3.

30. Annie E. Casey Foundation, http://www.aecf.org.

31. Federal Advisory Committee on Juvenile Justice, *Annual Report 2010*, 5.

32. Office of Juvenile Justice and Delinquency Prevention, "Juveniles in Adult Prisons," *Statistical Briefing Book*, https://www.ojjdp.gov/ojstatbb/corrections/qa08700.asp?qaDate=2014 (released December 13, 2015).

33. Office of Juvenile Justice and Delinquency Prevention, *Statistical Briefing Book*, https://www.ojjdp.gov/ojstatbb/

34. Bartollas and Miller, *Juvenile Justice in America*.

35. *Gregg v. Georgia*, 48 U.S. 153 (1976).

36. *Eddings v. Oklahoma*, 102 S. Ct. 869 (1982).

37. *Thompson v. Oklahoma*, 487 U.S. 815 (1988).

38. *Atkins v. Virginia*, 536 U.S. 304 (2002).

39. *Roper v. Simmons* (03-633), 112 SW 3d 397 (2003).

CHAPTER 6

1. Commonwealth v. Fisher, 27 Pa. Super. 175 (1905).

2. S. Hockenberry and C. Puzzanchera, *Juvenile Court Statistics* (Pittsburgh, PA: National Center for Juvenile Justice, April 2018).

3. National Center for Juvenile Justice, *Juvenile Offenders and Victims: 2014 Report* (2014), https://www.ojjdp.gov/ojstatbb/nr2014/downloads/chapter7.pdf; OJJDP, "Juvenile Probation" (1999), https://www.ojjdp.gov/pubs/jaibgbulletin/over.html.

4. Clemens Bartollas and Stuart J. Miller, *Juvenile Justice in America*, 8th ed. (Boston, MA: Pearson Education, 2017).

5. Lori Colley, Robert G. Culbertson, and Edward J. Latessa, "Juvenile Probation Officers: A Job Analysis," *Juvenile and Family Court Journal* 38 (1987): 1–12.

6. Douglas W. Young, Jill L. Farrell, and Faye S. Taxman, "Impacts of Juvenile Probation Training Models on Youth Recidivism," *Justice Quarterly* 30 (2013): 1068–1089.

7. *Mempa v. Rhay*, 339 U.S. 128, 2d Cir. 3023 (1968).

8. *Gagnon v. Scarpelli*, 411 U.S. 778 (1973).

9. Bartollas and Miller, *Juvenile Justice in America*; National Juvenile Defender Center, "Juvenile Court Terminology" (2017), http://njdc.info/juvenile-court-terminology/; Anne L. Schneider, "Restitution and Recidivism Rates of Juvenile Offenders: Results From Four Experimental Studies," *Criminology* 24 (1986): 533.

10. Patrick Griffin and Patricia Torbet, eds., *Desktop Guide to Good Juvenile Probation Practice* (Pittsburgh, PA: National Center for Juvenile Justice, 2002).

11. City of Baton Rouge, "Juvenile Services," http://brgov.com/dept/juvenile/isp.htm.

12. Sarah Hockenberry, Andrew Wachter, and Anthony Sladky, *Juvenile Residential Facility Census, 2014: Selected Findings* (Washington, DC: U.S. Department of Justice, September 2016), https://www.ojjdp.gov/pubs/250123.pdf.

13. Bartollas and Miller, *Juvenile Justice in America*.

14. Coalition for Juvenile Justice, *Juvenile Justice and Delinquency Prevention Act* (2017), http://www.juvjustice.org/federal-policy/juvenile-justice-and-delinquency-prevention-act; Office of Juvenile Justice and Delinquency Prevention, *The Mandates* (1994), https://www.ncjrs.gov/txtfiles/fs-9407.txt.

15. Ira M. Schwartz, Linda Harris, and Laurie Levi, "The Jailing of Juveniles in Minnesota: A Case Study," *Crime & Delinquency* 34 (1988): 146; David Steinhart, "California's Legislature Ends the Jailing of Children: The Story of Policy Reversal," *Crime & Delinquency* 34 (1988): 169–170; D. Steinhart and B. Krisberg, "Child in Jail," *State Legislature* 13 (1987): 12–16.

16. Office of Juvenile Justice and Delinquency Prevention, "Residential Programs," *Literature Review: A Product of the Model Programs Guide* (September 2010), https://www.ojjdp.gov/mpg/litreviews/Residential.pdf.

17. Office of Juvenile Justice and Delinquency Prevention, "Juvenile Justice Reform Initiatives in the States 1994–1996: Juvenile Boot Camps," https://www.ojjdp.gov/pubs/reform/ch2_g.html.

18. National Center for Juvenile Justice, *Juvenile Offenders and Victims: 2014 Report*.

19. Bartollas and Miller, *Juvenile Justice in America*.

20. National Center for Juvenile Justice, *Juvenile Offenders and Victims: 2014 Report*.

21. *White v. Reid*, 125 F. Supp. 647 (D.D.C. 1954).

22. Inmates of the Boys' Training School v. Affleck, 346 F. Supp. 1354 (D.R.I. 1972).

23. *Nelson v. Heyne*, 355 F. Supp. 451 (N.D. Ind. 1972).

24. *Morales v. Turman*, 364 F. Supp. 166 (E.D. Tex. 1973).

25. *Pena v. New York State Division for Youth*, 419 F. Supp. 203 (S.D.N.Y. 1976).

26. Morgan v. Sproat, 432 F. Supp. 1130 (S.D. Miss. 1977).

27. Federal Advisory Committee on Juvenile Justice, *Annual Report 2010* (Washington, DC: Office of Juvenile Justice and Delinquency Prevention, 2010).

28. Laura S. Abrams and Susan M. Snyder, "Youth Offender Reentry: Models for Intervention and Directions for Future Inquiry," *Children and Youth Services Review* 12 (2010): 1787–1795; Howard N. Snyder, "An Empirical Portrait of the Youth Reentry Population," *Youth Violence and Juvenile Justice* 2 (2004): 39–55.

29. National Juvenile Defender Center, "Juvenile Court Terminology."

30. D. A. Andrews and James Bonta, "Level of Security Inventory-Revised," *MHS Assessments* (2017), https://www.mhs.com/MHS-Publicsafety?prodname=lsi-r.

31. David Altschuler and Troy Armstrong, "Intensive Aftercare for the High-Risk Juvenile Parolee: Issues and Approaches in Reintegration and Community Supervision," in *Intensive Interventions With High-Risk Youths: Promising Approaches in Juvenile Probation and Parole*, ed. Troy Armstrong (Monsey, NY: Criminal Justice Press, 1991), 49–50.

32. Purdon's Pennsylvania Statutes Annotated 62 PS. Paragraph 731, 1968, 82.

33. T. Clear, M. Reisig, and G. Cole, *American Corrections*, 12th ed. (Boston, MA: Cengage Learning, 2018).

34. P. McCarthy, V. Schiraldi, and M. Shark, *The Future of Youth Justice: A Community-Based Alternative to the Youth Prison Model* (Washington, DC: National Institute of Justice, 2016).

CHAPTER 7

1. Luc Sante, *Low Life: Lures and Snares of Old New York* (New York: Vintage Books, 1991); Robert Redfield, *Folk Culture of Yucatan* (Chicago, IL: University of Chicago Press, 1941).

2. Frederic Thrasher, *The Gang: A Study of 1,313 Gangs in Chicago* (Chicago, IL: University of Chicago Press, 1927).

3. Walter B. Miller, "The Impact of a Total Community Delinquency Control Project," *Social Problems* 10 (1962): 168–191; Clemens Bartollas and Stuart J. Miller, eds., *Juvenile Justice in America*, 8th ed. (Boston, MA: Pearson Education, 2017).

4. National Youth Gang Center, *National Youth Gang Survey Analysis* (Washington, DC: Office of Juvenile Justice and Delinquency Prevention, National Youth Gang Center, 2007), https://www.nationalgangcenter.gov/survey-analysis.

5. U.S. Department of Justice, *About Violent Gangs*, https://www.justice.gov/criminal-ocgs/about-violent-gangs; James C. Howell, *Gangs in America's Communities* (Los Angeles, CA: Sage, 2012).

6. Arlen Egley, James C. Howell, and Meena Harris, "Highlights of the 2012 National Youth Gang Survey," *Juvenile Justice Fact Sheet* (Washington, DC: U.S. Department of Justice, December 2014).

7. National Council for Crime and Delinquency, "Girls and Gangs: Improving Our Understanding and Ability to Respond," June 2017, https://www.nccdglobal.org/sites/default/files/Girls%20and%20Gangs%20Executive%20Summary.pdf.

8. A. Sweeney, "Impact of Chicago's Violence on Girls in Toughest Neighborhoods Often Overlooked," *Chicago Tribune* (December 10, 2016).

9. E. Maxwell and A. Henning, "Female Gang Membership: Current Trends and Future Directions," *Police Chief Magazine* (2018), http://www.policechiefmagazine.org/female-gang-membership/.

10. Carl S. Taylor, *Dangerous Society* (East Lansing: Michigan State University Press, 1990).

11. C. Ronald Huff, "Youth Gangs and Public Policy," *Crime & Delinquency* 35 (1989): 528–529.

12. Jeffrey Fagan, "The Social Organization of Drug Use and Drug Dealing Among Urban Gangs," *Criminology* 27 (1989): 633–664.

13. As cited in Bartollas and Miller, *Juvenile Justice in America*.

14. National Gang Intelligence Center, *National Gang Report 2015* (2015), https://www.fbi.gov/file-repository/stats-services-publications-national-gang-report-2015.pdf/view.

15. Ibid.

16. Mike Carlie, *Into the Abyss: A Personal Journey Into the World of Street Gangs* (2002), http://people.missouristate.edu/michaelcarlie/.

17. Egley, Howell, and Harris, "Highlights of the 2012 National Youth Gang Survey"; Howell, *Gangs in America's Communities*.

18. Herbert Bloch and Arthur Niederhoffer, *The Gang: A Study in Adolescent Behavior* (New York, NY: Philosophical Library, 1958); Richard A. Cloward and Lloyd E. Ohlin, *Delinquency and Opportunity: A Theory of Delinquent Gangs* (New York, NY: Free Press, 1960); Albert K. Cohen, *Delinquent Boys: The Culture of the Gang* (Glencoe, IL: Free Press, 1955); Walter B. Miller, "Lower-Class Culture as a Generating Milieu of Gang Delinquency," *Journal of Social Issues* 14 (1958): 5–19; Lewis Yablonsky, *The Violent Gang* (New York, NY: Macmillan, 1963).

19. As cited in Bartollas and Miller, *Juvenile Justice in America*.

20. National Gang Intelligence Center, *National Gang Report 2015*.

21. G.R.E.A.T., "What Is G.R.E.A.T.?" 2017, https://www.great-online.org/Home/About/What-Is-GREAT.

22. Finn-Aage Esbensen, Dana Peterson, Terrance J. Taylor, and D. Wayne Osgood, *Is G.R.E.A.T. Effective? Does the Program Prevent Gang Joining? Results From the National Evaluation of G.R.E.A.T.* (2012), https://www.umsl.edu/ccj/pdfs/great/GREAT%20Wave%204%20Outcome%20Report.

23. National Gang Center, "Frequently Asked Questions About Gangs," 2018, https://www.nationalgangcenter.gov/About/FAQ#q10.

CHAPTER 8

1. Shibani Mahtani, "Profile of a School Shooter," *The Wall Street Journal* (June 3, 2018), https://www.wsj.com/articles/profile-of-a-school-shooter-1528023600.

2. Violence Prevention Alliance, "Definition and Typology of Violence," 2018, http://www.who.int/violenceprevention/approach/definition/en/.

3. Matt DeLisi and Alex R. Piquero, "New Frontiers in Criminal Careers Research, 2000–2011: A State-of-the-Art Review," *Journal of Criminal Justice* 39 (2011): 289–301; David P. Farrington, Rolf Loeber, and Mark T. Berg, "Young Men Who Kill: A Prospective Longitudinal Examination From Childhood," *Homicide Studies* 16 (2012): 99–128.

4. Michael Luca, Deepak Malhotra, and Christopher Poliquin, *The Impact of Mass Shootings on Gun Policy*, working paper 16-126 (Boston, MA: Harvard University, Harvard Business School, 2016).

5. Office of Juvenile Justice and Delinquency Prevention, *Gun Violence and Youth* (December 2016), https://www.ojjdp.gov/mpg/litreviews/gun-violence-and-youth.pdf.

6. Centers for Disease Control, *Web-Based Injury Statistics Query and Reporting System* (Atlanta, GA: Centers for Disease Control, National Center for Injury Prevention and Control, 2016), http://www.cdc.gov/injury/wisqars/index.html.

7. Ibid.

8. Luca, Malhotra, and Poliquin, *The Impact of Mass Shootings on Gun Policy*.

9. Kara E. Rudolph, Elizabeth A. Stuart, Jon S. Vernick, and Daniel W. Webster, "Association Between Connecticut's Permit-to-Purchase Handgun Law and Homicides," *American Journal of Public Health* 105, no. 8 (2015): e49–54.

10. Anthony A. Braga and David M. Hureau, "Strong Gun Laws Are Not Enough: The Need for Improved Enforcement of Secondhand Gun Transfer Laws in Massachusetts," *Preventive Medicine* 79 (2015): 37–42.

11. Office of Juvenile Justice and Delinquency Prevention, *Reducing Youth Gun Violence: An Overview of Programs and Initiatives* (Washington, DC: U.S. Department of Justice, Office of Justice Programs, 1996), https://www.ncjrs.gov/pdffiles/redyouth.pdf.

12. William G. Doerner and Steven P. Lab, *Victimology*, 7th ed. (New York, NY: Routledge, 2015).

13. Lauren Musu-Gillette, Anlan Zhang, Ke Wang, Jizhi Zhang, and Barbara A. Oudekerk, *Indicators of School Crime and Safety: 2016*, NCES 2017-064, NCJ 250650 (National Center for Education Statistics, U.S. Department of Education, U.S. Department of Justice Office of Justice Programs, 2017), https://nces.ed.gov/pubs2017/2017064.pdf.

14. Harlan Luxenberg, Susan P. Limber, and Dan Olweus, *Bullying in U.S. Schools: 2014 Status Report* (Center City, MN: Hazelden Publishing, 2015), http://www.violencepreventionworks.org/public/index.page.

15. Centers for Disease Control and Prevention, "School-Associated Violent Death Study" (2016), https://www.cdc.gov/ViolencePrevention/youthviolence/schoolviolence/SAVD.html.

16. George E. Higgins, Catherine D. Marcum, Jason Nicholson, and Phillip Weiner, "Predictors of Physical and Dating Violence in Middle and High School Students in the United States," *Crime & Delinquency* 64, no. 5 (2018): 625–649.

17. Michele C. Black, Kathleen C. Basile, Matthew J. Breiding, Sharon G. Smith, Mikel L. Walters, Melissa T. Merrick, Jieru Chen, and Mark R. Stevens, *The National Intimate Partner and Sexual Violence Survey: 2010 Summary Report* (Atlanta, GA: National Center for Injury Prevention and Control, Centers for Disease Control and Prevention, 2011), https://www.cdc.gov/violenceprevention/pdf/nisvs_executive_summary-a.pdf.

18. Kevin J. Vagi, Emily Rothman, Natasha E. Latzman, Andra Teten Tharp, Diane M. Hall, and Matthew J. Breiding, "Beyond Correlates: A Review of Risk and Protective Factors for Adolescent Dating Violence Perpetration," *Journal of Youth and Adolescence* 42 (2013): 633–649.

19. Daphne Bavelier, C. Shawn Green, Doug Hyun Han, Perry F. Renshaw, Michael M. Merzenich, and Douglas A. Gentile, "Brains on Video Games," *Nature Reviews Neuroscience* 12 (2011): 763–768; Gregory R. Mitchell, "Revisiting Truth or Triviality: The External Validity of Research in the Psychological Laboratory," *Perspectives on Psychological Science* 7 (2012): 109–117.

20. Tobias Greitemeyer and Neil McLatchie, "Denying Humanness to Others: A Newly Discovered Mechanism by Which Violent Video Games Increase Aggressive Behavior," *Psychological Science* 22 (2011): 659–665.

21. Christopher J. Ferguson, "The Good, the Bad and the Ugly: A Meta-Analytic Review of Positive and Negative Effects of Violent Video Games," *Psychiatric Quarterly* 78 (2007): 309–316; Christopher J. Ferguson, C. R. Torres San Miguel, Adolfo Garza, and Jessica M. Jerabeck, "A Longitudinal Test of Video Game Violence Influences on Dating and Aggression: A 3-Year Longitudinal Study of Adolescents," *Journal of Psychiatric Research* 46 (2012): 141–146; Christopher J. Ferguson, Claudia San Miguel, Richard D. Hartley, "A Multivariate Analysis of Youth Violence and Aggression: The Influence of Family, Peers, Depression, and Media Violence," *Journal of Pediatrics* 155 (2009): 904–908.

22. *Brown v. Entertainment Merchants Association*, 564 U.S. 786 (2011).

CHAPTER 9

1. Some of the details for this story come from Kevin Poulsen, "Former Teen Hacker's Suicide Linked to TJX Probe," *Wired*, July 7, 2009, https://www.wired.com/2009/07/hacker-3 (accessed July 21, 2018).

2. Stephen M. Rosoff, Henry N. Pontell, and Robert Tillman, *Profit Without Honor: White-Collar Crime and the Looting of America* (Upper Saddle River, NJ: Prentice Hall, 2002).

3. George E. Higgins and Catherine D. Marcum, *Digital Piracy: An Integrated Theoretical Approach* (Durham, NC: Carolina Academic Press, 2011).

4. Brandon Gaille, "23 Shocking Music Piracy Statistics," May 23, 2017, https://brandongaille.com/21-shocking-music-piracy-statistics/; information gathered from Columbia University, Freakonomics, BBC News, and other resources, courtesy of www.backgroundcheck.org.

5. George E. Higgins, Catherine D. Marcum, Tina L. Freiburger, and Melissa L. Ricketts, "Examining the Role of Peer Influence and Self-Control on Downloading Behavior," *Deviant Behavior* 33 (2012): 412–423; George E. Higgins, Scott E. Wolfe, and Catherine D. Marcum, "Digital Piracy: An Examination of Three Measurements of Self-Control," *Deviant Behavior* 29, no. 5 (2008): 440–461; George E. Higgins, Scott E. Wolfe, and Melissa L. Ricketts, "Digital Piracy: A Latent Class Analysis," *Social Science Computer Review* 27, no. 1 (2009): 24–40; Sameer Hinduja, "Neutralization Theory and Online Software Piracy: An Empirical Analysis," *Ethics and Information Technology* 5 (2007): 49–61; Sameer Hinduja and Jason R. Ingram, "Social Learning Theory and Music Piracy: The Differential Role of Online and Offline Peer Influences," *Criminal Justice Studies* 22, no. 4 (2009): 407–422.

6. Tonja R. Nansel, Mary Overpeck, Ramani S. Pilla, W. June Ruan, Bruce Simons-Morton, and Peter Scheidt, "Bullying Behaviors Among U.S. Youth: Prevalence and Association With Psychosocial Adjustment," *Journal of the American Medical Association* 285 (2001): 2094–2100. doi:10.1001/jama.285.16.2094

7. Justin W. Patchin and Sameer Hinduja, "Bullies Move Beyond the Schoolyard: A Preliminary Look at Cyberbullying," *Youth Violence and Juvenile Justice* 4, no. 2 (2006): 148–169.

8. Sameer Hinduja and Justin W. Patchin, "Offline Consequences of Online Victimization: School Violence and Delinquency," *Journal of School Violence* 6, no. 3 (2007): 89–112. doi:10.1300/J202v06n03_06

9. Catherine D. Marcum, George E. Higgins, Scott E. Wolfe, and Melissa L. Ricketts, "Becoming Someone New: Identity Theft Behaviors by High School Students," *Journal of Financial Crime* 22, no. 3 (2014): 318–328.

10. Peter K. Smith, Jess Mahdavi, Manuel Carvalho, Sonja Fisher, Shanette Russell, and Neil Tippet, "Cyberbullying: Its Nature and Impact in Secondary School Pupils," *Journal of Child Psychology and Psychiatry* 49, no. 4 (2008): 376–385.

11. Sameer Hinduja and Justin W. Patchin, "Social Influences on Cyberbullying Behaviors Among Middle and High School Students," *Journal of Youth and Adolescence* 42, no. 5 (2013): 711–722; Catherine D. Marcum, *Cybercrime* (New York, NY: Willan, 2013).

12. Sara Pabian and Heidi Vandebosch, "An Investigation of Short-Term Longitudinal Associations Between Social Anxiety and Victimization and Perpetration of Traditional Bullying and Cyberbullying," *Journal of Youth Adolescence* 45 (2016): 328–339.

13. Justin W. Patchin, "Teens Talk: What Works to Stop Cyberbullying," *Cyberbullying Research Center*, December 1, 2017, https://cyberbullying.org/teens-talk-works-stop-cyberbullying.

14. Bradford W. Reyns, Billy Henson, and Bonnie S. Fisher, "Stalking in the Twilight Zone: Extent of Cyberstalking Victimization and Offending Among College Students," *Deviant Behavior* 33, no. 1 (2012): 1–25.

15. Jordana N. Navarro, "Cyberabuse and Cyberstalking," in *The Intersection Between Intimate Partner Abuse, Technology and Cybercrime: Examining the Virtual Enemy*, eds. Jordana N. Navarro, Shelly Clevenger, and Catherine D. Marcum (Durham, NC: Carolina Academic Press, 2016), 125–140.

16. Catherine D. Marcum, George E. Higgins, and Jason Nicholson, "I'm Watching You: Cyberstalking Behaviors of University Students in Romantic Relationships," *American Journal of Criminal Justice* 42, no. 2 (2017): 373–388.

17. National Conference of State Legislatures, "Cyberbullying," December 14, 2010, http://www.ncsl.org/issues-research/educ/cyberbullying.aspx; National Conference of State Legislatures, "State Cyberstalking and Cyberharassment Laws," 2012, http://www.ncsl.org/issues-research/telecom/cyberstalking-and-cyberharassment-laws.aspx.

18. W. Weins, "Concepts and Context," in *Sexting and Youth*, eds. T. Heistand and W. J. Weins (Durham, NC: Carolina Academic Press, 2014), 63–76.

19. Karuppannan Jaishankar, "Sexting: A New Form of Victimless Crime?" *International Journal of Cybercriminology* 31, no. 1 (2009): 21–25.

20. Renée D. Lamphere and Kweilin T. Pikciunas, "Sexting, Sextortion, and Other Internet Sexual Offenses," in *The Intersection Between Intimate Partner Abuse, Technology and Cybercrime: Examining the Virtual Enemy*, eds. Jordana N. Navarro, Shelly Clevenger, and Catherine D. Marcum (Durham, NC: Carolina Academic Press, 2016), 141–165; Kimberly J. Mitchell, David Finkelhor, Lisa M. Jones, and Janis Wolak, "Prevalence and Characteristics of Youth Sexting: A National Study," *Pediatrics* 129 (2012): 13–20; Bradford W. Reyns, Billy Henson, and Bonnie S. Fisher, "Digital Deviance: Low Self-Control and Opportunity as Explanations of Sexting Among College Students," *Sociological Spectrum* 34 (2014): 273–292.

21. Sarah Wastler, "The Harm in Sexting? Analyzing the Constitutionality of Child Pornography Statutes That Prohibit the Voluntary Production, Possession, and Dissemination of Sexually Explicit Images by Teenagers," *Harvard Journal of Law & Gender* 33 (2010): 687–702.

22. Ibid.

23. Michael Arnold, "A Disturbing Picture: Revenge Porn Is a Vicious New Way to Smear Someone's Professional Reputation," *HR Magazine* 59, no. 8 (2014): 58, http://www.shrm.org/publications/hrmagazine/editorialcontent/2014/0814/pages/0814-revenge-porn.aspx; Natalie Webb, "End Revenge Porn Infographic," *Cyber Civil Right Initiative,* January 3, 2014, http://www.cybercivilrights.org/end_revenge_porn_infographic.

24. Pam Greenberg, "The Newest Net Threat," *State Legislatures Magazine,* May 1, 2017, http://www.ncsl.org/bookstore/state-legislatures-magazine/trends-in-state-policy-news.aspx.

25. Erica Goode, "Once Scorned, but on Revenge Sites, Twice Hurt," *New York Times,* September 24, 2013, A11; Michael Gregg, "Cyber-Random and Online Extortion: 5 Ways You Could Fall Victim," *Huffington Post,* July 2, 2014, http://www.huffingtonpost.com/michael-gregg/cyber-ransom-and-online-e_b_5548810.html.

26. Janis Wolak and David Finkelhor, *Sextortion: Findings From a Survey of 1,631 Victims* (Durham, NH: Crimes Against Children Research Center, University of New Hampshire, June 2016), https://27l51l1qnwey246mkc1vzqg0-wpengine.netdna-ssl.com/wp-content/uploads/2016/08/Sextortion_Report.pdf.

27. Matt Liebowitz, "Fake Justin Bieber Arrested for Sextortion," *NBC News,* May 3, 2012, http://www.nbcnews.com/id/47286244/ns/technology_and_science-security/t/fake-justin-bieber-arrested-sextortion/#.WjlxKq3Mw0Q.

28. Robert E. Taylor, Eric J. Fritsch, John R. Liederbach, and Thomas J. Holt, *Digital Crime and Digital Terrorism,* 2nd ed. (Upper Saddle River, NJ: Pearson Prentice Hall, 2010).

29. Thomas J. Holt, "Subcultural Evolution? Examining the Influence of On- and Off-Line Experiences on Deviant Subcultures," *Deviant Behavior* 28 (2007): 171–198.

30. Marc Rogers, Natalie D. Smoak, and Jia Liu, "Self-Reported Deviant Computer Behavior: A Big-5, Moral Choice, and Manipulative Exploitive Behavior Analysis," *Deviant Behavior* 27 (2005): 245–268.

31. Thomas J. Holt, "Exploring the Social Organisation and Structure of Stolen Data Markets," *Global Crime* 14 (2013): 155–174.

32. Thomas J. Holt and Adam M. Bossler, "Examining the Applicability of Lifestyle-Routine Activities Theory for Cybercrime Victimization," *Deviant Behavior* 28 (2009): 1–25; Hollis Stambaugh, David S. Beaupre, David J. Icove, Richard Baker, Wayne Cassaday, and Wayne P. Williams, *Electronic Crime Needs Assessment for State and Local Law Enforcement*, NCJ 186276 (Washington, DC: National Institute of Justice, 2001), https://www.ncjrs.gov/pdffiles1/nij/186276.pdf.

33. Catherine D. Marcum, George E. Higgins, Melissa L. Ricketts, and Scott E. Wolfe, "Hacking in High School: Cybercrime Perpetration by Juveniles," *Deviant Behavior* 35, no. 7 (2014), 581–591.

34. Steven Furnell, *Cybercrime: Vandalizing the Information Society* (Boston, MA: Addison-Wesley, 2002); Holt, "Subcultural Evolution? Examining the Influence of On- and Off-Line Experiences on Deviant Subcultures."

35. Holt, "Subcultural Evolution? Examining the Influence of On- and Off-Line Experiences on Deviant Subcultures"; Bernadette H. Schell and John L. Dodge, *The Hacking of America: Who's Doing It, Why, and How* (Westport, CT: Quorum Books, 2002).

36. Furnell, *Cybercrime: Vandalizing the Information Society*.

37. Catherine D. Marcum, *Cybercrime* (New York, NY: Wolters Kluwer, 2013).

CHAPTER 10

1. Bob Kalinowski and Bill Wellock, "Opioid Crisis Is Killing People Every Day," *The Citizens' Voice,* January 11, 2018, http://citizensvoice.com/news/opioid-crisis-is-killing-people-every-day-1.2289146.

2. National Institute for Drug Abuse, *Monitoring the Future 2016 Survey Results* (December 2016), https://www.drugabuse.gov/related-topics/trends-statistics/infographics/monitoring-future-2016-survey-results.

3. Centers for Disease Control, "Health Effects of Cigarette Smoking" (2017), https://www.cdc.gov/tobacco/data_statistics/fact_sheets/health_effects/effects_cig_smoking/index.htm.

4. National Institute for Drug Abuse, *Monitoring the Future 2016 Survey Results*.

5. Katy Steinmetz, "420 Day: Why There Are so Many Different Names for Weed," *TIME*, April 20, 2017, http://time.com/4747501/420-day-weed-marijuana-pot-slang/.

6. Lloyd D. Johnston, Patrick M. O'Malley, Jerald G. Bachman, and John E. Schulenberg, *Monitoring the Future: Nationals Results on Adolescent Drug Use: Overview of Key Findings, 2011* (Ann Arbor: Institute for Social Research, University of Michigan, 2012).

7. National Institute for Drug Abuse for Teens, "Heroin," July 2017, https://teens.drugabuse.gov/drug-facts/heroin; National Institute for Drug Abuse, *Monitoring the Future 2016 Survey Results*.

8. Foundation for a Drug Free World, "What Is Meth Made From?" 2017, http://www.drugfreeworld.org/drugfacts/crystalmeth/what-is-meth-made-from.html.

9. National Institute for Drug Abuse, *Monitoring the Future 2016 Survey Results*.

10. Richard Rawson, Rachel Gonzales, Jeanne L. Obert, Michael J. McCann, and Paul Brethen, "Methamphetamine Use Among Treatment-Seeking Adolescents in Southern California: Participant Characteristics and Treatment Response," *Journal of Substance Abuse Treatment* 29 (2005): 67–74.

11. National Institute on Drug Abuse for Teens, "Inhalants," February 2017, https://www.drugabuse.gov/publications/drugfacts/inhalants.

12. National Institute for Drug Abuse, *Monitoring the Future 2016 Survey Results*.

13. Ibid.

14. National Institute on Drug Abuse, "Hallucinogens," January 2016, https://www.drugabuse.gov/publications/drugfacts/hallucinogens.

15. National Institute on Drug Abuse for Teens, "Prescription Pain Medications (Opioids)," March 2017, https://teens.drugabuse.gov/drug-facts/prescription-pain-medications-opioids.

16. National Institute on Drug Abuse for Teens, "Prescription Depressant Medications," March 2017, https://teens.drugabuse.gov/drug-facts/prescription-depressant-medications.

17. National Institute on Drug Abuse for Teens, "Prescription Stimulant Medications (Amphetamines)," March 2017, https://teens.drugabuse.gov/drug-facts/prescription-stimulant-medications-amphetamines.

18. Clemens Bartollas and Frank Schmalleger, *Juvenile Delinquency*, 9th ed. (Upper Saddle River, NJ: Pearson, 2014); Melissa L. Ives, Ya-Fen Chan, Kathryn C. Modisette, and Michael L. Dennis, "Characteristics, Needs, Services, and Outcomes of Youths in Juvenile Treatment Drug Courts as Compared to Adolescent Outpatient Treatment," *Drug Court Review* 7, no. 1 (2010): 10–56.

19. Loretta E. Lynch, Karol V. Mason, and Robert L. Listenbee, *Juvenile Drug Treatment Court Guidelines* (Washington, DC: Office of Juvenile Justice and Delinquency Prevention, 2016), https://www.ojjdp.gov/pubs/250368.pdf.

20. Michael L. Dennis, Pamela Baumer, and S. Stevens, "The Concurrent Evolution and Intertwined Nature of Juvenile Drug Courts and Reclaiming Futures Approaches to Juvenile Justice Reform," *Drug Court Review* 10, no. 1 (2016): 2–26.

21. National Research Council, *Implementing Juvenile Justice Reform: The Federal Role* (Washington, DC: National Academies Press, 2014).

22. Bureau of Justice Assistance, *Juvenile Drug Courts: Strategies in Practice* (Washington, DC: U.S. Department of Justice, Office of Justice Programs, Bureau of Justice Assistance, 2003), www.ncjrs.gov/pdffiles1/bja/197866.pdf; Jacqueline G. van Wormer, *Understanding Operational Dynamics of Drug Courts*, unpublished doctoral dissertation (Pullman, WA: Washington State University, 2010).

23. Kevin M. Thompson, *An Outcome Evaluation of Juvenile Drug Court Using the Child and Adolescent Functional Assessment Scale* (Fargo, ND: North Dakota State University, 2006), http://jpo.wrlc.org/handle/11204/1393; P. J. Townsend, *Juvenile Drug Court Programs in Mississippi: An Examination of Judicial and Administrative Perceptions*, unpublished doctoral dissertation (Hattiesburg, MS: University of Southern Mississippi, 2011).

24. David Wilson, Ajima Olaghere, and Catherine S. Kimbrell, *Developing Juvenile Court Practices on Process Standards: A Systematic Review and Qualitative Synthesis* (Fairfax, VA: George Mason University, 2016).

25. University of Arizona, Southwest Institute for Research on Women, *National Cross-Site Evaluation of Juvenile Drug Courts and Reclaiming Futures: Final Report* (Tucson, AZ: University of Arizona, Southwest Institute for Research on Women, 2015).

26. Substance Abuse and Mental Health Services Administration, Center for Behavioral Health Statistics and Quality, *Behavioral Health Trends in the United States: Results From the 2014 National Survey on Drug Use and Health,* HHS Publication No. SMA 15-4927, NSDUH Series H-50 (Rockville, MD: Author, 2015), https://www.samhsa.gov/data/sites/default/files/NSDUH-FRR1-2014/NSDUH-FRR1-2014.pdf; Substance Abuse and Mental Health Services Administration, Center for Behavioral Health Statistics and Quality, *Treatment Episode Data Set (TEDS): 2002–2012. State Admissions to Substance Abuse Treatment Services*, BHSIS Series S-72, HHS Publication No. (SMA) 14-4889 (Rockville, MD: Author, 2014).

27. Margot Peeters, Wilma A. M. Vollebergh, Reinout W. Wiers, and Matt Field, "Psychological Changes and Cognitive Impairments in Adolescent Heavy Drinkers," *Alcohol and Alcoholism* 49 (2013): 182–186; Jennifer L. Winward, Karen L. Hanson, Susan F. Tapert, and Sandra A. Brown, "Heavy Alcohol Use, Marijuana Use, and Concomitant Use by Adolescents Are Associated With Unique and Shared Cognitive Decrements," *Journal of the International Neuropsychological Society* 20 (2014): 784–795.

28. Emily E. Tanner-Smith, Katarzyna T. Steinka-Fry, Heather Hensman Kettrey, and Mark W. Lipsey, *Adolescent Substance Use Treatment Effectiveness: A Systematic Review and Meta-Analysis* (Nashville, TN: Peabody Research Institute, 2016), https://www.ncjrs.gov/pdffiles1/ojjdp/grants/250440.pdf.

CHAPTER 11

1. Details for this story come from "Penn State Student Overcomes 'Juvenile Delinquent' Label to Earn Degree," *Penn State News*, December 11, 2013, https://news.psu.edu/story/297733/2013/12/11/academics/penn-state-student-overcomes-%e2%80%98juvenile-delinquent%e2%80%99-label-earn (accessed July 30, 2018).

2. Robert Martinson, "What Works? Questions and Answers About Prison Reform," *Public Interest* (June 1974): 22–54; Dennis A. Romig, *Justice for Our Children: An Examination of Juvenile Delinquency Rehabilitation Programs*, 3rd ed. (Troy, MI: Performance Resource Press, 1999).

3. Peter W. Greenwood, *Changing Lives: Delinquency Prevention as Crime Control Policy* (Chicago, IL: University of Chicago Press, 2006); Institute of Medicine, *Knowing What Works in Health Care: A Road Map for the Nation* (Washington, DC: National Academy Press, 2008); Lawrence W. Sherman, David P. Farrington, Brandon C. Welsh, and Doris L. MacKenzie, eds., *Evidence-Based Crime Prevention* (New York: Routledge, 2002).

4. Sharon F. Mihalic and Delbert S. Elliott, "Evidence-Based Programs Registry: Blueprints for Healthy Youth Development," *Evaluation and Program Planning* 48 (2015): 124–131; Office of Management Budget, *The President's Management Agenda* (Washington, DC: US Government Printing Office, 2001); Office

of Management Budget, *The President's Management Agenda* (Washington, DC: US Government Printing Office, 2002).

5. Coalition for Evidence-Based Policy, *What Works in Social Policy? Findings From Well-Conducted Randomized Controlled Trials* (2014), http://evidencebasedprograms.org; Delbert S. Elliott, "Crime Prevention and Intervention Over the Life Course," in *Handbook of Life-Course Criminology*, eds. Chris L. Gibson and Marvin D. Krohn (New York: Springer, 2013), 297–316; Sharon Mihalic, Abigail Fagan, Katherine Irwin, Diane Ballard, and Delbert Elliott, *Blueprints for Violence Prevention* (Boulder, CO: University of Colorado, Institute of Behavioral Science, Center for the Study and Prevention of Violence, 2004); William R. Shadish, Jr., Thomas D. Cook, and Laura C. Leviton, *Foundations of Program Evaluation* (Newbury Park, CA: Sage, 1991).

6. Office of Juvenile Justice and Delinquency Prevention, "About OJJDP," 2018, https://www.ojjdp.gov/about/about.html.

7. Mihalic and Elliott, "Evidence-Based Programs Registry: Blueprints for Healthy Youth Development."

8. Blueprints for Healthy Youth Development, "Lifeskills Training (LST)," 2018, http://www.blueprintsprograms.com/factsheet/lifeskills-training-lst.

9. Blueprints for Healthy Youth Development, "Functional Family Therapy (FFT)," 2018, http://www.blueprintsprograms.com/factsheet/functional-family-therapy-fft.

10. Youth.gov, 2018, https://youth.gov

11. Sara B. Heller, Anuj K. Shah, Jonathan Guryan, Jens Ludwig, Sendhil Mullainathan, and Harold A. Pollack, *Thinking, Fast and Slow? Some Field Experiments to Reduce Crime and Dropout in Chicago,* working paper no. 21178 (Cambridge, MA: National Bureau of Economic Research, 2015).

12. Joseph P. Tierney, Jean Baldwin Grossman, and Nancy L. Resch, *Making a Difference: An Impact Study of Big Brothers/Big Sisters* (Philadelphia, PA: Public/Private Ventures, 2000).

13. Boys & Girls Clubs of America, "About Us," 2018, https://www.bgca.org/about-us.

14. Finn-Aage Esbensen, Dana Peterson, Terrance J. Taylor, and D. Wayne Osgood, "Results From a Multisite Evaluation of the G.R.E.A.T. Program," *Justice Quarterly* 29, no. 1 (2012): 125–151.

15. M. Fraser, E. Walton, R. Lewis, P. Pecora, and W. Walton, "An Experiment in Family Reunification: Correlates of Outcomes at 1-Year Follow-Up," *Children and Youth Services Review* 18 (1996):

335–361; Raymond S. Kirk and Diane P. Griffith, "Intensive Family Preservation Services: Demonstrating Placement Prevention Using Event History Analysis," *Social Work Research* 28 (2003): 5–18.

16. Lawrence J. Schweinhart, Helen V. Barnes, and David P. Weikart, "Significant Benefits: The High/Scope Perry Preschool Study Through Age 27," in *Monographs of the High/Scope Education Research Foundation,* no. 10 (Ypsilanti, MI: High/Scope Press, 1993).

17. Janet G. Froeschle, Robert L. Smith, and Richard Ricard, "The Efficacy of a Systematic Substance Abuse Program for Adolescent Females," *Professional School of Counseling* 10, no. 5 (2007): 498–505.

18. Nancy G. Harrington, Steven M. Giles, Rick H. Hoyle, Greg J. Feeney, and Steven C. Yungbluth, "Evaluation of the All Stars Character Education and Problem Behavior Prevention Program: Effects on Mediator and Outcome Variables for Middle School Students," *Health Education Research* 28, no. 5 (2001): 533–546.

19. S. Mihalic, D. Huizinga, A. Ladika, K. Knight, and C. Dyer, *CASASTART Final Report* (Princeton, NJ: Robert Wood Johnson Foundation, 2011).

20. R. Clayton, A. Cattarello, and B. Johnstone, "The Effectiveness of Drug Abuse Resistance Education (Project DARE): 5-Year Follow-Up Results," *Preventive Medicine* 25 (1996): 307–318.

21. Lisa Sanbonmatsu, Jens Ludwig, Lawrence F. Katz, Lisa A. Gennetian, Greg J. Duncan, Ronald Kessler, Emma Adam, Thomas W. McDade, and Stacy Tessler Lindau, *Moving to Opportunity for Fair Housing Demonstration Program: Final Impacts Evaluation* (Washington, DC: U.S. Department of Housing and Urban Development, 2011), http://www.huduser.org/portal/publications/pubasst/MTOFHD.html.

22. Chudley E. Chad Werch, Deborah M. Owen, Joan M. Carlson, Carlo C. DiClemente, P. Edgemon, and M. V. Moore, "One-Year Follow-Up Results of the STARS for Families Alcohol Prevention Program," *Health Education Research* 18, no. 1 (2003): 74–87.

23. Pamela K. Lattimore and Christy A. Visher, *The Multisite Evaluation of SVORI: Summary and Synthesis* (Research Triangle Park, NC: RTI International, 2009), https://www.ncjrs.gov/pdffiles1/nij/grants/230421.pdf.

24. WNYC Radio, *Caught*, https://www.npr.org/podcasts/589480586/caught.

INDEX